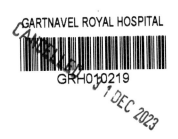

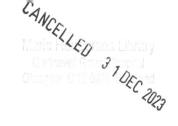

Metacognition and Severe Adult Mental Disorders

Many adults who experience severe mental illness also suffer from deficits in metacognition – put simply, thinking about one's own thought processes – limiting their abilities to recognize, express and manage naturally occurring painful emotions and routine social problems as well as to fathom the intentions of others.

This book presents an overview of the field, showing how current research can inform clinical practice. An international range of expert contributors provide chapters which look at the role of metacognitive deficit in personality disorders, schizophrenia and mood disorders, and the implications for future psychotherapeutic treatment.

Divided into three parts areas covered include:

- how metacognitive deficits may arise and the different forms they might take
- the psychopathology of metacognition in different forms of mental illness
- whether specific deficits in metacognition might help us understand the difficulties seen in differing forms of severe mental illness.

Offering varying perpsectives and including a wealth of clinical material, this book will be of great interest to all mental health professionals, researchers and practitioners.

Giancarlo Dimaggio is a psychiatrist and psychotherapist at the Third Center of Cognitive Psychotherapy in Rome. He is currently involved in clinical work and research on pathology and treatment of personality disorders.

Paul H. Lysaker is a clinical psychologist at the Roudebush VA Medical Center in Indianapolis, Indiana and an Associate Professor of Clinical Psychology in the Department of Psychiatry, Indianapolis School of Medicine. His current research interests include the development of metacognitive capacity through individual psychotherapy for persons with schizophrenia.

"Traditional cognitive domains, such as language, memory or perception, do not properly capture the problems experienced by people with severe mental disorders like schizophrenia. Their problems lie rather with insight and with the ability to monitor the mental and emotional states of themselves and others. In this book the editors have recognised that these disparate problems can be brought together under the heading of Metacognition. As the contents of the book so admirably show, this very important insight provides a framework for guiding both theory and practice in the study of severe mental disorders."

Chris Frith, UCL & University of Aarhus

"Dimaggio and Lysaker have assembled a stellar cast of contributors who apply the latest developments in theory and research on metacognition to our understanding of the both the development and treatment of severe mental disorders. Although all of the contributions are subsumed under the general topic of metacognition, the authors are in fact addressing a number of vitally important and timely areas. These include: theory of mind, reflective functioning, mentalization, attachment, affect regulation, and the therapeutic relationship. The end result is a lively, engaging and thought provoking collection of essays that will be of tremendous interest to theorists, researchers and psychotherapists of all orientations."

Jeremy D. Safran, Professor and Director of Clinical Psychology, New School for Social Research; President, International Association for Relational Psychoanalysis and Psychotherapy

Metacognition and Severe Adult Mental Disorders

From research to treatment

Edited by Giancarlo Dimaggio and Paul H. Lysaker

Routledge
Taylor & Francis Group
LONDON AND NEW YORK

First published 2010
by Routledge
27 Church Road, Hove, East Sussex BN3 2FA

Simultaneously published in the USA and Canada
by Routledge
270 Madison Avenue, New York NY 10016

Routledge is an imprint of the Taylor & Francis Group, an Informa business

Typeset in Times by Garfield Morgan, Swansea, West Glamorgan
Printed and bound in Great Britain by TJ International Ltd, Padstow, Cornwall
Cover design by Andrew Ward

This publication has been produced with paper manufactured to strict environmental standards and with pulp derived from sustainable forests.

British Library Cataloguing in Publication Data
A catalogue record for this book is available from the British Library

Library of Congress Cataloging-in-Publication Data
Metacognition and severe adult mental disorders : from research to treatment / edited by Giancarlo Dimaggio & Paul H. Lysaker.
p. ; cm.
Includes bibliographical references.
ISBN 978-0-415-48423-7 (hardback)
1. Mental illness. 2. Metacognition. I. Dimaggio, Giancarlo. II. Lysaker, Paul H.
[DNLM: 1. Mental disorders. 2. Adult. 3. Awareness. 4. Cognition. WM 140 M587 2010]
RC454.M474 2010
616.89–dc22

2009032563

ISBN: 978-0-415-48423-7 (hbk only)

Contents

Illustrations

Figures

Tables

Dialogue tables

Contributors

Mona Abdel-Hamid, PhD has been holding positions as a research and teaching assistant in the faculties of psychology and medicine of the University of Bochum, Germany as well as in the departments of psychiatry of the Universities of Bochum and Duisburg-Essen, Germany. Her primary research interests are social cognitive functioning in schizophrenic spectrum disorders and attention deficit hyperactivity disorder (ADHD) and cognitive behavioural therapy in ADHD. She is working as a cognitive behavioural therapist specializing in pain therapy.

Elliot M. Bell is a clinical psychologist and lecturer in the School of Medicine and Health Sciences at the University of Otago, Wellington. His research is focused on social cognition, particularly theory of mind and neurocognition in psychotic conditions.

Martin Brüne, MD is a specialist in neurology, psychiatry and psychotherapy and Professor of Psychiatry at the University of Bochum, Germany. His main research interests are social cognition in psychiatric disorders, and psychopathology in evolutionary perspective including cross-species comparison. He has conducted research into theory of mind and nonverbal behaviour in various psychopathological conditions. He edited *The Social Brain – Evolution and Pathology* (with Hedda Ribbert and Wulf Schiefenhövel, Wiley, 2003) and wrote *Textbook of Evolutionary Psychiatry. The Origins of Psychopathology* (Oxford University Press, 2008).

Kelly D. Buck is a clinical nurse specialist at the Roudebush VA Medical Center. She has over 20 years of experience in the treatment of severe mental illness and has a specialized interest in the provision and supervision of psychotherapy for adults with psychoses.

Jeremy I. M. Carpendale, Professor of Developmental Psychology at Simon Fraser University, has published in the areas of cognitive, social cognitive and moral development. His work focuses on the nature and development of thinking about social and moral matters and the role of language and social interaction in such development. He is author with Charlie Lewis of *How Children Develop Social Understanding* (Blackwell, 2006), co-editor of several books including the *Cambridge Companion to Piaget* and associate editor for *New Ideas in Psychology*.

Livia Colle, PhD is Lecturer in Cognitive Psychology, University of Torino, Faculty of Psychology, and a psychotherapist at the Third Center of Cognitive Psychotherapy in Rome. Her principal research interests are the cognitive process underlying the development of social cognition in normally developing population and in the autistic spectrum. She has also conducted research into metacognitive and communicative abilities in various psychopathological conditions.

Stefania D'Angerio, PhD is a psychologist and psychotherapist. She works as a clinician and researcher at the Third Center of Cognitive Psychotherapy in Rome. She works mainly with patients with personality disorders featuring dysregulated traits and eating disorders. She teaches at the Schools for Cognitive Psychotherapy – Associazione di Psicologia Cognitiva (APC) and Scuola di Psicoterapia Cognitiva (SPC).

Anthony S. David graduated in medicine from Glasgow University in 1980 and trained in psychiatry at the Maudsley Hospital, London and has been Professor of Cognitive Neuropsychiatry at the Institute of Psychiatry since 1996. He is author of over 350 publications including, *The Self in Neuroscience and Psychiatry* (2003) with T. Kircher, and *Insight and Psychosis* (2nd edn, 2004) with X. Amador.

Mattias Desmet is a postdoctoral researcher at the Department of Psychoanalysis and Clinical Consulting at Ghent University, Belgium. In 2007 he completed a PhD on psychometric characteristics of personality measures. His current research activities focus on psychotherapy research, with special interest in the interaction between personality characteristics and symptoms throughout the therapeutic process. Besides his academic work, he is a psychoanalytic psychotherapist in private practice.

Giancarlo Dimaggio is a psychiatrist and a psychotherapist at the Third Center of Cognitive Psychotherapy in Rome. He is currently involved in clinical work and research on pathology and treatment of personality disorders.

Pete M. Ellis is Professor of Psychological Medicine in the School of Medicine and Health Sciences at the University of Otago, Wellington. His research interests include aspects of affective disorders, health services research and phenomenology of major psychiatric disorders.

Donatella Fiore, MD is a psychiatrist and psychotherapist. She is a trainer at the Schools for Cognitive Psychotherapy – Associazione di Psicologia

Cognitiva (APC) and Scuola di Psicoterapia Cognitiva (SPC). She has written papers about the psychotherapeutic process and pathology and treatment of personality disorders in Italian and international journals.

Andrew Gumley is a clinical psychologist and is currently Chair of Psychological Therapy in the Section of Psychological Medicine, University of Glasgow. His main interests are the developmental, interpersonal and metacognitive determinants of emotional recovery and staying well after psychosis. He is particularly interested in the development and evaluation of group and individually based compassion focused psychotherapy for recovery after psychosis. He has co-authored with Matthias Schwannauer *Staying Well After Psychosis: A Cognitive Interpersonal Approach to Emotional Recovery and Relapse Prevention* and recently completed a major study of attachment states of mind, mentalisation and recovery in first episode psychosis funded by the Scottish government.

Ilanit Hasson-Ohayon is a rehabilitation psychologist, a lecturer in the Department of Psychology and co-director of the community psychological services clinic at the Bar-Ilan University. Her main theoretical, empirical and clinical interests include psychiatric rehabilitation and psycho-oncology.

Yumiko Inoue, MD, PhD is Assistant Professor, Department of Psychiatry, Tokyo Women's Medical University, Medical Center East, Tokyo.

Ruth Inslegers is a research assistant at the Department of Psychoanalysis and Clinical Consulting at Ghent University, Belgium. Her current research focuses on alexithymia, affect regulation processes and interpersonal functioning in psychiatric patients. She is currently pursuing further training in psychoanalytic psychotherapy from a Freudian-Lacanian perspective at Ghent University.

Shigenobu Kanba, MD, PhD is Chair and Professor at the Department of Neuropsychiatry. She graduated from the School of Medicine, Keio University, Tokyo in 1980. She had residency training in psychiatry at the Mayo Clinic, Rochester, USA and became a professor of psychiatry at Yamanashi University in 1996, moving to her current position in 2003. Her current interests are mood disorders, neurobiology and psychopharmacology.

Shlomo Kravetz is a Professor Emeritus at Bar-Ilan University's Department of Psychology. His theoretical, empirical and clinical interests include the relationship between dialogue, empathy and metacognition and the role that these phenomena play in recovery from severe mental illness.

Robyn Langdon is a Senior Research Fellow, Macquarie Centre for Cognitive Science, Macquarie University. Much of her research focuses on understanding why people with schizophrenia show theory-of-mind impairment, and how this impairment limits these individuals' opportunities.

Charlie Lewis has been Professor of Family and Developmental Psychology at Lancaster University since 1999. Since the late 1980s Charlie's research has focused increasingly on young children's social-cognitive development. He is interested in how social interactions and relationships influence the nature and rate of development. This ranges from the social influences on how young children learn early number skills, to the influences of television advertising on young children to the social interactional skills of children with autism. His main work in this area is on how infants and young children gain an understanding of themselves and others as social agents, which he conducted with Jeremy Carpendale. They are currently working towards a new edition of their book *How Children Develop Social Understanding* (Blackwell, 2006).

Giovanni Liotti is a psychiatrist and psychotherapist. He currently teaches in the APC School of Psychotherapy and in the Post-Graduate School of Clinical Psychology of the Salesian University, Rome, Italy. His interest in the clinical applications of attachment theory was first expressed in a book co-authored with V.F. Guidano, *Cognitive Processes and Emotional Disorders* (Guilford Press, 1983). This interest has more recently focused on the links between dissociation, trauma-related mental disorders and disorganization of attachment, a theme explored in a number of journal papers and book chapters. In 2005, this work was acknowledged with the Pierre Janet's Writing Award of the International Society for the Study of Dissociation.

Paul H. Lysaker is a clinical psychologist at the Roudebush VA Medical Center in Indianapolis, Indiana and an Associate Professor of Clinical Psychology in the Department of Psychiatry, Indianapolis School of Medicine. His current research interests include the development of metacognitive capacity through individual psychotherapy for persons with schizophrenia.

Reitske Meganck is a postdoctoral researcher at the Department of Psychoanalysis and Clinical Consulting at Ghent University, Belgium. She completed a PhD on the validity of alexithymia measures in 2009. Her current research mainly focuses on affective experience and affect regulation processes, and on the link between clinical practice and empirical research. She finished training in psychoanalytic psychotherapy from a Freudian–Lacanian perspective at Ghent University.

Kevin D. Morgan gained his BSc psychology degree at Brunel University and his PhD at the Institute of Psychiatry, London. He is a senior lecturer in psychology at the University of Westminster with research interests in insight and neurocognition in psychosis.

Giuseppe Nicolò, MD is a psychiatrist and psychotherapist and Director of Mental Health Outpatient Services Roma G. He is a past president of the European Chapter of the Society for Psychotherapy Research and Professor of Clinical Psychology at the LUMSA University, Rome. He is a teacher for the School of Cognitive Psychotherapy (SPC). He has written papers about the psychotherapeutic process and pathology and treatment of personality disorders in English, Spanish and Italian. He has edited *La ricerca in Psicoterapia* and co-authored *Psychotherapy of Personality Disorders* (Routledge). He leads a group investigating correlates of metacognition in long-term schizophrenia.

Shani Offen is a postdoctoral fellow at the Center for Neuroscience at New York University, New York. Her areas of interest include visual neuroscience, functional MRI, metacognition, decision making and the connection between normal and disordered brain function.

Els Ooms is a research and teaching assistant at the Department of Psychoanalysis and Clinical Consulting at Ghent University, Belgium. Her current research focuses on affect regulation processes and alexithymia in patients suffering from tinnitus. Besides her academic work, she is also a psychoanalytic psychotherapist in private practice, where she works with patients suffering from tinnitus.

Katerine Osatuke is the research director at the Veterans Health Administration National Center for Organization Development. She provides data analytic support to VA management initiatives and participates in organizational assessments and interventions at VA hospital facilities nationwide. She has a theoretical and research background in models of psychological change, including how change is defined, empirically measured and tracked across time. She co-authored 20 publications and made over four dozen national and international conference presentations on aspects of clinical and organizational change. She is particularly interested in tracking individual change in severely traumatized and personality disordered clients, and in studying organizational change within process-oriented, action-focused approaches.

Raffaele Popolo, MD is a psychiatrist and psychotherapist and past vice president of the Italian section of the Psychotherapy Research Society. He is a trainer at the Società Italiana di Psicoterapia Comportamentale e Cognitiva (SITCC) and the Schools for Cognitive Psychotherapy – Associazione di Psicologia Cognitiva (APC) and Scuola di Psicoterapia

Cognitiva (SPC). He has written works on the pathology of schizophrenia and on the psychotherapeutic process, particularly regarding patients suffering from social anxiety.

Michele Procacci, MD is a psychiatrist and psychotherapist, head of an outpatient mental health service in Rome, Professor of Psychopathology, University of Naples and a trainer at the SITCC and the Schools for Cognitive Psychotherapy – Associazione di Psicologia Cognitiva (APC) and Scuola di Psicoterapia Cognitiva (SPC). He has written papers about cognitive neuropsychiatry and the pathology of schizophrenia and personality disorders in Italian, Spanish and international journals. He co-authored *Psychotherapy of Personality Disorders* (Routledge).

Elena Prunetti, PhD is a psychotherapist and the coordinator of the Psychiatric Unit for Personality Disorders at the Villa Margherita Clinic Vicenza, where she has worked since 1994. She is a trainer at the SITCC and the Schools for Cognitive Psychotherapy – Associazione di Psicologia Cognitiva (APC) and Scuola di Psicoterapia Cognitiva (SPC). Her major fields of interest are treatment of personality disorders and clinical applications of attachment theory.

David Roe is a clinical psychologist and Associate Professor at the Department of Community Mental Health, Faculty of Social Welfare and Health Sciences at the University of Haifa. His research and clinical work focuses on processes of recovery from serious mental illness.

Giampaolo Salvatore, MD is a psychiatrist and psychotherapist. He is a trainer at the Schools for Cognitive Psychotherapy – Associazione di Psicologia Cognitiva (APC) and Scuola di Psicoterapia Cognitiva (SPC). He has written papers about the psychotherapeutic process, pathology and treatment of schizophrenia and of personality disorders, in particular of persons with dysregulated trait. He is the author of *Il Tao della psicoterapia* [Tao of psychotherapy].

Rebecca Saxe is the Fred and Carole Middleton Career Development Professor, in Brain and Cognitive Sciences, at MIT. Her research investigates the neural bases of abstract cognitive capacities that make the human mind unique, like language, social cognition and moral cognition.

Daniela Schaub, PhD specializes in clinical and social psychology. Since 2006 she has worked as a research assistant in the Department of Psychiatry, University of Bochum, Germany. Her main research interest is psychosocial functioning in patients with schizophrenia. She is in training for psychotherapy with focus on cognitive behavioural therapy.

Antonio Semerari, MD is a psychiatrist and psychotherapist and a trainer at the SITCC and the Schools for Cognitive Psychotherapy – Associazione di Psicologia Cognitiva (APC) and Scuola di Psicoterapia Cognitiva (SPC). He has been dealing with personality disorders psychotherapy, about which he has published many research papers. He has been president of the Italian Chapter of the Society for Psychotherapy Research (SPR). Included among his works are *Psicoterapia cognitiva del paziente grave* [Cognitive psychotherapy of severe patients] (ed.) (Milan, 1999); *Storia, teorie e tecniche della psicoterapia cognitiva* [History, theories and techniques of cognitive psychotherapy] (Rome, 2002). He co-authored *Psychotherapy of Personality Disorders* (Routledge).

Richard J. Siegert is a Senior Lecturer in Rehabilitation at King's College London in the Department of Palliative Care, Policy and Rehabilitation. His research interests include psychometrics, cognition in neurological and neuropsychiatric disorders and rehabilitation for neurological conditions.

Giovanni Stanghellini, MD, DHC is a psychiatrist and psychotherapist and Professor of Dynamic Psychology and Psychopathology at D'Annunzio University, Chieti, Italy. He is Chair of the WPA section Psychiatry and the Humanities and founding chair of the EPA section Philosophy and Psychiatry. He is co-editor of the Oxford University Press series *International Perspectives in Philosophy and Psychiatry* and associate editor of the journal *Psychopathology*. He has published extensively on the philosophical foundations of psychopathology and the phenomenology of the vulnerability to major psychoses.

William B. Stiles is a professor of psychology at Miami University in Oxford, Ohio, USA. He received his PhD from UCLA in 1972. He taught previously at the University of North Carolina at Chapel Hill and has held visiting positions at the universities of Sheffield and Leeds in England, at Massey University in New Zealand and at the University of Joensuu in Finland. He is the author of *Describing Talk: A Taxonomy of Verbal Response Modes*. He has been president of the Society for Psychotherapy Research. He has served as North American editor of *Psychotherapy Research*, associate editor of *British Journal of Clinical Psychology*, and co-editor of *Person-Centered and Experiential Psychotherapies*.

Stijn Vanheule, PhD is an associate professor of psychoanalysis and clinical psychodiagnostics at the Department of Psychoanalysis and Clinical Consulting at Ghent University, Belgium. His research on the one hand focuses on affect regulation, alexithymia and interpersonal functioning and on the other hand he is engaged in conceptual research in psychoanalysis. He is a psychoanalyst in private practice.

Kazuo Yamada, MD, PhD is Associate Professor, Department of Psychiatry, Tokyo Women's Medical University, Medical Center East, Tokyo.

Introduction

Giancarlo Dimaggio and Paul H. Lysaker

The metacognitive system

Theory, evidence and implications for treatment

Many adults with severe mental illness experience persistent difficulties in forming and scrutinizing complex ideas about themselves and others. This may involve deficits in many related but distinct psychological tasks. For instance, it may be problematic to recognize one's own thoughts and feelings. Emotions may be undetectable or characterized in a singular manner. I may, for instance, be unable to name what I feel. I may be able to know that I feel something but can only describe it as one intense internal state without any nuance that never wavers. It may seem impossible to intuit the feelings of another person who is talking to me or two other people who are talking to one another just a few feet away. The requirements of a social situation may appear hopelessly ambiguous. I may have no idea of how others will respond if I tell a joke. I may be unable to distinguish the good-natured joking of others from malicious slander. Personal reactions to complex events may appear as the impregnably true explanation of those events rather than individual beliefs. I may feel that I cannot possibly question my sense that another person loves or hates me. There may appear to be only one solution to an unexpected challenge, despite the fact that others can readily imagine a wide range of alternative possible courses of action or ways to cope.

Since the late 1970s, theoreticians and researchers from widely varying traditions and disciplines have described these sets of skills as falling under the general label of metacognition (e.g. Flavell, 1979). Metacognition refers to a thought which is about another thought or the process of thinking about thinking. Thinking about how I learn best, why I made a sarcastic remark to a loved one or why a rival made a friendly gesture to me are examples of metacognition. Interest in metacognition broadly developed as fields such as education, developmental psychology and cognitive sciences recognized that human beings do not merely process information or solve problems. Human beings may take in information but they also make meaning of that information. Human beings, for instance, form representations of their own mental states. They label their own overt and covert emotions. They think deeply about the desires and intentions of others and there are recognizable mechanisms and pathways which make this possible (Fodor, 1983). The study of metacognition was thus born out of the realization that the ability to think about thinking was not merely an unusual artifact of cognition but a uniquely human capacity which is necessary for successful adaptation to a changing social world.

While the initial work on metacognition offered unique insights into healthy function, it also pointed to the possibility that if these capacities were compromised less healthy function would ensue. Could deficits in metacognition explain some of the more persistent problems associated with various forms of psychiatric or neurodevelopmental conditions? In response to this, one of the first clinical applications concerned autism. In particular, as has now been widely studied, it was proposed that a profound inability to think about the mind of another person might explain why children with autism cannot relate to others because in part they are unable to form theories about what is transpiring in the minds of others (Baron-Cohen *et al.*, 1985).

Following the early work on autism, interest grew steadily in the 1990s regarding the possible roles that deficits in metacognitive capacity could play in adults with serious mental disorders. Chistopher Frith (1992) for instance, suggested that an inability to recognize and make sense of mental states, both one's own and the mental states of other persons, was a core and stable deficit in schizophrenia. Fonagy (1991) suggested that some of the same problems could also be observed in borderline personality disorders, though here these problems appear as state-dependent, as difficulties that emerge in only some intimate interpersonal circumstances. Stiles and colleagues (1990) noted how persons with depressive disorders possessed a minimal, at best, awareness of disturbing thoughts and most importantly had a limited ability to describe affects – a phenomenon similar to what earlier theoreticians and clinicians labelled alexithymia (Sifneos, 1973). Stiles also reported that as psychotherapy assisted depressed persons to develop more complex levels of awareness of their problematic mental states, they began to find a way to think more clearly about stressors and to cope with them, pointing to the causal role these deficits may play in dysfunction.

Since the beginning of the twenty-first century interest in metacognition and severe mental illness has grown in leaps and bounds. Articles and monographs have appeared with increasing frequency suggesting that deficits in metacognition are not merely the result of other symptoms of various mental disorders but are themselves key aspects of these disorders which may play a unique role in disability. Clearly emerging in the literature also is theory and evidence for a metacognitive system, with a set of functions that can operate or be damaged separately or in combination (Semerari, 1999). In the face of this, scientists, theoreticians, clinicians and the interested public have been faced with the increasingly daunting task of synthesizing material, which involves widely varying methods and foci. How should one bring together, for instance, studies of neuroimaging of metacognition, work on theory of mind (TOM) deficits in bipolar disorder and the development of metacognitive focused psychotherapy for persons with personality disorder?

It was in response to these issues that we first conceived an edited book, one which might lay different research findings and emerging theoretical and clinical issues side by side. To organize our initial thinking about this project we conceptualized emerging literature as posing at least two essential questions. First, are deficits in metacognition merely a general problem that occurs in no systematic manner across different forms of psychopathology? That is, are they a universal feature of disability? Are the deficits found in post traumatic stress disorder (PTSD), bipolar disorder and schizophrenia roughly equivalent? Alternatively, are different kinds of deficits linked to different disorders (Semerari *et al.*, 2007) such that, for instance, the disorders of PTSD, bipolar disorder and schizophrenia have different kinds of metacognitive profiles? Answers to this first question would appear to have a considerable number of practical and conceptual implications. Emerging evidence that the latter is in fact the case has led some to suggest that concepts related to metacognition should be included or woven into the categorization of adult mental disorders. Krueger (2005) has suggested that 'poor insight' be seen as a key aspect of the psychopathology of personality disorders – though with the caveat that there is not yet consistent evidence for this idea. One aim of our volume is to address this issue – while Brüne and colleagues (2007) have proposed a social cognitive deficit be included in the definition of schizophrenia.

The second question that also guided us to the current project regards the far-reaching issue of treatment. If dysfunctions in metacognition are at issue here, the possibility of treating them may hold out enormous promises for the rehabilitation of even the most severely ill. A complex account of these difficulties may lead to the refinement of existing treatments and creation of new treatments which could assist patients not only to become more aware of their own thinking but also to plot their own course towards recovery. We know, for example, that a limited ability to recognize and communicate one's own emotional state, alexithymia, has a negative impact on therapists' reactions and thus is a risk factor for a poor therapeutic alliance and a poor outcome (Ogrodniczuk *et al.*, 2005). It is clear that such a variable needs to be a target when it arises. But treatment probably should have a different target depending upon how that deficit is understood. A deficit in awareness of others linked to an inability to detach from the affect-induced information processing as in dissociative disorder vs. a lack of awareness of internal states as in schizophrenia might require different interventions. To date only a few programmes include metacognitive (or the related concept, mentalizing) dysfunctions as a barrier to recovery and a target of treatment. In the field of personality disorders, mentalization based therapy (Bateman and Fonagy, 2004) and metacognitive interpersonal therapy (Dimaggio *et al.*, 2007) directly seek to enhance the capacity to reflect about oneself and others. Transference-focused psychotherapy (Clarkin *et al.*, 2006) though not explicitly focused on metacognition, is able to improve patients' ability to reason on mental states (Levy *et al.*, 2006). Many other treatments of personality disorders largely neglect the importance of the problem. In schizophrenia, psychotherapy is rarely considered and, if so, it is often only presented as an innocuous supportive treatment that might be offered to any disadvantaged and stigmatized group (Lysaker *et al.*, 2007). An understanding of the role of metacognitive deficits in schizophrenia could pave the way for the refinement of psychotherapeutic practices.

Before tackling these issues, however, one immediate barrier to bringing together this burgeoning literature is that the traditions and fields actively studying this phenomenon have slowly developed their own language, labelling this ability to make sense of mental states in a variety of ways: *theory of mind*, *mentalizing*, *social cognition*, *social understanding*, *mind-reading* or *psychological mindedness*. On the other hand we had a sense, both from published papers and personal conversations, that these terms spoke to very similar processes (see Allen *et al.*, 2008; Choi-Kain and Gunderson, 2008). In response to this issue we have chosen to leave the authors free to adopt their preferred terminology, and we will use the term metacognition as an umbrella concept in a manner consistent with our view of its historical origins. We thus understand metacognition broadly to refer to reflections on self and social experience (Semerari *et al.*, 2003), to the set of skills which makes it possible to use cues such as bodily signals, facial expressions or overt behaviours to grasp one's own underlying emotions, thoughts and intentions as well as the emotions, thoughts and intentions of others (Semerari *et al.*, 2007). It includes the ability to reason about the contents of experience and, of the utmost importance, pragmatically to use knowledge of mental states to cope with suffering, to find solutions when faced with conflicting emotions, to negotiate with significant others the meaning of experience and to adapt to the social environment and find ways to reach goals.

A key point for us is that metacognition, as it is conceptualized here, operates across a number of semi-independent domains which differ from one another according to the subject which is the focus of each particular metacognitive act. For instance, metacognitive acts which involve making a judgement about oneself may be substantively different from metacognitive acts which involve deciding what another person is thinking. A metacognitive act which involves making a judgement about how to handle a certain dilemma may be qualitatively different than making a judgement about a relationship between two other people. Importantly, metacognitive acts with different foci are conceived of involving both different psychological processes as well as overlapping but distinct cortical processes. For example, research suggests that the cortical activity called for when reflecting about others who are like oneself differs from the cortical activity called for when reflecting about others not alike (Mitchell *et al.*, 2006). Similarly, reasoning about personality traits may result in different patterns of cortical activity than reasoning about the affective states of others (Heberlein and Saxe, 2005). The relative independence of the many aspects of metacognition might have an adaptive value. For example, evidence is mounting that the more automatic, quick and probably reliable way to grasp what others have in mind is using the self as a model (Gallese and Goldman, 1998). One price to pay for this though may be a bias toward attribution of similarity. Persons may tend to overestimate the degree to which others share mental contents with the self (Royzman *et al.*, 2003). As a welcome buffer against this and other similar biases, separate cognitive processes exist that help to correct misattributions via logical reasoning (Saxe, 2005).

In this way, metacognition is used in this volume to refer to a set of skills that can be conceived of as operating separetely. Certain situations may not only call for different kinds of metacognitive acts but it is also possible that a capacity for successfully making metacognitive judgements in one or more metacognitive domain is lesser or greater than the capacity for making metacognitive judgements in other domains. I may, for instance, have an aptitude for discerning the emotions of others but have little sense of my own emotions or not understand the nuances of a relationship which two other people have with one another which does not involve me. However, these metacognitive capacities also interact with each other, functioning as a system which allows for social adaptation and problem solving (Dimaggio *et al.*, 2008). The output of one metacognitive act, such as identifying one's own emotion, can serve as an input for another act, such as grasping the social or internal processes which elicited that emotion. The ability to create and later recall a broad and integrated picture of one's mental functioning may help people to turn back to moments in which they reacted in a manner that was unexpected and think about how they felt and why they felt that way. For example, I can know that I feel controlled by an outside force but not understand why I started feeling that way a couple of days ago. But it could help if I know I tend to dissociate under stressful social conditions such as moments when other people misunderstand what I need. This overall picture of one aspect of my mental life might prime me to more readily focus on elements of an episode formerly left unnoticed. It might cue me to think of a recent experience of distress and to link it to a situation in which I was refused a needed vacation day that I believe I deserved. I might then replay the scenario in which I was refused the vacation and slowly recognize that I felt a twinge of anger which I coped with by dissociating with the only thought in mind being that I was not in control of my life. This new thought about my own thinking might then help me to cope more effectively, leading to my finding new avenues to relax or to negotiate with my superiors about when I could take my vacation.

As an even wider illustration of the interplay among the many elements of the metacognitive system, consider the following. An unexpected psychological challenge has emerged one afternoon. I have been offered a significant promotion at work but this would require moving to another city and my spouse would have to change jobs and my child enrol in a new school. To move forward I must rely on my capacity for monitoring my own inner states and detect that I am in a state of distress. I want to take the job and do not want to hurt my spouse and so feel conflicted. When I sit down in the evening to talk to my spouse, I then have to rely on my capacity to infer her emotions and respond to them. The success of any conversation about what should be done, for instance, will depend upon my ability to see she is angry even though she is smiling or to make sense of her feelings about her career aspirations and whether they are being met at her current work. After that conversation I must then rely on my ability to create an integrated plan of action in which I recognize that I am not the centre of world, that others have their own independent relationships with one another and perhaps decide to seek advice from a friend or change the way I am thinking about the problem.

From this example we hope that two things are clear which have an immediate bearing on understanding metacognitive disturbances in severe mental illness. First, one might expect that a severe deficit in metacognition would lead to more severe personal or social dysfunction. More serious failures at the points along the chain of tasks of thinking about myself, thinking about others, thinking about how others relate to one another and thinking about problem solving may lead to more serious consequences in terms of interpersonal conflicts, psychosocial dysfunctions or emotional discomfort. A second point, however, is that different kinds of deficits in metacognitive capacity, alone and in combination with one another, might result in very different kinds of symptoms or challenges. A different set of difficulties might arise, for instance, if I am unable to recognize the thoughts and feelings of others as opposed to whether I cannot distinguish one emotion I feel from another.

In this volume we are interested in bringing to the table a range of international experts from different fields and orientations to pursue three aims:

- to provide an updated account of current models of metacognition in severe mental illness, including its biological and social underpinnings and current methods of assessment

- to offer detailed systematic descriptions of specific forms of metacognitive dysfunctions potentially linked with distinct disorders and the relationship of those dysfunctions with the symptoms and psychosocial deficits which define those disorders
- to provide an up-to-date account of ways in which treatments including psychotherapy and rehabilitation are being developed to target metacognition.

Researchers and academicians should be able to derive testable hypotheses from sections of this collection and clinicians should be able to supplement or reconceptualize ongoing work with their patients with severe mental illness.

The present book

Part I, composed of three chapters, attempts to tackle the basic underlying theoretical issues related to the social and neurocognitive bases of metacognition. Chapter 1 by Saxe and Offen exploits the parallel with the vision to illustrate how multidimensional deficits in self-awareness are found throughout human conscience and detail recent neuroimaging studies which point to the neural basis of these functions. Continuing to focus on the issues raised in Chapter 1, Chapter 2, by Carpendale and Lewis, examines how social understanding is constructed through relational processes and embedded in interpersonal relationships in which the meaning of mental states is jointly constructed. They also discuss the idea that mirror neurons, the neural system hypothesized to make possible how people can immediately grasp the feelings of others, may be laid down during early interactions with caretakers and others. In Chapter 3, Andrew Gumley continues this discussion focusing on the developmental origins of metacognitive disorders in adults.

Part II of this volume touches on the issue of psychopathology of metacognition in different adult disorders. In Chapter 4, Lysaker describes a programme of ongoing research which has explored the links between neurocognition and deficits in metacognition in schizophrenia. In Chapter 5, Schaub, Abdel-Hamid and Brüne continue this discussion by examining the complex manner in which various deficits in metacogntion may interact to serve as a unique barrier to function. In Chapter 6, Morgan and David present the complex and multidimensional processes involved in persons with schizophrenia coming to appraise the nature of their illness, to accept that they suffer from that illness and choose to seek and adhere to treatment. In Chapter 7, Elliot Bell and his colleagues perform a thorough review of the many tasks involved in assessing theory of mind in persons with schizophrenia, highlighting current methodological issues in the assessment of this domain of metacognition. In Chapter 8, Stanghellini discusses the phenomenological bases of the felt experience of disturbance in self experience and their relationship to delusions in schizophrenia. Chapter 9 by Kanba and colleagues deals with theory of mind impairments in mood disorders, underscoring how a subpopulation exists with poor performance in understanding others and how this is linked with worst prognosis. In Chapter 10, Vanheule and colleagues describe how the phenomenon of alexithymia can be conceuptalized as a fundamental form of metacognitive disturbance, one which may contribute to psychosocial dysfunction in many different forms of mental illness. They detail the potentially deep impact this form of metacognitive deficit has in terms of its impact on symptoms, social functioning, coping strategies and treatment response. Colle and colleagues – Chapter 11 – focus on the kinds of metacognitive dysfunctions found in personality disorders. They discuss how these can range from a prevasive metacognitive disorder to dysfunctions in specific unique functions. They also consider the possibility that a linear relationship may exist between the severity of metacognitive dysfunctions and the severity of the personalitiy disorder itself. In Chapter 12, Liotti and Prunetti turn to post traumatic disorders and discuss the existence of different metacognitive disturbances linked to trauma, including disruptions in the ability to monitor inner states and distinguish between fantasy and reality. They also underscore how difficulties with attachment may be implicated in cases of more severe forms of psychopathology.

In Part III the book turns to the issue of whether specific deficits in metacognition might help us to understand the difficulties seen in differing forms of severe mental illness. Authors from varying perspectives discuss the implications of the foregoing material for the treatment of these conditions. Clinical implications are explored in general and as applied to schizophrenia, trauma, personality disorders, psychotherapy and psychosocial rehabilitation and each chapter contains clinical material (session transcripts, semi-structured interviews or clinical vignettes). Chapter 13 by Lysaker and Buck discusses how an integrative individual psychotherapy can be adapted to focus on enhancing metacognitive capacity in schizophrenia. Hasson-Ohayon, Kravetz and Roe, Chapter 14, expand this discussion to talk about how psychosocial rehabilitation can be refined to also address metacognitive capacity for persons with severe mental illness. In Chapter 15, Dimaggio and colleagues explore the implications of the material presented in the first two parts of the book for enhancing the metacognition of persons with over-constricted personality disorder – that is with poor awareness and repression of affects and a restricted range of schemas for making sense of social relationships. In Chapter 16, Semerari offers an insight into how dysfunctional metacognition in its different presentations has an impact on the therapeutic relationship. He describes how the therapist found himself immersed in those relational problems and offers guidance as to how therapists may disentangle themselves from those dysfunctional patterns, offering opportunies for even great growth in the patient's metacognitive capacity. In Chapter 17, Osatuke and Stiles explore the implications of deficits in metacognition for assisting persons with post traumatic stress disorder to move towards recovery using an assimilation model.

In the Conclusion, written jointly by the editors, the findings of the three parts of the book are summarized and points of divergence and convergence are highlighted. A possible programme for future research and the development and application of technologies derived from the foregoing work is detailed.

References

Allen, J.G., Fonagy, P. and Bateman, A.W. (2008). *Mentalizing in clinical practice*. Washington, DC: American Psychiatric Publishing.

Baron-Cohen, S., Leslie, A. and Frith, U. (1985). Does the autistic child have a 'theory of mind'? *Cognition, 21*, 37–46.

Bateman, A.W. and Fonagy, P. (2004). *Psychotherapy for borderline personality disorder: Mentalization-based treatment*. Oxford: Oxford University Press.

Brüne, M., Abdel-Hamid, M., Lehmkämper, C. and Sonntag, C. (2007). Mental state attribution, neurocognitive functioning, and psychopathology: What predicts poor social competence in schizophrenia best? *Schizophrenia Research, 92*, 151–159.

Choi-Kain, L.W. and Gunderson, J.G. (2008). Mentalization: Ontogeny, assessment and application in the treatment of borderline personality disorder. *American Journal of Psychiatry, 165*, 1127–1135.

Clarkin, J.F., Yeomans, F. and Kernberg, O.F. (2006). *Psychotherapy of borderline personality: Focusing on object relations*. Washington, DC: American Psychiatric Press.

Dimaggio, G., Semerari, A., Carcione, A., Nicolò, G. and Procacci, M. (2007). *Psychotherapy of personality disorders: Metacognition, states of mind and interpersonal cycles*. London: Routledge.

Dimaggio, G., Lysaker, P.H., Carcione, A., Nicolò, G. and Semerari, A. (2008). Know yourself and you shall know the other . . . to a certain extent. Multiple paths of influence of self-reflection on mindreading. *Consciousness and Cognition, 17*, 778–789.

Flavell, J.H. (1979). Metacognition and cognitive monitoring: A new area of cognitive-developmental inquiry. *American Psychologist, 34*, 906–911.

Fodor, J.A. (1983). *The modularity of mind*. Cambridge, MA: MIT Press.

Fonagy, P. (1991). Thinking about thinking: Some clinical and theoretical considerations in the treatment of borderline patients. *International Journal of Psycho-analysis, 72*, 639–656.

Frith, C.D. (1992). *The cognitive neuropsychology of schizophrenia*. Hove, UK: Lawrence Erlbaum Associates Ltd.

Gallese, V. and Goldman, A. (1998). Mirror neurons and the simulation theory of mind-reading. *Trends in Cognitive Sciences, 2*, 493–501.

Heberlein, A.S. and Saxe, R. (2005). Dissociation between emotion and personality judgements: Convergent evidence from functional neuroimaging. *Neuroimage*, *28*, 770–777.

Krueger, R.F. (2005). Continuity of axes I and II: Toward a unified model of personality, personality disorders, and clinical disorders. *Journal of Personality Disorders*, *19*, 233–261.

Levy, K.N., Meehan, K.B., Kelly, K.M., Reynoso, J.S., Weber, M., Clarkin, J.F., *et al.* (2006). Change in attachment patterns and reflective function in a randomized control trial of transference-focused psychotherapy for borderline personality disorder. *Journal of Consulting and Clinical Psychology*, *74*, 1027–1040.

Lysaker, P.H., Buck, K.D. and Roe, D. (2007). Psychotherapy and recovery in schizophrenia: A proposal of critical elements for an integrative psychotherapy attuned to narrative in schizophrenia. *Psychological Services*, *4*, 28–37.

Mitchell, J.P., Macrae, C.N. and Banaji, M.R. (2006). Dissociable medial prefrontal contributions to judgments of similar and dissimilar others. *Neuron*, *50*, 655–663.

Ogrodniczuk, J.S., Piper, W.E. and Joyce, A.S. (2005). The negative effect of alexithymia on the outcome of group therapy for complicated grief: What role might the therapist play? *Comprehensive Psychiatry*, *46*, 206–213.

Royzman, E.B., Cassidy, K.W. and Baron, J. (2003). "I know, you know": Epistemic egocentrism in children and adults. *Review of General Psychology*, *7*, 38–65.

Saxe, R. (2005). Against simulation: The argument from error. *Trends in Cognitive Sciences*, *9*, 174–179.

Semerari, A. (ed.) (1999). *Psicoterapia cognitiva del paziente grave. Metacognizione e relazione terapeutica* [Cognitive psychotherapy of severe patients. Metacognition and therapy relationship]. Cortina: Milan.

Semerari, A., Carcione, A., Dimaggio, G., Falcone, M., Nicolò, G., Procacci, M., *et al.* (2003). How to evaluate metacognitive functioning in psychotherapy? The metacognition assessment scale and its applications. *Clinical Psychology and Psychotherapy*, *10*, 238–261.

Semerari, A., Dimaggio, G., Nicolò, G., Procacci, M. and Carcione, A. (2007). Understanding minds: Different functions and different disorders? The contribution of psychotherapeutic research. *Psychotherapy Research*, *17*, 106–119.

Sifneos, P.E. (1973). The prevalence of 'alexithymic' characteristics in psychosomatic patients. *Psychotherapy and Psychosomatics*, *24*, 151–155.

Stiles, W.B., Elliot, R., Lewelyn, S.P., Firth-Cozens, J.A., Margison, F.R., Shapiro, D.A., *et al.* (1990). Assimilation of problematic experiences by clients in psychotherapy. *Psychotherapy*, *27*, 411–420.

Part I

Theory

The neural and social basis for metacognition and its disorders

Chapter 1

Seeing ourselves

What vision can teach us about metacognition

Rebecca Saxe and Shani Offen

> When [split-brain patient] P.S. was asked, "Why are you doing that?", the verbal system of the left hemisphere was faced with the cognitive problem of explaining a discrete overt movement carried out for reasons truly unknown to it. In trial after trial, when queried, the left hemisphere proved extremely adept at immediately attributing cause to the action. When "laugh," for example, was flashed to the right hemisphere, the subject commenced laughing, and when asked why, [P.S.] said, "Oh, you guys are too much."
>
> (Gazzaniga *et al.*, 1977)

How do we know our own minds? Does knowing our minds allow us to use them better? Or to live better? These questions are old, and urgent, and at the heart of interest in metacognition. Unfortunately, the scientific answers remain fractionated and confusing.

Intuitively, knowledge of one's own mind seems simple and direct, quite unlike the effortful and error-prone inferences we make about other people, and more like visual perception of the world around us. To know one's own thoughts and desires, it seems, we need only 'look inward', introspect, and our true states will be clearly visible.

In the current chapter, we explore the analogy between metacognition and vision, and its perhaps unintuitive implications. The analogy serves to organize existing data concerning metacognition from many disciplines, and to suggest new hypotheses for future investigations. Visual perception, we show, is not as dissimilar from knowledge of other minds as it first seems. We will describe how the resulting account of metacognition unifies evidence from developmental psychology, social psychology, neuroimaging and from studies of patients with brain damage.

Two meanings of 'metacognition'

Metacognition has been studied in cognitive psychology in two largely unrelated literatures. The first literature concerns the ability to attribute beliefs and desires to oneself, to explain and justify actions and experiences. For example, I might explain that I ran home because I thought I left the keys in the door, or that I changed jobs because I wanted a shorter commute. We will call this aspect of self-knowledge 'attributive metacognition'. The second literature concerns the ability to monitor and control ongoing mental activities. For example, I could decide to rehearse a phone number in order to remember it better, or to switch to thinking about a different section of this chapter in order to get past a mental block. We will call this second aspect of self-knowledge 'strategic metacognition'.

Attributive and strategic metacognition differ from one another in both the objects of thought (beliefs and desires, versus mental activities and plans), and the actions taken (attribution in the service of explanation, versus monitoring in the service of control). In addition, they depend on largely independent neural substrates (as described below). In the psychological literature, strategic metacognition is closely related to work on executive function, the ability to switch flexibly between tasks and subgoals, and to inhibit unwanted options; attributive metacognition is closely related to work on 'theory of mind' (TOM), the ability to attribute psychological states to ourselves and to other people.

The current chapter concerns attributive metacognition, and the analogy with vision. At the end of the chapter, however, we will briefly return to the relation between the two aspects of metacognition: seeing one's own mind, and knowing how to change it.

Visual illusions

Visual perception feels simple; we just see the objects and scenes in the world around us, when light bounces off their surfaces and reaches our eyes. It seems to us that we couldn't possibly see anything else, given what's out there in the world. Moreover, visual perception feels complete and highly detailed; at every moment we feel as if we are seeing everything before us. Decades of experiments and computational models in vision science belie this experience.

Vision poses an inverse problem: there are infinitely many possible arrangements of surfaces and light sources consistent with any given pattern of light on the retina. The input to vision is ambiguous and sparse, containing many gaps; yet these inputs are somehow transformed into a perception of a stable and highly detailed reality. The way in which the solution is achieved reflects the visual system's goal: to quickly produce a single coherent interpretation, on which decisions and actions can be based. To make this possible, the inputs are disambiguated and completed by processes that take advantage of the system's cumulative knowledge, encoded as prior expectations. Some of these expectations may be learned during our lifetime, and others built into the structure of our brains through evolution. In general the algorithms are effective, efficiently representing external reality, and providing a basis for action. However, systematic illusions reveal that this representation of external reality is really an inference to the best explanation, and can occasionally be 'wrong'.

We suggest that metacognition shares these features of visual perception. As a consequence, the (relatively well understood) mechanisms of visual perception can provide a model for the mechanisms of metacognition. In particular, three features of the visual system provide instructive clues about the metacognitive system:

1 Perception depends both on current data and on prior expectations.
2 The subjective experience of a highly detailed, obligatory perception of the external world is an illusion.
3 Rapid construction of a single coherent interpretation is a central function of the visual system.

These features imply an intriguing fourth feature that may also be shared:

4 There is no dedicated mechanism for interpretation, separate from 'visual processing'; rather, interpretation is suffused into every component of the visual system.

We will illustrate each of these four points in the visual domain, and then consider their extension to metacognition.

Prior expectations let us both disambiguate and go beyond the current data. For example, the visual system enforces a single coherent geometry, populated with smooth surfaces and few edges. It also discounts illumination sources when computing brightness, to achieve brightness constancy. These constraints are revealed by the Adelson plaid illusion (Adelson, 1993), in which the global geometric interpretation leads to big differences in the perceived 'brightness' of two patches of the image with equal luminance (see Figure 1.1). The visual system also enforces what it knows about statistical probabilities. If three dark pac-man shapes are suitably aligned on a light background, the visual system rules out coincidence. Instead, subjects perceive an illusory white triangle occluding the three black disks (Figure 1.2). This perception is rich: there is perceived depth (the white triangle looks as if it is above the black disks), as well as shading and contours (the triangle appears brighter than the background, and its boundaries are clear). In each of these illusions, at least one alternative interpretation of the scene, completely unlike the perceived interpretation, is equally consistent with the incoming data – namely, the true interpretation. Nevertheless, our visual system generates one stable percept, not a bistable percept or a mixture of both interpretations, and the percept is not uncertain or ambiguous. The

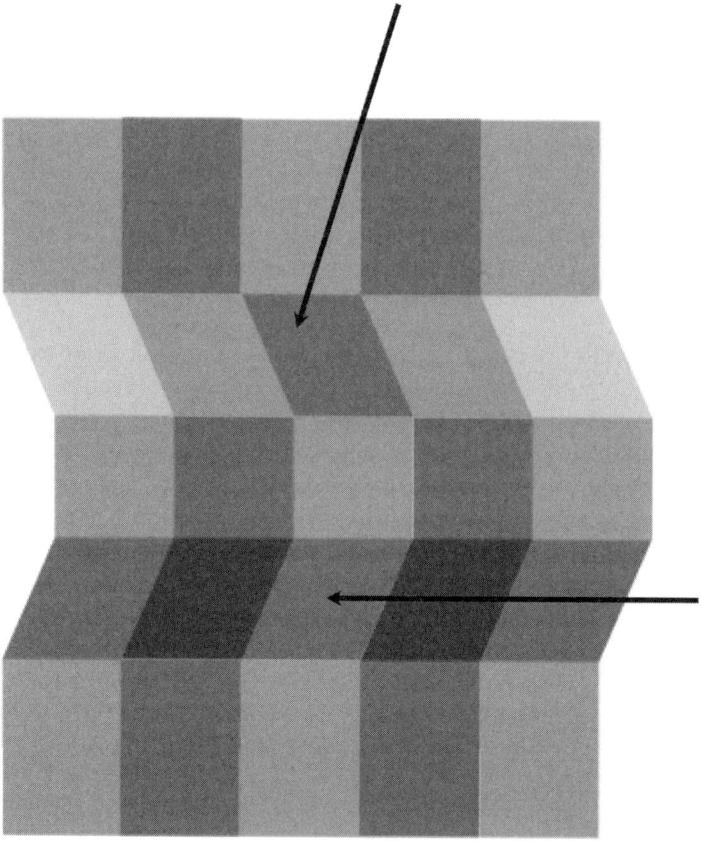

Figure 1.1 The Adelson plaid illusion. The two indicated squares have the same luminance but different perceived brightness. Rotating the image reduces the difference in perceived brightness, demonstrating the dependence of the effect on the 3-D interpretation of the scene.

Source: Image courtesy of Edward Adelson.

mechanisms involved 'cover their own tracks', and the intermediate, inferential stages of processing are inaccessible to introspection.

Also inaccessible to introspection is the extent to which even in the most unambiguous images we may retain only a small amount of the information afforded by the scene, and fill in the rest with untested expectations of what should be there. In change-blindness experiments (Rensink *et al.*, 1997), for example, a visual scene is flashed on and off repeatedly. Successive frames are similar but not identical; the differences between the two frames can be large, central, and quite obvious when the two frames are shown simultaneously. When they are flashed in succession (even very slowly), though, it is often extremely difficult to detect the change. This demonstration

Figure 1.2 A Kanizsa triangle. Although there is no triangle-shaped object in the image, we nevertheless perceive a triangle.

suggests that our introspective experience of continuously seeing a whole scene is itself an illusion. We experience a rich and detailed perception of the visual world; we don't experience the gaps and ambiguities that our visual system is designed to cover. Change blindness doesn't feel like anything. The world we perceive is just a fraction of what's out there, but we are designed not to notice.

Visual illusions are not simply mistakes. Prior expectations are necessary for the visual system to fulfil its function: rapidly producing stable percepts that generalize across contexts, upon which decisions and actions can be based. Moreover, in most situations, the incoming data are consistent with prior expectations, so the single interpretation chosen by the visual system is usually 'accurate'. To expose the hidden mechanisms, experimental situations have to be carefully constructed.

The nature of these hidden mechanisms may be particularly revealing for the analogy with metacognition. Naively, one might conceive of 'input processing' and 'interpretation' as two separate components of the visual system, housed in distinct brain regions and arranged serially. By contrast, experimental evidence from both humans and animals suggests that interpretation of the visual input is built into the architecture of the visual system at every level.

Illusions of metacognition

Like vision, metacognition feels simple; we just know our own thoughts and beliefs. Our introspection feels complete and highly detailed; we feel as if we have reliable access to our entire internal life. This surface of simplicity and directness is an illusion in metacognition, just as it is in vision. We suggest that metacognition shares the structural features we described in the visual system:

1 Metacognition depends on both current data and prior expectations.
2 The subjective experience of a highly detailed, obligatory perception of one's own mind is an illusion.
3 Rapid construction of a single coherent interpretation is a central function of the metacognitive system.

These shared features suggest the possibility of a fourth:

4 There is no separate mechanism for self-interpretation; rather, interpretation is suffused into every component of the metacognitive system.

Attributive metacognition produces the best interpretation of our own behaviours in terms of mental states, based on the current data and prior expectations. Given data that strongly favour a single interpretation consistent with past experience, the system will settle on an accurate attribution. However, equally compelling interpretations will arise when the data are ambiguous, incomplete or inconsistent, or when strong prior expectations are violated by the context. These interpretations are metacognitive illusions; just as in the visual domain, such illusions provide a critical window on the hidden mechanisms.

Relevant input for metacognition may be missing for many reasons. For Gazzaniga *et al.*'s (1977) split-brain patient in our epigraph, the left hemisphere was missing information because it was surgically disconnected from the right hemisphere. When asked why she was laughing, the patient confabulated the most plausible explanation given the data her left hemisphere did have, along with prior expectations (people usually laugh for a reason, the experimenters are fairly odd people, etc.). As in visual illusions, an alternative interpretation is consistent with the incoming data: namely, 'a scientist has surreptitiously instructed my right hemisphere to laugh, and I am unaware of the instruction because my brain is split'. This alternative interpretation is rejected because it is too inconsistent with prior expectations of the system.

Metacognitive illusions are by no means restricted to such exotic cases. Sometimes metacognitive data are missing because the input has been surreptitiously manipulated in a way that even an intact brain cannot detect. For example, Maier (1931) asked people to tie together the ends of two strings that were suspended from the ceiling too far apart to be grasped simultaneously. The solution is to make one string a pendulum. As participants struggled ineffectively, the experimenter would (seemingly inadvertently) brush one of the strings to set it swinging. Shortly after receiving this hint, a large percentage of participants were suddenly able to solve the puzzle. Nevertheless, these participants were unaware of receiving or using the hint. Instead, they offered alternative plausible explanations of their mental processes: that they got the idea from a physics class, or that they had spontaneously visualized monkeys swinging from vines.

'Choice blindness' is a related illusion (Johansson *et al.*, 2005). Participants were shown two pictures of similar, but not identical faces and asked to pick the more attractive one. The participants were given the chosen photo, and then asked to explain their choice. Through a sleight of hand, the experimenter occasionally gave the participant the rejected picture. Participants detected the swap very rarely. What's more, the justifications that participants gave for choosing the rejected photograph were indistinguishable from justifications they gave for choosing the selected one, in length, confidence, emotional intensity, detail and number of embarrassed laughs.

As in the split-brain example, the metacognitive system chooses between two alternative interpretations: one includes current sensory and emotional responses to the (unchosen) picture; the other includes the hypothesis that the experimenter has, by an invisible sleight of hand, switched the two pictures. Prior expectations make the second interpretation very unlikely, so it is excluded. Participants then generate equally compelling interpretations of the wrong choice as they do of the right choice, with no sign of ambiguity or hesitation. Characterizing choice blindness this way also allows for the reasonable prediction that participants will not be blind to swaps between two pictures that differ significantly in attractiveness or emotional response, or when either of the images is easy to recognize. In those cases, the strong evidence from internal states would outweigh prior expectations, and participants would instead conclude that the experimenter was being sneaky.

An experimenter's manipulation can go undetected because it is literally hard to see, as in the examples above, but it can also be neglected in plain view, if the effect of the manipulation is inconsistent with prior expectations. One example is the induced compliance effect (a case of 'cognitive dissonance', Bem, 1967). Participants are requested to do an action that doesn't fit well with their prior beliefs and attitudes (e.g. tell a fellow student that a boring task is interesting). There seems to be little pressure or incentive to comply (i.e. no punishment for non-compliance, and little reward for compliance). Nevertheless, almost all participants comply. Afterwards, they (mis)report having found the task interesting. In contrast, well-paid participants (high reward for compliance) correctly continue to report that they found the task boring. The difference occurs because people's prior expectations substantially underrate the persuasive power of a mere request (Milgram, 1974). Compliance without reward thus seems inconsistent with performing an undesired behaviour (Lepper, 1973). Given this conflict, participants revise their mental state self-attributions, to make them consistent with prior expectations. That is, self-attributing 'I found the task interesting' provides an acceptable retroactive explanation of why they told someone else it was interesting. Induced compliance is thus analogous to a visual illusion: one source of evidence is discarded because it contradicts stronger prior expectations.

The analogy to vision shows that such confabulation is not necessarily a failure. Metacognitive 'errors' may really be illusions, the result of normal attributional processing in the presence of incomplete or conflicting patterns of information. Metacognitive illusions, like visual illusions, arise when the system for attributive metacognition is missing information but, blissfully unaware of its own ignorance, generates an interpretation as if it had all the relevant information. This view explains why we misattribute, rather than simply fail to generate an attribution, when we are not aware of the true causes of our behaviours, and why these misattributions have the subjective feel of 'truth'. Furthermore, attributional processing may not require a separate 'Interpreter' mechanism, but may be inherent in the cortical mechanisms that underlie all self-representations.

To understand (and even predict) metacognitive illusions, though, we need to understand: what are the typical inputs to metacognition? In vision, the 'input data' can be understood to be the pattern of light currently on the retina, or any of the intermediate representations created during visual processing (e.g. oriented edges can be conceived as the 'input' in the Kanisza figures). Nevertheless, in each case, it seems relatively straightforward to distinguish these inputs from the outputs of visual perception, which include the three-dimensional interpretation of the scene, and recognition of the objects in it.

We suggest that for attributive metacognition, the input data include current and remembered actions, physiological states, and sensory states, but not categorized mental states like belief, or anger. Schooler *et al.* (2003) provide a clear statement of this view, for the specific case of happiness or pleasure:

> [There is a] fundamental distinction between individuals' continuous hedonic experience and their intermittent reflective appraisal (alternately referred to as 'meta-awareness' or 'meta-consciousness' (Schooler, 2002)) of that experience. [. . .] *In short, we suggest that individuals' hedonic experiences are typically represented as visceral and non-verbal feeling states. However, when compelled to make hedonic judgments, individuals draw on inferencing processes in order to translate these visceral states into an explicit hedonic appraisal.*
>
> (Schooler *et al.*, 2003: 45, original italics)

The classic data supporting this claim come from an elegant series of studies by Schachter and others (Schachter and Singer, 1962; Reisenzein, 1983). In these studies, changes in the context can lead to widely different self-attributions, e.g. of anger or bemusement, based on the same visceral arousal state (Schachter and Singer, 1962). Likewise, artificially changing inputs about physiological states (e.g. with false feedback about heart rate), in the same context, can systematically alter self-attributions: e.g. of sexual attraction (Liebhart, 1979). These results thus constitute another class of metacognitive illusions: the same internal data are interpreted very differently depending on the context, resulting in widely different, but equally compelling, self-attributions.

We propose that the same distinction applies to all metacognition. The process of attributive metacognition integrates memorial, sensory and physiological inputs with prior expectations. The output is an attribution to oneself of mental states: beliefs, thoughts, desires, emotions, intentions and motivations. Importantly, the outputs of metacognition are never simple 'mirror images' of the inputs. It is in this sense that attributive metacognition is always an act of interpretation (see Carruthers, 2009) and discussion.

Note that we are not proposing that the difference between the inputs and outputs of metacognition is a difference in availability to conscious awareness. Rather, we are proposing that the inputs are different in content from the resulting attribution. People can be made aware of physiological states, just as under some conditions they can be made visually aware of a meaningless jumble of surfaces and edges; this jumble is nonetheless different from the proper output of visual perception.

In sum, the analogy with vision highlights the inferential nature of metacognition that allows for illusions. Of course, in non-clinical populations, the adult metacognitive system is highly effective. Noticeable 'errors' generally arise only in the highly artificial situations devised by social psychologists, or because of neurological damage or neuropsychological disorders. Clinical disorders associated with confabulation might either compromise the integrity of the patient's incoming information, or the patient's ability to know that he or she doesn't know. In everyday life, data may be missing for other reasons: for example, we may be motivated to 'miss' some information about our own minds if it's too unsettling to detect. Future research should investigate these different classes of illusions. As in visual perception, we expect such illusions will provide a critical window on the typical inferential mechanisms for attributive metacognition.

The analogy with vision also suggests another route of inquiry. Unlike the naive intuition that we 'just see' the world, or our own minds, we have argued that both visual perception and introspection are inferential processes. If so, then the divide between knowledge of one's own mind and knowledge of other minds may be due to a difference in inputs, rather than a difference in processing. We suggest that knowledge of our own minds depends on similar mechanisms to our (necessarily inferential) knowledge of other minds, but differs from knowledge of other minds because we have privileged access to our own internal physiological states (as well as more extensive prior experience with ourselves).

Expectations and other minds

How do we know what someone else is thinking? Commonly, lots of clues are available: people talk about their thoughts and feelings, show emotional expressions on their face and body, turn their eyes towards the objects or people they're thinking about, and choose actions based on their beliefs and desires. If your friend keeps looking across the table at your glass of wine, she probably wants some wine; a stranger who is standing by a locked door and reaching into his empty pocket probably doesn't yet realize that he forgot his keys at home.

Like vision, though, inferring other people's thoughts poses an inverse problem (Csibra and Gergely, 2007): there are infinitely many combinations of beliefs and desires that are consistent with any given action. The friend looking at your wine might (truly or falsely) believe the wine has been poisoned, and be waiting for you to drink it and die. The infinite possibilities are excluded based on prior experience, both of how people's minds work in general and of the specific mind of the person in question.

In the last 30 years, hundreds of studies have investigated children's growing understanding of how minds work (Gergely *et al.*, 1995; Wellman *et al.*, 2001; Saxe *et al.*, 2004; Astington and Baird, 2005; Russell, 2005; Surian *et al.*, 2007). Mental states are never directly observed. During development, children must therefore simultaneously learn that other people have internal mental states, the kinds of mental states that people have, and the individual mental states that predict or explain specific actions and events. Children's expectations about other minds are not adult-like from the start; rather, children develop successive mental models of how beliefs and desires are formed, and when they can change, and the role that beliefs and desires have in determining action.

Developmental change thus provides a key window on one component of attributive metacognition: expectations about how minds work. Experimentally, scientists can provide children of different ages with the same current data; that is, the same scenario, and the same information about a person's actions. Developmental change in the inferences, explanations and predictions that children make for these scenarios therefore reflect the changes in the children's expectations about how minds work.

The most commonly studied example of children's changing mental model of other minds is the False Belief task. In one version of this task, a child watches while a puppet places a toy in location A. The puppet leaves the scene, and the toy is transferred to location B. Then the puppet returns, and the child is asked to predict where the puppet will look for the toy. Three year olds predict the puppet will look in location B, where the toy actually is; older children predict the puppet will look in location A, where the puppet last saw the toy (Wimmer and Perner, 1983; Wellman *et al.*, 2001).

Importantly, the younger children's expectations are just as systematic and coherent as the older children's; the difference in their responses generalizes to many different tasks and contexts. For example, instead of asking for an action prediction, Goodman and colleagues (2006) actually showed children where the puppet looked for the toy. In one condition, young children were given evidence against their expectation: the puppet looked for the toy in location A, where the puppet last saw the toy (the 'standard' outcome). In another condition, older children were given evidence against their interpretation: the puppet looked for the toy in location B, where the toy really was (the 'psychic' outcome). In both cases, the children were asked to explain why the puppet was looking in that location; and in both cases, they generated novel but consistent explanations. Younger children, seeing the standard outcome, inferred that the puppet had a different desire (e.g. 'well, that's where she wants to look', or 'she doesn't want the toy'). Older children, seeing the psychic outcome, inferred that the puppet had some other source of access to the true location (e.g. 'I think he heard his sister going over there').

Younger children are also very confident in their answers. For example, Ruffman and colleagues (2001) taught children to bet, to express their confidence in their predictions. Children of all ages learned to use betting to express confidence, and three year olds bet all of their chips that the puppet would look for the toy in location A. In sum, at each developmental stage, children interpret the data of other people's behaviour in light of their prior knowledge and expectations of how minds work. Younger children, like older children, have coherent and organized expectations about minds, and have high confidence in the inferences they make using these expectations. Note that both younger and older children are very frequently accurate, in their behaviour predictions and explanations. People usually do look for objects in the right locations. Careful experimental situations, however, can reveal the developmental changes in children's expectations and inferences.

In these experiments, the younger children's answers are often categorized as 'errors', so that three year olds are often described as 'failing' the False Belief task; five year olds are correspondingly described as 'passing' the task, and even as 'having' a theory of mind. We suggest that these descriptions are misleading. At every age, people use expectations and mental models to guide their interpretations of others' actions. These expectations are very useful, but can also be biased or oversimplified. In experimental circumstances, adults can likewise be induced to give systematically biased predictions and explanations of others' actions (Saxe, 2005).

Since the same expectations about how minds work contribute to people's interpretation of both others' actions and of their own, the same systematic biases appear in both cases. Versions of the False Belief task have been developed explicitly to tap children's ability to attribute false beliefs to themselves. On direct tests, three year olds neglect their own past false beliefs, just as they neglect the false beliefs of other people (Gopnik and Astington, 1988; Gopnik, 1993). In one study, children saw a candy box, and then discovered that it was filled with pencils. They were asked what they thought was in the box when they first saw it. Three-year-old children reported that they initially thought the box contained pencils and predicted that other people would think the box contained pencils; success on the first- and third-person versions was correlated. These results are counter-intuitive. We might expect children just to remember their previous thoughts, and so to have qualitatively different, and better, access to the mental state explanations of their own actions than those of others. But the evidence suggests that they do not.

In an elegant study, Atance and O'Neill (2004) gave three year olds an opportunity to make plans and act based on a false belief. Then, immediately after the action, the children discovered the true state of affairs and were asked to explain their own immediately past action. On one trial, for example, the child was shown a crayon box and asked to say what she thought was inside. When she said 'crayons', the experimenter pointed out a piece of paper and suggested the child retrieve the paper so she could draw with the crayons. Then the box was opened to reveal candles. The child was asked what she initially thought was in the box and, consistent with prior work (Gopnik and Astington, 1988), most children said 'candles'. Amazingly, though, when asked to explain why they picked up the piece of paper, these children still failed to refer to their prior belief (saying instead, e.g. 'there it was on the floor').

The developmental pattern suggests that expectations about how minds work is used to help resolve the inverse problem both for other minds, and one's own mind. Recently, converging evidence for this shared mechanism has come from neuroimaging studies of adults. Following developmental psychology, early neuroimaging experiments identified brain regions showing higher metabolism when participants reasoned about another person's false belief (Gallagher *et al.*, 2000; Saxe and Kanwisher, 2003). A reliable group of brain regions was implicated in the 'false belief' condition (relative to a variety of control conditions, described below), including right and left temporo-parietal junction (right and left TPJ), medial parietal cortex (PC, including posterior cingulate and precuneus), and medial prefrontal cortex (MPFC, not including anterior cingulate cortex).

In many of these regions, the response is specific to thinking about thoughts relative to thinking about other facts about people. In one study (Saxe and Powell, 2006), participants read stories from three conditions, each highlighting a different aspect of reasoning about another person: (a) 'Appearance' stories that described information about a person that is visible from the outside, like hair style and clothing; (b) 'Bodily Sensations' stories that described internal states, like hunger and tiredness; (c) 'Thoughts' stories that described another person's thoughts, beliefs and desires. The right and left TPJ and PC all showed a significantly greater response to the thoughts stories than to the appearance or bodily sensations stories.

When participants attribute beliefs and desires to themselves, the same brain regions are implicated. For example, Lombardo and colleagues (2008) showed participants brief statements of attitudes (e.g. 'thinks it's important to keep a diary') and physical traits (e.g. 'has blond hair'); participants judged whether these properties applied to themselves, or to another person (the Queen of England). The right and left TPJ, PC and MPFC all showed higher metabolic responses during mental compared to physical traits, but did not differentiate between mental states applied to oneself versus another (Vogeley *et al.*, 2001).

Neuroimaging studies of attributive metacognition are still in their infancy, and many questions remain to be answered. What, if any, distinct contribution is made by each of these brain regions, remains in dispute (Frith and Frith, 2003; Amodio and Frith, 2006; Saxe, 2006). Perhaps more importantly, no study has yet elicited attributive metacognition in a natural context. One possible experimental design would be an adult version of Atance and O'Neill (2004): participants should be induced to believe and act on one idea, then learn the truth and be asked to explain their previous actions. Nothing like this design has yet been used with neuroimaging. Developmental and neuroimaging evidence provide a window on one piece of attributive metacognition: prior expectations about how minds work, whether our own or others'. These expectations are combined with perceptions of current and past actions, the context, and the history of the specific individual, as the basis for attributing mental states like beliefs, intentions and emotions to both oneself and to other people. As mentioned above, additional inputs are sometimes available in the first person, including physiological and cognitive states. But in all cases, for self as for others, mental state attributions are inferences to the best explanation, not direct mirrors of internal truth.

We have shown thus far that the analogy to vision, with its focus on illusions that reveal the mechanisms underlying normal processing, helps unite the evidence from social psychology, developmental psychology and neuroimaging. This point of view provides a single framework for thinking of attributive metacognition for both self and other, as an inherently inferential process that takes in inputs (e.g. current perception, physiological states, etc.), evaluates them in the context of prior experience and expectations, and heuristically infers the best explanation for the current data in the given context. In the final section, we consider the question of how attributive metacognition is related to strategic metacognition.

Separating and reuniting metacognition

A first glance at the psychological literature suggests that attributive and strategic metacognition might share a label only by mistake (but see Flavell, 1999). As described above, attributive and strategic metacognition differ from one another in both the objects of thought (beliefs and desires, versus mental activities and plans), and the actions taken (attribution, versus monitoring and control). Many experiments concerning strategic metacognition thus investigate how people estimate their current familiarity with some material, how they choose what kind of studying to do before a test, and how they implement those strategies while avoiding distraction. These experiments share little, superficially, with experiments on attributive metacognition, and indeed are usually conducted by an unrelated group of psychologists.

Developmental studies appear to confirm the impression of two unrelated functions. Studies of attributive metacognition tend to focus on children aged two to six years. 'Theory of mind' is described as 'mature' once children can reliably reason about the causes and consequences of people's differing beliefs and desires. By contrast, the development of strategic metacognition – especially for learning and memory strategies – is usually studied in much older children, from elementary all the way through high school and beyond.

In functional neuroimaging, it is possible to compare (somewhat indirectly) the brain regions implicated in strategic and attributive metacognition, and again, the results point to two unrelated neural systems. Strategic metacognition is often studied under the guise of 'executive functions', including monitoring conflict between competing responses, selecting the correct response, and inhibiting the incorrect response. Across a range of tasks, conflict monitoring and inhibition of responses are correlated with activity in anterior cingulate cortex (ACC), dorsolateral prefrontal cortex, superior parietal lobule, and ventralateral prefrontal cortex (e.g. Braver *et al.*, 2001; Wager *et al.*, 2005). Selecting the appropriate response is also associated with activity in bilateral frontal eye fields, intraparietal sulcus and frontal operculum (e.g. Jiang and Kanwisher, 2003; Lau *et al.*, 2006).

The important point, for our current purposes, is that these brain regions are different from the brain regions implicated in attributive metacognition (and in understanding others' minds): the right and left TPJ, PC and MPFC. In one study, we (Saxe *et al.*, 2006) replicated two previous experiments, one tapping components of executive function including response selection and inhibitory control (Jiang and Kanwisher, 2003) and the other a False Belief task (Saxe and Kanwisher, 2003), within the same individual subjects.

In both individual participants, and in the group average, almost entirely non-overlapping brain regions were implicated in the two tasks.

These results suggest that knowing one's own mind, and controlling it, are completely separable psychological capacities. Nevertheless, clinical experience and common sense both suggest that attributive and strategic metacognition are more deeply linked than the corresponding scientific disciplines. The ability to name our own mental states (attribution) is widely recognized as a necessary step towards developing ways to deliberately alter those states. Parents teach toddlers names for their emotions as a tool to help them productively master them, and avoid tantrums. Similarly, psychotherapy may function partly by identifying and encouraging self-attribution of introspectively inaccessible mental states, in order to make them accessible to strategic manipulation. The distinction we drew earlier, between the inputs to and the outputs of the attributive system, may help describe the link between attributive and strategic metacognition. Just as the goal of visual perception is to identify objects so as to allow the organism to monitor and control those objects, the goal of attributive metacognition may be to identify mental states so as to allow the person to monitor and control those mental states.

The key questions about metacognition thus remain open for future research: under what circumstances does knowing our minds allow us to use them better? Or to live better?

Acknowledgements

The authors would like to thank Nava Rubin and Laura Schulz for extensive conversations about the ideas in this chapter.

References

Adelson, E. H. (1993). Perceptual organization and the judgment of brightness. *Science*, *262*(5142), 2042–2044.

Amodio, D. M. and Frith, C. D. (2006). Meeting of minds: The medial frontal cortex and social cognition. *National Review of Neuroscience*, *7*(4), 268–277.

Astington, J. W. and Baird, J. A. (2005). *Why language matters for theory of mind.* Oxford: Oxford University Press.

Atance, C. M. and O'Neill, D. K. (2004). Acting and planning on the basis of a false belief: Its effects on 3-year-old children's reasoning about their own false beliefs. *Developmental Psychology*, *40*(6), 953–964.

Bem, D. J. (1967). Self-perception: An alternative interpretation of cognitive dissonance phenomena. *Psychological Review*, *74*(3), 193–200.

Braver, T. S., Barch, D. M., Gray, J. R., Molfese, D. L. and Snyder, A. (2001). Anterior cingulate cortex and response conflict: Effects of frequency, inhibition and errors. *Cerebral Cortex (New York, N.Y. : 1991)*, *11*(9), 825–836.

Carruthers, P. (2009). How we know our own minds: The relationship between mindreading and metacognition. *Behavioral and Brain Sciences*, *32*, 121–128.

Csibra, G. and Gergely, G. (2007). 'Obsessed with goals': Functions and mechanisms of teleological interpretation of actions in humans. *Acta Psychologica*, *124*(1), 60–78.

Flavell, J. H. (1999). Cognitive development: Children's knowledge about the mind. *Annual Review of Psychology*, *50*, 21–45.

Frith, U. and Frith, C. D. (2003). Development and neurophysiology of mentalizing. *Philosophical Transactions of the Royal Society of London. Series B: Biological Sciences*, *358*(1431), 459–473.

Gallagher, H. L., Happe, F., Brunswick, N., Fletcher, P. C., Frith, U. and Frith, C. D. (2000). Reading the mind in cartoons and stories: An fmri study of 'theory of mind' in verbal and nonverbal tasks. *Neuropsychologia*, *38*(1), 11–21.

Gazzaniga, M. S., LeDoux, J. E. and Wilson, D. H. (1977). Language, praxis, and the right hemisphere: Clues to some mechanisms of consciousness. *Neurology*, *27*(12), 1144–1147.

Gergely, G., Nádasdy, Z., Csibra, G. and Bíró, S. (1995). Taking the intentional stance at 12 months of age. *Cognition*, *56*(2), 165–193.

Goodman, N. D., Baker, C. L., Bonawitz, E. B., Mansinghka, V. K., Gopnik, A., Wellman, H., *et al.* (2006). Intuitive theories of mind: A rational approach to false belief. In *Proceedings of the twenty-eighth annual conference of the cognitive science society*. Vancouver, Cananda.

Gopnik, A. (1993). How we know our minds: The illusion of first-person knowledge of intentionality. *Behavioral and Brain Sciences*, *16*(1), 1–14.

Gopnik, A. and Astington, J. W. (1988). Children's understanding of representational change and its relation to the understanding of false belief and the appearance–reality distinction. *Child Development*, *59*(1), 26–37.

Jiang, Y. and Kanwisher, N. (2003). Common neural substrates for response selection across modalities and mapping paradigms. *Journal of Cognitive Neuroscience*, *15*(8), 1080–1094.

Johansson, P., Hall, L., Sikström, S. and Olsson, A. (2005). Failure to detect mismatches between intention and outcome in a simple decision task. *Science*, *310*(5745), 116–119.

Lau, H., Rogers, R. D. and Passingham, R. E. (2006). Dissociating response selection and conflict in the medial frontal surface. *Neuroimage*, *29*(2), 446–451.

Lepper, M. R. (1973). Undermining children's intrinsic interest with extrinsic reward: A test of the 'overjustification' hypothesis. *Journal of Personality and Social Psychology*, *28*, 129–137.

Liebhart, E. H. (1979). Information search and attribution: Cognitive processes mediating the effect of false autonomic feedback. *European Journal of Social Psychology*, *9*(1), 19–37.

Lombardo, M. V., Chakrabarti, B., Sadek, S. A., Pasco, G., Wheelwright, S. J., Suckling, J., *et al.* (2008). 'You' and 'I': Shared neural systems for the self and others during mentalizing or physical judgments. Poster presented at Cognitive Neuroscience Society, San Francisco, April.

Maier, N. R. F. (1931). Reasoning in humans: II. The solution of a problem and its appearance in consciousness. *Journal of Comparative and Physiological Psychology*, *12*, 181–194.

Milgram, S. (1974). *Obedience to authority: An experimental view*. New York: Harper & Row.

Reisenzein, R. (1983). The Schachter theory of emotion: Two decades later. *Psychological Bulletin*, *94*(2), 239–264.

Rensink, R. A., O'Regan, J. K. and Clark, J. J. (1997). To see or not to see: The need for attention to perceive changes in scenes. *Psychological Science*, *8*(5), 368–373.

Ruffman, T., Garnham, W., Import, A. and Connolly, D. (2001). Does eye gaze indicate implicit knowledge of false belief? Charting transitions in knowledge. *Journal of Experimental Child Psychology*, *80*(3), 201–224.

Russell, J. (2005). Justifying all the fuss about false belief. *Trends in Cognitive Sciences*, *9*(7), 307–308.

Saxe, R. (2005). Against simulation: The argument from error. *Trends in Cognitive Sciences*, *9*(4), 174–179.

Saxe, R. (2006). Uniquely human social cognition. *Current Opinion in Neurobiology*, *16*(2), 235–239.

Saxe, R. and Kanwisher, N. (2003). People thinking about thinking people. The role of the temporo-parietal junction in 'theory of mind'. *Neuroimage*, *19*(4), 1835–1842.

Saxe, R. and Powell, L. J. (2006). It's the thought that counts: Specific brain regions for one component of theory of mind. *Psychological Science*, *17*(8), 692–699.

Saxe, R., Carey, S. and Kanwisher, N. (2004). Understanding other minds: Linking developmental psychology and functional neuroimaging. *Annual Review of Psychology*, *55*, 87–124.

Saxe, R., Schulz, S. and Jiang, Y. (2006). Reading minds versus following rules: Dissociating theory of mind and executive control in the brain. *Social Neuroscience*, *1*(3/4), 284–298.

Schachter, S. and Singer, J. E. (1962). Cognitive, social, and physiological determinants of emotional state. *Psychological Review*, *69*, 379–399.

Schooler, J. W. (2002). Re-representing consciousness: Dissociations between experience and meta-consciousness. *Trends in Cognitive Sciences*, *6*(8), 339–344.

Schooler, J. W., Ariely, D. and Loewenstein, G. (2003). The pursuit and assessment of happiness can be self-defeating. In J. Carrillo and I. Brocas (eds), *Psychology and economics* (pp. 41–70). Oxford: Oxford University Press.

Surian, L., Caldi, S. and Sperber, D. (2007). Attribution of beliefs by 13-month-old infants. *Psychological Science*, *18*(7), 580–586.

Vogeley, K., Bussfeld, P., Newen, A., Herrmann, S., Happe, F., Falkai, P., *et al.* (2001). Mind reading: Neural mechanisms of theory of mind and self-perspective. *Neuroimage*, *14*(1 Pt 1), 170–181.

Wager, T. D., Sylvester, C. Y., Lacey, S. C., Nee, D. E., Franklin, M. and Jonides, J. (2005). Common and unique components of response inhibition revealed by fmri. *Neuroimage*, *27*(2), 323–340.

Wellman, H. M., Cross, D. and Watson, J. (2001). Meta-analysis of theory-of-mind development: The truth about false belief. *Child Development*, *72*(3), 655–684.

Wimmer, H. and Perner, J. (1983). Beliefs about beliefs: Representation and constraining function of wrong beliefs in young children's understanding of deception. *Cognition*, *13*(1), 103–128.

Chapter 2

Social understanding through social interaction

Jeremy I. M. Carpendale and Charlie Lewis

Understanding human activity in psychological terms is such an important aspect of our everyday lives that, ironically, it tends to be overlooked. This is because such an understanding is a taken for granted and essential part of our ability to engage in typical interaction – it is the medium of our everyday exchanges. This crucial part of our social fabric becomes noticeable, however, when it is missing. There may be serious consequences for individuals who lack the easy understanding of others that is typically assumed. This is a topic that developmentalists have returned to again and again, and various literatures have employed terms such as 'person perception', 'perspective taking', 'role-taking', 'metacognition', or, more recently, 'theory of mind' (TOM) (Flavell, 1992). Although metacognition can have a broader meaning concerning understanding cognitive processes, what these terms have in common is not only a concern with how children and then adults think about what others may be thinking, but also how they reflect on their own thinking about social matters.

The goal of our chapter is to outline an approach to the development of understanding of human activity in psychological terms which assumes that the roots of such understanding are embedded in children's interpersonal relationships. In order to do this, we must first outline the problem to be addressed, then critique current theoretical accounts of the association between social understanding and language, and present our approach to the development of children's understanding of human activity in psychological terms as emerging in social interaction. (For further discussion see Carpendale and Lewis, 2006.) We suggest that earlier forms of competence in coordinating attention with others, referred to as joint attention, can be thought of as social skills in particular forms of interaction that are gradually combined. Mastering these forms of triadic interaction then makes language possible, and the verbal or reflective forms of knowledge that are required to pass supposed critical tests of 'theory of mind' meant to assess the understanding that beliefs can be false. We then consider recent research employing neuroimaging methodology and speculation about the possible role of mirror neurons in social development.

Social understanding and social interaction

Much of the current work on social cognitive development has focused on four- to five-year-old children's understanding that they and others can hold beliefs that may be mistaken. This area is now generally referred to as 'theory of mind'. This phrase derives from a particular theoretical perspective on this problem, that is, the theory that children come to understand their own and others' minds through formulating a theory (e.g. Gopnik and Wellman, 1992). Two other popular approaches have vied for dominance with what has become known as 'theory theory' (TT). One of these is the view that such a theoretical understanding of the mind is not formulated by each individual child, but instead is based on innate modules that have evolved through natural selection (e.g. Baron-Cohen, 1995; German and Leslie, 2000). According to a third theory, children's understanding regarding social matters is not derived theoretically but rather through the process of simulation in which children use their own minds to reason analogically about others (Harris, 1991).

The current literature on what has come to be known as 'theory of mind' has centred around particular research procedures known as false belief tasks. In these tasks children must either make predictions about the actions of a story character who, in the course of the experimental procedure, ends up with a belief that is out of date, or provide explanations for the character's actions based on such a false belief. The false belief research paradigm captivated attention partly because this was seen as assessing a critical step in children's development of an understanding of mind, and was considered the 'litmus test' that indicates if children had acquired a 'representational theory of mind'. The initial research was aimed at charting this transition as well as developing modifications of the tasks that might be easier for young children.

Some of the subsequent research and theoretical debate has focused more broadly on the nature and development of children's social understanding. In particular, considerable evidence was reported that links this social understanding with children's history of social experience and language (for a review see Carpendale and Lewis, 2006, Chapters 6 and 7). This shows that there are several social predictors of false belief performance in young children. For example, Dunn *et al.* (1991) found that individual differences in children's social understanding were linked to different forms of family interaction. Furthermore, preschoolers with more siblings were found to be advanced in false belief understanding relative to their age mates (e.g. Perner *et al.*, 1994). This finding was built on by research which in general found that it was primarily having older siblings, although not too old, that was associated with advanced false belief understanding (e.g. Peterson, 2000). This 'sibling effect', however, has not always been replicated, suggesting that what is important is not just the number of bodies in the house, but rather the nature of the social interaction and the relationships children experience. Supporting this position, attachment security (e.g. Fonagy *et al.*, 1997), maternal sensitivity as indicated by the language used by mothers when talking to their children (Meins *et al.*, 2002) and child-centred parenting styles (e.g., Pears and Moses, 2003) have all been shown to relate to advanced false belief performance. Evidence like this confirms Dunn's (1996) claim that a number of aspects of children's social experience are linked to their social development.

Another source of evidence of the role of social interaction in development is that deaf children of hearing parents are delayed in their development of an understanding of false beliefs compared to other children their age. In contrast, deaf children with deaf parents are not delayed. These parents are fluent in sign language, and would thus expose their children to complex language and interaction that may be missing for those deaf children with hearing parents who lack fluency in sign language (e.g. Peterson and Siegal, 1995). This evidence raises the issue of the role of language in social development (Astington and Baird, 2005). For example, it has been found that the 'sibling effect' did not hold for children who were advanced in their linguistic ability (Jenkins and Astington, 1996). More generally, there is evidence that children who are linguistically advanced are also precocious in false belief understanding (Astington and Baird, 2005). Language, of course, is very complex and many different aspects can be considered including syntax, semantics and pragmatics. Thus we could ask what aspect of language is important for children's false belief understanding.

A number of proposals have been advanced. These include the argument that the aspect of linguistic competence required for false belief understanding is complementation. Statements like "he thought *the earth is flat*" necessarily involve complementary clauses (i.e. '*the earth is flat*'). It has been argued that this aspect of grammar, in which although the overall sentence is true a phrase within it is false, is involved in talking about false beliefs and is a prerequisite for understanding false beliefs (de Villiers, 2005). An alternative view is that the role of conversation in exposing young children to differing perspectives is what supports their development of the insight that others can have false beliefs (Harris, 1996). In a training study designed to sort out the relative roles of these different aspects of language, it was found that both complementation and the conversational aspect of language facilitate the development of false belief understanding and, when combined, the largest improvement in performance was found (Lohmann and Tomasello, 2003). This may be because both forms of training facilitate children's understanding of situations involving differing beliefs.

Furthermore, there is interest in the possible role played by the language that children are exposed to in their homes in how they develop social understanding. The research has focused particularly on the mental state terms that children hear in conversation with their parents. Longitudinal studies have found that the amount of mental state terms that children are exposed to appears to plays a causal role in the development of children's false belief understanding (e.g. Ruffman *et al.*, 2002). However, what appears to be more important in social cognitive development than just exposure to mental state terms is mothers' explanatory talk about social events (Slaughter *et al.*, 2007). A way to think of the convergence evident in the roles of both social interaction and language in social development is with the idea of the connectedness of conversation. This is the extent to which turns in conversation are in response to the previous turn. This may indicate something about the nature of the relationship and the likelihood that such conversations will lead to understanding. Ensor and Hughes (2008) found that the extent to which mothers and their two-year-old children engaged in such connected conversation was associated with the children's advanced false belief understanding at age four.

How does this evidence that many aspects of social interaction are associated with the development of children's false belief understanding fit with the three popular theories mentioned above? At first glance such evidence does not appear to fit well with the predominantly individualistic approaches that we summarized above, but they must offer some explanation for how forms of social interaction and language may facilitate the development of social understanding. Some, like German and Leslie (2004), claim that modularity theory has no difficulty in accounting for this social evidence in the development of children's social understanding. There are grounds for questioning their argument on the basis of its oversimplicity. They weaken their theory to the general claim that 'the capacity to acquire an understanding of mind is innate' (p. 107). Much depends on what is meant by the term 'innate', but on face value such a statement is merely a truism and no one would or could disagree. Yet on the other hand they claim that 'maturation of hardwired mechanisms enables the child to make appropriate sense of social inputs and hence to learn about the social and mental worlds' (p. 107), and that the 'theory of mind' mechanism 'allows the young brain to attend to . . . mental states despite the fact that such states cannot be seen, heard, felt or otherwise sensed' (p. 107). The problem with accounts like this is that is not clear how 'the young brain' can attend to something that 'cannot be seen, heard, felt or otherwise sensed'. Something must be manifest in the child's interaction with others and it is this that we build on. This is even to set aside the problem of how 'the young brain' can attend to anything rather than the young child (Bennett and Hacker, 2003). Such an individualistic, mentalistic approach depicts the brain as being somewhat detached from the body in a new form of 'brain–body' dualism bereft of a grasp of how we as embodied selves relate to other embodied selves.

Other approaches are more amenable to accommodating the social correlates of social understanding. Yet this accommodation seems to modify their theories in interesting ways. Bartsch and Estes (2004) account for the evidence by noting that social interaction provides data for the young 'theory theorist'. Ruffman (2004: 120) agrees that this evidence is not a threat to theory theory (TT) because 'scientific theories, the very basis for TT, are typically constructed both gradually and as the result of community (social) efforts'. However, for us all statements like this do is to accentuate the problem they have in accommodating the social evidence. Not only does this approach depict the child as being capable of formulating theoretical arguments, but it also now places him or her in the hubbub of 'scientific' debate. Yet it does not go far enough. But first it is important to see how the problem is set up to lead to such conundrums.

The poverty of individualism

The problem that is of common interest in this field, described above, is how children come to understand others and themselves in psychological terms. This problem is often set up in a particular way, and how a question is framed already contains assumptions about what an acceptable answer should look like. Although there is much debate about how to explain children's social development, there has been general agreement about the problem that children face in coming to understand the mind, beliefs and intentions. It is the following. People's actions can be explained and predicted in terms of their beliefs and desires and these aspects of their mind are hidden and private. Therefore, there are limited ways in which such an understanding may develop. The three general approaches have been the source of much debate over the last two decades. We, and others, have critiqued these theories (Carpendale and Lewis, 2004, 2006; Hutto, 2008; Leudar and Costall, 2009). Here we point out that all these critical perspectives begin from a common way of setting up the problem that children must solve, and this is problematic. In fact, it is this very problem that the philosopher Ludwig Wittgenstein (1968) grappled with.

The common approach to the problem which children have to solve is that they must come to understand that the mind consists of mental entities such as beliefs, desires and intentions which underlie and cause outer behaviour. Although this view of the mind can be traced to earlier roots, it is usually attributed to Descartes (Ryle, 1949). This 'picture of a purely mental willing entity trapped, as it were, inside the body, able, if it pulls the right levers, to cause the body to move as it intends it to move' (Russell, 1996: 173) has been described as the 'ghost in the machine' (Ryle, 1949).

This position assumes that what needs to be explained is how children learn about other minds that are hidden and inaccessible and begin to communicate from one inner, private mind to another. It is assumed that 'there is a special mystery about how we publish our thoughts instead of realizing that we employ a special artifice to keep them to ourselves' (Ryle, 1949: 28). In contrast, others have argued that, in fact, 'keeping our thoughts to ourselves is a sophisticated accomplishment' (Ryle, 1949: 28). It is this view of the mind as private and accessible only to the self that Wittgenstein argued against, especially in his 'private language argument', making his ideas highly relevant for views regarding how children come to understand others and themselves. Wittgenstein questioned the possibility of a language that is necessarily private – that is, no one else could learn the meaning of the words if they were based on the individual's inner, private experience which is inaccessible to others. In such a private language, links between words and meaning are formed through introspection. Wittgenstein's arguments concern how children learn the meaning of sensation words, and in this context of social cognitive development we can extend this argument to how they learn to use psychological terms. These are at the same time arguments against a particular view of the mind, and it is the view assumed in much of the 'theory of mind' literature.

There are a number of difficulties with such a private language. An empiricist might be concerned that there would be no way for parents to indicate for the child which inner entity should be labelled as pain, happy, sad, or afraid, and would not be able to determine if the child has acquired the correct 'mapping' from word to sensation. Beyond this apparent difficulty, the more fundamental problem concerns how such words are meaningful. The claim that a private language is possible is based on the view of language as words being linked to objects, and in the case of a private language words would be linked to an individual's private inner experience. In order for such a private language to work, the individual would concentrate attention on an inner sensation and label it. Wittgenstein's general argument about language raises problems with the idea that such ostensive definitions can provide meaning. Although pointing can be used to convey meaning, this is only within a regular use or a custom. A private ostensive definition is no better than a public ostensive definition; the act of fixing attention cannot give meaning. Instead, a lot of stage setting is involved, requiring human practices or ways of acting or public practices, regular use or customs.

Wittgenstein's famous beetle box story shows that if one assumes a Cartesian position according to which sensation words refer to inner entities, then such entities drop out of the equation and become irrelevant. In Wittgenstein's story everyone has a beetle box but cannot show anyone else what is inside. But if people have a way of talking about beetles it doesn't matter if what everyone has in their boxes is different, or is constantly changing, or, in fact, is nothing at all. The moral of this story is that if one takes the Cartesian view of the mind then private inner sensation drops out as irrelevant.

Wittgenstein argued against the idea that introspection could be a way in which children could learn the meaning of psychological terms. But he did not deny that adults have the ability to introspect in the sense of thinking about how they might feel in various imagined situations. However, the adult's experience of an inner mental world is a developmental outcome, and therefore cannot be the source of this development. Since we as adults have this experience it is a natural tendency to attribute this to infants, but doing so leads to many theoretical difficulties and toward an individualistic position; that is, a view of the infant as trapped in his or her own body attempting to learn how to communicate with others – a view evident in *The Confessions of St Augustine*. In contrast, from a relational perspective that we have been arguing for (e.g. Mead, 1934) it is communication that develops first and infants develop a sense of self and other only through this process.

An alternative account

In proposing an alternative account we first describe the development of the forms of interaction on which such language is based. This is the area of infant social development known as joint attention. Here we take a constructivist, action-based approach. Earlier social understanding is practical, or lived social understanding – that is, understanding is first within action, it is practical, sensorimotor knowledge. These various terms are attempts to capture a form of knowledge that is different from and earlier than the form of verbal knowledge children need to pass a false belief test. These are various social skills that are gradually combined (Carpendale and Lewis, 2004, 2006; Racine and Carpendale, 2007; Bibok *et al.*, 2008).

If Wittgenstein's arguments are valid how, then, do children learn about beliefs, desires, intentions and the mind? Wittgenstein suggests that one possibility is that 'words are connected with the primitive, the natural, expression of the sensations and used their place' (Wittgenstein, 1968: §244). Children have natural reactions of joy, fear, sadness, etc. It is clear to adults when a child is afraid of a dog, or happy in playing a game. Adults talk about this and children gradually learn to use words in such situations. Infants' desires may be manifest in their bodily orientation toward objects, such as reaching toward a bottle or an out-of-reach teddy bear. Adults respond to these actions and infants may develop 'protoimperatives', that is, pointing gestures used to make requests. This shared routine of interaction in which the infant and adult understand what is going on is the type of interaction in which words can be used, so that later on children can make a request. Infants may first reach, then point to make a request, then say 'juice' and later say, 'I want some juice'.

The infant may not always receive what she is wanting in such settings. This might be due to the adult misunderstanding and thus the child persisting with the request may finally be successful. Alternatively, a parent may attempt to explain why the request cannot be granted, and in the process attempt to achieve mutual understanding regarding the situation. However, it is also possible that the failure of communication might be due to the parent not being responsive. In this case the infant may give up. This not a good sign for future development. If this form of interaction persists between infant and parent, the infant, and later child, will have reduced opportunity to reach understanding of social situations and how to talk about such patterns of human activity. As such children grow up they will interact with age-mates who have relatively advanced social understanding compared to themselves. This could result in problematic interaction in which they may not understand their peers and their peers may therefore reject them. This, of course, could lead to a negative spiral because rejected children are deprived of interaction in which they could learn about the social world. Deficits in social understanding may also result in reduced insight regarding the children's own experience.

What about children's use of what are considered cognitive terms such as 'think', 'know' and 'remember'? These are very complex terms with many different uses. But they, like other psychological terms, redescribe people's activity (Bennett and Hacker, 2003). In accounting for children's mastery of such words elsewhere we have suggested beginning with simpler terms such as 'look' and 'see' (Carpendale *et al.*, 2009). These words are used to talk about attention. They must be based on earlier competence in coordinating attention with others in so-called joint attention behaviours such as using pointing gestures and gaze following (Carpendale and Lewis, 2006; Racine and Carpendale, 2008).

In objecting to a Cartesian view of the mind we are not denying that people believe things, desire things and act intentionally, etc. When infants' activity reaches a certain level of complexity we can say that they are acting intentionally; that is, their actions can be thought of in terms of means and ends. In many circumstances an infant's intention is clear to her parents. In situations of shared understanding parents and children talk about whether an action was accidental or 'on purpose', and thus children learn how to talk about intentions. However, we want to be clear that an intention is not an individual mental entity that causes behaviour but is, rather, a way of talking about an individual's activity embedded in events and interactions (Racine and Carpendale, 2008).

The approach we take is relational in nature and thus it is important to consider how characteristics of the parent and the child may influence the interaction in which development occurs. On the parent's side we have reviewed research above on how aspects of parenting, language and interaction may facilitate social cognitive development. Our way of making sense of the evidence concerns aspects of social relationships and parents' use of language, as well as the child's linguistic ability. These are all related to advanced false belief understanding in that what is essential for social development is understanding, and all of these factors may play a role in the child achieving understanding of social situations. Furthermore, parents who do not understand their children's experience would not be able to respond to them in appropriate ways.

On the child's side, we have mentioned linguistic ability but we must also assume an ability to learn from experience as well as motivation and interest in social matters. A child who did not find other people and social interaction to be salient and interesting might, therefore, not engage in the forms of interaction that are essential to learn about the social world (Klin *et al.*, 2003). Emotional reactivity is another factor that might influence infants' and children's engagement in social interaction. Infants who are over-reactive might turn away from interaction, whereas under-reactivity might result in lack of interest (Shanker, 2004). These examples are drawn from discussion regarding autism, but it might be possible that less dramatic effects might be found in typically developing infants and children.

Social cognitive neuroscience

Recent interest in social cognition has concerned an attempt to localize brain areas involved in social cognition as well as excitement about the potential of the mirror neuron system to explain social cognitive development. Attempts to perform this localization are based on neuroimaging investigations as well as lesion studies (see Saxe and Offen, this volume, Chapter 1). There are a number of issues to keep in mind in the careful interpretation of neuroimaging studies. First, the same area of the brain can be active in different tasks for different functions (Kagan, 2006; Page, 2006; Miller, 2008). Caution is also important regarding interpreting fMRI data because it is mass changes in blood flow that is the signal not the firing of neurons (Logothetis, 2008); thus, 'a brain region can activate according to the fMRI measure without producing any outputs' (Page, 2006: 432). Claims regarding particular brain regions involved in social understanding are controversial, and this ability probably involves 'the activation of large regions of our brain, certainly larger than a putative and domain-specific theory of mind module' (Gallese, 2007: 667).

Although there must obviously be an important neurological level of explanation in a complete account of social cognition, from the perspective outlined above we argue that this level of explanation is far from complete – we contend that such neurological data are the product of the complexity of social exchange that we have outlined above, not simply their cause. For over two thousand years it has been known that damage to the left hemisphere tends to be linked with language difficulties, but this knowledge of the tendency for aspects of language to be localized in the left hemisphere has not helped in evaluating views of language differing as radically as

Chomsky compared to Tomasello (2003) or Wittgenstein (1968). Although we now have more fine-grained descriptions of blood flow to different parts of brains when people are asked to think about particular topics, it is not yet clear what this contributes to our understanding of the nature and development of social cognition (see Page, 2006). We have argued that a grasp of self and others in psychological terms requires a social process of development. That is, forms of thinking are not simply innately given but rather develop and the brain structures that casually underlie such thinking are shaped through experiences. Social cognition is driven by social interaction.

There are two possible families of approaches to neuroscience and social cognitive development. The first view is that cognitive neuroscience is 'the study of the mind through the brain' and that it 'holds the promise of explaining the operations of the mind in terms of the physical operations of the brain' (Greene and Cohen, 2004: 1775): that is, to reduce psychological processes to neurological processes. A difficulty with this is that at a psychological level, actions are performed for reasons, whereas neurology can only deal with causes. To form and act on an intention requires a brain, and neurological processes must be involved. However, intentions cannot be studied solely by studying the brain because they are always embedded in social situations (Bennett and Hacker, 2003; Racine and Carpendale, 2007). The second type of approach is to explore the neurological causal prerequisites for thinking about social matters, and the ways in which social experience shapes neurological processes, taking a developmental systems approach (e.g. Griffiths and Stotz, 2000). In this approach psychological concepts define what it is we are looking for.

Another aspect of neuroscience viewed as relevant for explaining social cognitive development are mirror neurons, first discovered in the macaque premotor cortex. This has resulted in the re-emergence of the simulation view in accounts of social understanding, where there has been much speculation about the role of mirror neurons in social development. It has been claimed that 'in our brain, there are neural mechanisms (mirror mechanisms) that allow us to directly understand the meaning of the actions and emotions of others by internally replicating ("simulating") them without explicit reflective mediation' (Gallese *et al.*, 2004: 396). It is important to remember that these types of neurons were first discovered in macaques, and macaques do not develop an understanding of others' beliefs. Thus we should expect to add levels of complexity in going from the firing of neurons to the experience of understanding someone.

A strength of Gallese's (e.g. 2005, 2007) approach is that it roots understanding in activity, and these neuronal systems may well play a role in social understanding, but we should be cautious about claims that they enable us to 'directly understand the meaning of the actions and emotions of others' (Gallese *et al.*, 2004: 396). We encounter complications in moving from the firing of neurons in the macaque's premotor cortex when seeing or hearing another grasp or crack a nut, to the simple example of communicative interaction such as using pointing gestures. That is, there are further levels of complexity in accounting for human forms of meaning requiring explanation. Even if the same neurons fire when either we or someone else makes a pointing gesture, this will not generally help us understand the intended meaning because such gestures can be used to convey many different meanings in different situations (Carpendale and Lewis, 2008). At 18 months, infants can understand that the same pointing gesture to the same object can convey different meaning when made by different persons with which the infants have shared different experiences (Liebal *et al.*, 2009). Although research on mirror neurons is not yet able to explore this level of complexity, Iacoboni *et al.* (2005: 533) now write that in addition to mirror neurons coding the observed action there will also be '"logically related" mirror neurons coding the motor acts that are most likely to follow the observed one in a given context. To ascribe an intention is to infer a forthcoming new goal.'

Such systems of neurons may be outcomes of social development through which brain structures are shaped. From a Hebbian view of neurological development we would expect that neurons that fire together would wire together (Keysers and Perrett, 2004). So, in fact, if we consider the mirror neuron system to be a developmental outcome (Del Giudice *et al.*, 2009) then it would seem to be consistent with an action-based view of development. There is a necessary neurological side to the story of social cognitive development. However, from the position we outline above, it should be clear that an account focused only at the level of neurons is insufficient because children's understanding of their social world is necessarily rooted in their social interaction and language development. In spite of the importance of this line of research on mirror neurons in potentially providing part of the causal story in explaining social cognition, we should keep in mind what remains to be explained in accounting for understanding human action.

Conclusion and implications

We have argued that the development of children's social understanding is necessarily embedded in social interaction and that development is gradual and piecemeal rather than monolithic. It would be difficult, however, to find a theorist who disagrees with this general statement. What is needed is to go further in specifying the process involved. We emphasize that thinking, and in this case thinking about social matters, is formed in interaction. We have reviewed Wittgenstein's arguments against the view of the mind assumed by many approaches in the 'theory of mind' literature. Instead, we have argued that psychological words redescribe people's activity. Children learn the meaning of mental state terms not by introspection and mapping psychological words on to private inner experience, but rather based on the child's natural reactions in situations when, for example, they are happy, sad or afraid. Within these routine patterns of interaction children learn to talk about human activity in psychological terms. This approach is essentially relational. Children construct their social understanding within social interaction. This then provides a means for children to understand their experience in psychological terms.

Much of the current research on social cognitive development has focused on the important developments occurring during the preschool years as well as the earlier development of joint attention skills in infancy. The older literature on role taking, however, as well as some current research (see Carpendale and Lewis, 2006, Chapter 8) concerns further developments occurring after children have mastered an understanding of false beliefs. It is here that there may be more variability in individuals' social competence, and this may have either positive or negative consequences for these individuals' social lives. We have suggested that children learn about their experience of interacting with others in this social process and gradually learn to talk about this aspect of their world. It follows from this argument that children who lack the forms of social interaction which facilitate such development will be delayed in social cognitive development. Since human life is embedded in interpersonal relationships, this delay could hinder their successful social interaction as well as affect their self-reflective ability to understand themselves, and thus affect their social and emotional health. We have focused on increases in sophistication of social understanding, but biases or distortions in the way people make sense of their social experience (Sharp *et al.*, 2007) may also have detrimental effects on mental health through leading to, resulting from or maintaining emotional or behavioural disorders.

References

Astington, J. W. and Baird, J. A. (eds) (2005). *Why language matters for theory of mind.* New York: Oxford University Press.

Baron-Cohen, S. (1995). *Mindblindness: An essay on autism and theory of mind.* Cambridge, MA: MIT Press.

Bartsch, K. and Estes, D. (2004). Articulating the role of experience in mental state understanding: A challenge for theory-theory and other theories. *Behavioral and Brain Sciences*, *27*, 99–100.

Bennett, M. R. and Hacker, P. M. S. (2003). *Philosophical foundations of neuroscience.* Oxford: Blackwell.

Bibok, M. B., Carpendale, J. I. M. and Lewis, C. (2008). Social knowledge as social skill: An action based view of social understanding. In U. Müller, J. I. M. Carpendale, N. Budwig and B. Sokol (eds), *Social life and social knowledge:*

Toward a process account of development (pp. 145–169). New York: Taylor & Francis.

Carpendale, J. I. M. and Lewis, C. (2004). Constructing an understanding of mind: The development of children's social understanding within social interaction. *Behavioral and Brain Sciences, 27*, 79–151.

Carpendale, J. I. M. and Lewis, C. (2006). *How children develop social understanding*. Oxford: Blackwell.

Carpendale, J. I. M. and Lewis, C. (2008). Imitation cannot explain understanding. *Behavioral and Brain Sciences, 31*, 23–24.

Carpendale, J. I. M., Lewis, C., Susswein, N. and Lunn, J. (2009). Talking and thinking: The role of speech in social understanding. In A. Winsler, C. Fernyhough and I. Montero (eds), *Private speech, executive function, and the development of verbal self-regulation* (pp. 83–94). Cambridge: Cambridge University Press.

Del Giudice, M., Manera, V. and Keysers, C. (2009). Programmed to learn? The ontogeny of mirror neurons. *Developmental Science, 12*, 350–363.

de Villiers, J. G. (2005). Can language acquisition give children a point of view? In J. W. Astington and J. A. Baird (eds), *Why language matters for theory of mind* (pp. 186–219). New York: Oxford University Press.

Dunn, J. (1996). Children's relationships: Bridging the divide between cognitive and social development. *Child Psychology and Psychiatry, 37*, 507–518.

Dunn, J., Brown, J., Slomkowki, C., Tesla, C. and Youngblade, L. (1991). Young children's understanding of other people's feelings and beliefs: Individual differences and their antecedents. *Child Development, 62*, 1352–1366.

Ensor, R. and Hughes, C. (2008). Content or connectedness? Mother–child talk and early social understanding. *Child Development, 79*, 201–216.

Flavell, J. H. (1992). Perspectives on perspective taking. In H. Beilin and P. B. Pufall (eds), *Piaget's theory: Prospects and possibilities* (pp. 107–139). Hillsdale, NJ: Lawrence Erlbaum Associates, Inc.

Fonagy, P., Redfern, S. and Charman, T. (1997). The relationship between belief-desire reasoning and a projective measure of attachment security (SAT). *British Journal of Developmental Psychology, 15*, 51–61.

Gallese, V. (2005). Embodied simulation: From neurons to phenomenal experience. *Phenomenology and the Cognitive Sciences, 4*, 23–48.

Gallese, V. (2007). Before and below 'theory of mind': Embodied simulation and the neural correlates of social cognition. *Philosophical Transactions of the Royal Society, B, 362*, 659–669.

Gallese, V., Keysers, C. and Rizzolatti, G. (2004). A unifying view of the basis of social cognition. *Trends in Cognitive Science, 8*, 396–403.

German, T. P. and Leslie, A. M. (2000). Attending to and learning about mental states. In P. Mitchell and K. J. Riggs (eds), *Children's reasoning and the mind* (pp. 229–252). Hove, UK: Psychology Press.

German, T. P. and Leslie, A. M. (2004). No (social) construction without (meta) representation: Modular mechanisms as a *basis* for the capacity to acquire an understanding of mind. *Behavioral and Brain Sciences, 27*, 106–107.

Gopnik, A. and Wellman, H. M. (1992). Why the child's theory of mind really is a theory. *Mind and Language, 7*, 145–171.

Greene, J. and Cohen, J. (2004). For the law, neuroscience changes nothing and everything. *Philosophical Transactions of the Royal Society*, *359*, 1775–1785.
Griffiths, P. E. and Stotz, K. (2000). How the mind grows: A developmental perspective on the biology of cognition. *Synthese*, *122*, 29–51.
Harris, P. L. (1991). The work of the imagination. In A. Whiten (ed.), *Natural theories of mind* (pp. 283–304). Oxford: Blackwell.
Harris, P. L. (1996). Desires, beliefs, and language. In P. Carruthers and P. K. Smith (eds), *Theories of theories of mind* (pp. 200–220). Cambridge: Cambridge University Press.
Hutto, D. D. (2008). *Folk psychological narratives: The sociocultural basis of understanding reasons*. Cambridge, MA: MIT Press.
Iacoboni, M., Molnar-Szakacs, I., Gallese, V., Buccino, G., Mazziotta, J. C. and Rizzolatti, G. (2005). Grasping the intentions of others with one's own mirror neuron system. *PLoS Biology*, *3*, 529–535.
Jenkins, M. J. and Astington, J. W. (1996). Cognitive factors and family structure associated with theory of mind development in young children. *Developmental Psychology*, *32*, 70–78.
Kagan, J. (2006). Biology's useful contribution: A comment. *Human Development*, *49*, 310–314.
Keysers, C. and Perrett, D. I. (2004). Demystifying social cognition: A Hebbian perspective. *Trends in Cognitive Science*, *8*, 501–507.
Klin, A., Jones, W., Schultz, R. and Volkmar, F. (2003). The enactive mind, or from actions to cognition: Lessons from autism. *Philosophical Transactions of the Royal Society, London B*, *358*, 345–360.
Leudar, I. and Costall, A. (Eds) (2009). *Against theory of mind.* Basingstoke: Palgrave Macmillan.
Liebal, K., Behne, T., Carpenter, M. and Tomasello, M. (2009). Infants use shared experience to interpret pointing gestures. *Developmental Science*, *12*, 264–271.
Logothetis, N. (2008). What we can and what we cannot do with fMRI. *Nature*, *453*, 869–878.
Lohmann, H. and Tomasello, M. (2003). The role of language in the development of false belief understanding: A training study. *Child Development*, *74*, 1130–1144.
Mead, G. H. (1934). *Mind, self and society*. Chicago: University of Chicago Press.
Meins, E., Fernyhough, C., Wainwright, R., Das Gupta, M., Fradley, E. and Tuckey, M. (2002). Maternal mind-mindedness and attachment security as predictors of theory of mind understanding. *Child Development*, *73*, 1715–1726.
Miller, G. (2008). Growing pains for fMRI. *Science*, *320*, 1412–1414.
Page, M. P. A. (2006). What can't functional neuroimaging tell the cognitive psychologist? *Cortex*, *42*, 428–443.
Pears, K. C. and Moses, L. J. (2003). Demographics, parenting, and theory of mind in preschool children. *Social Development*, *12*, 1–20.
Perner, J., Ruffman, T. and Leekam, S. R. (1994). Theory of mind is contagious: You catch it from your sibs. *Child Development*, *65*, 1228–1238.
Peterson, C. C. (2000). Kindred spirits: Influences of siblings' perspectives on theory of mind. *Cognitive Development*, *15*, 435–455.
Peterson, C. C. and Siegal, M. (1995). Deafness, conversation and theory of mind. *Journal of Child Psychology and Psychiatry*, *36*, 459–474.

Racine, T. P. and Carpendale, J. I. M. (2007). The role of shared practice in joint attention. *British Journal of Developmental Psychology*, *25*, 3–25.

Racine, T. P. and Carpendale, J. I. M. (2008). The embodiment of mental states. In W. F. Overton, U. Müller and J. Newman (eds), *Developmental perspectives on embodiment and consciousness* (pp. 159–190). Mahwah, NJ: Lawrence Erlbaum Associates, Inc.

Ruffman, T. (2004). Children's understanding of mind: Constructivist but theory-like. *Behavioral and Brain Sciences*, *27*, 120–121.

Ruffman, T., Slade, L. and Crowe, E. (2002). The relation between children's and mothers' mental state language and theory-of-mind understanding. *Child Development*, *73*, 734–751.

Russell, J. (1996). *Agency: Its role in mental development*. Hove, UK: Erlbaum (UK) Taylor & Francis.

Ryle, G. (1949). *The concept of mind*. Harmondsworth: Penguin.

Shanker, S. G. (2004). Autism and the dynamic developmental model of emotions. *Philosophy, Psychiatry & Psychology*, *11*, 219–233.

Sharp, C., Croudace, T. J. and Goodyer, I. M. (2007). Biased mentalizing in children aged seven to 11: Latent class confirmation of response styles to social scenarios and associations with psychopathology. *Social Development*, *16*, 181–202.

Slaughter, V., Peterson, C. C. and Mackintosh, E. (2007). Mind what mother says: Narrative input and theory of mind in typical children and those on the autism spectrum. *Child Development*, *78*, 839–858.

Tomasello, M. (2003). *Constructing a language: A usage-based theory of language acquisition*. Cambridge, MA: Harvard University Press.

Wittgenstein, L. (1968). *Philosophical investigations*. Oxford: Blackwell.

Chapter 3

The developmental roots of compromised mentalization in complex mental health disturbances of adulthood

An attachment-based conceptualization

Andrew Gumley

Metacognitive function refers to how individuals make sense of their own and others' behaviour in terms of mental states and their utilization of this capacity to solve problems and to cope with specific mental states that are a source of distress (Semerari *et al.*, 2003). Related to this, mentalization which has been defined as the 'process by which an individual implicitly or explicitly interprets his own actions and those of others as meaningful on the basis of intentional mental states (e.g. desires, needs, feelings, beliefs and reasons)' (Bateman and Fonagy, 2004: 302). Problems in metacognition have been implicated in schizophrenia (Frith, 1992), borderline personality disorder (BPD; Fonagy and Bateman, 2006) and personality disorders in general (see Colle *et al.*, this volume, Chapter 11), complex trauma and post traumatic stress disorder (PTSD; Liotti and Prunetti, this volume, Chapter 12). This chapter explores the developmental roots of compromised metacognition and mentalization in severe adult mental disorders. It focuses on how metacognitive processes have been differentially conceptualized in different adult psychological disturbances and explores how an attachment-based approach to understanding the development of metacognition can help us understand these processes from a normative perspective. This approach is in line with Sroufe (1997: 252) who argued that 'behavioural and emotional disturbance is viewed as a developmental construction, reflecting a succession of adaptations that evolve over time in accord with the same principles that govern normal development'. I propose that these normative developmental pathways, which are important to metacognition, are compromised amongst people who are later diagnosed with complex mental health problems, particularly trauma-related disorders, personality disorders and psychotic disorders including schizophrenia. These groups of disorders in many ways typify the tension between a predominant medical model which emphasizes the interplay between neurobiology and environment (as in schizophrenia) versus a developmental model which places emphasis on the interplay between the environment and the individual's history of successive adaptations in the context of risk and protective factors and the individual's progressively active role in these adaptations over time.

The chapter will conclude by considering the implications of this analysis for the further development of research and theory of metacognition in complex adult psychological problems. I propose that personality disorders and psychotic disorders including schizophrenia can be conceived as disorders of affect regulation underpinned by weakened or compromised metacognition and mentalization. A crucial implication of this model is that change is possible at many points despite earlier unsuccessful attempts at adaptation and the return to positive functioning also remains possible. This has important implications for the development of psychological therapies focused upon recovery from complex mental health problems.

Mentalization in complex adult mental health problems

Mentalization or metacognition has been variously referred to as the capacity to conceive of one's own and others' mental states as explanations of behaviour (Fonagy and Target, 2006), the cognitive ability to attribute mental states such as thoughts, beliefs and intentions to people allowing an individual to explain, manipulate and predict behaviour (Sprong *et al.*, 2007) or the ability to think about one's own inner states, and the inner states of others, allowing for complex self-experience and coping with distress (Semerari *et al.*, 2003). Whilst these various conceptualizations of metacognition appear to reflect a degree of commonality in approach, this masks significant complexity and differences in the underlying disorder specific models of mentalization.

Schizophrenia

Impairments in mentalization have been shown to be closely linked to impairments in social and interpersonal functioning observed in schizophrenia (Schaub *et al.*, this volume, Chapter 5). Frith (1992) proposed that mentalization develops adequately amongst individuals later diagnosed with schizophrenia and in line with the cognitive development of 'normal' children, but that abnormalities in brain function and circuitry gave rise to specific abnormalities in meta-representation expressed as symptoms of schizophrenia. In this model, the role of the individual themselves in responding, shaping and evolving adaptation and the influence and constraints imposed by the context of their development was minimized. Sprong *et al.* (2007) found robust evidence of problems in mentalization compared to non-patient controls and those individuals with more severe and complex symptoms including disorganization, negative symptoms and paranoia experienced the most profound difficulties in mentalization. Contrary to Frith's position, individuals in remission also showed mentalization problems in comparison to non-clinical controls. Performance on mentalization tasks was not accounted for by intellectual or executive functioning (Bell *et al.*, this volume, Chapter 7). Mentalizing abilities are also impaired amongst those at genetic high risk for schizophrenia (Schiffman *et al.*, 2004) and those with at risk mental states for developing psychosis (Pickup, 2006). Some have argued that the data are so robust with respect to impairments of metacognition and mentalization in schizophrenia that these impairments should be incorporated into diagnostic criteria (Bell *et al.*, this volume, Chapter 7).

Lab-based tests of metacognition and theory of mind (TOM) have been criticized for their lack of ecological validity. Metacognition and mentalization processes are involved in the ebb and flow of daily life and are particularly involved in emotionally laden interpersonal situations (Lysaker, this volume, Chapter 4). Lysaker has shown in a series of studies (Lysaker *et al.*, 2005a, 2005b, 2007a, 2007b, 2008) how narrative-based approaches to the assessment of metacognition (Metacognition Assessment Scale, MAS; Semerari *et al.*, 2003) capture the way in which individuals diagnosed with schizophrenia utilize mentalization processes including understanding self and other mental states, and the ability to use mental state information to solve problems. Greater difficulties in metacognition as assessed using the MAS were linked to greater cognitive impairment in attention, verbal memory and executive function. Keri and Kelemen (2009) have found that individuals diagnosed with schizophrenia who had more difficulties in attention and memory experienced a greater increase in unusual thoughts during critical interactions with their relatives than those individuals with less cognitive impairment. Although metacognition and mentalization were not assessed in this study, the results highlighted the impact of emotionally laden interactions on increasing psychotic experiences and the possible mediating role that neurocognition (and probably metacognition) have in buffering the stressful impact of harsh criticism. That is, the moment-by-moment capacity to reflect on painful experiences, events and memories without loss of narrative coherence is a key marker of resilience to interpersonally stressful events. As we will see later, this capacity has its roots in early development and attachment security.

Personality disorders

Fonagy and Target (2006) have argued that the capacity for metacognition and mentalization evolves through the experience of social interaction and caregiving and it has been hypothesized that early disruption of affectional bonds will increase the risk of later maladaptation through impaired mentalization. In this sense, mentalization is crucial to the maintenance of a coherent sense of self and acts as a buffer between early adversity on the one hand and later emotional and interpersonal adaptation on the other hand. Bateman and Fonagy (2004) have argued that in BPD there is an inhibition of mentalization where individuals will defensively avoid thinking about the mental states of self and others, as these are linked to experiences in the past (e.g. trauma and maltreatment) which have been associated with extreme pain. In this sense there is a distinction between capacity for mentalization and utilization of mentalization. For those who have experienced trauma in the past and for whom capacity for mentalization is already weakened, the collapse of mentalization in the face of further stress (e.g. increased emotional arousal) leads to the loss of awareness and an inability to differentiate internal and external experiences. This results in extreme states of affect combined with dissociative responding, thus creating the affective and interpersonal instability which characterizes BPD. Liotti and Prunetti (this volume, Chapter 12) have shown evidence that early interpersonal trauma is linked to the metacognitive deficits in identifying the source and nature of mental states and emotions.

Semerari *et al.* (2005) have proposed that there are three core metacognitive impairments in monitoring, reasoning and integration, and differentiation in BPD. First is the ability to identify and describe inner mental states, particularly negatively laden affect states. Second is the integration of mental states and processes into a coherent and organized narrative. Third, is the failure to distinguish between pretend modes and reality-based models of functioning. Impairments in the capacity to step back and reflect on the separateness of others' mental states and their independence to the person's own self (decentration; see Colle *et al.*, this volume, Chapter 11) are a key feature of a range of personality disorders. Semerari *et al.* (2005) have found that whilst individuals diagnosed with BPD were able to identify mental states, they experienced failures in metacognitive functions involving the integrating mental states and distinguishing between imagination and reality reflected in confused and chaotic therapeutic narratives. In contrast, Dimaggio *et al.* (2007) found that individuals with narcissistic and avoidant personality disorders, including those with schizoid traits, had little ability to identify internal states or their casual antecendents. These contrasting results are intriguing and point to the role of metacognition in affect regulation. On the one hand we observe BPD individuals having the capacity to identify mental states but being unable to utilize this information to integrate and differentiate subjective and intersubjective experiences, whereas those with more avoidant states of mind are unable to access mental states and infer causality in their development.

Approaches to mentalization in schizophrenia, complex trauma and personality disorders share a number of key principles. First, mentalization is regarded as an evolved mental capacity designed to enable primates and particularly humans to function in complex social environments requiring the development of affiliative and affectional bonds and necessitating competition for resources (Brüne and Brüne-Cohrs, 2006; Fonagy and Target 2006). Second, these approaches map mentalization closely to brain development and organization. Brüne and Brüne-Cohrs (2006) identified that theory of mind studies have indicated that theory of mind tasks appear to map on to a neural network comprising temporal lobes, inferior parietal cortex and the frontal lobes. Saxe and her colleagues (Saxe and Wexler, 2005; Saxe *et al.*, 2006) have found a role for the right temperoparietal junction (TPJ) for performance on theory of mind, self-reflective and autobiographical memory tasks which is consistent with the developmental evidence on the interrelationship amongst these functions. Fonagy *et al.* (2007) have suggested that the brain structures underpinning social cognition are also implicated in emotion processing and suggest that a two-component model of mentalizing based on implicit (automatic) and explicit (reflective and controlled) processing systems with separate but related underlying neurobiological systems. Mentalization-based approaches to schizophrenia have tended to emphasize the cognitive components of theory of mind, that is, those systems involved in belief reasoning, whereas in mentalization-based approaches to personality disorder the emphasis has been on affect regulation and emotional reflectivity. In addition, few investigators (e.g. Salvatore *et al.*, 2007) have considered the intersubjective dimensions of impoverished understanding of mental states in schizophrenia. The contrasting perspectives on metacognition and mentalization in the psychoses and personality disorders are not incompatible though. Baron-Cohen's (2005) model and the evidence from Saxe and colleagues (2005, 2006) allow us to consider developmentally the evolution of mentalization in the early years of life and its possible role as a risk factor for the development of problems diagnosed as schizophrenia or personality disorders.

Development of mentalization in context of secure attachment

The fundamental tenet of Bowlby's (1969, 1973, 1980) formulation of attachment theory concerned the primacy of the human need for security – 'the secure base'. Infants can best explore and take an active interest in the world if they feel they have a secure base to which they can return if threatened. Initially this base is provided by the attachment figure. It is an evolutionary necessity for infants to be able to secure the interests and attention of adults, and for adults to maintain the care and empathy for the infant. This describes a reciprocal control system. Therefore, when infants are separated from their caregiver, if their caregiver is unresponsive, or if an infant detects some danger and feels frightened or distressed then the attachment system is switched on and the infant seeks proximity. The reciprocal of this is the switching on of the caregiver's attachment system. The goal of the attachment system is defence, safety and self-regulation including the regulation of affect. Once this goal has been achieved, the system switches off again. Ainsworth and colleagues (1978) identified two main attachment styles, secure and insecure. Secure attachment strategies are observed when an infant can confidently rely on his or her caregiver for security. Insecure attachment styles can be further subdivided into avoidant and ambivalent patterns. In infants, these insecure behaviour patterns are attempts to maintain security in the absence of an optimal attachment situation (e.g. an inconsistently available or even rejecting caregiver) by either over-amplifying (ambivalent) or deactivating (avoidant) attachment behaviours. A fourth dimension referred to the disorganized/disorientated group which is characterized by bizarre or conflicted behaviour. It is often observed in infants who have experienced high levels of loss, separation, abuse or highly chaotic parenting behaviour. Attachment (dis)organization is addressed later by Liotti and Prunetti (this volume, Chapter 12). The focus in this chapter is on the relevance of attachment (in)security and organization to the development of metacognition and mentalization.

Infant attachment provides the basis for the development of internal working models, which provide the basis for adult relational functioning, metacognition, mentalization and affect regulation. Infant attachment security is strongly related to the way in which attachment-related experiences are portrayed by caregivers using the Adult Attachment Interview (AAI; George *et al.*, 1985). The AAI provides an adult analogue of the infant Strange Situation Test and based on the analysis of narratives provides a two category (freely autonomous and secure/insecure), three category (freely autonomous and secure/avoidant/preoccupied) and four category (freely autonomous and secure/avoidant/preoccupied/disorganized) classification system. These categories map on to infant attachment organization and behaviour. Freely autonomous and secure speakers tend to value attachment relationships, regard attachment experiences as influential, appear relatively independent and autonomous and appear free to explore both positive and painful thoughts and feelings. Avoidant or dismissing speakers tend to limit the influence of attachment-related experiences by denying, closing down or minimizing these experiences. These speakers will often implicitly claim strength, normality and independence and provide a very positive description of early development, which is not substantiated by episodic memories. Preoccupied speakers often appear confused. Discussions of attachment and other relational experiences are often prolonged, vague and uncritical or angry and conflicted. Discussions are rarely fruitful and are sometimes fearfully preoccupied with or overwhelmed by trauma and loss. Unresolved or disorganized speakers portray marked lapses in metacognitive monitoring of discourse and reasoning during discussion of loss or trauma. In a recent meta-analysis, Fraley (2002) found moderate stability of attachment from infancy to adulthood and showed that representations of early experiences continue to have an influential role in attachment behaviour across the lifespan. These findings are important here given the close relationships between attachment security and the development of metacognition and mentalization.

Maternal attunement, reflective functioning and mind-mindedness

Correspondence between security of caregiver attachment organization and infant security is high in normative samples with rates of 83 per cent when using the secure–insecure distinction falling to around 45 per cent correspondence when using four category classifications (18 per cent predicted by chance) (Hesse, 1999). Rates of correspondence found in prebirth studies are also striking. Fonagy *et al.* (1991a) found 75 per cent concordance for the secure insecure classification, and 66 per cent for the three-way classification (avoidant, preoccupied, secure). These findings have been subsequently replicated in three-generation studies (grandmother, daughter, granddaughter), high-risk studies and confirmed in subsequent meta-analyses (Hesse, 1999).

The lack of perfect correspondence between maternal and infant attachment classifications has prompted further studies into additional factors promoting attachment security in infancy. Fonagy *et al.* (1991b) explored maternal reflective functioning as assessed by the AAI and its relation to infant attachment security at 12 and 18 months. Reflective functioning (RF) refers to the psychological processes underlying the capacity to mentalize and 'involves both a self reflective and an interpersonal component that ideally provides the individual with a well-developed capacity to distinguish inner from outer reality, pretend from "real" modes of functioning, intrapersonal mental and emotional processes from interpersonal communications' (Fonagy *et al.*, 1998: 4). RF is also related to the quality of affective elaboration of others' mental states (Bouchard *et al.*, 2008). Fonagy *et al.* (1991b) found that maternal RF was strongly associated with infant security and was a more powerful predictor of infant security that maternal narrative coherence (a key predictor of attachment security on the AAI). These results showed the crucial importance of mentalization processes in the intergenerational transmission of attachment security. Maternal RF has also been associated with more accurate and appropriate affective communication between mothers and their infants. Lower RF is associated with more affective communication errors, greater boundary confusion, increased intrusiveness and more fearful, disorientated and disorganized behaviour (Grienenberger *et al.*, 2005). Furthermore, Grienenberger *et al.* (2005) found that affective communication partially mediated the relationship between maternal attachment and infant attachment. Caregiver infant communication is therefore understood as a key vehicle through which parental RF and affect regulation is translated and communicated to the child. Related to this, maternal mind-mindedness (MM) has been an important focus of study in the development of security in infancy and childhood and the evolution of mentalization capacity (Meins, 2003). MM refers to the tendency to treat infants as individuals with minds reflected in how the mother frames interactions with her infant in terms of her infant's desires, intentions, beliefs and emotions. In this sense it also closely accords with RF. MM is stable over time (Meins and Fernyhough, 1999) and greater MM has been associated with more sensitivity, less intrusiveness and less hostility during play (Lok and McMahon, 2006), security of attachment (assessed using the AAI) and higher RF (Arnott and Meins, 2007). In a longitudinal study, Arnott and Meins (2007) found that autonomous maternal AAI was associated with high MM and subsequent secure infant attachment and non-autonomous insecure maternal AAI was associated with low MM and insecure infant attachment. High MM appeared to ameliorate the effects of insecure AAI on infant attachment security. MM has also been linked to mothers' use of mind-related comments in communication with their infants, and is a predictor of infant security at twelve months (Meins *et al.*, 2001).

Infant attachment security has been associated with a number of improved outcomes in childhood including better problem solving, greater use of symbolic play, greater independence and autonomy, greater persistence on tasks and improved peer competence in comparison to insecurely attached infants (Meins, 2003). For example, children developing in families where there is a tendency to discuss feelings and use mental state language (a feature of attachment security) are more likely to pass age-appropriate theory of mind tasks (Dunn *et al.*, 1991). Maternal MM at six months has been associated with children's understanding of mind assessed using both TOM tasks and narrative at 45 and 55 months (Meins *et al.*, 2003) and that mothers' use of mental state language predicts TOM performance (at 45 and 48 months) independent of the child's attachment security at twelve months (Meins *et al.*, 2002). Importantly, these findings with respect to the development of children's mentalizing abilities are not accounted by their language acquisition (Meins and Fernyhough, 1999).

Pretend play and understanding minds

A further key aspect of metacognitive development of mentalizing and metarepresentational capacities is the role of pretence and pretend play. Pretence provides an opportunity for the child to explore a 'decoupled' imagined world that retains many of the properties of the real world but also allows for change in chosen parameters (e.g. pretending to use a banana as a telephone; Twin Earth theory, Lillard, 2001). A crucial aspect of pretend play in children is the construction of a mental representation that is intentionally projected into reality. Lillard (2001) has highlighted the importance of parental social referencing during early pretend play.

Amongst infants of parents who engage frequently in pretence, there is a tendency amongst those infants to become particularly attuned to the social signals of the parent. She has shown that pretend play and the use of pretence in parental or peer relationships promotes the development of metacognitive skills involved in mentalizing and theory of mind during early to middle childhood. Pretend play has its basis in security of attachment, which promotes and stimulates playful exploration. The attachment relationship provides the basis for the transformation of objects, intentions and affects into pretend and 'nonconsequential' modes of expression and communication, which are 'decoupled' from physical reality (Fonagy *et al.*, 2004). Indeed Fonagy and his colleagues (2004) have argued that marked parental mirroring in the context of pretend play or in the context of empathic positive social interactions provides the infant with the experiences which facilitate the development of metacognitive skills while later underpin emotional regulation.

Evidence for compromised developmental experiences in BPD and schizophrenia

Liotti and Gumley (2009) have reviewed the role of early infant disorganization, childhood loss and trauma and its possible relationship to compromised mentalization in people with schizophrenia. Their position is consistent with Bateman and Fonagy's (2004) formulation of the ontogeny of mentalization problems in BPD (for a review see Choi-Kain and Gunderson, 2008).

Parental trauma and loss

A key component of an attachment theory is the intergenerational transmission of security and insecurity. A major risk factor for adult disorganization of attachment is the experience of loss and trauma. A number of studies are emerging exploring the BPD, dissociative disorders and severe trauma and loss suffered by the mothers of adult patients in the two years before or after the individual's birth. Liotti *et al.* (2000) found that the risk of developing BPD, rather than another type of mental disorder (anxiety, affective and cluster C personality disorders), was increased by: (a) the individual's mother was mourning over a loss (or dealing with a serious trauma) during the individual's infancy and (b) the patient's childhood had been plagued by severe traumatic experiences (losses and/or sexual, emotional and physical abuse). This combination of risk factors may also be relevant to understanding the developmental pathways of individuals diagnosed with schizophrenia. Miti and Chiaia (2003) did not find any differences between those diagnosed with dissociative disorders or BPD and schizophrenia, with regard to the amount of losses and traumas experienced by the mothers, which was high in all three groups.

Parental separation and Loss

In those who are diagnosed with BPD, rates of parental separation and loss (80 per cent) through divorce, parental illness or death are elevated. Similarly, we also observe high rates of parental loss in childhood through death, divorce and separation amongst those who are later diagnosed as having schizophrenia (for a review see Read and Gumley, 2008).

Childhood abuse and maltreatment

Elevated rates of childhood trauma, abuse and maltreatment amongst individuals diagnosed with BPD have been noted (Bateman and Fonagy, 2004). Evidence is also emerging from longitudinal studies showing that childhood abuse and neglect substantially increase the risk of BPD specifically and cluster B symptoms generally (Johnson *et al.*, 1999, 2000). A recent review of 46 studies of individuals diagnosed with schizophrenia found that around one half had been subjected to childhood sexual abuse (CSA) and to childhood physical abuse (CPA). The majority had been subjected to either CSA or CPA (Read *et al.*, 2005). Bebbington *et al.* (2004) identified psychiatric disorders amongst 8580 individuals living in the UK. Compared to respondents with other psychiatric disorders, the prevalence of lifetime victimization amongst people with definite or probable psychosis was elevated. These experiences included sexual abuse, running away from home, expulsion from school, bullying, local authority care and being a victim of assault. These relationships were robust and remain significant after controlling for depression and for the interrelationship between these life events. What is apparent from these data are that severe disruption in early attachment and bonding experiences increases individuals' vulnerability to developing psychosis. In a general population sample of 4045 participants, who were followed up over two years, Janssen and colleagues (2004) found that experience of CSA associated with psychosis. This relationship remained despite different types of measurements of psychosis. In addition more frequent sexual abuse was associated with greater risk of developing psychosis and having need for care. Liotti and Gumley (2009) and Read and Gumley (2008) have argued that these high rates of trauma are likely to impact on the development of metacognition and mentalization in a way that may help explain the relationship between early childhood trauma and later complex mental health problems, particularly schizophrenia, personality disorder and dissociative disorders.

Studies using the AAI in schizophrenia and personality disorder

Studies using the AAI in individuals diagnosed with BPD have found that participants tend to be classified as preoccupied with attachment. That is, their narratives tend to be long and confusing and reflect angry, fearful or passive accounts of attachment experiences. In addition the vast majority of these transcripts are unresolved for loss and trauma (Dozier *et al.*, 1999; Bateman and Fonagy, 2004). These AAI transcripts tend to show impoverished RF (Fonagy *et al.*, 1996). Fonagy *et al.* (1996) found that RF was particularly impoverished in individuals diagnosed with BPD compared to those with Axis I disorders, and that low RF was predictive of diagnosis of BPD in the context of early childhood abuse.

In contrast, studies using the AAI in people diagnosed with schizophrenia have been limited. Dozier *et al.* (1992) found that individuals with schizophrenia (n = 21) relied on more repressing attachment strategies than those with affective disorder (n = 19). In a later study, Dozier and Tyrrell (1997) investigated individuals diagnosed with bipolar disorder (n = 7), schizoaffective disorder (n = 8) and schizophrenia (n = 27). Using the three-way classification of attachment organization (autonomous, preoccupied and dismissing), most of these participants were classified as dismissing of attachment. In terms of the four-way classification (which includes disorganized attachment), almost 50 per cent of those diagnosed with schizophrenia were classified as disorganized. No studies of RF in persons with a diagnosis of schizophrenia or other psychoses have been published.

Conclusions and implications for understanding recovery and persistence of psychosis and personality disorder

Both schizophrenia and personality disorders share common developmental pathways characterized by the lack of secure base and/or the presence of relational trauma and loss during childhood and adolescence. What is striking about the AAI studies reported above is the contrasting way in which affect regulation is organized in BPD and schizophrenia. Affect dysregulation is understood in BPD in the context of early attachment insecurity and disorganization, complex and relational trauma, and weakened reflective functioning or mentalization. In BPD affect is under-regulated producing states of fear and intense pain, leading to dissociative and disorganized responding and maladaptive coping including self-harm and suicidal behaviour. In contrast, we observe that in schizophrenia affect regulation strategies tend to close down, limit or minimize affect and affectively laden memories. Although to date there have not been reported studies of RF in individuals diagnosed with schizophrenia, theory of mind studies show that mentalization is weakened in schizophrenia. In addition, we also draw upon a substantial and growing body of evidence from Lysaker and colleagues (Lysaker, this volume, Chapter 4) showing that metacognitive deficits reflected in individuals' narrative accounts of their experiences are characterized by difficulties in awareness of self and other mental states and utilization of mental state information. Research in personality disorders (e.g. Semerari *et al.*, 2005; Dimaggio *et al.*, 2007). show that on the one hand individuals with BPD experience greater difficulties in integrating mental states and distinguishing between mental states, those with narcissistic and avoidant personality disorders, including those with schizoid traits, were severely impaired in identifying internal states and in relating internal states to their causal mechanisms. In schizophrenia we observe a tendency towards greater difficulties in identifying and relating internal states. Therefore in schizophrenia this combination of a predominance of avoidant or shut down affect regulation strategies with weakened mentalization may begin to help us understand the development and persistence of negative symptoms, disorganization and vulnerability to relapse (which is characterized by affect dysregulation). Attachment disorganization, dissociative responding and impaired mentalization may also help us understand psychotic experiences such as auditory, visual and other forms of hallucinations.

Recovery

This is not to say that all individuals who are diagnosed with schizophrenia lack a secure base or are insecure in their attachment organization. In fact, this account would accommodate that individuals can develop psychosis in the context of severe life events, which overwhelm mentalization producing intense unbearable affects, dissociative responding and psychotic experiences. It would be predicted that these individuals experience an acute onset, short duration of untreated psychosis (DUP) and have good premorbid functioning. It would also be predicted that these individuals are more likely to express affective disturbance during their recovery, be more likely to engage with services and seek help in a crisis and have a positive emotional and symptomatic recovery. This formulation would explain the important findings related to DUP and premorbid functioning (Macbeth and Gumley, 2008) and attachment security, sealing over and recovery from psychosis (Tait *et al.*, 2004). Tait *et al.* (2004) explored the hypothesis that individuals who seal over (or avoid thinking about the implications of their 'illness') have greater psychological vulnerability and lowered resilience, defined by more negative beliefs about themselves, more problematic early parenting experiences and less secure self-reported attachment attitudes.

Compared to integrators, individuals who sealed over had more negative views of themselves, felt more insecure and rated their mothers and fathers as less caring and more abusive. In addition, individuals who used a sealing over recovery style described their attitudes to attachment as less close, less dependable and rated themselves as having greater fear of rejection by others. Insecure attachment attitudes were related to service engagement; that is those who felt less close had greater fear of rejection and saw others as less dependable and were less engaged with services. Attachment attitudes correlated with parental bonding, where insecure attachment attitudes were related to more perceived parental abuse and less perceived parental care. These data provide a helpful framework from which to view engagement, whereby individual attitudes to adult attachment (derived from early parental attachment experiences) mediate how individuals cope with their psychosis and engage with services.

Psychotherapy

Holmes (2001) has likened psychotherapy to a playful pretend mode of functioning facilitated by the secure relationship with a therapist, which facilitates exploration of real and imagined modes of function within interpersonal problems. From this viewpoint, metacognition provides a key framework to begin to understand processes of change and this has been found in psychotherapy of personality disorders (Dimaggio *et al.*, 2007) and schizophrenia (Lysaker *et al.*, 2005b). In addition, RF has been found to improve with some psychotherapies in individuals with BPD (Levy *et al.*, 2006). Cognitive therapy has been shown to be effective for persistent and distressing psychotic symptoms. Cognitive interpersonal therapy may have an important role to play in facilitating affect regulation, interpersonal functioning and emotional recovery (Gumley and Schwannauer, 2006) Preliminary evidence suggests that RF is a key aspect of therapeutic change in the psychotherapy of psychosis. Dilks *et al.* (2008) conceptualized the central activity of psychological therapy as a process of building bridges to observational perspectives. These activities involved opening up topics where the therapist prompted service users to elaborate different views of the experience under consideration; negotiating shared understandings between the therapist and service user; utilizing the relationship to develop new insights and meanings; and finally managing the expression and climate of emotional experience. Crucial to these psychotherapeutic processes, Dilks *et al.* observed the emergence of greater reflectivity that was embedded in the security of the therapeutic relationship, which provided a scaffold to the emergence of reflectiveness. In addition a number of case studies have provided some preliminary evidence that psychotherapy may enhance mentalizing in individuals with schizophrenia and thereby promote recovery (Lysaker *et al.*, 2005a, 2007a).

Much can be learned by a research and clinical focus on transdiagnostic processes in psychosis and personality disorders. Metacognition provides a key construct to allow the development of research and clinical practice focused on acquiring a greater understanding of the developmental roots of these complex mental health problems, our understanding of core psychological processes associated with the persistence of these disorders, and provides a promising focus for the development of innovative and effective psychotherapies.

References

Ainsworth, M.D.S., Blehar, M.C., Waters, E. and Wall, S. (1978). *Patterns of attachment: A psychological study of the strange situation*. Hillsdale, NJ: Lawrence Erlbaum Associates, Inc.

Arnott, B. and Meins, E. (2007). Links among antenatal attachment representations, postnatal mind mindedness, andingant attachment security: A preliminary study of mothers and fathers. *Bulletin of the Menninger Clinic*, *71*, 132–149.

Baron-Cohen, S. (2005). Autism. In B. Hopkins, R.G. Barr, G.F. Michel and P. Rochat (eds), *Cambridge encyclopaedia of child development* (Vol 28, pp. 109–126). Cambridge: Cambridge University Press.

Bateman, A. and Fonagy, P. (2004). *Psychotherapy for borderline personality disorder: Mentalization based treatment*. Oxford: Oxford University Press.

Bebbington, P.E., Bhugra, D., Brugha, T., Singleton, N., Farrell, M., Jenkins, G., *et al.* (2004). Psychosis, victimisation and childhood disadvantage: Evidence from the second British national survey of psychiatric morbidity. *British Journal of Psychiatry*, *185*, 220–226.

Bouchard, M.-A., Target, M., Lecours, S., Fonagy, P., Tremblay, L.-M., Schachter, A., *et al.* (2008). Mentalization in adult attachment narratives: Reflective functioning, mental states and affect elaboration compared. *Psychoanalytic Psychology*, *25*, 47–66.

Bowlby, J. (1969). *Attachment and Loss Vol. 1: Attachment*. London: Hogarth Press.

Bowlby, J. (1973). *Attachment and Loss Vol. 2: Separation, anger and anxiety*. London: Hogarth Press.

Bowlby, J. (1980). *Attachment and Loss Vol. 3: Loss, sadness and depression*. London: Hogarth Press.

Brüne, M. and Brüne-Cohrs, U. (2006). Theory of mind – evolution, ontogeny, brain mechanisms and psychopathology. *Neuroscience and Biobehavioural Reviews*, *30*, 437–455.

Choi-Kain, L.W. and Gunderson J.G. (2008). Mentalization: Ontogony, assessment and application in the treatment of borderline personality disorder. *American Journal of Psychiatry*, *165*, 1127–1135.

Dilks, S., Tasker, F. and Wren, B. (2008). Building bridges to observational perspectives: A grounded theory of therapy processes in psychosis. *Psychology and Psychotherapy: Theory, Research and Practice*, *81*, 209–229.

Dimaggio, G., Procacci, M., Nicolò, G., Popolo, R., Semerari, A., Carcione, A., *et al.* (2007). Poor metacognition in narcissistic and avoidant personality disorders:

Four psychotherapy patients analysed using the metacognition assessment scale. *Clinical Psychology and Psychotherapy*, *14*, 386–401.

Dozier, M. and Tyrrell, C. (1997). Attachment and communication among persons with serious psychopathological disorders. In J. Simpson and W. Rholes (eds), *Attachment theory and close relationships*. New York: Guilford Press.

Dozier, M., Stevenson, A., Lee, S. and Velligan, D. (1992). Attachment organizaton and familial overinvolvement for adults with serious psychopathological disorders. *Development and Psychopathology*, *3*, 475–489.

Dozier, M., Stovall, K.C. and Albus, K.E. (1999). Attachment and psychopathology in adulthood. In J. Cassidy and P.R. Shaver (eds), *Handbook of attachment: Theory, research and clinical applications*. New York: Guilford Press.

Dunn, J., Brown, J., Slomkowski, C., Tesla, C. and Youngblade, L.M. (1991). Young childrens' understanding of other people's feelings and beliefs: Individual differences and their antecedents. *Child Development*, *62*, 1352–1366.

Fonagy, P. and Bateman, A.W. (2006). Mechanisms of change in mentalization based treatment of BPD. *Journal of Clinical Psychology*, *62*, 411–430.

Fonagy, P. and Target, M. (2006). The mentalization-focussed approach to self pathology. *Journal of Personality Disorders*, *20*, 544–576.

Fonagy, P., Steele, H. and Steele, M. (1991a). Maternal representations of attachment during pregnancy predict organisation of infant–mother attachment at one year of age. *Child Development*, *62*, 891–905.

Fonagy, P., Steele, M., Steele, H., Moran, G.S. and Higgitt, A.C. (1991b). The capacity for understanding mental states: The reflective self in parent and child and its significance for security of attachment. *Infant Mental Health Journal*, *12*, 201–218.

Fonagy, P., Leigh, T., Steele, M., Steele, H., Kennedy, R., Mattoon, G., *et al.* (1996). The relation of attachment status, psychiatric classification and response to psychotherapy. *Journal of Consulting and Clinical Psychology*, *64*, 22–31.

Fonagy, P., Target, M., Steele, H. and Steele, M. (1998). Reflective functioning manual (version 5). Unpublished manuscript. University College London.

Fonagy, P., Gergely, G., Jurist, E.L. and Target, M. (2004). *Affect regulation, mentalization and the development of the self*. London: Karnac.

Fonagy, P., Gergely, G. and Target, M. (2007). The parent–infant dyad and the construction of the subjective self. *Journal of Child Psychology and Psychiatry*, *48*, 288–328.

Fraley, R.C. (2002). Attachment stability from infancy to adulthood: Meta-analysis and dynamic modelling of developmental mechanisms. *Personality and Social Psychology Review*, *6*, 123–151.

Frith, C.D. (1992). *The cognitive neuropsychology of schizophrenia*. Hove, UK: Lawrence Erlbaum Associates Ltd.

George, C., Kaplan, N. and Main, M. (1985). The adult attachment interview. Unpublished manuscript. University of California at Berkeley.

Grienenberger, J., Kelly, K. and Slade, A. (2005). Maternal reflective functioning, mother–infant affective communication, and infant attachment: Exploring the link between mental states and observed caregiving behaviour in the intergenerational transmission of attachment. *Attachment and Human Development*, *7*, 299–311.

Gumley, A.I. and Schwannauer, M. (2006). *Staying well after psychosis: A cognitive interpersonal approach to relapse prevention and emotional recovery*. Chichester: Wiley.

Hesse, E. (1999). The Adult Attachment Interview: Historical and current perspectives. In J. Cassidy and P.R. Shaver (eds), *Handbook of attachment* (pp. 395–433). New York: Guilford Press.

Holmes, J. (2001). *The search for a secure base: Attachment theory and psychotherapy*. London: Brunner-Routledge.

Janssen, I., Krabbendam, L., Bak, M., Hanssen, M., Vollebergh, W., de Graaf, R., *et al.* (2004). Childhood abuse as a risk factor for psychotic experiences. *Acta Psychiatrica Scandinavica, 109*, 38–45.

Johnson, J.G., Cohen, P., Brown, J., Smailes, E.M. and Bernstein, D.P. (1999). Childhood maltreatment increases risk for personality disorders during early childhood. *Archives of General Psychiatry, 56*, 600–605.

Johnson, J.G., Smailes, E.M., Cohen, P., Brown, J. and Bernstein, D.P. (2000). Associations between four types of neglect and personality disorder symptoms during adolescence and early adulthood: Findings of a community based longitudinal study. *Journal of Personality Disorders, 14*, 171–187.

Keri, S. and Kelemen, O. (2009). The role of attention and immediate memory in vulnerability to interpersonal criticism during family interactions in schizophrenia. *British Journal of Clinical Psychology, 48*, 21–30.

Levy, K.N., Meehan, K.B., Kelly, K.M., Reynoso, J.S., Weber, M., Clarkin, J.F., *et al.* (2006). Change in attachment patterns and reflective function in a randomized control trial of transference-focused psychotherapy for borderline personality disorder. *Journal of Consulting and Clinical Psychology, 74*, 1027–1040.

Lillard, A. (2001). Pretend play as twin earth: A social cognitive analysis. *Developmental Review, 21*, 495–531.

Liotti, G. and Gumley, A.I. (2009). An attachment perspective on schizophrenia: Disorganized attachment, dissociative processes, and compromised mentalization. In A. Moskowitz, M. Dorahy and I. Schaefer (eds), *Dissociation and psychosis: Converging perspectives on a complex relationship* (pp. 117–133). Chichester: Wiley.

Liotti, G., Pasquini, P. and Italian Group for the Study of Dissociation (2000). Predictive factors for borderline personality disorder: Patients' early traumatic experiences and losses suffered by the attachment figure. *Acta Psychiatrica Scandinavica, 102*, 282–289.

Lok, S.M. and McMahon, C.A. (2006). Mothers' thoughts about their children: Links between mind-mindedness and emotional availability. *British Journal of Developmental Psychology, 24*, 477–488.

Lysaker, P.H., Carcione, A., Dimaggio, G., Johannesen, J.K., Nicolò, G., Procacci, M., *et al.* (2005a). Metacognition amidst narratives of self and illness in schizophrenia: Associations with insight, neurocognition, symptom and function. *Acta Psychiatrica Scandinavica, 112*, 64–71.

Lysaker, P.H., Davis, L.D., Eckert, G.J., Strasburger, A., Hunter, N. and Buck, K.D. (2005b). Changes in narrative structure and content in schizophrenia in long term individual psychotherapy: A single case study. *Clinical Psychology and Psychotherapy, 12*, 406–416.

Lysaker, P.H., Buck, K.D. and Ringer, J. (2007a). The recovery of metacognitive capacity in schizophrenia across thirty two months of individual psychotherapy: A case study. *Psychotherapy Research*, *17*, 713–720.

Lysaker, P.H., Dimaggio, G., Buck, K.D., Carcione, A. and Nicolò, G. (2007b). Metacognition within narratives of schizophrenia: Associations with multiple domains of neurocognition. *Schizophrenia Research*, *93*, 278–287.

Lysaker, P.H., Warman, D.M., Dimaggio, G., Procacci, M., LaRocco, V., Clark, L.K., *et al.* (2008). Metacognition in schizophrenia: Associations with multiple assessments of executive function. *Journal of Nervous and Mental Disease*, *196*, 384–389.

Macbeth, A. and Gumley, A.I. (2008). Premorbid adjustment, symptom development and quality of life in first episode psychosis: A systematic review and critical reappraisal. *Acta Psychiatrica Scandinavica*, *117*, 85–99.

Meins, E. (2003). *Security of attachment and the social development of cognition.* Hove, UK: Psychology Press.

Meins, E. and Fernyhough, C. (1999). Linguistic acquisitional style and mentalising development: The role of maternal mind mindedness. *Cognitive Development*, *14*, 363–380.

Meins, E., Fernyhough, C., Fradley, E. and Tukey, M. (2001). Rethinking maternal sensitivity: Mothers' comments on infants' mental processes predict security of attachment at 12 months. *Journal of Clinical Psychology and Psychiatry*, *42*, 637–648.

Meins, E., Fernyhough, C., Wainwright, R., Das Gupta, M., Fradley, E. and Tukey, M. (2002). Maternal mind-mindedness and attachment security as predictors of theory of mind understanding. *Child Development*, *73*, 1715–1726.

Meins, E., Fernyhough, C., Wainwright, R., Clark-Carter, D., Das Gupta, M., Fradley, E., *et al.* (2003). Pathways to understanding the mind: Construct validity and predictive validity of maternal mind mindedness. *Child Development*, *74*, 1194–1211.

Miti, G. and Chiaia, E. (2003). Patterns of attachment and the etiology of dissociative disorders and borderline personality disorder. *Journal of Trauma Practice*, *2*, 19–35.

Pickup, G.J. (2006). Theory of mind and its relation to schizotypy. *Cognitive Neuropsychiatry*, *11*, 177–199.

Read, J. and Gumley, A.I. (2008). Can attachment theory help explain the relationship between childhood adversity and psychosis? *Attachment: New Directions in Psychotherapy and Relational Psychoanalysis*, *2*, 1–35.

Read, J., van Os, J., Morrison, A. and Ross, C. (2005). Childhood trauma, psychosis and schizophrenia: A literature review with theoretical and clinical implications. *Acta Psychiatrica Scandinavica*, *112*, 330–350.

Salvatore, G., Dimaggio, G. and Lysaker, P.H. (2007). An inter-subjective perspective on negative symptoms of schizophrenia: Implications of simulation theory. *Cognitive Neuropsychiatry*, *12*, 144–164.

Saxe, R. and Wexler, A. (2005). Making sense of another mind: The role of the right temporo-parietal junction. *Neuropsychologica*, *43*, 1391–1399.

Saxe, R., Moran, J.M., Scholz, J. and Gabrieli, J. (2006). Overlapping and non-overlapping brain regions for theory of mind and self reflection in individual subjects. *SCAN*, *1*, 229–234.

Schaub, D., Abdel-Hamid, M. and Brüne, M. (2010). Schizophrenia and social functioning: The role of impaired metacognition. In G. Dimaggio and P.H. Lysaker, *Metacognition and severe adult mental disorders: From research to treatment*. London: Routledge.

Schiffman, J., Lam, C.W., Jiwatram, T., Ekstrom, M., Sorensen, H. and Mednick, S. (2004). Perspective taking deficits in people with schizophrenia spectrum disorders: A prospective study. *Psychological Medicine*, *38*, 1518–1586.

Semerari, A., Carcione, A., Dimaggio, G., Falcone, M., Nicolò, G., Procaci, M., *et al.* (2003). How to evaluate metacognitive function in psychotherapy? The metacognition assessment scale its applications. *Clinical Psychology and Psychotherapy*, *10*, 238–261.

Semerari, A., Carcione, A., Dimaggio, G., Nicolò, G., Pedone, R. and Procacci, M. (2005). Metarepresentative functions in borderline personality disorder. *Journal of Personality Disorders*, *19*, 690–710.

Sprong, M., Scothorst, P., Vos, E., Hox, J. and van Engeland, H. (2007). Theory of mind in schizophrenia. *British Journal of Psychology*, *191*, 5–13.

Sroufe, L.A. (1997). Psychopathology as an outcome of development. *Development and Psychopathology*, *9*, 251–268.

Tait, L., Birchwood, M. and Trower, P. (2004). Adapting to the challenge of psychosis: Personal resiliance and the use of sealing-over (avoidant) coping strategies. *British Journal of Psychiatry*, *185*, 410–415.

Part II

Metacognitive disorders in different clinical populations

Its relation with symptoms, interpersonal functioning and adaptation

Chapter 4

Metacognition in schizophrenia spectrum disorders

Methods of assessing metacognition within narrative and links with neurocognition

Paul H. Lysaker

As discussed at length earlier in this volume, the term "metacognition" can be used in a variety of ways. In this chapter we use metacognition to refer to a person's general capacity to think about thinking. This capacity is thought to reflect a general aptitude that involves a wide range of semi-independent faculties which allow the individual to perform discrete tasks such as forming representations of his or her own mental states and the mental states of others, and to form, question and revise ideas of what is believed, felt, dreamt of, feared, feigned or pretended in any of a number of rapidly evolving contexts. Metacognition refers both to implicit and explicit knowledge. It allows the individual to form and then accept or reject ideas about him or herself in the moment and also to sustain more enduring ideas about the kind of person he or she is across different situations. Metacognitive capacities consequently allow people to place disappointments and triumphs in a given perspective, to see growth from pain, opportunity in disappointment and to construct with others consensual meaning about daily activities.

Over the last 15 years, interest has grown rapidly in determining whether deficits in metacognitive capacity play a central role in the course and potential outcomes of schizophrenia. It has been suggested that deficits in metacognition may be a risk factor for more severe cases of illness and prolonged dysfunction. One reason for initially thinking that schizophrenia might involve metacognitive deficits is that many of the symptoms of schizophrenia involve a failure to draw plausible conclusions about the motives of others and the origins of one's internal states. Delusional certainty that another person wants to kill me because he is wearing an orange hat could be linked to difficulties discerning the intentions and emotions of others as well as a failure to see that my own thoughts are fallible. A lack of affect or volition could be linked to a failure to perceive myself as an active agent in the world or to detect others' emotional responses. A second phenomenon that early on also pointed to a consideration of metacognitive deficits is that many with schizophrenia commonly lack of awareness of their illness (Amador *et al.*, 1994). They may also experience a reduced vitality of self-experience or even feel that their very core being or most personal sense of identity has been diminished (Stanghellini, 2004). These unusual kinds of self-experience, which exist independent of symptoms, seem almost synonymous with a loss of metacognitive capacity.

The overall question of whether schizophrenia is in part a disorder of metacognition, however, has import which reaches far beyond explaining unusual experiences and beliefs. Understanding whether the loss of metacognitive capacities is a key feature of schizophrenia as well as identifying its contributing factors could illuminate the processes that undermine function across the course of the illness. Intuition would suggest that if the capacity for thinking about thinking is reduced, solving unexpected problems should become more difficult, especially for persons already faced with distressing symptoms and social stigma. With reduced self-awareness it could only be more trying to construct a meaningful picture of mental illness, making successful adaptation to that illness an even more distant possibility (Lysaker and Lysaker, 2008). If I struggle to recognize my emotions, or I cannot see my conclusions about myself and others as subjective and possibly inaccurate, how could I develop a working idea of my mental illness and chart a course towards wellness?

Indeed, research has confirmed that many with schizophrenia experience difficulties apprehending their own thoughts and the thoughts of others. Further, greater levels of these difficulties are linked with heightened levels of paranoia, negative symptoms and thought disorder as well as with poor levels of function (e.g. Franck *et al.*, 2001; Corcoran and Frith, 2003; Brune, 2005; Stratta *et al.*, 2007). This is not to suggest that metacognitive deficits are reducible to symptoms or other aspects of psychopathology; a delusion, for instance, is not synonymous with impaired metacognition.

While the existence of metacognitive deficits in schizophrenia and their theoretical import has been subsequently well established, both as discussed here and in previous chapters, one issue awaiting clarification regards exactly what factors contribute to the development of metacognitive deficits. A nuanced understanding of the factors that contribute to compromises in different forms of metacognition could have important implications for clinical issues ranging from prevention to remediation as well as for emerging neurobiological models of social function.

In response to this question, this chapter will describe our research into whether there are consistent patterns of association between metacognition in schizophrenia and one possible causal factor: impairments in neurocognitive function. To that end we will first present a rationale for why impairments in neurocognition may play a role in the development of deficits in metacognition. Next, we will describe limitations in the existing literature regarding the assessment of metacognition and our attempts to address these by rating different possible foci of metacognition within spontaneously generated personal narratives. Finally, we will present findings from a program of study aimed at uncovering the links between metacognitive capacity as revealed in those narratives and concurrent assessments of neurocognition.

Determinants of metacognition

The possible relationship of neurocognition and metacognition

Impairments in neurocognition are believed to appear early in the course of schizophrenia and include losses in previously held levels of ability to sustain attention, to sort out relevant from irrelevant stimuli, to recall and recognize visual and verbal material and to think in a flexible and abstract manner. The loss of these capacities has been widely suggested as limiting the ability to learn new material and to successfully solve problems. As a result, persons with schizophrenia may quickly find it challenging to function in vocational and interpersonal settings (Lysaker and Buck, 2007). As these previously held capacities deteriorate, tasks such as mastering new assignments on the job or managing conflicts with family may inexplicably become baffling and overwhelming.

Turning to the issue of the development of deficits in metacognition, one possibility is that as neurocognitive abilities are degraded, there may be a point at which this loss imperils ability to perform certain metacognitive acts. As noted above, performance on tests of neurocognition does not fully predict levels of metacognition, nor explain the impact of deficits in metacognition on function (Roncone *et al.*, 2002). Intact neurocognitive function is not necessarily sufficient for full metacognitive function. Yet, certain levels of neurocognitive function may be necessary to perform some basic metacognitive acts. Evidence of this includes findings that more severe deficits in flexibility of abstract thought limit social cognition (Lancaster *et al.*, 2003), and the acquisition of social skills in rehabilitation (Lysaker *et al.*, 1995). Other studies have more directly linked performance on assessments of metacognition with performance on tests of verbal and visual memory (Greig *et al.*, 2004), visual memory span (Langdon *et al.*, 2001), intelligence (Brüne, 2003), executive function (Langdon *et al.*, 2002; Greig *et al.*, 2004) and learning ability in schizophrenia (Doody *et al.*, 1998).

The possibility that cognitive decline in schizophrenia could underpin some deficits in metacognition is also consistent with studies of other conditions. Following general cognitive loss, many may experience familiar social situations as increasingly confusing and difficult to decode (Frank *et al.*, 2006). In cases involving loss of neurocognitive abilities as a result of head injury, it has been suggested that there may follow a reduced ability to perform basic self-monitoring tasks (Ownsworth and Fleming, 2005) or to shift mentally between different self-representations resulting in an impoverished sense of self (Heller *et al.*, 2006). In the case of Asperger's syndrome, an inability to appreciate the thoughts and feelings of others has been linked to difficulties with integrating contextual information and impairments in executive function that compromise persons' abilities to shift back and forth from two viewpoints (Frith and Vignemont, 2005). Also supporting this contention are studies of young children which suggest that executive functions emerge prior to, and are a basis for, the ability to think about the mental states of others (Moses, 2005).

Limitations of current research on metacognition and neurocognition

While there is a solid basis for looking to neurocognitive impairments as a contributory factor to development of metacognitive deficits in schizophrenia, research on this subject has been hampered to date by a range of different factors. For one, most studies have assessed metacognition along a singular continuum from "intact" to "impaired" by observing performance on a laboratory task which simulates social interaction or a self-reflective task. For instance, a participant might be asked to make a guess about someone's intention on the basis of a story or cartoon or to determine whether movements they were watching were mimicking the movement of their arm (Brüne, 2005; Harrington *et al.*, 2005). Yet, in daily life, metacognitive acts can occur in emotion-laden contexts, often involving others for whom we have strong feelings. Thus, assessment of metacognition using impersonal stimuli may not speak to an individual's ability to engage in metacognitive acts outside of the laboratory and especially when sensitive personal issues are involved, for instance, when facing a loved one during a confrontation.

A second problem with this research is that these tasks cue or call for specific metacognitive acts at specific times. Specific facts or images are presented and the participant is asked to make an explicit judgment. Here the problem is that these tasks may be measuring how persons respond to cues for metacognition but not necessarily what they tend to do spontaneously. For instance, it might be possible for those with diminished metacognitive capacity to accurately judge an emotion which a person is feeling when cued at a specific moment to do so but not when no one is providing a request to do so.

A third difficulty is that metacognition is often studied as a one-dimensional phenomenon. Metacognitive acts, however, which have different foci (thoughts about my own thinking versus thoughts about another person's thinking) may involve capacities which are not only conceptually distinct but also involve semi-independent neurocognitive functions. Research suggests, for example, that creating a mental image of oneself may utilize a range of cortical activities, some of which are similar to those utilized when creating an image of another but others which may be unique (Saxe *et al.*, 2004; Saxe, 2005; Mitchell *et al.*, 2006). Thus, studying the larger problem of metacognition as varying along one axis carries the risk of missing the possibility that the capacity to perform metacognitive acts with different foci may in part be sustained by the activation of different brain areas.

The assessment of metacognition within narratives

The Indiana Psychiatry Illness Interview and the modified Metacognition Assessment Scale

To address some of the difficulties associated with tasks that utilize cued responses or personally/emotionally neutral stimuli, we have proposed a method to rate metacognition from a spontaneously generated speech sample. That speech sample is obtained through a semi-structured interview called the Indiana Psychiatry Illness Interview (IPII; Lysaker *et al.*, 2002). Lasting typically between 30 and 60 minutes, the interview elicits a narrative of self and illness that is tape recorded and later transcribed. The interview is divided conceptually into four sections. First, participants are asked to tell the story of their lives in as much detail as they can. Second, participants are asked if they think they have a mental illness, and if so, how they understand it. This is followed with questions about what has and has not been affected by their condition in terms of interpersonal, vocational, and psychological life. In the third section, participants are asked if their condition "controls" their life as well as if and how effectively they "control" their condition. Fourth, participants are asked how much their illness is affected by others and how much others have been affected by their illness. Finally, participants are asked what they expect to stay the same and what will be different in the future, again in terms of interpersonal and psychological function.

The IPII differs in procedure from other psychiatric interviews in that the interviewer is instructed not to introduce content. Commonly, most psychiatric interviews ask participants if they have certain experiences. Do they, for instance, hear or see things other people do not hear or see? In the IPII, the interviewer does not inquire about specific symptoms. He or she may ask for minor clarification when confused and may query non-directivity but does not pose questions about specific matters. The interviewer, for example, will not ask if the participant has hallucinations or ask for historical details to anchor the life narrative.

The IPII thus results in a self-narrative in which specific metacognitive acts may appear spontaneously. As a life story is told, there are a number of turns in that story where participants may choose or not choose to think about their own thinking, the thinking of others, or how certain challenges are best faced. In this way the IPII may provide a behavior sample of metacognitive acts which are related to real and potentially emotion-laden life experiences. Furthermore, because a larger story is being told which includes the individual participant, other people in relation to him or her and other people in relation to each other, it is also a sample in which different kinds of metacognitive capacity can be separately estimated.

To assess metacognition within IPII narratives we have used a modified version of the Metacognition Assessment Scale (MAS; Semerari *et al.*, 2003). The MAS is a rating scale that assesses metacognitive abilities as manifest in an individual's verbalizations. It was originally designed to detect within psychotherapy transcripts changes in the ability of persons with severe personality disorders to think about their own thinking. In consultation with the authors, the modified MAS has been adapted for the study of IPII transcripts (Lysaker *et al.*, 2005). The MAS focuses on metacognitive functions rather than contents and conceptualizes metacognition as the set of abilities that allows persons to understand mental phenomena and use that understanding to tackle tasks that are sources of distress.

The modified MAS contains four scales that pertain to different foci of metacognitive acts: Understanding of One's Own Mind or the comprehension of one's own mental states, Understanding of Others' Minds or the comprehension of other individuals' mental states, Decentration or the ability to see the world as existing with others having independent motives, and Mastery or the ability to work through one's representations and mental states to implement effective action strategies in order to accomplish cognitive tasks or cope with problematic mental states.

The modified MAS treats each of these different metacognitive capacities as semi-autonomous phenomenon. Individuals are assumed to possess capacities in each of its metacognitive domains which vary along a continuum. Accordingly, each of the four MAS subscales are composed of a series of smaller capacities, or steps, which are arranged in hierarchical order. These steps range in order from the least complex to the most complex level of metacognition in that domain. In this sense, once a capacity is not attained on a given step, no higher capacities should be possible. For instance, within the Understanding of One's Own Mind subscale, if one does not recognize one's emotions (step four out of a total of nine), then it should not be possible to successfully perform what is required by the next and more complex step, which is to understand links between one's thoughts and feelings (step five out of a total of nine).

To make ratings using the modified MAS, the rater looks for evidence of each step within each scale. If evidence is found that a capacity is present, a point is awarded and the rater then searches for evidence that the participant can perform the next step. If no evidence is found that the participant is capable of performing the metacognitive act described in the next step, no evidence is sought for the subsequent higher capacities and the score for that scale is the number of capacities already achieved. As an example, after a rater has judged that a participant had achieved the first three steps of the MAS Understanding of One's Own Mind scale, the rater would turn to the next step: awareness of one's own emotions. To do this the rater would search the IPII transcript for places where the participant described different ways he or she felt. If the rater then found several places in the transcript where the participant described his or her own emotions, this would constitute evidence that the participant was able to identify their own emotions and a point would be awarded. The rater would then start to search for evidence of the next step of this scale, which is awareness that one's views of the world are fallible. If the next step was rated as achieved, another point would be awarded (giving the subject five points so far). Next, the rater would search for evidence of the sixth step. In this way, increasing scores reflect increasingly complex metacognitive operations.

Once a participant is judged not to be able to perform what is required by a particular step, no further steps are considered. If a participant does not show evidence, for example, of the sixth step of the Understanding of One's Own Mind subscale, which is an awareness that expectations, thoughts, and desires do not necessarily dictate reality, further capacities would attain a zero. The final score then would be a five for this scale. In this way a score of five would reflect more complex levels of metacognition in this domain than a four but less complex metacognition than a six.

Evidence of the reliability of these methods for assessing and rating metacognition includes findings of good interrater reliability for blind raters separately assessing the same narratives and internal consistency among the four modified MAS scales (Lysaker *et al.*, 2007). Concerning its validity, the modified MAS has been linked with Amador and colleagues' (1994) Scale to Assess Unawareness of Mental Disorder, which is a measure of the ability to evaluate one's own mental illness (Lysaker *et al.*, 2005). Regarding convergent and divergent validity performance of the modified MAS, MAS scores have been found to be correlated with performance on the Scale to Assess Narrative Development (STAND), a scale which measures depth of personal narrative while being uncorrelated with theoretically unrelated aspects of self-experience such as internalized stigma (Lysaker *et al.*, 2008a). In a study that we have submitted for publication we have found modified MAS scores linked with assessment of social cognition using the Social Cognition and Object Relations Scale (Westen, 1991), a scale which allows for assessments based on responses to the Thematic Apperception Test (Murray, 1943) of the extent to which persons construct a story that appreciates the complex roots and mutuality necessary in social interactions.

Four studies: neurocognition and metacognitive capacities as assessed with personal narratives

To study the possible relationship of neurocognitive and metacognitive capacities, we have undertaken a series of studies in which we have concurrently gathered IPII narratives and assessments of neurocognition from adults with schizophrenia entering rehabilitation. The purpose of these studies has been to search for associations between the metacognitive capacities assessed by the MAS and different forms of neurocognitive capacities. Results of these studies and their implications will be detailed in this section of the chapter.

Study 1

In our first study (Lysaker *et al.*, 2005) we sought to determine whether ratings on three of the domains assessed by the modified MAS were linked with performance on a range of neurocognitive functions. Our central questions were whether poorer levels of metacognitive functions assessed within narratives of persons with schizophrenia were associated with poorer neurocognitive test performance, and if so, on which types of tests? Participants were 61 men with *DSM-IV* diagnoses of schizophrenia (n = 40) or schizoaffective disorder (n = 21) enrolled in a larger study seeking to develop a cognitive behavioral therapy targeting working function with schizophrenia. All were initially recruited from the outpatient psychiatry service of a VA medical center in the Midwestern United States and were in a post-acute phase of illness as defined by having no hospitalizations or changes in medication or housing in the month prior to entering the study.

Participants were administered the IPII along with a battery of neurocognitive tests that included the Wisconsin Card Sorting Test (WCST; Heaton, 1981), a test which assesses flexibility in abstract thought by presenting the participant with a problem which to successfully solve requires them to form an idea about how to solve that problem, hold on to that idea and shift to another idea when the first idea no longer successfully solves the problem. Two commonly generated scores are the total number of categories correct, which reflects the number of times the participant was able to grasp the key idea and then shift to another idea when necessary as well as the number of persevering responses, or times a participant could not flexibly shift to another idea when the current idea no longer successfully solves the problem. The second test of the battery was the Hopkins Verbal Learning Test (HVLT; Brandt, 1991), an auditory verbal memory test which presents participants with a list of words they are asked to repeat back and then later to recognize. The HVLT score used for this study was the total number of correctly recalled words across all the trials.

The third group of neurocognitive tests gathered were from the Wechsler Adult Intelligence Scale III (WAIS III; Wechsler, 1997a), the most widely used assessments of intellectual function. From this test, we used two subscales: Vocabulary, which assesses participants' global verbal intellectual function (and is also believed to tap premorbid intelligence in schizophrenia) and the Digit Symbol subtest, which assesses processing speed. Finally, we also assessed visual memory using the Visual Reproduction subtest of the Wechsler Memory Scale III (WMS III; Wechsler, 1997b).

To assess the relation of metacognition and neurocognition we next correlated modified MAS scores for Awareness of One's Own Mind, Awareness of Other's Mind and Mastery. Results of this revealed that participants rated as having a greater metacognitive capacity for awareness of one's own mind had better performance on the HVLT, the Vocabulary and Digit Symbol subtest of the WAIS III, and the Visual Reproduction subtest of the WMS III. When entered into a regression, the Vocabulary and Digit Symbol scores predicted a quarter of the variance in Understanding of One's Own Mind. Participants rated as having greater metacognitive capacities for knowing the other's mind and for mastery tended have better performance on the HVLT. No measures were related to the WCST.

We concluded that these results can be taken to suggest that deficits in metacognition that impact one's ability to make judgments about one's own mental states may be influenced by possible risk factors for schizophrenia such as premorbid intellectual function and cognitive impairments linked to disease progress such as processing speed. The finding that verbal memory was linked with all three domains may suggest that these deficits also interfere with the ability to hold on to a mental representation of mental or emotional states as objects for contemplation. Perhaps with greater difficulty encoding verbal material, it may be more difficult to maintain the larger cognitive structures needed to make meaning of experience and frame a personal sense of self.

Study 2

To follow up on these findings we conducted a second study exploring whether certain levels of specific metacognitive function were related to corresponding levels of neurocognition (Lysaker *et al.*, 2007). Here the question was: Do certain elements of metacognition require minimal levels of neurocognitive function? Do persons who possess versus do not possess the capacity for performing basic metacognitive acts have different neurocognitive profiles. To respond to this issue, we divided a second sample of adults with schizophrenia enrolled in rehabilitation into different groups based on whether they had or had not achieved basic self-reflectivity and decentration and then compared their performance on neurocognitive tests.

Participants in this second IPII sample were 61 men and eight women with diagnoses of schizophrenia (*n* = 43) or schizoaffective disorder (*n* = 26), recruited from the outpatient psychiatry service of a VA medical center or community mental health center. As in Study 1, all were in a post-acute phase of illness. The neurocognitive testing battery differed slightly from the first study in that we utilized additional subtests of the WAIS III, including the Block Design subtest, which assesses visual spatial processing and is often used as a non-verbal measure of intelligence. The Arithmetic subtest calls on persons to mentally manipulate numbers in order to solve mathematical problems and thus is understood to involve working memory. From the WMS III, we again used the Visual Reproduction subtest and this time the Logical Memory subtest, which is a test of verbal memory in which participants hear stories and are then asked to recall as many different units of meaning from those stories. As before, we included the WCST.

To divide participants into those who possessed versus did not possess basic self-reflectivity and Decentration we used the Understanding of One's Own Mind scale and the Decentration scale of the modified MAS. Participants were rated on an a priori basis as having basic self-reflective capacity if they obtained scores of four or higher and as not having basic self-reflectivity if their score was lower than four on the MAS Understanding of One's Own Mind scale. They were rated on an a priori basis as having achieved decentration if they achieved a score of two or higher and as not having achieved decentration if they achieved scores of less than two on the MAS Decentration scale. This resulted in participants being placed into three groups: (a) minimal self-reflectivity/not decentered (*n* = 25); (b) basic self-reflectivity/not decentered (*n* = 33); (c) basic self-reflectivity/decentered (*n* = 11).

The three groups were then compared on background variables and neurocognitive testing. Groups were not found to differ according to diagnosis or other demographic information. Comparisons of test scores between the three groups revealed participants with basic self-reflectivity had generally better performance on the WCST, and WAIS III Arithmetic subtest, while participants rated as having achieved basic decentration had better performance on the Visual Reproduction subtest of the WMS III. The basic self-reflectivity/decentered group also had better performance on the Vocabulary and Block Design subtest than the minimal reflectivity group.

We interpreted these results as suggesting that difficulties distinguishing internal states in schizophrenia can emerge when there are significant deficits in executive function, such as in persons who have greater difficulties holding abstract matters in mind and then shifting fluidly from one abstract concept to another. Beyond this, the ability to see that others have their unique views requires relatively intact visual memory, perhaps to be able to represent social relations in a complex spatial manner, though not necessarily greater capacities for flexibility in abstract thought. Such assertions are possibly consistent with the Frith and Vignemont's (2005) observation that the egocentrism in Asperger's syndrome may result from an inability to form representations of others as having spatially a relation to one another which is fully independent of the individual's relationship to others.

Study 3

In our third study (Lysaker *et al.*, 2008b) we planned to follow up our previous findings linking self-awareness with deficits in executive function. One of the limitations of the previous study is that it assessed executive function exclusively using the WCST. Though a reasonable measure of global executive function, the WCST is widely seen as unable to distinguish between the multiple and semi-independent elements of executive function (Dimitrov *et al.*, 1999). Success at the task, for instance, requires a range of different capacities, including the ability to form an idea then to inhibit that idea and shift to another. If used alone to determine executive functioning, the WCST may not be able to determine which of these specific, semi-independent elements are responsible for successes or deficiencies in completing the test. Thus, the previous studies cannot determine whether specific aspects of executive function are more closely linked than others to different forms of metacognition. This seems to be especially important, because of all the neurocognitive capacities studied so far, executive function would intuitively seem likely to play a significant role in the construction of a complex and flexible idea of the self.

To address this issue, we examined whether MAS scores were linked with selected subtests of the Delis Kaplan Executive Function System (DKEFS; Delis *et al.*, 2001). The DKEFS assesses multiple domains of executive function potentially relevant for metacognitive acts, including: (a) tests of inhibition and set shifting (the ability to wilfully inhibit a thought or feeling and switch to another in a goal directed manner); (b) mental flexibility, that is the ability to form and reform ideas about how different stimuli can be related to one another in a goal directed manner (Baldo *et al.*, 2004). In this study, we chose six specific DKEFS subtests, three because of their links to inhibition switching (i.e. tests which require making responses according to alternating principles) and three because of their links with mental flexibility (i.e. tests which require moving between abstractions to solve problems). The inhibition switching tests we considered were:

- design fluency switching – how many different designs can be generated on a piece of paper by alternately connecting dots that are filled with dots which are open
- category switching on Verbal Fluency Task – how many words from alternating categories can be produced verbally in 60 seconds

- inhibition switching from the Color-Word Task – the capacity to alternately name the color of the ink a word is printed in (which spells out a different color) and then read the word ignoring the color it is printed in.

The tasks requiring mental flexibility we chose were:

- total correct sorts from the Sorting Task – the number of different ways participants arrange cards into two groups based on the card's attributes
- total score for the Word Context Task – how quickly the meaning of nonsense words are grasped from increasingly precise contextual hints
- the total correct score of the Twenty Questions Test – how many yes/no questions it takes for a participant to correctly identify an object chosen by the examiner from a picture of an array of objects.

Participants in this sample were 49 participants drawn from the first two IPII studies above based on whether they completed the DKEFS as part of a study of the correlates of anxiety and the IPII as part of one of the first two studies. For this reason it is notable that the DKEFS and IPII were not administered concurrently but could have taken place potentially up to six months apart (something likely to attenuate our findings but not to bias us to find significant correlations).

Two specific analyses were undertaken. First Spearman Rho correlations were calculated between the six DKEFS scores and the Modified MAS Understanding One's Own Mind, Understanding the Other's Mind, Mastery and Total score. These revealed that greater levels of Understanding One's Own Mind were linked to better performance on the Sorting, Word Context, and Twenty Questions tests. Higher levels of Understanding the Other's Mind were linked to better performance on the Design Fluency Switching and Twenty Questions tests. Greater Mastery was linked to better performance on the Verbal Fluency Switching and Twenty Questions tests.

Since the modified MAS Decentration scores showed a highly skewed range, with 76 per cent of the sample having a score of one or less, in our second analysis we treated this as a categorical variable and classified participants as having high decentration if their decentration scores were greater than one or low decentration if the scores were one or less. Scores of greater than one suggest the ability to see the world as involving others' unique thoughts and feelings. An ANOVA was then conducted comparing the DKEFS scores of participants with high (n = 7) versus low (n = 42) decentration. Results revealed that participants with higher levels of decentration had significantly higher scores on the Verbal Fluency, Color Word switching, and Word Context tests.

The pattern of results may suggest that awareness of one's own mind is more closely linked to mental flexibility than the other domains assessed by the MAS and is consistent with the findings of Study 2. The DKEFS tests linked to the ability to inhibit a response were more closely linked to Decentration and somewhat to Awareness of the Other's Mind and Mastery. While causality cannot be determined in any of the cross-sectional designs we have employed, results are at least consistent with the possibility that as persons with schizophrenia are less able to move flexibly between abstract ideas, they cannot detect the nuances and different patterns present in how they think and feel. They might be less able, for instance, to see how a feeling of anger could be reframed as sadness or vulnerability, and also how those feelings of anger are like the feelings of anger they have felt in some past situations but not others. Without being able to define thoughts and feelings in multiple ways, awareness of internal complexity may be difficult to sustain. Results also support the speculation that with a reduced capacity to inhibit one's immediate thoughts or reactions, preoccupation with one's own needs may serve as a barrier to recognizing the needs of others. Without an ability to inhibit thoughts about one's own needs, some may find it difficult to call to mind the perspectives of others and to detect a range of different meanings in rapidly evolving but ambiguous situations.

Study 4

In our final study – now being prepared for publication – we have turned to the issue of the neurocognitive correlates of the modified MAS Mastery subscale. In this study we have asked whether different levels of metacognition as applied to psychological challenges require basic levels of different forms of neurocognition. For instance, recognizing and plausibly describing psychological challenges may require basic levels of executive function, while complex forms of coping which involve actively changing one's own thinking might require basically intact levels of other more complex aspects of neurocognition.

To explore this we have divided our latest sample of participants who have completed the IPII into three groups on the basis of their score on the Mastery scale. The first group contained participants with Mastery scores of zero to two. These scores reflect at most the ability to plausibly define a psychological state to be coped with without mention of any coping responses. The second consisted of participants with Mastery scores from between three to five. These scores reflect an attempt to cope by trying to calm oneself, seeking support, or inhibiting a habitual response to it. The third group was made up of participants with Mastery scores from six to nine. These scores reflect coping in which persons flexibly adjust their own thinking about themselves and others.

In this study we sought to determine whether participants who attained these different levels of metacognition as it pertained to Mastery showed a different pattern of performance on neurocognitive testing. The sample used here is one which contained the same 69 participants as the second study plus an additional 24 participants (meeting the same inclusions criterion as above) bringing the complete total for this study to 93. The neurocognitive tests are the same as in Study 2: The Vocabulary, Arithmetic, Digit Symbol and Block Design subtests of the WAIS III, the WMS III Visual Reproduction and Logical Memory subtest, and the WCST.

To determine if participants with these different levels of mastery had different levels of neurocognitive function, a MANOVA was conducted. This was followed by individual ANOVA comparing groups on each of these tests. Results revealed that groups differed on the WCST and Digit Symbol subtest. Comparisons of individual groups revealed that the group who could not produce either a coherent account of psychological challenges or a coping strategy performed significantly more poorly on the WCST than the other groups who report some form of coping strategy. By contrast, the group who were able to report higher order coping strategies (e.g. to at a minimum adjust their own thinking about the psychological challenge) had superior performance on the Digit Symbol subtest.

As in the case of the first three studies, the correlational nature of this study precludes drawing conclusions about causality. Results, however, could be taken to suggest that difficulties framing plausible challenges or formulating any coping strategies may emerge when there are significant deficits in executive function. By contrast, the ability to form complex coping responses which involve thinking about thinking may require relatively more intact abilities to process information. Both the data and intuition seem to suggest that in order for an individual to be able to recognize and challenge his or her own thinking as it pertains to coping with psychological challenges, it must necessary for this person to be able to manage large amounts of incoming information in a quick and effective manner.

Summary, limitations and conclusions

In sum, there are many reasons to believe that impairments in neurocognition may play a role in the development of metacognitive deficits in schizophrenia. In this chapter we have described four studies which have examined whether the capacity to perform different kinds of metacognitive acts during an interview eliciting a personal narrative of self and illness were concurrently linked to performance on neurocognitive tests. Results suggested better performance on tests of neurocognition was linked to better performance on a range of scales assessing metacognitive capability within a narrative of self and illness. Specific findings were suggestive of the possibility that certain levels of neurocognitive capacity are necessary for successfully performing certain metacognitive acts. For instance, awareness of one's own thoughts and feelings as well as the ability to plausibly frame psychological challenges and respond with a meaningful coping response may both require a certain level of executive function. The ability to see others as having independent relationships with one another may require intact visual memory and employing more complex coping strategies may require relatively fewer impairments in processing speed.

As already noted, the correlational nature of each of these studies precludes drawing firm conclusions and all interpretations of the observed relationships are intended as speculative and a basis for future study. Furthermore, alternative hypotheses cannot be ruled out. It is possible that different neurocognitive deficits in schizophrenia are in part the result of different forms of metacognitive deficits. Perhaps different metacognitive dysfunctions interact with each other to generate neurocognitive dysfunctions or possibly deficits in neurocognition and metacognition magnify one another in the manner of a vicious cycle. It is also possible that relationships observed here were the products of other biological or socio-cultural variables not measured.

Generalization of findings is also limited by sample composition. Participants were mostly persons in their forties, all of whom were involved in treatment. It may well be that a different relationship exists between neurocognition and metacognition among younger persons with schizophrenia, or in particular persons who decline treatment. We additionally examined only several of many possible aspects of metacognitive capacity in schizophrenia and more study is called for to explore a wide range of other possible patterns of deficit. Thus, more research is necessary which involves the collection of data at multiple time points using broader samples and exploring other aspects of neurocognition and metacognition. Finally, results should not be taken to suggest that impairments in neurocognition are the only or even main causal force in the development of deficits in metacognition. As highlighted across this entire volume, current evidence suggests that there are multiple paths which lead to deficits in metacognition among adults with severe mental illness and neurocognitive impairments at best play a role among many competing forces in the development of metacognitive deficits.

Regarding the clinical implications of this work, our comments will be brief given that work in this area is just beginning and also because a chapter on psychotherapy for schizophrenia follows in Part III. Nevertheless, it seems worth noting that if impairments in different aspects of neurocognition are linked to decrements in certain metacognitive acts, then interventions in general might be thought of as having to assist persons to perform neurocognitive tasks which are intrinsically difficult for them (e.g. flexibly shift set or process information quickly) in order to better think about their own thinking. At the very least, this would suggest that progress in the development of metacognitive capacities might be expected to occur slowly and incrementally given the recalcitrant nature of these difficulties.

Beyond this, however, interventions might furthermore be conceptualized as providing prostheses to help persons learn to perform the neurocognitive tasks linked to specific aspects of metacognition. If impairments, for instance, in the ability to shift set or to form an abstract idea about a set of events and then change that idea when dealing with the next set of events are linked to problems discerning one's own thoughts and feelings, then interventions may be necessary which help persons to recognize they are applying the same abstractions to different internal states. As an illustration, if internal states are repeatedly only understood as anger, interventions may be necessary to help that person to challenge his or her perseverative interpretations.

Implied in these speculations is that cognitive impairments in schizophrenia are likely to be persistent barriers to the engagement in metacognitive acts. This is certainly an empirical question, however, and one that has yet to be tested. Additionally, lurking here is also the question of what happens if neurocognitive deficits are remediated. Would the remediation of neurocognitive impairments automatically lead to improved metacognition or even just to the opportunity for improved metacognition with time? These and many other questions await longitudinal research.

References

Amador, X.F., Flaum, M., Andreasen, N.C., Strauss, D.H., Yale, S.A., Clark, S.C., *et al.* (1994). Awareness of illness in schizophrenia and schizoaffective and mood disorders. *Archives of General Psychiatry*, *51*, 826–836.

Baldo, J.V., Delis, D.C., Wilkins, D.P. and Shimamura, A.P. (2004). Is it bigger than a breadbox? Performance of frontal patients on a new executive function test. *Archives of Clinical Neuropsychology*, *19*, 407–419.

Brandt, J. (1991). The Hopkins verbal learning test: Development of a new memory test with six equivalent forms. *Clinical Neuropsychologist*, *5*, 125–142.

Brune, M. (2003). Theory of mind and the role of IQ in chronic disorganized schizophrenia. *Schizophrenia Research*, *60*, 57–64.

Brune, M. (2005). Theory of mind in schizophrenia: A review of the literature. *Schizophrenia Bulletin*, *31*, 21–42.

Corcoran, R. and Frith, C.D. (2003). Autobiographical memory and theory of mind: Evidence of a relationship in schizophrenia. *Psychological Medicine*, *33*, 897–905.

Delis, D.C., Kaplan, E. and Kramer, J.H. (2001). *Delis Kaplan executive function system: Technical manual*. San Antonio, TX: Psychological Corporation.

Dimitrov, M., Grafman, J., Soares, A.H. and Clark, K. (1999). Concept formation and concept shifting in frontal lesions and Parkinson's disease patients assessed with the California Card Sorting Test. *Neuropsychology*, *13*, 135–143.

Doody, G.A., Gotz, M., Johnstone, E.C., Frith, C.D. and Owens, D.G. (1998). Theory of mind and psychosis. *Psychological Medicine*, *28*, 397–405.

Franck, N., Farrer, C., Geirgueff, N., Marie-Cardine, M., d'Amato, T. and Jeannerod, M. (2001). Defective recognition of one's own actions in patient with schizophrenia. *American Journal of Psychiatry*, *158*, 454–459.

Frank, L., Lloyd, A., Flynn, J.A., Kleinman, L., Matza, L.S., Margolis, M.K., *et al.* (2006). Impact of cognitive impairment on mild dementia patients and mild cognitive impairment patients and their informants. *International Psychogeriatrics*, *11*, 1–12.

Frith, U. and Vignemont, F. (2005). Egocentrism, allocentrism, and Asperger syndrome. *Consciousness and Cognition*, *14*, 719–738.

Greig, T.C., Bryson, G.J. and Bell, M.D. (2004). Theory of mind performance in schizophrenia: Diagnostic, symptoms and neuropsychological correlates. *Journal of Nervous and Mental Disease*, *192*, 12–18.

Harrington, L., Seiger, R.J. and McClure, J. (2005). Theory of mind in schizophrenia: A critical review. *Cognitive Neuropsychiatry*, *10*, 249–286.

Heaton, R.K. (1981). *The Wisconsin card sorting test, manual.* Odessa, FL: Psychological Assessment Resources.

Heller, W., Levin, R.L., Mukerjee D. and Reis, J.P. (2006). Characteristics in contexts: Identity and personality processes that influence individual and family adjustment to brain injury. *Journal of Rehabilitation*, *72*, 44–49.

Lancaster, R.S., Evans, J.D., Bond, G.R. and Lysaker, P.H. (2003). Social cognition and neurocognitive deficits in schizophrenia. *Journal of Nervous and Mental Disease*, *191*, 295–300.

Langdon, R., Coltheart, M., Ward, P.B. and Catts, S.V. (2001). Mentalizing, executive planning and disengagement in schizophrenia. *Cognitive Neuropsychiatry*, *6*, 81–108.

Langdon, R., Coltheart, M., Ward, P.B. and Catts, S.V. (2002). Disturbed communication in schizophrenia: The role of poor pragmatics and poor mind-reading. *Psychological Medicine*, *32*, 1273–1284.

Lysaker, P.H. and Buck, K.D. (2007). Neurocognitive deficits as a barrier to psychosocial function: Multidirectional effects on learning, coping and self conception. *Journal of Psychosocial Nursing and Mental Health Services*, *45*, 24–30.

Lysaker, P.H. and Lysaker, J.T. (2008). *Schizophrenia and the fate of the self.* Oxford: Oxford University Press.

Lysaker, P.H., Bell, M.D., Zito, W.S. and Bioty, S.M. (1995). Social skill impairments at work: Deficits and predictors of improvement in schizophrenia. *Journal of Nervous and Mental Disease*, *183*, 688–692.

Lysaker, P.H., Clements, C.A., Plascak-Hallberg, C.D., Knipscheer, S.J. and Wright, D.E. (2002). Insight and personal narratives of illness in schizophrenia. *Psychiatry*, *65*, 197–206.

Lysaker, P.H., Carcione, A., Dimaggio, G., Johannesen, J.K., Nicolò, G., Procacci, M., *et al.* (2005). Metacognition amidst narratives of self and illness in schizophrenia: Associations with insight, neurocognition, symptom and function. *Acta Psychiatrica Scandinavica*, *112*, 64–71.

Lysaker, P.H., Dimaggio, G., Buck, K.D., Carcione, A. and Nicolò, G. (2007).

Metacognition within narratives of schizophrenia: Associations with multiple domains of neurocognition. *Schizophrenia Research*, *93*, 278–287.

Lysaker, P.H., Buck, K.D., Taylor, A.C. and Roe, D. (2008a). Associations of metacognition, self stigma and insight with qualities of self experience in schizophrenia. *Psychiatry Research*, *157*, 31–38.

Lysaker, P.H., Warman, D.M., Dimaggio, G., Procacci, M., LaRocco, V., Clark, L.K., *et al.* (2008b). Metacognition in prolonged schizophrenia: Associations with multiple assessments of executive function. *Journal of Nervous and Mental Disease*, *196*, 384–389.

Mitchell, J.P., Macrae, N.C. and Banaji, M.R. (2006). Dissociable medial prefrontal contributions to judgments of similar and dissimilar others. *Neuron*, *50*, 655–663.

Moses, J.L. (2005). Executive functioning and children's theories of mind. In B.F. Malle and S.D. Hodges (eds), *Other minds: How humans bridge the divide between self and others* (pp. 11–25). New York: Guilford Press.

Murray, H.A. (1943). *Thematic apperception test manual.* Cambridge, MA: Harvard University Press.

Ownsworth, T. and Fleming J. (2005). The relative importance of metacognitive skills, emotional status and executive function in psychosocial adjustment following acquired brain injury. *Journal of Head Trauma Rehabilitation*, *20*, 315–332.

Roncone, R., Falloon, I.R., Mazza, M., De Risio, A., Necozione, S., Morosini, P., *et al.* (2002). Is theory of mind in schizophrenia more strongly associated with clinical and social function than with neurocognitive deficit? *Psychopathology*, *35*, 280–288.

Saxe, R. (2005). Against simulation: The argument from error. *Trends in the Cognitive Sciences*, *9*, 174–179.

Saxe, R., Carey, S. and Kanwisher, N. (2004). Understanding other minds: Linking developmental psychology and functional neuroimaging. *Annual Review of Psychology*, *55*, 87–124.

Semerari, A., Carcione, A., Dimaggio, G., Falcone, M., Nicolò, G., Procacci, M., *et al.* (2003). How to evaluate metacognitive functioning in psychotherapy? The metacognition assessment scale and its applications. *Clinical Psychology and Psychotherapy*, *10*, 238–261.

Stanghellini, G. (2004). *Disembodied spirits and deanimated bodies: The psychopathology of common sense.* Oxford: Oxford University Press.

Stratta, P., Riccardi, I., Mirabilio, D., Di Tommaso, S., Tomassini, A. and Rossi, A. (2007). Exploration of irony appreciation in schizophrenia: A replication study on an Italian sample. *European Archives of Psychiatry and Clinical Neuroscience*, *257*, 337–339.

Wechsler, D. (1997a). *Wechsler adult intelligence scale – III.* San Antonio, TX: Psychology Corporation.

Wechsler, D. (1997b). *Wechsler memory scale – III.* San Antonio, TX: Psychology Corporation.

Westen, D. (1991). Clinical assessment of the object relations using the TAT. *Journal of Personality Assessment*, *56*, 56–74.

Chapter 5

Schizophrenia and social functioning

The role of impaired metacognition

Daniela Schaub, Mona Abdel-Hamid and Martin Brüne

Introduction

The term schizophrenia – coined by Eugen Bleuler in a scientific meeting in 1908 – embraces a clinically heterogeneous group of psychotic syndromes that are characterized by positive symptoms such as delusions and hallucinations, negative symptoms including abulia and affective flattening, symptoms pertaining to expressive behaviors a subset of which is labeled catatonic, and neurocognitive deficits (American Psychiatric Association, 2000). One common feature of the various types of schizophrenia is that many individuals suffering from the condition(s) are impaired in their social functioning. That is, patients with schizophrenia often have difficulties in meeting societal defined roles, in maintaining social relationships and in self-care. Impaired social functioning is not only a (non-specific) core feature of manifest schizophrenia, but may also precede the onset of the disorder, and hence be already present in the prodromal stage. Moreover, social functioning often worsens over the course of the disorder, and poor social functioning contributes to the rate of relapse and need of rehospitalization (Pinkham *et al.*, 2003). Put differently, social functioning in schizophrenia is an important outcome parameter and crucial for the evaluation of treatment (Burns and Patrick, 2007).

In the past decade, clinicians have increasingly recognized the need to focus on means to improve social functioning in schizophrenia, to some extent independent of mere symptom reduction. Even though attempts to improve social functioning by general cognitive remediation therapy have been partially successful, research into the underlying cognitive deficits associated with poor social functioning in schizophrenia has lent support to the assumption that impaired social cognition has greater explanatory power than deficits in non-social cognition in terms of predicting social competence in schizophrenia (Penn *et al.*, 1997; Green *et al.*, 2005; Brüne *et al.*, 2007). In other words, social cognition seems to be strongly linked to functional outcome areas such as social skills or independent living skills, including communication with others, maintaining employment, and functioning in the community (Couture *et al.*, 2006).

The term social cognition concerns the perception and processing of social signals to construct representations of the relation between oneself and others and to use those representations flexibly to guide social behavior (Lysaker *et al.*, 2005). The concept has somewhat vague boundaries to the domains of motivation, emotion, attention, memory and decision-making (Adolphs, 2001). Narrowly defined, social cognition involves the ability to form mental representations of one's own and others' mental experiences such as beliefs, desires, intentions, feelings, and dispositions, a process that involves the presence of a "theory of mind" (TOM; Premack and Woodruff, 1978; Leslie, 1987) or "metacognition" (Lysaker *et al.*, 2005). Metacognition also includes the ability "to imagine oneself in a different situation from the here-and-now, and to evaluate one's current thoughts and emotions non-subjectively, as if looking at oneself from the outside" (Roberts and Penn, 2006). As far as the representation of other minds is concerned, metacognitive processes are highly inferential in nature and therefore clearly bear the risk to err (Gigerenzer, 1997). That is, during discourse the attributed mental states to one's interlocutor require permanent checking for their validity. Otherwise, a conversation can quickly move into an unintended direction leading to all sorts of misinterpretations and misunderstandings. By contrast, representation of one's own mental states is a prerequisite for the ability to experience the self as an agent such that behavior can be initiated on the basis of one's perceived intentions. For example, if someone intends to execute a complex task he or she needs to develop a mental plan of how to sequence individual steps in a logical way, otherwise task performance would go wrong.

Both the representation of other minds and the representation of one's own mentality are frequently disrupted in schizophrenia and are supposed to be one cause of symptoms and social problems (Frith, 1992, 2004). For example, misinterpreting other person's intentions due to an inability to discriminate between reality and subjective representation may cause delusional ideation. Conversely, difficulties in understanding one's own behavior as the result of self-generated intentions may lead to the conviction of being under alien control. Finally, the inability to initiate an action on the basis of one's own intentions may manifest in the form of disorganized behavior (Frith, 1992). Since conscious self-representation including the ability to reflect upon one's mental and physical integrity overlaps with the concept of insight, impaired metacognition could also be the "missing link" between unawareness of illness and poor social functioning in schizophrenia.

From an empirical standpoint, metacognitive processes in schizophrenia have been examined using questionnaires that target attributional styles such as the Attributional Style Questionnaire (ASQ; Peterson *et al.*, 1982) or its successor the Internal, Personal and Situational Attribution

Questionnaire (IPSAQ; Kinderman and Bentall, 1996), rating scales like the Metacognition Assessment Scale (MAS) that examine individuals' ability to recognize own and others' mental states and their ability to work through one's representations and mental states (termed "mastery") as revealed by analysis of narratives of individuals' verbalizations (Semerari *et al.*, 2003), and a variety of tasks designed to explore individuals' capacity to comprehend mental states of story or cartoon characters (Happé, 1994; Langdon *et al.*, 1997; Sarfati *et al.*, 1997; Stone *et al.*, 1998; Brüne, 2005b). These approaches to assess patients' metacognition are, by and large, quite diverse in design and therefore, obviously, measure different aspects of this cognitive faculty. However, as will be outlined in the following paragraphs, studies seem to converge on the finding that impaired metacognitive functioning in schizophrenia is tightly linked with poor social functioning, irrespective of how exactly metacognitive capacities are measured, and also largely independent of which particular aspect of social functioning is being examined (Burns and Patrick, 2007).

This chapter reviews the evidence for a link of impaired metacognition in schizophrenia with social functioning. Specifically, the chapter will summarize studies that have addressed the association of attributional style, objective ratings of metacognition, and studies into patients' ability to infer mental states of story characters (i.e. "theory of mind" or "mentalizing") with social functioning. In addition, we will review recent approaches that have explored the relationship of schizophrenic patients' metacognitive impairment with poor insight with possible implications for social functioning. The chapter concludes by suggesting that metacognitive training is a useful non-pharmacological tool to improve social functioning in patients with schizophrenia.

Social functioning and metacognition

Social functioning in schizophrenia has traditionally been linked with deficits in information processing including working memory, verbal memory or executive functioning. The view that "non-social" cognition can sufficiently account for functional deficits in schizophrenia has, however, repeatedly been challenged for the limited statistical power of deficits in non-social information processing in explaining poor social functioning (Penn *et al.*, 1997). In several seminal articles it has been argued instead that social cognitive processes – of which metacognition represents an important aspect – are superior in explaining impaired functioning in schizophrenia (Pinkham *et al.*, 2003; Green *et al.*, 2005; Penn *et al.*, 2008). It now seems empirically well supported that poor metacognition in schizophrenia represents a domain on its own that can be distinguished from neurocognition (Van Hooren *et al.*, 2008), and that the former is more strongly linked with patients' compromised social functioning (Brüne *et al.*, 2007).

Research into attributional styles of patients with paranoid ideation, for example, has repetitively demonstrated that patients with delusional beliefs tend to attribute negative events to other persons, whereas positive events are attributed to one's self (Kinderman and Bentall, 1996). Although only quantitatively distinct from attributional styles of healthy individuals (Penn *et al.*, 2008), the extreme of such a "self-serving bias" has been interpreted as the attempt to reduce the discrepancy between actual-self and ideal-self to stabilize fragile ego boundaries (Bentall *et al.*, 2001). This comes at the expense of being able to accurately evaluate differences between one's self-perception and the apparent perception of self by others. In other words, an extreme self-serving bias reduces the ability to use contextual information such that others' perception of one's self is rigidly believed to be hostile in nature. Accordingly, the social consequences of such a personalizing bias may include aggressive outbursts or the inability to carry out work-related activities because of general discomfort at work (reviewed in Couture *et al.*, 2006). In line with these assumptions, Waldheter and colleagues (2005) found a significant association of an externalizing and personalizing attributional style with aggressive behavior in acute inpatients with schizophrenia. In contrast, patients with schizophrenia in remission tend to make more stable attributions, which predicts more frequent social contacts, a higher quality of social interaction, and better community participation (Lysaker *et al.*, 2004).

In a subsequent study, Lysaker *et al.* (2005) chose a different approach by rating patients' narratives according to their ability to understand their own minds, to understand the mental life of others, and patients' ability to work through their own mental states in a constructive and problem-solving way. These dimensions can be assessed using the Metacognition Assessment Scale (MAS; Semerari *et al.*, 2003) during conversation with individual patients who are encouraged to reflect on own and others' life histories and illnesses. According to this study, impaired metacognition is strongly linked with measures of neurocognition such as executive functioning and verbal learning. Most importantly, poor social functioning was best explained by deficits in "mastery", that is, the ability to purposefully regard a particular problem or source of distress (Lysaker *et al.*, 2005).

The majority of studies into the association of social functioning with social cognition in schizophrenia – at least within the broader concept of metacognition – have used cartoon picture stories or short stories to examine patients' ability to comprehend the mental states of story characters, referred to as "mentalizing" or "theory of mind" (reviewed in Brüne, 2005a). A wealth of studies has demonstrated that schizophrenic patients have specific difficulties in inferring what others intend, think, or pretend, and in understanding false beliefs, intentions, deception, metaphor, irony, and faux pas situations (Penn *et al.*, 2008).

Roncone and colleagues (2002) were the first to reveal a direct relationship between impaired mentalizing and poor social functioning. Specifically, patients' compromised mentalizing abilities were the second-best predictor (after duration of illness) of poor social functioning in the community, and contributed a greater statistical variance to explain impaired social competence compared with verbal fluency, executive functioning and negative or positive symptoms. This finding could be confirmed in a study into the comprehension of cartoon story characters, with the differences that impaired mentalizing predicted poor social competence best, accounting for more than a quarter of the variance (Brüne, 2005b). More recently, a replication in an independent sample of patients with schizophrenia spectrum disorders (which included a small number of patients with schizoaffective disorders and "pure" delusional disorder) demonstrated that impaired metacognition (i.e. mentalizing) accounted for 50 per cent of the variance of social functioning (Brüne *et al.*, 2007). Interestingly, while positive symptoms and duration of illness contributed only small percentages of additional variance, these findings were independent of general intelligence, executive functioning and medication. In a similar vein, Bora and colleagues (2006) found a significant association of poor mentalizing with impaired social functioning. They also discovered that mental state decoding and mental state reasoning might represent two separable aspects of mentalizing. The authors hypothesized that mental state decoding from basic facial expressions of emotion or from more complex and ambiguous cues as, for example, required in the detection of sarcasm from prosody, involves the ability to use contextual information perhaps with greater immediacy than mental state reasoning. By contrast, the latter more specifically relies on the ability to decipher verbally transmitted information, which does not even require the presence of the person to which mental states are to be ascribed. Accordingly, Bora *et al.* (2006) used a task showing the facial region surrounding the eyes from which the mental state has to be inferred (Baron-Cohen *et al.*, 2001), and a task designed to recognize the hidden meaning behind indirect speech (Corcoran *et al.*, 1995). Only the former predicted poor social functioning when neurocognition was statistically controlled.

Taken together, these studies strongly support the assumption of a causal link between social cognitive abilities such as metacognition and social functioning (overview in Brüne, 2005a; Couture *et al.*, 2006). Since insight into illness constitutes a crucial factor in social functioning and outcome measures, we will explore in the next section as to what extent poor metacognition could mediate the association between insight and functioning in schizophrenia.

Social functioning, insight and metacognition

In potentially debilitating disorders such as schizophrenia, social functioning critically depends on patients' ability to recognize symptoms and to correctly attribute source or cause to symptoms. Both awareness and attribution are key components of insight (Amador *et al.*, 1993), which, in turn, are seen as prerequisites for consent to treatment (Rusch and Corrigan, 2002; Koren *et al.*, 2005; Osatuke *et al.*, 2008). Empirical evidence supports the view that poor insight in patients with schizophrenia is associated with reduced treatment achievements (Schwartz, 1998), and, most importantly, poor social functioning (Francis and Penn, 2001). The underlying cognitive deficits of poor insight in schizophrenia are, however, only partially understood. Whilst some studies have failed to demonstrate an association of impaired insight with poorly developed cognitive skills (Freudenreich *et al.*, 2004; Cuesta *et al.*, 2006), others revealed that executive functioning, attention, cognitive flexibility, perceptual organizational skills, working memory, identification of facial emotions and learning skills were linked to insight (Keshavan *et al.*, 2004; Goodman *et al.*, 2005; Simon *et al.*, 2006; Lysaker *et al.*, 2007; Ritsner and Blumenkrantz, 2007). According to a recent meta-analysis of 35 studies (Aleman *et al.*, 2006) the impact of neurocognitive skills on insight is marginal but significant, which leaves open to speculation whether or not other cognitive domains are potentially involved in insight in patients with schizophrenia. Since causal attribution of symptoms is distorted in schizophrenia and often part of delusional thinking (Warman *et al.*, 2007), it is well conceivable that impaired metacognition contributes to poor insight and may also mediate the association of poor insight with compromised social functioning. For example, a patient with schizophrenia who experiences voice-commenting hallucinations or that his movements are not under his own volitional control usually interprets such passivity symptoms as alien-made rather than as the result of some brain dysfunction. Consequently, such a patient would reject alternative explanations and not be able to gain insight. However, empirical studies have only begun to address this question.

Without referring to social functioning, a couple of recent studies have shown that poor metacognitive abilities in patients with schizophrenia are consistently associated with poor insight and awareness of illness. For example, Koren and colleagues (2004) demonstrated that the association between insight and metacognitive skills (as assessed using a metacognitive version of the Wisconsin Card Sorting Test) was higher compared to the relationship between insight and basic cognitive flexibility. Similarly, several recent studies have underscored the association of impaired metacognition and poor insight using a variety of measures tapping into the domain of metacognition and social cognition respectively (Lysaker *et al.*, 2007). Langdon and colleagues (2006) found that a strong self-serving bias as expressed by a high number of externalizing and personalizing attributions of negative events seems to exacerbate poor insight. Moreover, although mentalizing deficits do not increase the personalization bias, it is associated with impaired insight (Langdon *et al.*, 2006). Similarly, Bora and colleagues

(2007), as well as Langdon and Ward (2008), found that impaired mentalizing predicted poor insight and symptom misattribution best.

In summary, these findings indicate that metacognitive functioning contributes to at least certain aspects of insight such as awareness of symptoms and attribution of causation. However, even though this suggests that impaired metacognition in schizophrenia could mediate the association of poor insight and poor social functioning, this issue needs to be carved out in detail in future studies that take direct measures of social functioning into account. Such an approach should ideally involve various measures of metacognition including attributional style, mentalizing, and mastery, as well as measures of different aspects of social functioning such as the quality of interpersonal relationships, occupational performance and self-care.

Social functioning and metacognitive training

The previous sections have shown that social functioning is tightly linked with patients' ability to entertain metacognitive abilities such as perspective taking, thinking about thinking and intact self-reflection. This, in turn, emphasizes the necessity to search for new intervention strategies to achieve improvements in this domain, particularly in the light of ambiguous findings regarding the potential for improvement of metacognition of psychopharmacological treatment (Penn *et al.*, 2008). Previous intervention studies have typically focused on one aspect of social cognition, but have not examined whether or not findings of improved social cognition after training can be generalized to improvements in social functioning (Combs *et al.*, 2007).

According to this therapeutic gap, Roberts and Penn (2006) developed a Social Cognitive Interaction and Treatment (SCIT) program that targets several key components of social cognition including various aspects of metacognition. A pilot study revealed improvements in mentalizing, and a reduced externalizing and personalizing bias in patients with schizophrenia (Penn, Corrigan *et al.*, 2007). The same group could demonstrate in a subsequent study that social cognitive training leads to improved social relationships and a decrease in aggressive incidents in forensic inpatients. These changes were independent of changes in clinical symptoms (Combs *et al.*, 2007).

A similar program (Metacognitive Training for Schizophrenia Patients, MCT), devised by Moritz and Woodward (2008), yielded comparable results including a strengthening of metacognitive competences and relapse prevention (Aghotor *et al.*, 2007). This program comprises training modules designed to help patients modify their attributional styles and to develop more flexibility in evaluating ambiguous social information in order to reduce patients' tendency to accept conclusions based on insufficient information. Unlike Combs *et al.* (2007), the study by Aghotor *et al.* (2007) showed that metacognitive training might also be helpful in reducing the amount of positive symptoms. Although at this stage preliminary, these findings suggest that social cognitive training can serve as a useful tool to induce changes in real-world behavior beyond the effects of psychopharmacological treatment.

Summary and conclusions

In the past, poor social functioning has been one of the most critical aspects of schizophrenia that has proven difficult to improve effectively by means of psychopharmacological treatment or cognitive remediation therapy. Recent research suggests that impaired social functioning – regardless of whether social communication, performance at work or functioning in the community is the prime target of measurement – can at least in part be attributed to impaired metacognitive abilities in patients with schizophrenia. Several subprocesses may be involved. First, deficits in emotion and social cue perception may cause difficulties in identifying relevant social cues. Second, cognitive biases foster certain attributional styles and, if combined with impaired mentalizing, may influence an individual's interpretation of incoming communications in a misleading way. Finally, deficits in social or communication skills can bring about ineffective interpersonal performance, which reflects a part of poor social functioning (Dickinson *et al.*, 2007). Whether or not this is similar across schizophrenia subtypes is subject to further empirical work. Metacognitive deficits seem to be most severe in patients with prominent disorganization symptoms (Sprong *et al.*, 2007; Abdel-Hamid *et al.*, 2009). Accordingly, it is equally unknown whether patients with different subtypes respond differentially to social cognitive remediation therapy.

Future studies should include standardized functional outcome measures and multiple measures of metacognition and insight to elucidate the relationships between these constructs. It would also be desirable to devise longitudinal studies of the association of social functioning, metacognition and insight in individuals at risk of developing schizophrenia to evaluate the potentially predictive value of these domains for transition into full-blown psychosis and to examine whether early social cognitive interventions can even contribute to prevent the transition into manifest schizophrenia.

It is clear that communication of psychoeducative facts alone is not sufficient to effectively treat patients with schizophrenia and improve their social functioning. In addition, supporting patients in social issues and everyday life may eventually not only prove to be a fruitful endeavour, but also enhance insight into the illness (Lysaker *et al.*, 2007).

References

Abdel-Hamid, M., Lehmkämper, C., Sonntag, C., Juckel, G., Daum, I. and Brüne, M. (2009). Theory of mind in schizophrenia: The role of clinical symptomatology and neurocognition in understanding other people's thoughts and intentions. *Psychiatry Research, 165*, 19–26.

Adolphs, R. (2001). The neurobiology of social cognition. *Current Opinion in Neurobiology, 11*(2), 231–239.

Aghotor, J., Moritz, S., Pfüller, U., Gmehlin, D., Rösch-Ely, D. and Weisbrod, M. (2007). Evaluation eines Metakognitiven Trainingsprogramms für schizophrene Patienten: Effekte auf die Positivsymptomatik. Poster at DGPPN-Kongress, Berlin.

Aleman, A., Agrawal, N., Morgan, K.D. and David, A.S. (2006). Insight in psychosis and neuropsychological function: Meta-analysis. *British Journal of Psychiatry, 189*, 204–212.

Amador, X.F., Strauss, D.H. and Yale, S.A. (1993). Assessment of insight in psychosis. *American Journal of Psychiatry, 150*, 873–879.

American Psychiatric Association (2000). *Diagnostic and statistical manual of mental disorders, 4th edn, DSM-IV*. Washington DC: American Psychiatric Association.

Baron-Cohen, S., Wheelwright, S., Hill, J., Raste, Y. and Plumb, I. (2001). The 'Reading the Mind in the Eyes' test revised version: A study with normal adults, and adults with Asperger Syndrome or high-functioning autism. *Journal of Child Psychology and Psychiatry, 42*, 241–251.

Bentall, R.P., Corcoran, R., Howard, R., Blackwood, N. and Kinderman, P. (2001). Persecutory delusions: A review and theoretical integration. *Clinical Psychology Reviews, 21*, 1143–1192.

Bora, E., Eryavuz, A., Kayahan, B., Sungu, G. and Veznedaroglu, B. (2006). Social functioning, theory of mind and neurocognition in outpatients with schizophrenia: Mental state decoding may be a better predictor of social functioning than mental state reasoning. *Psychiatry Research, 145*, 95–103.

Bora, E., Sehitoglu, G., Aslier, M., Atabay, I. and Veznedaroglu, B. (2007). Theory of mind and unawareness of illness in schizophrenia: Is poor insight a mentalizing deficit? *European Archives of Psychiatry and Clinical Neuroscience, 257*(2), 104–111.

Brüne, M. (2005a). 'Theory of mind' in schizophrenia: A review of the literature. *Schizophrenia Bulletin, 31*(1), 21–42.

Brüne, M. (2005b). Emotion recognition, 'theory of mind', and social behavior in schizophrenia. *Psychiatry Research, 133*, 135–147.

Brüne, M., Abdel-Hamid, M., Lehmkämper, C. and Sonntag, C. (2007). Mental state attribution, neurocognitive functioning, and psychopathology: What predicts poor social competence in schizophrenia best? *Schizophrenia Research, 92*, 151–159.

Burns, T. and Patrick, D. (2007). Social functioning as an outcome measure in schizophrenia studies. *Acta Psychiatrica Scandinavica, 116*, 403–418.

Combs, D.R., Adams, S.D., Penn, D.L., Roberts, D.L., Tiegreen, J. and Stem, P. (2007). Social cognition and interaction training (SCIT) for inpatients with schizophrenia spectrum disorders: Preliminary findings. *Schizophrenia Research, 91*, 112–116.

Corcoran, R., Mercer, G. and Frith, C.D. (1995). Schizophrenia, symptomatology and social inference: Investigating 'theory of mind' in people with schizophrenia. *Schizophrenia Research, 17*, 5–13.

Couture, S.M., Penn, D.L. and Roberts, D.L. (2006). The functional significance of social cognition in schizophrenia: A review. *Schizophrenia Bulletin*, *32*, S44–S63.

Cuesta, M.J., Peralta, V., Zarzuela, A. and Zandio, M. (2006). Insight dimensions and cognitive function in psychosis: A longitudinal study. *BMC Psychiatry*, *31*, 6–26.

Dickinson, D., Bellack, A.S. and Gold, J.M. (2007). Social/communication skills, cognition, and vocational functioning in schizophrenia. *Schizophrenia Bulletin*, *33*(5), 1213–1220.

Francis, J.L. and Penn, D.L. (2001). The relationship between insight and social skill in persons with severe mental illness. *Journal of Nervous and Mental Disease*, *189*, 822–829.

Freudenreich, O., Deckersbach, T. and Goff, D.C. (2004). Insight into current symptoms of schizophrenia: Association with frontal cortical function and affect. *Acta Psychiatrica Scandinavica*, *110*, 14–20.

Frith, C.D. (1992). *The cognitive neuropsychology of schizophrenia*. Hove, UK: Lawrence Erlbaum Associates Ltd.

Frith, C.D. (2004). Schizophrenia and theory of mind. *Psychological Medicine*, *34*(3), 385–389.

Gigerenzer, G. (1997). The modularity of social intelligence. In A. White and R.W. Byrne (eds), *Machiavellian intelligence II: Extensions and evaluations*. Cambridge: Cambridge University Press.

Goodman, C., Knoll, G., Isakov, V. and Silver, H. (2005). Insight into illness in schizophrenia. *Comprehensive Psychiatry*, *46*, 284–290.

Green, M.F., Olivier, B., Crawley, J.N., Penn, D.L. and Silverstein, S. (2005). Social cognition in schizophrenia: Recommendations from the Measurement and Treatment Research to Improve Cognition in Schizophrenia New Approaches Conference. *Schizophrenia Bulletin*, *31*(4), 882–887.

Happé, F.G.E. (1994). An advanced test of theory of mind: Understanding of story characters' thoughts and feelings by able autistic, mentally handicapped and normal children and adults. *Journal of Autism and Developmental Disorders*, *24*, 129–154.

Keshavan, M.S., Rabinowitz, J. and DeSmedt, G. (2004). Correlates of insight in first episode psychosis. *Schizophrenia Research*, *70*, 187–194.

Kinderman, P. and Bentall, R.P. (1996). A new measure of causal locus: The internal, personal and situational attributions questionnaire. *Personality and Individual Differences*, *20*, 261–266.

Koren, D., Seidman, L.J., Poyurovsky, M., Goldsmith, M., Viksman, P., Zichel, S., *et al.* (2004). The neuropsychological basis of insight in first-episode schizophrenia: A pilot metacognitive study. *Schizophrenia Research*, *70*(2–3), 195–202.

Koren, D., Poyurovsky, M., Seidman, L.J., Goldsmith, M., Wenger, S. and Klein, E.M. (2005). The neuropsychological basis of competence to consent in first-episode schizophrenia: A pilot metacognitive study. *Biological Psychiatry*, *57*, 609–616.

Langdon, R. and Ward, P. (2008). Taking the perspective of the other contributes to the awareness of illness in schizophrenia. *Schizophrenia Bulletin*, *35*(5), 1003–1011.

Langdon, R., Michie, P.T., Ward, P.B., McConaghy, N., Catts, S. and Coltheart,

M. (1997). Defective self and/or other mentalising in schizophrenia: A cognitive neuropsychological approach. *Cognitive Neuropsychiatry*, *2*, 167–193.

Langdon, R., Corner, T., McLaren, J., Ward, P.B. and Coltheart, M. (2006). Externalizing and personalizing biases in persecutory delusions: The relationship with poor insight and theory-of-mind. *Behaviour Research and Therapy*, *44*(5), 699–713.

Leslie, A. (1987). Pretence and representation: The origins of 'theory of mind'. *Psychological Review*, *94*, 412–426.

Lysaker, P.H., Lancaster, R.S., Nees, M.A. and Davis, L.W. (2004). Attributional style and symptoms as predictors of social function in schizophrenia. *Journal of Rehabilitation Research and Development*, *41*(2), 225–232.

Lysaker, P.H., Carcione, A., Dimaggio, G., Johannesen, J.K., Nicolò, G., Procacci, M., *et al.* (2005). Metacognition amidst narratives of self and illness in schizophrenia: Associations with neurocognition, symptoms, insight and quality of life. *Acta Psychatrica Scandinavica*, *112*, 64–71.

Lysaker, P.H., Daroyanni, P., Ringer, J.M., Beattie, N.L., Strasburger, A.M. and Davis, L.W. (2007). Associations of awareness of illness in schizophrenia spectrum disorder with social cognition and cognitive perceptual organization. *Journal of Nervous and Mental Disease*, *195*(7), 618–621.

Moritz, S. and Woodward, T.S. (2008). *Metacognitive training for schizophrenia patients (MCT). Manual.* Hamburg: VanHam Campus.

Osatuke, K., Ciesla, J., Kasckow, J.W., Zisook, S. and Mohamed, S. (2008). Insight in schizophrenia: A review of etiological models and supporting research. *Comprehensive Psychiatry*, *49*, 70–77.

Penn, D.L., Corrigan, P.W., Bentall, R.P., Racenstein, J.M. and Newman, L. (1997). Social cognition in schizophrenia. *Psychological Bulletin*, *121*, 114–132.

Penn, D.L., Roberts, D.L., Combs, D. and Sterne, A. (2007). Best practices: The development of the social cognition and interaction training program for schizophrenia spectrum disorders. *Psychiatric Services*, *58*(4), 449–451.

Penn, D.L., Sanna, L.J. and Roberts, D.L. (2008). Social cognition in schizophrenia: A review. *Schizophrenia Bulletin*, *34*(3), 408–411.

Peterson, C., Semmel, A., von Baeyer, C., Abramson, L., Metalsky, G.I. and Seligman, M.E.P. (1982). The attributional style questionnaire. *Cognitive Therapy and Research*, *3*, 287–300.

Pinkham, A.E., Penn, D.L., Perkins, D.O. and Lieberman, J. (2003). Implications for the neural basis of social cognition for the study of schizophrenia. *American Journal of Psychiatry*, *160*, 815–824.

Premack, D. and Woodruff, G. (1978). Does the chimpanzee have a 'theory of mind'? *Behavioral and Brain Sciences*, *4*, 515–526.

Ritsner, M.S. and Blumenkrantz, H. (2007). Predicting domain-specific insight of schizophrenia patients from symptomatology, multiple neurocognitive functions, and personality related traits. *Psychiatry Research*, *149*(1–3), 59–69.

Roberts, D.L. and Penn, D.L. (2006). Social cognition and interaction training (SCIT), training manual. Unpublished manuscript.

Roncone, R., Falloon, I.R.H., Mazza, M., De Risio, A., Pollice, R., Necozione, S., *et al.* (2002). Is theory of mind in schizophrenia more strongly associated with clinical and social functioning than with neurocognitive deficits? *Psychopathology*, *35*, 280–288.

Rusch, N. and Corrigan, P.W. (2002). Motivational interviewing to improve insight and treatment adherence in schizophrenia. *Psychiatric Rehabilitation Journal, 26*(1), 23–32.

Sarfati, Y., Hardy-Baylé, M.C., Brunet, E. and Widlöcher, D. (1997). Investigating theory of mind in schizophrenia: Influence of verbalization in disorganized and non-disorganized patients. *Schizophrenia Research, 37*, 183–190.

Schwartz, R.C. (1998). The relationship between insight, illness and treatment outcome in schizophrenia. *Psychiatric Quarterly, 69*, 1–22.

Semerari, A., Carcione, A., Dimaggio, G., Falcone, M., Nicolò, G., Procacci, M., *et al.* (2003). How to evaluate metacognitive funtioning in psychotherapy? The metacognition assessment scale and its applications. *Clinical Psychology and Psychotherapy, 10*, 238–261.

Simon, A.E., Berger, G.E., Giacomini, V., Ferrero, F. and Mohr, S. (2006). Insight, symptoms and executive functions in schizophrenia. *Cognitive Neuropsychiatry, 11*(5), 437–451.

Sprong, M., Schothorst, P., Vos, E., Hox, J. and van Engeland, E. (2007). Theory of mind in schizophrenia. *British Journal of Psychiatry, 191*, 5–13.

Stone, V.E., Baron-Cohen, S. and Knight, R.T. (1998). Frontal lobe contributions to theory of mind. *Journal of Cognitive Neuroscience, 10*, 640–656.

Van Hooren, S., Versmissen, D., Janssen, I., Myin-Germeys, I., à Campo, J., Mengelers, R., *et al.* (2008). Social cognition and neurocognition as independent domains in psychosis. *Schizophrenia Research, 103*, 257–265.

Waldheter, E.J., Jones, N.T., Johnson, E.R. and Penn, D.L. (2005). Utility of social cognition and insight in the prediction of inpatient violence among individuals with a severe mental illness. *Journal of Nervous and Mental Disease, 193*(9), 609–618.

Warman, D., Lysaker, P.H. and Martin, J.M. (2007). Cognitive insight and psychotic disorder: The impact of active delusions. *Schizophrenia Research, 90*, 325–333.

Chapter 6

Awareness is not the same as acceptance

Exploring the thinking behind insight and compliance

Kevin D. Morgan and Anthony S. David

> "Yeah, the radio talks to me, it's like the radiators – they're telling me something, it's pretty scary but I am away from the house now, so I don't need any treatment. The evil was in the house. There is nothing wrong with me."
>
> (Female aged 45 subsequently diagnosed with paranoid schizophrenia)

Introduction

It is through an integration of sensory information and stored knowledge in memory that we perceive and interpret the objects, events and emotions that make up our world. Thus, we may perceive a state of happiness in the self, or another, when inner cues such as a feeling of elation, or external signs like a smiling face, are detected and associated with previously held conceptions about what a state of happiness is. In patients with psychosis, however, this transaction between external and internal environmental cues and knowledge of the self and the world can be disrupted at any point. Indeed, psychosis is a mental state where there is, proverbially, some loss of contact with reality and where there are disturbances to the normal processes of thought and perception. When the normal mechanisms of mental appraisal are impaired, it is not only the perception and appraisal of external behaviours and events that is at risk of misinterpretation. The realization and understanding of the psychotic state in the self is likely to be distorted. In respect of auditory hallucinations, for example, patient explanations of the phenomena may range from claims of possessing a special power to hear such voices, to a belief that the voices are normal and that others can hear them too. If anomalous mental events such as hallucinations are adjudged in this way, the consequences can extend from disagreement with those who contest that interpretation, to a failure to recognize that help may be needed to manage such disordered and often distressing thought processes. In this chapter we focus on the link between the self-appraisal of psychotic states, the impact that has on perceived treatment needs and how that is reflected in treatment-related behaviour.

In psychiatric terminology, the word 'insight' describes the level of awareness that patients have with respect to their symptoms and illness status. Poor insight is a common feature of the functional psychoses and has been consistently reported as one of the most characteristic features in the clinical presentation of people with psychotic disorders such as schizophrenia (WHO, 1973; Amador *et al.*, 1994; Peralta and Cuesta, 1998; Chen *et al.*, 2001). In addition to lacking an awareness of illness and symptoms, poor treatment compliance is also an important factor associated with insight. Treatment compliance is an attitudinal and behavioural dimension of insight. It is concerned with the way in which a person responds to the management of their illness while placed in a patient role. Specifically, the term compliance refers to an individual's adherence to a recommended regimen of treatment.

In the psychoses, medical care may involve hospitalization, the prescription of antipsychotic medication, psychosocial treatments (e.g. cognitive behavioural therapy) and a requirement to attend regular outpatient appointments. High levels of non-compliance with treatment are a cause for concern in the management of psychotic disorders. In a review of 26 studies, Young *et al.* (1986) estimated a median default rate of 41 per cent (range 10 per cent to 76 per cent) in oral medication usage among outpatients with schizophrenia. A 15-study review, reported similar rates of medication refusal in schizophrenia (i.e. the median rate of refusal was 55 per cent, with a range of 24 per cent to 88 per cent) (Fenton *et al.*, 1997).

Psychotic patients who do not believe they are ill are less likely to comply with treatment than those who acknowledge they have a psychological disorder (Amador *et al.*, 1993; Lysaker *et al.*, 1994; Kemp and David, 1996; Smith *et al.*, 1999). A lack of illness awareness and non-compliance with treatment have also been associated with a poorer outcome and increased chance of relapse (van Os *et al.*, 1996; Schwartz *et al.*, 1997; Kemp *et al.*, 1998). It is also evident that people who are not aware, or deny that they are ill are more likely to be admitted to hospital on an involuntary basis (McEvoy *et al.*, 1989b; Kemp and David, 1996; Owen *et al.*, 2008). A study of first-episode psychotic patients found that during the acute phase of psychosis, insight and attitudes toward treatment were the only factors that could reliably predict treatment compliance (Kampman *et al.*, 2002). On this basis it might be reasonable to depict a relatively straightforward sequence of decision making leading from a self-judgement of illness towards a given pattern of treatment behaviour (Figure 6.1).

However, a model of health behaviour such as this is almost certainly too simplistic (i.e. treatment adherence is likely to be affected by other factors). These may include the perceived benefits of treatment and also the detrimental effects (or 'costs') of adopting the proposed programme of therapy. The term Health Belief Model has been used to describe these sometimes competing influences that steer patients towards a particular

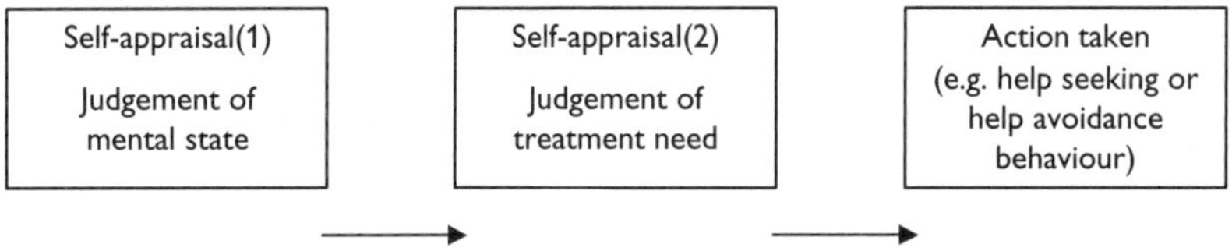

Figure 6.1 Decision-making sequence.

mode of treatment behaviour. These may include 'non-psychiatric' factors evident also in physical conditions such as heart disease, cancer, renal failure, tuberculosis and diabetes, whereas in the psychotic disorders, patients frequently fail to acknowledge their illness status and comply with treatment (Goldbeck, 1997). A range of factors unrelated to awareness of illness has been attributed to non-adherence in physical illnesses:

- fear of medication dependence or side effects
- poor patient–practitioner relationship
- conflicting medical advice
- poor understanding of treatment
- conflicting cultural or religious beliefs
- substance abuse
- feelings of low self-esteem and lack of personal autonomy
- complex medication regime (leading to forgetfulness)
- everyday life management takes priority over treatment adherence
- low risk perception of the illness
- lack of supportive family or peers.

It is probable that all these factors may also influence non-compliance in the psychoses. In view of this it is perhaps not surprising that in psychiatric illnesses such as schizophrenia studies of treatment adherence have not always found a simple linear association between illness awareness and treatment compliance (Garavan *et al.*, 1998; McCabe *et al.*, 2000). In a study of patients with a range of psychotic disorders it was found that while increased insight was significantly associated with a more positive attitude about medication, insight was not associated with medication compliance (Goldberg *et al.*, 2001). It would appear therefore that some patients with high levels of illness awareness refuse to engage with recommended treatment programmes. It is also evident that some patients with very low illness awareness are willing to accept medication and derive benefit from it (McEvoy *et al.*, 1989a).

In relation to the Health Belief Model and its applicability to the psychoses, it has been suggested that neurocognitive deficits may also affect a person's capacity to comply with treatment (Perkins, 2002). The factors affecting treatment compliance in psychotic disorders appear, therefore, to be particularly complex. On the one hand the patient is dealing with a series of pragmatic, personal, social and cultural issues that may influence their readiness to engage with treatment recommendations, much the same as patients in non-psychiatric settings. On the other hand there is an increased potential of confusion where the self-appraisal of the symptoms of psychosis may lead to a belief that there is no illness in the first place.

In this chapter we consider the extent to which the self-appraisal of mental and emotional states in psychotic disorders impacts on attitudes and beliefs about treatment and how in turn that is reflected in treatment behaviour. This will be examined through a study of illness and symptom appraisal and treatment attitudes and behaviour in a sample of 232 first-onset psychosis patients. The focus of the study is on the verbal accounts provided by the patients when asked about their beliefs and attitudes about needs for treatment. The first strand of this analysis is to consider the way in which patients describe the following:

1 How they appraise their psychotic state.
2 The extent to which external help is needed to manage that state.
3 The action taken in relation to those appraisals.

The intention of this qualitative analysis is to discover whether different compliance profiles or 'types' could be identified and which reflected the different ways in which need for treatment was conceptualized and acted upon.

As the mechanisms by which the thoughts and mental events of patients with psychosis are self-appraised are likely to be disrupted, we also sought to examine whether the different compliance 'types' we identified could be characterized by different patterns or levels of cognitive functioning. In recent years, a considerable amount of research has been devoted to understanding the neuropsychological determinants of poor illness and symptom awareness (Morgan and David, 2004; Aleman *et al.*, 2006) but few studies have considered how cognitive function relates to treatment behaviour in the psychoses beyond relatively basic dichotomous analyses of patients rated as being either 'compliant' or 'non-compliant'. In the second strand of the analysis, we therefore set out to scrutinize the cognitive performance of the different compliance profiles we identified with the aim of establishing whether variations in neuropsychological abilities such as fronto-executive functioning were associated with those different attitude-behaviour profiles.

Context of the interviews and analysis of the dialogue

The accounts of illness appraisal and attitudes towards treatment were based on a series of interviews conducted with 232 people presenting to psychiatric services with a psychotic illness for the first time in their lives.

Table 6.1 Sample background characteristics (*n* = 232)

	Mean	sd ±
Age	31.1	11.4
	n	%
Sex		
Female	95	41
Male	137	59
Ethnicity		
White British	116	50
Not White British	116	50
Diagnosis		
Schizophrenia	101	43
Schizoaffective disorder	9	4
Bipolar disorder	36	16
Depressive psychosis	44	19
Other psychosis	42	18

Participants were drawn from the Aetiology and Ethnicity in Schizophrenia and Other Psychoses (AESOP) study of first-onset psychosis conducted September 1997 to September 2000.

The interviewees were patients participating in an epidemiological study of first-onset psychosis (diagnosed according to F10–F29 and F30–F33 codings in *ICD-10*, WHO, 1993), taking place in three UK inner city areas: South-East London, Nottingham and Bristol (see Table 6.1 for background characteristics of the sample). The interviews took place as soon as possible after the patients had presented to psychiatric services providing the eligibility status of the patient had been verified (i.e. that they were experiencing a first-episode of psychosis). Informed consent was obtained from the patients along with permission from the treating clinician. The majority of the interviews were conducted either in a hospital or outpatient care setting by members of the research project team using the Schedule for the Assessment of Insight – Expanded Version (SAI-E, Kemp and David, 1997). The SAI-E is a semi-structured interview instrument that allows the interviewer to inquire of the patients about how they view their current psychological and emotional state, whether they see themselves as experiencing a psychological disorder, how they identify and account for specific psychotic symptoms and their beliefs about their treatment needs. Responses to the individual items on the schedule can be scored to reflect higher or lower levels of insight but the SAI-E is also designed so that the interviewer can record the patient's verbatim response to each question item. The interview is relatively brief (nine main question items) and in most instances completed within 15 minutes.

The first five items cover awareness of change in mental functioning; recognition of illness; explanations for illness; and the identification of life problems arising from the illness condition. Questions are put to the interviewee in terms such as 'Do you think you have been experiencing any psychological or emotional changes or difficulties?' and 'Do you think there is something wrong with you?' Attitudes and beliefs towards treatment are assessed according to each patient's expressed opinion about his or her treatment needs when the patient is asked: 'Do you think your condition or the problem resulting from it (or whatever term the patient used to describe their situation) needs treatment?' Actual treatment behaviour (as opposed to attitudes towards treatment) is rated through an interview with the patient's primary nurse, key worker or the clinical worker with whom they have had closest contact. These comprise an objective rating of the patient's attitude and behaviour towards treatment and these questions are asked as closely as possible to the time of the patient interview. The clinician concerned is asked questions such as: 'How does the patient accept the treatment provided?', and 'Does the patients ask or enquire about the treatment unprompted?'

The analysis of the interview dialogue was guided by two main issues. The first of these was in relation to evidence of the patient's thinking about his or her thoughts (metacognition). (Note our usage of the term metacognition in contrast to the other common usage to denote awareness of another person's thoughts, feelings and desires, i.e. theory of mind.) The second issue was centred on how attitudes and behaviour towards treatment are influenced by: (a) the way in which the patients conceptualized their current psychological and emotional state; and (b) other factors such as medication side effects. All of the analysis was conducted through a manual examination of the interview transcripts. In respect to metacognition, the dialogue was initially studied for any evidence that patients were thinking about (reflecting upon) their thought or emotional processes. Any element of dialogue identified as such was coded accordingly. Once all the transcripts had been reviewed the elements of dialogue coded in the way described were examined further and compared with each other in order to identify different ways in which thinking about thinking may influence illness and treatment behaviour. A similar scrutiny was applied to dialogue relating to treatment attitudes (with or without evidence of metacognition). For example, a female patient in her twenties with bipolar disorder commented:

> 'I don't know, I have never really believed in pills for treatment, but obviously I have taken medicine which has made a huge difference. There was a total rot in my brain and I wasn't going to get rid of it myself . . . it was part memory of some bad experiences and part of being ill.'

This extract was coded both in relation to treatment attitudes and also in respect of metacognition. The patient expresses a view that despite having previous misgivings about taking medication she feels she has benefited from the drugs provided. This view appears also to be related in some way to the self-appraisal of her thoughts in that she identifies the 'rot in my brain' to be resulting at least in part from the memory of bad experiences and that it was not a situation she could manage by herself.

How the patients think about their own psychosis

Through the analysis of the interview transcripts it emerged that a large number of the patients gave no overt indication that they were currently reflecting (or had previously reflected) on their own thoughts. This included responses where the presence of psychosis was not acknowledged. In such instances the accounts provided by the patients were sometimes expressed as outright denials of anything being wrong and on some occasions as delusional accounts of the current situation. For other patients an apparent failure to recognize their own disordered thinking arose, perhaps not surprisingly from their current state of confusion or in some instances a refusal to consider their current mental state. It could be considered that in respect of those particular patients, while the capacity for metacognitive thought was not entirely absent, a combination of motivational denial and a confused mental state severely reduced the ability to self-reflect on one's own thought processes (see Dialogue Table 6.1).

Lower levels of metacognitive processing did not inevitably lead to a failure to recognize (or at least acknowledge) the presence of illness or psychological change. In some instances, patients described at a relatively superficial level (in terms of how they reflected on their thought processes) the belief that they have some form of mental illness. However, while

Dialogue Table 6.1 Presence of illness not accepted – no clear evidence of metacognition

Denial	'There's nothing wrong, nothing's changed . . . I don't care what the doctors say, there's nothing wrong.'
	'The only thing that's been wrong with me in the past is a lack of confidence. I've got all the confidence I need now, but everyone else sees that as wrong, they just can't accept it.'
Delusion accounts	'They put stuff in the food, I know it . . . my husband put bugs all over the house, in the radio, in the clock.'
	'An impostor who claimed to be my son told the doctors I was ill . . . My son was in France at the time.'
Confusion	'I haven't got a clue [*what's wrong*]. People want to keep me in hospital for some reason.'
Refusal/inability to self-appraise	'I don't know what to think. I don't want to think about it.'

patient views expressed in this way are informative at one level, they provide little indication of the thinking processes taking place that underlie those views. In the absence of knowing the rationale behind the views expressed, it may prove very difficult to understand any subsequent behaviour that may be at odds with what has been said. A patient may, for example, appear to agree simply because that is what they have been told or because they wish to appear non-confrontational (see Dialogue Table 6.2).

Dialogue Table 6.2 Presence of illness accepted – no clear evidence of metacognition

Acceptance by self	'Yes, I've been sick. I'm not sure what sort of illness, but I've been lonely and sick.'
Based on others' opinion	'I respect the doctors' views above my own.'
	'If they say so then it must be true. I don't know what I feel really, maybe I suffer from this illness.'
Uncertainty	'Not when I'm at work, but when I'm finished I sometimes think there is [*something wrong*].'

Some patients when appraising their current psychological state are able to go beyond a 'face value' analysis of what they are experiencing and recognizably engage in a form of metacognition. This can range from a general identification that there are difficulties in their thinking processes, for example:

> 'I know I haven't been able to keep track of my thoughts.'

They can also take the form of more specific appraisals of thought processes involved or affected:

> 'At the time I had a disturbance in the way in which I perceive sounds from things like the CD player.'

Interestingly, the action of metacognition does not (at least by itself) lead to a realization that one's thought processes are in a pathological state:

> 'Sometimes my thinking is stagnated, but other times it's much clearer, more positive – often people can hear them.'

Indeed, the rationalization of aberrant thoughts may in itself lead to a sense of empowerment or intensify an existing delusional interpretation of the mechanisms driving the pathological state (see Dialogue Table 6.3).

Dialogue Table 6.3 Accounts of illness status with evidence of metacognition

Evidence of metacognition – presence of illness accepted	
Less specific identification of disruption to thought processes	'I've been upset, angry, my thinking gets stuck sometimes, and fluent at others . . . Yes I'm mixing reality with unreality.'
	'Instead of thinking – I was just putting it all on to my life, making everything refer to me. I know now this was very silly and my mind was playing tricks.'
	'My brain's weak – I don't know why . . . my thoughts and emotions are muddled . . . I need to clear up the problem with my brain . . . my brain is causing the other problems.'
More specific identification of disruption to thought processes	'I think it was something to do with my imagination. Because of my loneliness I'd started using my imagination more to talk to people in my head, I can make out any situation I wanted to . . . they were characters I had created myself, I don't have any stress, it was loneliness.'
	'No it was another level of understanding . . . I am seeing things in a more whole sort of way. I have been picking up more cues . . . a higher perception in my thinking – I am just more aware, picking things up.'
Evidence of metacognition – presence of illness not accepted	
Non-specific identification of disruption to thought processes	'There is something that is not connecting inside my head – yeah, it's a mental problem . . . I am controlled through television and phones, I can't trust anyone . . . I know it's not real, but I can't explain it – sometimes I think they're really there . . . I know it's real – it's not about being ill – someone or some people wants me to die.'
	'It happened to me just before I came here. My head got full of knowledge – it gave me the power to invoke spirits. I don't want to use it again, but it might happen another time. I can use it against certain people.'

Taking a different perspective

As can be seen from the analysis so far, the study of metacognition in the psychoses is complex. Some patients will identify that their thought processes may be erratic, anomalous and unpredictable, while others, although often troubled by the content of their thoughts and feelings, do not appear to reflect on the processes of those thoughts and emotions either through lack of motivation or an incapacity to do so. The approach of most studies of insight in the psychoses is to ask patients directly what they believe, what they feel and what they are thinking. It would be of particular value to know how patients would perceive their psychotic state, if they were asked to appraise from another person's viewpoint. A recent study conducted by

Gambini *et al.* (2004) on a sample of patients with schizophrenia who lacked any insight into their delusions considered this very question. Gambini *et al.* asked the patients to consider the reality of their delusional beliefs, for example, 'My neighbours influence my life with X-rays passing through the floor' (Gambini *et al.*, 2004: 43), by taking the perspective of the interviewer asking the questions. When the patients moved their perspective from the first to the third person, a significant number of them said that they no longer considered their delusions to be reasonable.

We asked a similar question of the patients in our study. A 'hypothetical contradiction' (Brett-Jones *et al.*, 1987) item is included in the SAI-E which ascertains the patient's capacity to encompass another person's view of their illness experience such as the inability of other people to hear 'the voices' that the patient is experiencing. The interviewer asks the patient: 'How do you feel when people do not believe you, when you talk about . . . [delusions or hallucinations]?' Asking questions in this way did allow some patients to think about their thoughts and other aspects of their mental state in a more insightful way than they had been able to previously, while for others taking the third person perspective did not appear to facilitate a deeper or more self-reflective view of their psychosis and in some only served to provide confirmation of delusional beliefs (see Dialogue Table 6.4).

Dialogue Table 6.4 Accounts of illness status when presented with hypothetical contradiction

No evidence of further insight or closer appraisal of mental state	'I'm sure my boyfriend was lying when he denied hearing the voices.' 'It doesn't alter the way I feel, it just means I wouldn't be able to talk to them again. I wouldn't be able to trust them.'
Little or no change in appraisal of mental state	'It sometimes makes me think about it in a different way – but it doesn't really change my mind.' 'I wouldn't care. It wouldn't change my mind.'
Confusion about what to think	'I CAN hear the people talking – I do sometimes get confused when someone questions it.'
Questions whether thought processing is normal	'I'd agree with them – I'd have to question what's going on with me.'
Full realisation that thought processes are disrupted	'Obviously, it's a hallucination.' 'I wouldn't expect anyone to believe it, although it felt real enough at the time. I realize now that something strange was happening to my thoughts.'

Treatment attitudes and treatment behaviour

The focus of the textual analysis was now shifted from accounts of how psychotic states were thought about to how attitudes to treatment were influenced by those appraisals. As would be expected, for many patients when a pattern of abnormal thinking was recognized in the self it led to a recognition of need. Conversely, for some patients, when disordered thinking processes or belief systems were not identified there was a failure to recognize any need. However, in some circumstances a reflection on one's thought processes was seen to lead to confusion and (an albeit erroneous) realization that treatment is not the correct course of action.

> 'I know what I hear and see – that's real, I don't lie but I guess my mind could be playing tricks . . . Perhaps there is no treatment. Perhaps my character is flawed and I'm a basket case.'

Perhaps most difficult to explain was the relatively poor predictive value of expressed treatment attitudes in respect of the actual treatment behaviour that was observed (see Dialogue Table 6.5). Of the sample 88 (38 per cent) acknowledged a need for treatment but based on the observations of their primary nurses were non-compliant. Conversely, 44 patients (19 per cent) stated that they did not require any form of therapy or help from health professionals, but nonetheless complied with the treatment programmes provided. In other words over half of the sample (57 per cent) expressed beliefs about treatment needs that were at odds with their actual treatment behaviour (or else their beliefs oscillated between two poles at a high frequency). Indeed, these sometimes conflicting forms of attitude and behaviour towards treatment could be characterized into five broad compliance profiles or types:

1. No need acknowledged – no engagement with treatment (n = 30).
2. No need acknowledged – engagement with treatment (n = 44).
3. Unsure of need – partial engagement with treatment (n = 21).
4. Need acknowledged – engagement with treatment (n = 88).
5. Need acknowledged – no engagement with treatment (n = 49).

There were no significant differences between these groups in terms of age, sex, diagnosis and ratings for positive and negative psychotic symptoms. There were significant differences between the groups, however, in terms of ratings for mania and depression. Patients in the group where no treatment need was acknowledged and who were non-compliant score significantly higher for ratings of mania than all the other groups except for the group who did not acknowledge a need for treatment but were nonetheless compliant. In terms of depression ratings, the group who acknowledged a

Dialogue Table 6.5 Mismatch between treatment attitudes and treatment behaviour

Primary nurse account	**Patient account**
Patient shows no reluctance to comply with the programme of medication and other treatment.	'I shouldn't be in this hospital. I should be at home. I don't need any pills.'
He always took the medication, there was never a problem.	'No – believe me I need nothing from anyone. I can deal with things myself.'
Patient repeatedly questions the need to take medication and remain on the hospital ward.	'I'd like to change to stronger medication yes, I . . . need to be in hospital.'

need for treatment and were treatment compliant were significantly more depressed than all the other groups except for group of patients unsure of treatment needs and only partially engaging with treatment (see Dialogue Table 6.5).

Other factors affecting treatment attitudes

Earlier we considered that a range of other factors might impact on levels of compliance above and beyond the realization that one is experiencing a state of disordered thinking and emotional and behavioural flux. In our study of the interview transcripts, one issue that concerned many patients and appeared to impact on their treatment attitudes and behaviour was that of compulsion. This was not unexpected as refusal to accept treatment may in some cases be a factor that is sufficient to determine a compulsory admission to hospital. Furthermore, previous studies have shown that psychotic patients admitted to hospital on a compulsory basis do appear to have lower levels of illness awareness and compliance than patients admitted voluntarily (McEvoy *et al.*, 1989b; Kemp and David, 1996; Owen *et al.*, 2008). Consequently, the proportion of people with the most severely impaired insight and greatest reticence towards treatment is likely to be higher amongst detained patients. However, admission status may not only be a reflection of lower insight levels. Being a detained patient could also contribute to them. The experience of being subject to compulsory admission, possibly involving the police service and the sometimes unpleasant side effects of forced antipsychotic medication may exacerbate negative attitudes towards engagement with services that were evident before admission. This could result in an even greater reluctance to comply with care programmes and provoke an increased likelihood of a failure to acknowledge one's illness. It was evident in the accounts provided by our patients that many of them were complying with their treatment regimens because they felt they had no choice, even though they had serious reservations about therapy (usual medication)

Dialogue Table 6.6 The impact of compulsion and deference to medical professionals on attitudes toward treatment

Compulsory admission	'I shouldn't be in hospital and I don't need any medicine – I take it because I have to, but I shouldn't be here.'
	'I could do it myself, but I go along with the doctors. I just play their game.'
	'They've put me on treatment, but I don't agree with that – but there's nothing I can do about it.'
Patient–doctor deference	'I thought that the hospital would be bad because you don't know what the medication could do to you. The doctor said I needed medication, so I trusted the doctor.'
	'Well yes, [*I must need the medication*] otherwise they wouldn't be giving it to me.'

they were subjected to. For other patients, including those admitted on a voluntary basis, it was apparent that a sense of deference towards the treating clinician was an important factor guiding treatment behaviour, even if a decision to comply ran contrary to personal reservations about the perceived benefits of taking prescribed medication (see Dialogue Table 6.6).

The examples in Dialogue Table 6.6 may explain in part why there is engagement with treatment when illness itself is not necessarily acknowledged. There were many instances, however, where, although a state of psychosis or illness in the self was recognized, patients expressed strong reservations about complying with treatment. The majority of patient comments about this were related to the issue of medication side effects and other potentially detrimental consequences of taking prescribed drugs (although attitudes to illness were likely to precede attitudes to medication). The majority of studies that have investigated possible relationships between insight and antipsychotic medication (Young *et al.*, 1993; Cuesta *et al.*, 1995; Lysaker *et al.*, 1998) have reported negative findings for any association between those factors. Macpherson *et al.* (1996) did find a correlation between insight and both antipsychotic dose and duration of use. However, the correlation was weak and neither the dose nor duration of use emerged as predictors for insight in a subsequent regression analysis. Anti-parkinsonian drugs are often prescribed to control the extrapyramidal side effects of antipsychotic drugs. Patients taking anti-parkinsonian medication are therefore likely to have recently experienced unpleasant side effects and may show more reluctance to continue taking antipsychotic medication. Cuesta and Peralta (1994) and Lysaker *et al.* (1998) found no association between anti-parkinsonian dosage and insight or compliance. The influence that other psychotropic medication may have on insight is relatively unknown.

Dialogue Table 6.7 Experiences and expectations of medication side effects on treatment attitudes and behaviour

Responses to question: 'Do you think your condition [*or patient's own term*] needs treatment?'	
Patients' reservations about medication side effects	'No but I've been ill because of the meds I'm taking [*making me feel*] . . . sick and dizzy.'
	'These drugs are okay but they make me restless. They're not addictive are they?'
	'I tried the largactyl but it just flattened me.'
	'One set was a nightmare, bad side effects, wasn't sure why I was given them. Felt as if I was being used as a guinea pig.'
	'The side effects might have made me ill. I don't really think that it was a mental illness, maybe it was I am not sure.'
Patient proposed alternatives	'I need a skunk, spliff and a joint to treat me. The doctor's treatment is crap.'
	'The only thing I need is to take some herbal preparations. That makes me feel better.'
	'I don't know if I need treatment. I need to talk to a spiritualist to find that out. The medication hasn't helped.'

In our study several of the patients expressed a reluctance to take prescribed medication based on either experiences or expectations of side effects. Interestingly, some of them suggested alternatives to conventional forms of medication offered providing some evidence that mismatches between treatment attitudes and treatment behaviour may be dependent on the type of treatment and the environmental context in which it is administered (see Dialogue Table 6.7).

Cognitive appraisal of the compliance profiles

While factors such as admission status and drug side effects will clearly have a bearing on compliance behaviour, the degree to which any disruption in the normal processes of cognition and self-appraisal impacts on treatment attitudes and behaviour is unclear. In recent years, research into the determinants of poor insight has focused on neuropsychological functioning where patterns of association have been observed between the self-appraisal of illness and symptom status alongside reduced fronto-executive functioning and to a lesser extent a more general disruption to cognition. It is rare, however, that similar associations have been found with the same neuropsychological measures and variations in attitudes and behaviour towards recommended treatment regimens. It could be implied from this that cognition has a less important role in this aspect of insight, when compared to factors such as symptom attribution. On the other hand, it might be that the cognitive mechanisms which contribute to how psychosis patients perceive a need for treatment and subsequently engage with programmes of care are different from those of other insight components and may have a more complex link with other psychological, social and cultural factors. In the final part of our analysis we considered this question. Specifically, we wanted to examine the cognitive function of the five compliance profile types that were identified in the textual analysis by making a cross-profile group comparison of performance on a brief battery of neuropsychological tests that measured general intellectual functioning (premorbid [National Adult Reading Test] and current IQ) and executive functioning (working memory, verbal fluency and set-shifting [Trail Making B]). This analysis comprised a total of 178 patients as not all of the sample had completed the neuropsychological test battery. As was found with the main sample, there were no significant differences between the five compliance profile groups in this analysis in terms of age, sex, diagnosis and ratings for positive and negative psychotic symptoms. Ratings for mania, however, were higher in the group that did not acknowledge a need for treatment and were non-compliant, while ratings for depression were highest in patients that did acknowledge a need for treatment and were compliant.

The analysis of neuropsychological test performance showed different patterns of cognitive functioning across the compliance profile groups. Further statistical analysis did not reveal significant between-group differences but the patterns of cognitive performance observed were nonetheless of interest (see Figure 6.2). The patients with greatest uncertainty of treatment need and only partial treatment engagement and the those who did not acknowledge acceptance of need but were nonetheless treatment compliant were the most cognitively impaired, performing poorer than the other compliance groups in measures of premorbid IQ, current IQ, working memory and verbal fluency. The comparison of both estimated premorbid IQ and current IQ scores was also of interest. The two compliance profile groups who acknowledged a need for treatment scored higher on both these measures compared to the other groups where no treatment need was acknowledged or where there was an uncertainty of treatment need. Of the two groups who accepted a need for treatment, one was compliant with their recommended treatment regimens and the other group, despite acknowledging a treatment need, were non-compliant. Of course, as previously stated, the analysis did not reveal statistically significant differences and any interpretation of the findings must be cautious. However, an indication is given that cognitive function might be more closely related to the appraisal of need rather than levels of compliance. Thus, patients who recognized that treatment would be of benefit had higher levels of general

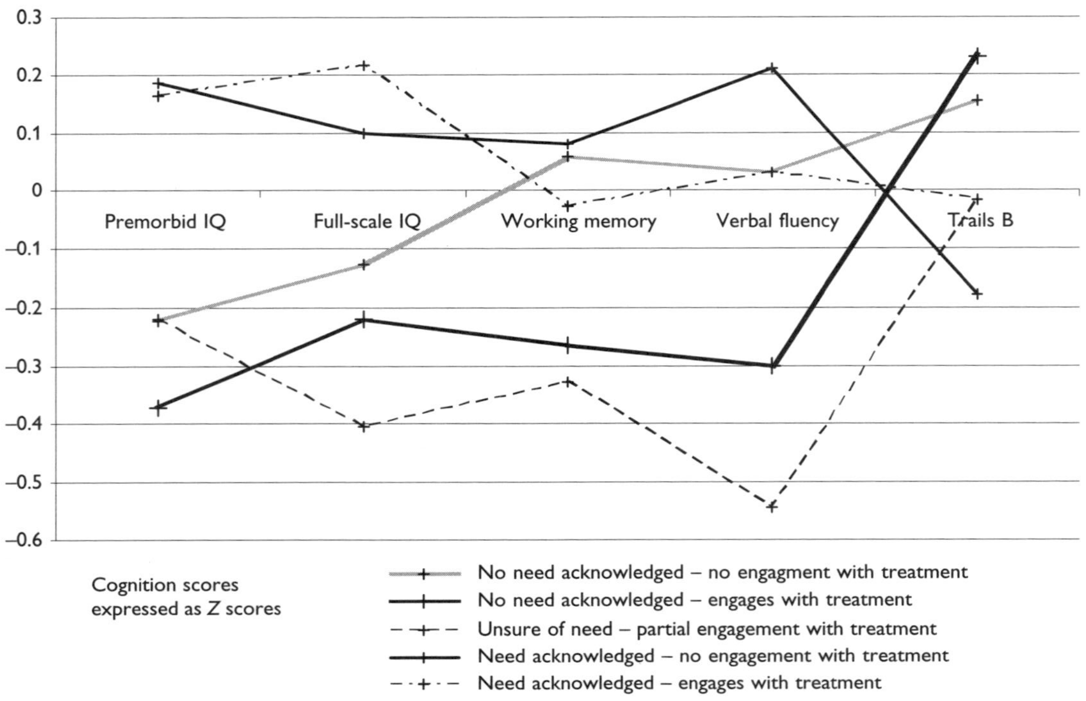

Figure 6.2 Cognition across the compliance profile groups.

intellectual functioning, irrespective of whether their actual treatment behaviour was compliant or non-compliant.

Conclusion

The analysis of the interview transcripts revealed that the degree to which patients engaged in metacognitive thought varied considerably across the sample. For some patients, the intrusion of factors such as delusional thought processes and pronounced emotional and motivational states appeared to substantially reduce the extent to which they were able to make self-judgements. In these cases it is likely that metacognitive thought occurred at a relatively residual level. In other patients there was clearer evidence of metacognition taking place although this appeared at times to be a fragmented or contradictory process. Finally, it was evident in many patients that the process of metacognition was integral to the self-appraisal of illness and treatment needs. In this respect, it was of interest that the act of metacognition was not necessarily a reliable predictor of illness recognition as several patients appraised their thinking to be 'abnormal' but not pathological. In the light of this it was perhaps not unexpected therefore to find that the identification of abnormal mental states did not always lead to a belief or acknowledgement that treatment was a necessary or desirable course of action. In the analysis we also considered whether taking a third person perspective might engender a more metacognitive stance in terms of illness appraisal and treatment need. While there were some signs that taking a third person perspective did influence some patients in the way they viewed their situation, the majority of patients did not appear to change their views.

The path between the appraisal of illness, recognition of need and treatment behaviour was one of complexity. We identified five compliance profile types that included groups of patients who acknowledged a need for treatment but were non-compliant and patients who did not believe themselves to be ill or require medical help but were nonetheless engaging with prescribed treatment regimens. It was evident that issues of compulsion and the experience (or fear of) medication side effects played a role in these seemingly contradictory stances. It also emerged that affective states had an impact on treatment behaviour where manic symptoms were associated with a failure to acknowledge treatment needs (but not necessarily compliance itself) and depressive symptoms were associated with acknowledgement of need and positive engagement with treatment. Finally, we looked at cognitive functioning across the five compliance profile types and observed that the two groups of patients with the highest levels of general intellectual functioning were those that acknowledged a need for treatment but while one of those groups was treatment compliant, the other was non-compliant. The accumulation of evidence from this study therefore supports the concept of a modified health belief model of adherence behaviour which is influenced by a range of factors including appraisal of illness and treatment needs, a 'cost-benefit' assessment of treatment engagement, affective states and neurocognitive functioning.

References

Aleman, A., Agrawal, N., Morgan, K. D. and David, A. S. (2006). Insight in psychosis and neuropsychological function: Meta-analysis. *British Journal of Psychiatry*, *189*, 204–212.

Amador X. F., Flaum M., Andreasen N. C., Strauss D. H. and Gorman J. M. (1994). Insight into illness in schizophrenia, schizoaffective disorder and mood disorders – results from the DSM IV Field Trials. *Archives of General Psychiatry*, *51*(10), 826–836.

Amador, X. F., Strauss, D. H., Yale, S. A., Flaum, M. M., Endicott, J. and Gorman, J. M. (1993). Assessment of insight in psychosis. *American Journal of Psychiatry*, *150*, 873–879.

Brett-Jones, J., Garety, P. and Hemsley, D. (1987). Measuring delusional experiences: A method and its application. *British Journal of Clinical Psychology*, *26*(Pt 4), 257–265.

Chen, E. Y., Kwok, C. L., Chen, R. Y. and Kwong, P. P. (2001). Insight changes in acute psychotic episodes: A prospective study of Hong Kong Chinese patients. *Journal of Nervous and Mental Disease*, *189*, 24–30.

Cuesta, M. J. and Peralta, V. (1994). Lack of insight in schizophrenia. *Schizophrenia Bulletin*, *20*, 359–366.

Cuesta, M. J., Peralta, V., Caro, F. and de Leon, J. (1995). Is poor insight in psychotic disorders associated with poor performance on the Wisconsin card sorting test? *American Journal of Psychiatry*, *152*, 1380–1382.

Fenton, W. S., Blyler, C. R. and Heinssen, R. K. (1997). Determinants of medication compliance in schizophrenia: Empirical and clinical findings. *Schizophrenia Bulletin*, *23*, 637–651.

Gambini, O., Barbieri V. and Scarone, S. (2004). Theory of mind in schizophrenia: first person vs third person perspective. *Consciousness and Cognition*, *13*, 39–46.

Garavan, J., Browne, S., Gervin, M., Lane, A., Larkin, C. and O'Callaghan, E. (1998). Compliance with neuroleptic medication in outpatients with schizophrenia: Relationship to subjective response to neuroleptics; attitudes to medication and insight. *Comprehensive Psychiatry*, *39*, 215–219.

Goldberg, R. W., Green-Paden, L. D., Lehman, A. F. and Gold. (2001). Correlates of insight in serious mental illness. *Journal of Nervous and Mental Disease*, *189*, 137–145.

Kampman, O., Laippala, P., Vaananen, J., Koivisto, E., Kiviniemi, P., Kilkku., N., *et al.* (2002). Indicators of medication compliance in first-episode psychosis. *Psychiatry Research*, *110*, 39–48.

Kemp, R. and David, A. S. (1996). Psychological predictors of insight and compliance in psychotic patients. *British Journal of Psychiatry*, *169*, 444–450.

Kemp, R. and David, A. S. (1997). Insight and compliance. In B. Blackwell (ed.), *Treatment compliance and the therapeutic alliance* (pp. 61–84). London: Informa Healthcare.

Kemp, R., Kirov, G., Everitt, B., Hayward, P. and David, A. S. (1998). Randomised controlled trial of compliance therapy. 18-month follow-up. *British Journal of Psychiatry*, *172*, 413–419.

Lysaker, P., Bell, M., Milstein, R., Bryson, G. and Beam-Goulet, J. (1994). Insight and psychosocial treatment compliance in schizophrenia. *Psychiatry*, *57*, 307–315.

Lysaker, P. H., Bell, M. D., Bryson, G. J. and Kaplan, E. (1998). Insight and interpersonal function in schizophrenia. *Journal of Nervous and Mental Disease*, *186*, 432–436.

McCabe, R., Quayle, E., Beirne, A. and Duane, M. (2000). Is there a role for compliance in the assessment of insight in chronic schizophrenia? *Psychology, Health and Medicine*, *5*, 173–178.

McEvoy, J. P., Apperson, L. J., Appelbaum, P. S., Ortlip, P., Brecosky, J., Hammill, K., *et al.* (1989a). Insight in schizophrenia. Its relationship to acute psychopathology. *Journal of Nervous and Mental Disease*, *177*, 43–47.

McEvoy, J. P., Applebaum, P. S., Apperson, L. J., Geller, J. L. and Freter, S. (1989b). Why must some schizophrenic patients be involuntarily committed? The role of insight. *Comprehensive Psychiatry*, *30*, 13–17.

Macpherson, R., Jerrom, B. and Hughes, A. (1996). Relationship between insight, educational background and cognition in schizophrenia. *British Journal of Psychiatry*, *168*, 718–722.

Morgan, K. D. and David, A. S. (2004). Neuropsychological studies of insight in patients with psychotic disorders. In X. Amador and A. S. David (eds), *Insight and psychosis* (pp. 177–196). Oxford: Oxford University Press.

Owen, G. S., Richardson, G., David, A. S., Szmukler, G., Hayward, P. and Hotopf, M. (2008). Mental capacity to make decisions on treatment in people admitted to psychiatric hospitals: Cross sectional study. *British Medical Journal*, *337*, a448.

Peralta, V. and Cuesta, M. J. (1998). Lack of insight in mood disorders. *Journal of Affective Disorders*, *49*, 55–58.

Perkins, D. O. (2002). Predictors of noncompliance in patients with schizophrenia. *Journal of Clinical Psychiatry*, *63*, 1121–1128.

Schwartz, R. C., Cohen, B. N. and Grubaugh, A. (1997). Does insight affect long-term inpatient treatment outcome in chronic schizophrenia? *Comprehensive Psychiatry*, *38*, 283–288.

Smith, T. E., Hull, J. W., Goodman, M., Hedayat-Harris, A., Willson, D. F., Israel, L. M., *et al.* (1999). The relative influences of symptoms, insight, and neurocognition on social adjustment in schizophrenia and schizoaffective disorder. *Journal of Nervous and Mental Disease*, *187*, 102–108.

van Os, J., Fahy, T. A., Jones, P., Harvey, I., Sham, P., Lewis, S., *et al.* (1996). Psychopathological syndromes in the functional psychoses: Associations with course and outcome. *Psychological Medicine*, *26*, 161–176.

WHO (1973). *Report of the international pilot study of schizophrenia*. Geneva: World Health Organization.

WHO (1993). *The ICD-10 classification of mental and behavioural disorders: Diagnostic criteria for research*. Geneva: World Health Organization.

Young, D. A., Davila, R. and Scher, H. (1993). Unawareness of illness and neuropsychological performance in chronic schizophrenia. *Schizophrenia Research*, *10*, 117–124.

Young, J. L., Zonana, H. V. and Shepler, L. (1986). Medication noncompliance in schizophrenia: Codification and update. *Bulletin of the American Academy of Psychiatry and Law*, *14*, 105–122.

Chapter 7

The assessment of theory of mind in schizophrenia

Elliot M. Bell, Robyn Langdon, Richard J. Siegert and Pete M. Ellis

Introduction

Premack and Woodruff (1978) introduced the term theory of mind (TOM) to describe the ability to infer one's own and others' mental states. The process (or the demonstrated performance) of making such inferences may be referred to as 'mentalizing' (Frith *et al.*, 1991). TOM is a crucial aspect of metacognition underpinning meaningful social interaction. Frith (1992) first proposed that TOM deficits accompany schizophrenia and are central in explaining the symptoms. There is now substantial evidence of TOM impairment in people with schizophrenia (see Harrington *et al.*, 2005), and resultant disruption of social functioning (see Schaub *et al.*, this volume, Chapter 5), such that many people with schizophrenia cannot fulfil major social roles like marriage, parenting and work. The significance of TOM for understanding and treating this social impairment is now recognized by the National Institute of Mental Health (NIMH, Green *et al.*, 2008) and clinicians (see Lysaker and Buck, this volume, Chapter 13, Hasson-Ohayon *et al.*, Chapter 14). We consider assessment of TOM will soon become a regular part of formulating treatment plans for people with schizophrenia. This chapter provides an overview of current approaches to the assessment of TOM in schizophrenia (and related conditions) for clinicians and researchers not expert in TOM. We conclude with recommendations for a pragmatic yet informative TOM assessment protocol, while acknowledging the psychometric limitations of current tests. We hope this will stimulate interest in establishing increasingly robust ways of assessing TOM.

We also outline a taxonomy of different approaches to assessing TOM in schizophrenia that categorizes subdomains of TOM and appraises the more prominent tasks used to evaluate them. Information about the psychometric properties of TOM tasks is sparse. Consequently we applied the following criteria to select and discuss the TOM assessment approaches:

1 The number of times a task has been used in published research (a form of "conferred" validity).

2 The discriminant validity of the tasks (i.e. the extent to which they demonstrate significant differences between schizophrenia samples and healthy control groups with regard to key theoretical issues).
3 Utility (e.g. administration time, suitability for adults).
4 Floor or ceiling effects (i.e. tests with a reasonable bandwidth are desirable for sensitivity and specificity).
5 The number and quality of the items in each test (which relates to content validity and face validity).
6 Availability of norms (i.e. whether a test has been used several times and means for healthy controls reported).

This chapter also touches on three important theoretical issues in current research on TOM in schizophrenia:

1 Are there links between TOM deficits and specific symptoms?
2 Are the TOM deficits in schizophrenia domain specific, meaning irreducible to common, more generalized cognitive deficits?
3 Are the TOM deficits a state or a trait?

Theory of mind assessment in schizophrenia

Taxonomy of tasks

Slaughter and Repacholi (2003) argue that several measures might be necessary to capture the complex, multidimensional nature of TOM. This section catalogues the different paradigms used to evaluate TOM in schizophrenia, grouping the various measures conceptually into a taxonomy (Table 7.1) that distinguishes between social-cognitive and social-perceptual subdomains. A third subdomain covers 'real-world' (i.e. ecologically valid) measures, which tap both these aspects of TOM.

The distinction between these two subdomains draws upon Tager-Flusberg and Sullivan (2000), who conceived these components as functionally and neurologically distinct. They contended that the social-cognitive facets (also referred to as mental state reasoning) require assimilation of contextual aspects about individuals (e.g. what they know or what they have done) in order to infer mental states. Social-cognitive TOM tasks include: assessing false belief; deception and intention understanding; and pragmatic language comprehension. By contrast, the social-perceptual aspects of TOM (also termed mental state decoding) involve inferring mental states via cues, such as bodily movements. This facet of TOM enables individuals to differentiate people from objects, and to form quick impressions of others' mental states on the basis of their physical appearance and/or movement. Social-cognitive TOM tasks also draw upon additional cognitive functions,

Table 7.1 Operationalizing theory of mind (TOM): classification of TOM tasks used in research on schizophrenia and related psychotic illnesses of adulthood

A. Social-cognitive TOM tasks
  1 Understanding of false belief and deception
    • Traditional vignettes, visual joke appreciation, picture sequencing
  2 Intention-inferencing story completion
  3 Pragmatic speech comprehension
    • Irony and metaphor, Gricean maxims, faux pas (FP), hints

B. Social-perceptual TOM tasks
  1 Inferring mental states from eye expressions
  2 Mental state inferences cued by observation of animated shapes

C. Real-world and more ecologically valid TOM assessments
  1 Structured interview
  2 Conversation analysis
  3 Analysis of video scenes of realistic social interactions

particularly language, whereas social-perceptual TOM may be related to more automatic affective systems.

Of course, many TOM tasks involve elements of both mental state reasoning and decoding. Consequently, we describe TOM tasks below under headings classifying them as primarily social-cognitive or social-perceptual, alongside discussion of real-world measures. For each subdomain, we describe: (a) how the tasks tap TOM; (b) further distinctions within each subdomain; (c) key examples of the tasks; (d) the strengths and weaknesses of these with reference to the theoretical and conceptual issues and psychometric criteria noted above.

A. Social-cognitive measures

1. Understanding of false belief and deception

Assessing TOM using the false belief and deception paradigm is based on the premise that intact TOM draws on a capacity to 'decouple' mental states from reality; allowing for the appreciation that people can believe things that misrepresent the true state of affairs. Consequently, this capacity enables deception. Many TOM studies on schizophrenia have combined tasks assessing understanding of both false belief and deception to produce composite TOM scores. These tasks typically use vignettes about interacting characters. Two types of task are commonly distinguished: (a) first-order tasks that typically involve identifying the mistaken beliefs held by a character in a story; (b) more complex second-order tasks requiring detection of one character's false belief about another's mental state. In their meta-analysis of the assessment of TOM in schizophrenia, Sprong *et al.* (2007) calculated large effect sizes for all first-order false belief tasks ($d = -1.193$), and second-order tasks ($d = -1.443$). The following subsections describe three different paradigms used to assess false belief and deception understanding in schizophrenia.

1.1 Traditional false belief and deception stories

FRITH AND CORCORAN'S FALSE BELIEF AND DECEPTION STORY (FBDS) TASK

This is the most frequently used false belief and deception task in schizophrenia research (see below). In the original version, Frith and Corcoran (1996) read the story vignettes aloud while presenting illustrative cartoons. Scoring assesses understanding of first-order and second-order false belief and deception stories. Participants are also asked 'reality questions' to assess their basic comprehension of the situations.

The psychometric properties of this task are unexplored in schizophrenia research, but similar tasks used in child development research generally show adequate test-retest reliability and internal consistency, albeit focusing mainly on first-order tests. Its utility is high, taking only ten to fifteen minutes to complete. It was designed to maximize straightforwardness and acceptability for adults. A potential weakness is likely ceiling effects for adults.

This task (or variants) has been used to examine links between TOM deficits and specific symptoms in schizophrenia, particularly a proposed link with paranoia (Frith, 1992), although findings are equivocal. Pickup and Frith (2001) used a FBDS task adapted to improve its ecological validity for chronic inpatients and found no evidence of such a link. Corcoran *et al.* (2008) compared the performance of patients with and without paranoid delusions, diagnosed with either schizophrenia or depression, on a FBDS task and the false belief trials from Langdon's picture sequencing task (see below). They found the paranoid participants were most impaired on the FBD stories regardless of diagnosis, while those diagnosed with schizophrenia were most impaired on the picture-sequencing task, whether or not they had paranoid delusions. These findings suggest that, within the same TOM subdomain, subtle differences in items or presentation format may alter sensitivity to deficits and discrimination between symptom and diagnostic groups.

The state–trait debate remains unresolved, with task selection again implicated in the divergent findings. Pickup and Frith (2001) found patients with schizophrenia in remission performed at the same level on their FBDS task as healthy controls. However, Janssen *et al.* (2003) observed that both patients with schizophrenia and their first-degree relatives showed deficits on Frith and Corcoran's FBDS task, consistent with the trait model. Similarly, Pickup (2008) found that positive schizotypal traits (e.g. magical thinking) were associated with subtle impairments in TOM, when using a story task more difficult than the FBDS task.

1.2 Visual joke appreciation tasks

Corcoran *et al.* (1997) developed a joke appreciation task to assess TOM, comprising two sets of ten cartoon jokes. The first (control) set is slapstick/behavioural jokes while the second (TOM) set requires understanding of false belief or deception to appreciate the humour. Participants have to explain each joke, so for the TOM set they must generate accurate mental-state descriptions, scored correct/incorrect for each joke. Corcoran and colleagues showed that schizophrenic patients found the mental-state jokes significantly more difficult to understand than the control jokes, this effect being most marked in patients with 'behavioural disorders' (negative and disorganized symptoms) and passivity experiences. Those with paranoid delusions had more subtle difficulties and symptom-free patients had none, supporting the state hypothesis. A longer 31-item version (Marjoram *et al.*, 2005a) discriminated between groups with and without schizophrenia, but could not link performance with specific symptoms. Langdon and colleagues (Langdon and Ward, in press; Langdon *et al.*, in press) also demonstrated TOM impairment in people with schizophrenia compared to healthy controls using a visual joke appreciation task. They graded the appropriateness of the explanation, which may have improved task sensitivity. However, such tasks must recognize the effects of cultural factors on appreciation of humour, potentially necessitating different cartoons for different groups. Furthermore, accurate differential scoring may require training to enhance interrater reliability.

1.3 Sequencing picture card stories

False belief and deception comprehension has also been evaluated using tasks requiring subjects to correctly order cartoon drawings to make logical stories. A large number of schizophrenia studies have used either Langdon's (Langdon *et al.*, 1997; Langdon and Coltheart, 1999) or Brüne's (2003a, 2003b) picture sequencing tasks (PST).

LANGDON'S PICTURE SEQUENCING TASKS

These incorporate a series of four-card picture stories, with the original version (Langdon *et al.*, 1997) updated to provide greater discrimination between patients with schizophrenia and controls (Langdon and Coltheart, 1999). The current version includes: False Belief sequences (to assess TOM by requiring identification of a false belief); Mechanical sequences (requiring only cause and effect reasoning); Social Script sequences (requiring appreciation of everyday social routines without needing to infer mental states); and Capture sequences (designed to assess disengagement – the capacity to inhibit misleading cues). The Capture sequences enabled the domain specificity of TOM deficits in schizophrenia to be examined (see below). The test is scored for both response time and correct ordering of cards. While nonverbal in its updated form, the verbal component of the original version, in which participants are asked to 'tell the story the cards tell', can be added.

BRUNE'S PICTURE SEQUENCING TASKS (PST)

Brüne (2003b) developed a PST to examine the relationship between intelligence and TOM in schizophrenia. It included a nonverbal sequencing component; questions to assess understanding of first-order false belief, second-order false belief, and tactical deception tasks; and reality control questions. Brüne (2003a) has extended this task to include further picture stories with questions probing comprehension of: (a) first-order and second-order belief and false belief; (b) third-order false belief; (c) reciprocity (based on two scenario types, one involving co-operative action based on mutual agreement, and the other co-operation to deceive); (d) deception; (e) cheating detection (requiring comprehension of one character's detection of another's intention to deceive them). Reality questions are also included. Though based on Langdon's format, Brüne's updated task always includes a verbal component and is untimed. Versions of Brüne's PST have been widely used in studies on schizophrenia and related psychotic illnesses (see below).

Both Langdon and Brüne's PSTs consistently demonstrate TOM deficits in people with schizophrenia, are quick to administer, and are relatively culture free. Langdon's task also assesses aspects of general cognition, minimizing additional cognitive testing, while Brüne's evaluates more challenging third-order TOM, potentially reducing ceiling effects.

Neither Langdon's nor Brüne's PSTs have consistently demonstrated symptom-specific discriminant validity (Langdon *et al.*, 2001, 2006; Brüne, 2005), in contrast to findings with the FBDS tasks. The PSTs may tap a component of TOM impairment which is present in all patients (and also in people with a vulnerability to schizophrenia, see below), while the FBDS task, at least in part, might tap TOM features which discriminate between symptom subtypes.

TOM impairment in schizophrenia, assessed via PSTs, appears independent of executive impairment, supporting the domain specificity of TOM deficits in schizophrenia. A systematic review of the association between TOM and executive functioning in schizophrenia (Pickup, 2008) found eight studies showed robust evidence of independence, with seven using either Langdon's or Brüne's PSTs (e.g. Langdon *et al.*, 2001; Brüne,

2005). The only other task in our TOM taxonomy demonstrating similar independence of TOM and executive impairment in schizophrenia assesses pragmatic language comprehension (see Section 3.1).

Results from both PSTs support the trait model of TOM deficits in schizophrenia. People with high levels of schizotypy perform worse on the false belief stories (but not the other stories) in Langdon's PST (Langdon and Coltheart, 1999). Marjoram and colleagues (2006) reported TOM deficits in relatives of people with schizophrenia using Brüne's PST. However, those same patients and controls did not differ on Corcoran's 'Hinting' task (see Section 3), suggesting the PSTs may be more sensitive TOM measures of schizophrenia vulnerability.

2. *Intention-inferencing story completion tasks*

A somewhat similar task to the PSTs – the Attribution of Intentions Task (AIT, Brunet *et al.*, 2003) – focuses on the capacity to infer others' intentions. This is conceived as less demanding than inferring false beliefs and deception, because intentions (about the future), while distinct from current reality, do not misrepresent the current reality in the same way as mistaken beliefs. Somewhat like PSTs, the AIT presents participants with a sequence of three cartoon pictures and requires them to choose the most logical option to complete a four-picture sequence. The first three pictures show a character performing an action with a particular intention, which is intimated at, but vague without the fourth card (e.g. a character digs in the ground and the fourth card reveals the intention is to find a worm for fishing). The fourth card alternatives include the correct answer, a contextually absurd pictorially similar option and other distracters.

The AITs are easy to administer and typically but not always (e.g. Sarfati *et al.*, 2000) nonverbal. One version can be administered in ten to fifteen minutes. Sprong *et al.*'s meta-analysis of TOM deficits in schizophrenia (2007) calculated a strong effect size (d = –0.959) for discrimination between people with schizophrenia and controls on intention-inferencing tasks (almost exclusively Sarfati's task), and is similar to the d's calculated for first-order false belief tasks, if weaker than the second-order tasks (–1.193 and –1.443 respectively).

In terms of discriminant validity between symptoms, Sarfati's group find the AIT consistently identifies links between TOM deficits and disorganized symptoms (mainly thought disorder) rather than with reality distortion and psychomotor poverty. However, other TOM tasks demonstrate different associations. For example, Mazza *et al.* (2001) found the psychomotor poverty group most impaired on traditional false belief and deception tasks, while Langdon *et al.* (1997) found TOM impairment most marked in patients with negative symptoms. Again, we infer that TOM has multiple components. Intention-inferencing tasks may be more sensitive to the TOM impairment most involved in the thought disorder of schizophrenia.

3. Pragmatic (non-literal) language comprehension

Pragmatics refers to 'the ability to use language to communicate effectively in a range of social contexts' (Tager-Flusberg, 2000: 124). Competent pragmatic communication requires the ability to transcend the mere literal meanings of words to infer and consider the conversational partner's beliefs and intentions. Pragmatic language assessment in TOM research emphasizes understanding of non-literal speech, in particular metaphor, irony, sarcasm and indirect hints. Tasks assessing the appreciation of a faux pas (FP) in conversational situations, and the Gricean maxims of conversational conduct, can also be considered pragmatic TOM tasks. We review these separately before considering them as a group.

3.1 Metaphor, irony and sarcasm

Both irony (Mitchley *et al.*, 1998) and combined irony and metaphor (Langdon *et al.*, 2002) tasks have been used to investigate pragmatic TOM abilities in schizophrenia. Mitchley and colleagues (1998) used a 'comprehension of irony task' in their schizophrenia study. Participants read short stories containing a remark and had to choose from three alternatives: a correct ironic interpretation, an incorrect interpretation related to the ironical interpretation, and an incorrect literal interpretation.

Identification of sarcasm has been assessed by Leitman *et al.* (2006) using the Attitudinal Subtest of the Aprosodia Battery (APT). This requires identification of recorded utterances as sincere or sarcastic, based on the 'manner' of the speaker. This format allows usage of the prosodic cues of sarcasm. Like Mitchley and colleagues, Langdon *et al.* (2002) asked participants to read stories and then judge 'yes/no' the appropriateness of the story character responding with a given statement. Half the statements are appropriate, with correct responses including ironical, metaphorical and literal utterances.

3.2 Indirect hints

Corcoran *et al.* (1995) developed the 'Hinting' task; the most frequently used pragmatic test of TOM in schizophrenia research. Ten short stories are read aloud. One character makes a hint to a second and participants are asked to identify the real meaning intended. Incorrect responses lead to a prompt. Administration takes five to 15 minutes. It has been used across a range of schizophrenia related disorders and related family studies.

Marjoram *et al.* (2005b) added extra trials to prevent ceiling effects in control participants (see later).

3.3 Faux pas tasks

Understanding of faux pas (FP) is included in the pragmatic TOM domain because it requires appreciation of the consequences of a FP in conversational context. One FP task (Stone *et al.*, 1998) assesses FP comprehension in schizophrenia (e.g. Martino *et al.*, 2007). Participants are asked if a FP is present and, if so, their cognitive and affective understanding of it – a measure of affective empathy as well as TOM.

3.4 Gricean maxims

Pragmatic tests of TOM include evaluating adherence to the 'general rules of conversation' (Grice, 1978): the maxims of quality (tell the truth), quantity (contribute only as much information as needed), relation (be relevant), and manner (be clear). An appreciation of the listener's mental state is necessary to comply with these rules. In Corcoran and Frith's (1996) 'Maxims' test, participants listen to a story and then choose a response for one of its characters from two alternatives – one of which adheres to each of the maxims. Such tasks are less commonly used in schizophrenia research. However, Tenyi *et al.* (2002) used a similar test focusing exclusively on understanding of the maxim of relevance.

3.5 Overview of pragmatic language tasks

Sprong *et al.*'s (2007) meta-analysis focused on appreciation of irony/sarcasm and indirect hints in evaluating pragmatic TOM abilities. They reported an overall large effect size (d = –1.040) for such tasks when discriminating between people with and without schizophrenia. This is comparable to the AITs and first-order False Belief tests, if not as strong as the second-order False Belief tasks.

In terms of discriminant validity, both the Hinting task (Corcoran *et al.*, 1995) and Gricean maxim appreciation (Corcoran and Frith, 1996) link TOM impairment more specifically to negative and behavioural signs of the illness. They found a more subtle link with paranoia, but this has not been replicated in subsequent studies assessing comprehension of hints (Greig *et al.*, 2004) and irony (Mitchley *et al.*, 1998).

Although Langdon *et al.* (2002) found people with schizophrenia had difficulties understanding both irony and metaphor, only the former was associated with another measure of TOM (the PST measure). They speculated that difficulties in understanding metaphors in schizophrenia might be more closely associated with impairments of semantic processing rather than TOM deficits. Similarly, Herold *et al.* (2002) found that irony, but not metaphor recognition, was related to a false belief story test of TOM in people with schizophrenia.

According to Pickup's (2008) review, some pragmatic TOM tasks appear to tap domain-specific processes. For example, poor appreciation of irony (e.g. Langdon *et al.*, 2002) and difficulty on the Hinting task (Janssen *et al.*, 2003) appear independent of executive deficits.

Findings are less clear in relation to the state/trait issue. Studies using the Hinting task (Corcoran *et al.*, 1995; Corcoran, 2003), found no TOM deficits for those in remission, but ceiling effects may have influenced these results (Corcoran, 2003). While Drury *et al.* (1998) also found no impairment in remitted patients using an irony and metaphor appreciation task, Herold *et al.* (2002) reported deficits in remitted paranoid patients using the very same irony task. This may reflect differences in the samples across studies, or that irony comprehension tasks are more sensitive than other types of pragmatic TOM task. Among family studies, both Janssen *et al.* (2003) and Mazza *et al.* (2008) used the Hinting task and found some impairment in the relatives of people with schizophrenia (compared to healthy controls), though the relatives were less impaired than patients. A spectrum of impairment on the Hinting task was shown by Fiszdon and colleagues (2007) between those with schizophrenia and schizoaffective disorder, with both impaired relative to controls, although Fernyhough *et al.* (2008) found no relationship between levels of schizotypy in a non-clinical sample and TOM. Longitudinal studies incorporating tasks with adequate retest reliability are required to resolve this question.

B. Social-perceptual measures

1. Inferring mental states from eye expressions

Baron-Cohen *et al.* (1997) developed the original 'Reading the Mind in the Eyes' task (hereafter the Eyes task), based on the theory that the eyes are the part of the face most involved in expressing complex emotions. It involves participants choosing which of two mental state terms best describe photographs of the eye region. They contended this task is an 'advanced' TOM test because the participant has access to only the eyes, not the whole face. In support of their view, they found adults with Tourette's disorder and high functioning adults with autistic or Asperger's disorders were impaired on the Eyes task but not on basic emotion or gender recognition tests. A revised Eyes task (Baron-Cohen *et al.*, 2001) has enhanced psychometric properties and is unlikely to suffer from ceiling or practice effects.

The Eyes task takes ten to 15 minutes, is available in paper and pencil or computerized format and has published norms. It is suitable for higher functioning individuals. It sits somewhere between classical TOM tasks and emotion recognition tasks and (like the Faux Pas test) allows a broader examination of social cognition by tapping both TOM and more basic emotion recognition. (Other emotion cue recognition tasks are not reviewed here.)

The Eyes task has consistently shown that schizophrenia participants have performed worse than controls (e.g. Craig *et al.*, 2004), indicating good discriminant validity. This task has rarely been used to examine associations with specific symptoms (Craig *et al.*, 2004).

Findings of impairment in this task among remitted patients with schizophrenia (Bora *et al.*, 2008) suggest it taps a trait marker. However, results among people with a genetic risk for schizophrenia have been inconsistent (e.g. Kelemen *et al.*, 2004; Meyer and Shean, 2006). Impaired performance has been reported among those with psychotic depression compared to depression alone (Wang *et al.*, 2008), suggesting sensitivity to psychotic symptoms, rather than the specific diagnosis.

2. *Analysis of the movement of animated shapes*

Blakemore *et al.* (2003) suggested the identification of agency (possessing a mental state motivated by intentions) is a basic TOM ability; one simpler than attributing beliefs. They examined this in computer-based tasks requiring the identification of agency in movements of animated shapes. Even abstract shapes can convey a sense of agency if they show animate (self-propelled) movement and causal relationships, for example, moving in response to each other (Blakemore *et al.*, 2003). Russell *et al.* (2006) argue that these tasks have the advantage of displaying dynamic stimuli, unlike traditional story-based tasks. Although little used to date, Russell and colleagues have used the 'Triangles' task. They presented geometric shapes moving in 'random', 'goal-directed' and 'socially complex' (TOM) ways, where shapes appear to interact with and manipulate each other. Participants describe their observations, with responses rated for accuracy, appropriateness of terms used, and use of 'target' terms pertaining to the conditions (e.g. mental-state terms for the TOM animations). All patients with schizophrenia performed poorly in terms of using suitable mental-state language. Those with behavioural signs and (to a lesser extent) paranoid symptoms were able to be distinguished from controls on all three conditions. Of note the paranoid patients appeared to over-interpret random animations. Blakemore and colleagues (2003) also found that people with persecutory delusions over-attributed agency relative to non-paranoid schizophrenia and controls on a similar ('Contingency') task requiring the rating of perceived intentionality in the movements of shapes in relation to each other. Fyfe *et al.* (2008) used the Triangles and Contingency tasks with a non-clinical sample, and found over-mentalizing on both measures in participants with higher self-report scores on delusional thinking, but not general schizotypy. These studies suggest that these agency identification tasks may be sensitive to both TOM and attributional bias. This adds to their utility given the significance of attributional style for understanding social cognition, more generally, in schizophrenia.

C. Real world and more ecologically valid measures

There are increasing efforts to develop 'real world' TOM measures with greater ecological validity. These use structured interviews, discourse analysis, and tasks showing video scenes of real world social interactions.

1. Structured interview

Bazin *et al.* (2005) revised a structured interview, developed by Oliver *et al.* (1997), to create the Scale for the Evaluation of Communication Disorders in Patients with Schizophrenia (SCD). Informed by Hardy-Bayle *et al.*'s (2003) model of disorganized speech, the SCD is designed to elicit both contextual processing (three items) and TOM (four items) deficits. The TOM items assess difficulties in: (a) attributing intentions to others (e.g. 'What would your friend think of your problems?'); (b) describing the clinician's intention during the interview (e.g. 'What do you think I meant by that?'); (c) attributing an intention to one's own speech (e.g. 'What were you trying to tell me by saying that?'); and (d) attributing an erroneous belief to a character in a story (i.e. that Little Red Riding Hood mistakenly believes that her grandmother is in her grandmother's bed). Responses are scored on a four-point scale. It takes 30 minutes to administer. With regard to our taxonomy, the first three of the TOM items appear to assess intention inferencing, while the fourth taps comprehension of false belief and deception. Not yet incorporated extensively into clinical or research work, it was used by Kayser *et al.* (2006) in a therapeutic intervention targeting TOM, and it appears particularly promising as a screen for TOM deficits in initial interviews.

2. Conversation analysis

McCabe *et al.* (2004) analyzed clinical interviews using conversation analysis to detect TOM abilities and deficits (i.e. difficulties explaining ascriptions of beliefs to others) and were unable to find impairment of TOM abilities among people with schizophrenia in this context. Clearly this work needs to be expanded in order to incorporate the McCabe technique with more traditional TOM tasks in the same study, and in interviews incorporating 'TOM probes' such as Bazin and colleagues' SCD. If results for the conversational analysis are replicated, alongside evidence of TOM deficits using other tasks, this may prove a way forward for informing how TOM might be remediated in people with schizophrenia – what is it about the interview situation that provides support for people with schizophrenia to show the sorts of TOM abilities that they do appear to have?

3. Analysis of video scenes showing real world social exchanges

While showing videos of real world social interactions is only a proxy for observing real world TOM ability, we include these tasks because of their more ecologically valid nature. Clearly they combine all aspects of understanding TOM – social cognitive and social perceptual – as well as drawing on more basic emotion recognition abilities. Kayser and colleagues (2006) used videotaped scenes from French movies to assess TOM functioning by asking participants to explain the actions of characters in various scenes with reference to their mental states. Jahshan and Sergi (2007) used the 'Awareness of Social Inference Test' (TASIT, McDonald *et al.*, 2003) to assess TOM in university students scoring high or low on schizotypy. TASIT uses video scenes of characters interacting to assess both emotion recognition and TOM. The TOM component of the test has two parts involving pragmatic communication: (a) 'social inference–minimal', involving nonliteral speech (sarcasm) comprehension; and (b) 'social inference–enriched', requiring identification of a character's true beliefs when they are lying to be kind. While these components clearly tap pragmatic TOM abilities, we include the TASIT here since it presents videos of actors simulating real world social interactions.

Schizophrenia research has used these 'real world' (or more ecologically valid) measures of TOM infrequently thus far. This is surprising given the design and ecological validity of the TASIT. It certainly warrants validation with people with psychotic illnesses. Jahshan and Sergi (2007) found no evidence of TOM impairments with the TASIT in high schizotypy students relative to low schizotypy students, but clearly family and community studies are needed before making inferences about the state/trait issue.

Conclusions and recommendations

Quantitative and narrative reviews have concluded that there is TOM impairment in schizophrenia. However, firm conclusions concerning symptom specificity, domain specificity and the state/trait distinction seem premature. Nevertheless, the more consistent observations suggest that TOM is multidimensional, with different symptoms associated with different performance profiles across the various dimensions. Thus, it seems desirable to include multiple tasks in assessing TOM in schizophrenia and other disorders with paranoid symptoms. Using multiple measures will promote better psychometric investigation of TOM through validation of the tests used.

In this chapter we propose a conceptual taxonomy of TOM tasks that clinicians and researchers can now use to specify and to operationalize those dimensions of TOM that they intend to measure in people with schizophrenia. This taxonomy provides a conceptual framework for approaching TOM tasks based on the most widely used tasks in schizophrenia research. In outlining this taxonomy we also reviewed the, admittedly limited, psychometric work on this array of tasks. Future psychometric studies are essential to resolve some of the inconsistent findings to date and to support the development of clinical trials to translate theory into practical assistance for those with schizophrenia. Future examinations of construct validity and TOM dimensionality could, for example, incorporate factor analysis and/or item response theory (e.g. Shryane *et al.*, 2008). Such studies are needed to demonstrate that the various putative dimensions of TOM, as well as making theoretical sense, can actually be measured as latent variables.

While findings suggest that TOM impairment is independent of executive dysfunction in schizophrenia, there is also evidence that executive deficits can contribute to and possibly exacerbate the TOM difficulties. Therefore, TOM assessments ought to be combined with a more general cognitive battery that includes executive measures (see Table 7.2). Longitudinal

Table 7.2 Areas of coverage in a proposed approach to the clinical evaluation of schizophrenia, with focus on a brief assessment of theory of mind

1 Clinical and diagnostic interview (incorporate probes for TOM functioning, as in the SCD).
2 Schizophrenia symptom severity and general psychopathology.
3 Neurocognitive functioning (particularly verbal and visual learning/memory, working memory, attention, executive functioning, and speed of information processing).
4 Social cognition
   - emotion recognition
   - attributional style (questionnaire to assess)
   - theory of mind
      - Story-based and nonverbal (PS) tests of false belief/deception (recommendation: different tests to maximize range of stimuli used to assess TOM; the same PST stimuli used with both verbal and nonverbal components if time is limited).
      - Tests of pragmatic language comprehension (recommendation: focus on indirect hints and irony or sarcasm; include faux pas task if interested in affective empathy).
      - Social-perceptual task (recommendation: Eyes task if interested in TOM and emotion recognition; Triangles task if interested in paranoid attributional biases; or both).
5 Interpersonal skills.
6 Adaptive functioning in community.
7 Cultural and family assessment.

studies incorporating TOM measures with good reliability and responsiveness are also necessary to resolve the state/trait question.

In the meantime, clinicians should be aware of the implications of TOM for their practice and the impact that TOM impairment can have on patients' lives. While acknowledging limited psychometric validation at this time, we cautiously propose a brief TOM battery in our recommended clinical assessment approach (Table 7.2). For further detail of neurocognitive assessment, refer to the National Institute of Mental Health Measurement and Treatment Research to Improve Cognition in Schizophrenia (MATRICS) battery (Green *et al.*, 2008). In accord with Combes *et al.* (2008), we have aimed for a broad, integrated schizophrenia assessment which will inform clinical diagnosis and meaningful case conceptualizations with a treatment and rehabilitation focus, and which incorporates TOM assessment as a critical component of a broader assessment approach.

Finally, the TOM tasks reviewed in this chapter focus on patients' ability to infer others' mental states. As TOM assessment enters clinical practice it will be important also to examine how these TOM measures relate to other metacognitive tasks where patients must think about their own thoughts. Such metacognitive processes relate to core clinical phenomena including insight (e.g. Langdon and Ward, in press) and self-reflection (e.g. Lysaker *et al.*, 2007). Dimaggio *et al.* (2008) have outlined the potential complexities in the interactions between impairments of self-reflection and TOM in schizophrenia and their treatment. Establishing robust measures of TOM will be required to obtain a sophisticated understanding of this important relationship in interventions such as psychotherapy and social cognitive remediation.

References

Baron-Cohen, S., Jolliffe, T., Mortimore, C. and Robertson, M. (1997). Another advanced test of theory of mind: Evidence from very high functioning adults with autism or Asperger Syndrome. *Journal of Child Psychology and Psychiatry and Allied Disciplines*, *38*, 813–822.

Baron-Cohen, S., Wheelwright, S., Hill, J., Raste, Y. and Plumb, I. (2001). The 'Reading the mind in the eyes' Test revised version: A study with normal adults, and adults with Asperger syndrome or high-functioning autism. *Journal of Child Psychology and Psychiatry and Allied Disciplines*, *42*, 241–251.

Bazin, N., Sarfati, Y., Lefrere, F., Passerieux, C. and Hardy-Bayle, M-C. (2005). Scale for the evaluation of communication disorders in patients with schizophrenia: A validation study. *Schizophrenia Research*, *77*, 75–84.

Blakemore, S.-J., Sarfati, Y., Bazin, N. and Decety, J. (2003). The detection of intentional contingencies in simple animations in patients with delusions of persecution. *Psychological Medicine*, *33*, 1433–1441.

Bora, E., Gokcen, S., Kayahan, B. and Veznedaroglu, B. (2008). Deficits of social-cognitive and social-perceptual aspects of theory of mind in remitted patients with schizophrenia. Effect of residual symptoms. *Journal of Nervous and Mental Disease*, *196*, 95–99.

Brüne, M. (2003a). Social cognition and the behaviour in schizophrenia. In M. Brüne, H. Ribbert and W. Schienfenhovel (eds), *The social brain: Evolution and pathology* (pp. 277–313). Chichester: Wiley.

Brüne, M. (2003b). Theory of mind and the role of IQ in chronic disorganised schizophrenia. *Schizophrenia Research*, *60*, 57–64.

Brüne, M. (2005). Emotion recognition, 'theory of mind' and social behaviour in schizophrenia. *Psychiatry Research*, *133*, 135–147.

Brunet, E., Sarfati, Y. and Hardy-Bayle, M.-C. (2003). Reasoning about physical causality and other's intentions in schizophrenia. *Cognitive Neuropsychiatry*, *8*, 129–139.

Combes, D. R., Basso, M. R., Warner, J. L. and Ledet, S. N. (2008). Schizophrenia. In M. Hertsen and J. Rosqvist (eds), *Handbook of psychological assessment, case conceptualisation and treatment* (pp. 352–402). New York: Wiley.

Corcoran, R. (2003). Inductive reasoning and the understanding of intention in schizophrenia. *Cognitive Neuropsychiatry*, *8*, 223–235.

Corcoran, R. and Frith, C. D. (1996). Conversational conduct and the symptoms of schizophrenia. *Cognitive Neuropsychiatry*, *1*, 305–318.

Corcoran, R., Mercer, G. and Frith, C. D. (1995). Schizophrenia, symptomatology, and social inference: Investigating theory of mind in people with schizophrenia. *Schizophrenia Research*, *17*, 5–13.

Corcoran, R., Cahill, C. and Frith, C. D. (1997). The appreciation of visual jokes in people with schizophrenia: A study of mentalizing ability. *Schizophrenia Research*, *24*, 319–327.

Corcoran, R., Rowse. G., Moore, R., Blackwood, N., Kinderman, P., Howard, R., *et al.* (2008). A transdiagnostic investigation of 'theory of mind' and 'jumping to conclusions' in patients with persecutory delusions. *Psychological Medicine*, *38*, 1577–1583.

Craig, J. S., Hatton, C., Craig, F. B. and Bentall, R. P. (2004). Persecutory beliefs, attributions and theory of mind: Comparison of patients with paranoid delusions, Asperger's syndrome and healthy controls. *Schizophrenia Research*, *69*, 29–33.

Dimaggio, G., Lysaker, P. H., Carcione, A., Nicolo, G. and Semerari, A. (2008). Know yourself and you shall know the other . . . to a certain extent: Multiple paths to influence of self-reflection on mindreading. *Consciousness and Cognition*, *17*, 778–789.

Drury, V. M, Robinson, E. J. and Birchwood, M. (1998). 'Theory of mind' skills during an acute episode of psychosis and following recovery. *Psychological Medicine*, *28*, 1101–1112.

Fernyhough, C., Jones, S. R., Whittle, C., Waterhouse, J. and Bentall, R. (2008). Theory of mind, schizotypy, and persecutory ideation in young adults. *Cognitive Neuropsychiatry*, *13*, 233–249.

Fiszdon, J. M., Richardson, R., Greig, T. and Bell, M. (2007). A comparison of basic and social cognition between schizophrenia and schizoaffective disorder. *Schizophrenia Research*, *91*, 117–121.

Frith, C. (1992). *The cognitive neuropsychology of schizophrenia*. Hove, UK: Lawrence Erlbaum Associates Ltd.

Frith, C. D. and Corcoran, C. (1996). Exploring 'theory of mind' in people with schizophrenia. *Psychological Medicine*, *26*, 521–530

Frith, U., Leslie, A. and Morton, J. (1991). The cognitive basis of a biological disorder: Autism. *Trends in Neurosciences*, *14*, 433–438.

Fyfe, S., Williams, C., Mason, O. J. and Pickup, G. J. (2008). Apophenia, theory of mind and schizotypy: Perceiving meaning and intentionality in randomness. *Cortex*, *44*, 1316–1325.

Green, M. F., Nuechterlein, K. H., Gold, J. G., Barch, D. M., Cohen, J., Essock, S., *et al.* (2008). Approaching a consensus cognitive battery for clinical trials in schizophrenia: The NIMH-MATRICS conference to select cognitive domains and test criteria. *Biological Psychiatry*, *56*, 301–307.

Green, M. F., Penn, D. L., Bentall, R., Carpenter, W. T., Gaebel, W., Gur, R. C., *et al.* (2008). Social cognition in schizophrenia: An NIMH workshop on definitions, assessment, and research opportunities. *Schizophrenia Bulletin*, *34*, 1211–1220.

Greig, T. C., Bryson, G. J. and Bell, M. D. (2004). Theory of mind performance in schizophrenia: Diagnostic, symptom, and neuropsychological correlates. *Journal of Nervous and Mental Disease*, *192*, 12–18.

Grice, H. P. (1978). Further notes on logic and conversation. In P. Cole (ed.), Syntax and semantics. *Psychological Medicine*, *24*, 557–564.

Hardy-Bayle, M.-C., Sarfati, Y. and Passerieux, C. (2003). The cognitive basis of disorganisation symptomatology in schizophrenia and its clinical correlates: Toward a pathogenic approach to disorganisation. *Schizophrenia Bulletin*, *29*, 459–471.

Harrington, L., Siegert, R. J. and McClure, J. (2005). Theory of mind in schizophrenia: A critical review. *Cognitive Neuropsychiatry*, *10*, 249–286.

Herold, R., Tenyi, T., Lenard, K. and Trixler, M. (2002). Theory of mind deficit in people with schizophrenia during remission. *Psychological Medicine*, *32*, 1125–1129.

Jahshan, C. S. and Sergi, M. J. (2007). Theory of mind, neurocognition, and functional status in schizotypy. *Schizophrenia Research*, *89*, 278–286.

Janssen, I., Krabbendam, L., Jolles, J. and van Os, J. (2003). Alterations in theory of mind in patients with schizophrenia and non-psychotic relatives. *Acta Psychiatrica Scandinavica*, *108*, 110–117.

Kayser, N., Sarfati, Y., Besche, C. and Hardy-Bayle, M-C. (2006). Elaboration of a rehabilitation method based on a pathogenetic hypothesis of 'theory of mind' impairment in schizophrenia. *Neuropsychological Rehabilitation*, *16*, 83–95.

Kelemen. O., Kéri, S., Must, A., Benedek, G. and Janka, Z. (2004). No evidence of impaired 'theory of mind' in unaffected first-degree relatives of schizophrenia patients. *Acta Psychiatrica Scandinavica*, *110*, 146–149.

Langdon, R. and Coltheart, M. (1999). Mentalizing, schizotypy, and schizophrenia. *Cognition*, *71*, 43–71.

Langdon, R. and Ward, P. B. (in press). Taking the perspective of the other contributes to awareness of illness in schizophrenia. *Schizophrenia Bulletin*.

Langdon, R., Michie, P. T., Ward, P. B., McConaghy, N, Catts, S. V. and Coltheart, M. (1997). Defective self and/or other mentalizing in schizophrenia: a cognitive neuropsychological approach. *Cognitive Neuropsychiatry*, *2*, 167–193.

Langdon, R., Coltheart, M., Ward, P. B. and Catts, S. V. (2001). Mentalizing,

executive planning and disengagement in schizophrenia. *Cognitive Neuropsychiatry*, *6*, 81–108.
Langdon, R., Coltheart, M., Ward, P. B. and Catts, S. V. (2002). Disturbed communication in schizophrenia: The role of poor pragmatics and poor mind-reading. *Psychological Medicine*, *32*, 1273–1284.
Langdon, R., Corner T., McLaren, J., Ward, P. B. and Coltheart, M. (2006). Externalizing and personalizing biases in persecutory delusions: The relationship with poor insight in theory-of-mind. *Behaviour Research and Therapy*, *44*, 699–713.
Langdon, R., Coltheart, M. and Ward, P. B. (in press). Reasoning anomalies associated with delusions in schizophrenia. *Schizophrenia Bulletin*.
Leitman, D. I., Ziwich, R., Pasternak, R. and Javitt, D. C. (2006). Theory of mind (ToM) and counterfactuality deficits in schizophrenia: Misperception or misinterpretation? *Psychological Medicine*, *36*, 1075–1083.
Lysaker, P. H., Buck, K. D. and Ringer, J. (2007). The recovery of metacognitive capacity in schizophrenia across 32 months of individual psychotherapy: A case study. *Psychotherapy Research*, *17*, 713–720.
McCabe, R., Leudar, I. and Antki, C. (2004). Do people with schizophrenia display theory of mind deficits in clinical interactions? *Psychological Medicine*, *34*, 401–412.
McDonald, S., Flanagan, S., Rollins, J. and Kinch, J. (2003). TASIT: A new clinical tool for assessing social perception after traumatic brain injury. *Journal of Head Trauma Rehabilitation*, *18*, 219–238.
Marjoram, D., Tansley, H., Miller, P., MacIntyre, D., Owens, D. G. C., Johnstone, E. C., *et al.* (2005a). A theory of mind investigation into the appreciation of visual jokes in schizophrenia. *BioMed Central Psychiatry*, *5*, 12.
Marjoram, D., Gardner, C., Burns, J., Miller, P., Lawrie, S. M. and Johnstone, E. C. (2005b). Symptomatology and social inference: A theory of mind study of schizophrenia and psychotic affective disorder. *Cognitive Neuropsychiatry*, *10*, 347–359.
Marjoram, D., Miller, P., McIntosh, A. M., Owens, D. G. C., Johnstone, E. C., *et al.* (2006). A neuropsychological investigation into 'theory of mind' and enhanced risk of schizophrenia. *Psychiatry Research*, *144*, 29–37.
Martino, D. J., Bucay, D., Butman, J. T. and Allegri, R. F. (2007). Neuropsychological frontal impairments and negative symptoms in schizophrenia. *Psychiatry Research*, *152*, 121–128.
Mazza, M., De Risio, A., Surian, L., Roncone, R. and Casacchia, M. (2001). Selective impairments of theory of mind in people with schizophrenia. *Schizophrenia Research*, *47*, 299–308.
Mazza, M., Di Michele, V., Pollice, R. and Casacchia, M. (2008). Pragmatic language and theory of mind deficits in people with schizophrenia and their relatives. *Psychopathology*, *41*, 254–263.
Meyer, J. and Shean, G. (2006). Social-cognitive functioning and schizotypal characteristics. *Journal of Psychology*, *140*, 199–207.
Mitchley, N. J., Barber, J., Gray, J. M., Brooks, D. N. and Livingstone, M. G. (1998). Comprehension of irony in schizophrenia. *Cognitive Neuropsychiatry*, *3*, 127–138.
Oliver, V., Hardy-Bayle, M. C., Lancrenon, S., Fermanian, J. Sarfati, Y., Paserieux,

C., *et al.* (1997). Rating scale for the assessment of communication disorders in schizophrenics. *European Psychiatry*, *12*, 352–361.

Pickup, G. J. (2008). Relationship between theory of mind and executive function in schizophrenia: A systematic review. *Psychopathology*, *41*, 206–213.

Pickup, G. J. and Frith, C. D. (2001). Theory of mind impairments in schizophrenia: Symptomatology, severity, and specificity. *Psychological Medicine*, *31*, 207–220.

Premack, D. and Woodruff, G. (1978). Does the chimpanzee have a theory of mind? *Behavioral and Brain Sciences*, *1*, 515–526.

Russell, T. A., Reynaud, E., Herba, C., Morris, R. and Corcoran, R. (2006). Do you see what I see? Interpretations of intentional movement in schizophrenia. *Schizophrenia Research*, *81*, 101–111.

Sarfati, Y., Passerieux, C. and Hardy-Bayle, M-C. (2000). Can verbalisation remedy the theory of mind deficit in schizophrenia? *Psychopathology*, *33*, 246–251.

Shryane, N. M., Corcoran, R., Rowse, G., Moore, R., Cummins, S., Blackwood, N., *et al.* (2008). Deception and false belief in paranoia: Modelling theory of Mind stories. *Cognitive Neuropsychiatry*, *13*, 8–32.

Slaughter, V. and Repacholi, B. (2003). Introduction: Individual differences in theory of mind – what are we investigating? In B. Repacholi and V. Slaughter (eds), *Individual differences in theory of mind: Implications for typical and atypical development* (pp. 1–12). Hove, UK: Psychology Press.

Sprong, M., Schothorst, P., Vos, E., Hox, J. and Van Engeland, H. (2007). Theory of mind in schizophrenia: Meta-analysis. *British Journal of Psychiatry*, *191*, 5–13.

Stone, V., Baron-Cohen, S. and Knight, R. (1998). Frontal lobe contributions to theory of mind. *Journal of Cognitive Neuroscience*, *10*, 640–656.

Tager-Flusberg, H. (2000). Language and understanding minds: Connections in autism. In S. Baron-Cohen, H. Tager-Flusberg and D. Cohen (eds), *Understanding other minds* (pp. 124–149). Oxford: Oxford University Press.

Tager-Flusberg, H. and Sullivan, K. (2000). A componential view of theory of mind: Evidence from Williams syndrome. *Cognition*, *76*, 59–89.

Tenyi, T., Herold, R., Szili, I. M. and Trixler, M. (2002). Schizophrenics show a failure in the decoding of violations of conversational implicatures. *Psychopathology*, *35*, 25–27.

Wang, Y.-G., Wang, Y.-Q., Chen, S.-L., Zhu, C.-Y. and Wang, K. (2008). Theory of mind disability in major depression with or without psychotic symptoms: A componential view. *Psychiatry Research*, *161*, 153–161.

Chapter 8

Commonsense, disembodiment and delusions in schizophrenia

Giovanni Stanghellini

An established theory in the phenomenological tradition is that a key feature of schizophrenia is a 'crisis of commonsense', that is, a loss of the meaning and significance that we usually attach without conscious reflection to everyday objects and situations. In an extensive study on 405 persons with schizophrenia, Blankenburg (1971) pointed out that these persons can no longer typify their experiences along commonsense categories. For them, the rootedness that accompanies us in our everyday life is absent. They seem to ignore, or sometimes to refuse, commonsense categories to typify their everyday experiences with – so that they are sometimes puzzled by ordinary situations and unable to think or act according to what is commonly expected. For Blankenburg, the fundamental character of schizophrenic abnormal experiences is the loss of natural evidence of commonsensical everyday reality.

In this chapter, I provide an account of how a crisis of commonsense may be involved in schizophrenia (Stanghellini, 2005, 2008; Stanghellini and Ballerini, 2004, 2007). Many of the phenomena that I discuss as parts of commonsense (e.g. self-awareness, object-awareness, other-awareness) are referred to in other parts of this book as related to metacognition, a construct that in general terms embraces the ability to think about thinking (e.g. Flavell, 1979). Frith (1992) suggested that deficits in metacognitive capacity are a core and stable feature in schizophrenia. I will not discuss here the overlap between these facets of metacognition and my own, phenomenological account of the core anomalies in persons with schizophrenia. I consider the phenomenological understanding of self-awareness and other-awareness as integrative, provided that we have in mind that phenomenology conceives of the lived body as the centre of all the main dimensions of human experience: the experience of my self as my own, object-experience and meaning-bestowing, and the experience of other people's behaviour as meaningful. The main assumption of this chapter is that commonsense and its disorders may be better understood as related to the notion of embodiment. Consistently with this view, I will propose an interpretation of delusions as disorders of the embodied attunement between the Self and the World.

What is commonsense?

A short review of 'commonsense' shows it may be conceptualized in two main ways. First, commonsense is a kind of body of knowledge shared by the members of a given culture or society, a set of rules that discipline behaviours in ordinary life situations. Second, commonsense is a 'sense' useful for attuning with what is 'common', i.e. a form of embodied practice aimed at understanding the others' actions in current social situations. We may refer to the former as commonsense as social knowledge and to the latter as commonsense as attunement (for a list of references see Stanghellini, 2008).

Taken as a whole there are a number of basic features of commonsense as social knowledge. This includes the postulate that one understands oneself, the meanings of worldly objects and situations and other persons' behaviours by implicitly employing a theoretical stance. Commonsense in this way is a set of knowledge, a sort of 'primary theory' of the world including the bulk of constructs we use to typify others' behaviours, courses of actions and one's own attitudes. It may include a set of knowledgeable facts as well as a set of interpretative procedures. This set of knowledge is of the kind I-know-that, that is it is in principle translatable into propositional terms and shared by the members of a given group or community. Commonsense is all that the members of a given society are disposed to take as obvious. Every person participates in this primary theory of the world spontaneously, intuitively, in an unreflected and implicit manner. Its purpose is not theoretical (knowing about something), but adaptive and pragmatic (doing something) being the medium for organizing the everyday experiences of individuals and social groups – in order to achieve survival and adaptation, and the foundation of people's expectations and of meaning attributions. As far as social situations are concerned, their conceptualization is mainly a process of attribution of intentional states to the others in order to explain their behaviours.

The commonsense world enjoys relative stability and consistency among individuals belonging to the same group since in it abnormalities undergo assimilation. Abnormal (i.e. non-typical) instances are as a rule assimilated to 'circles of similar' or 'normal kinds'. As a rule, experiences that fit commonsense categorizations are felt as more real than those that are idiosyncratic. If an experience does not fit commonsense schemata, it is not the schemata that is put at jeopardy, but the new character of the experience is ruled out and normalized. In contrast to commonsense as social knowledge, the basic features of commonsense as attunement theory include the postulate that one understands oneself, the meanings of worldly objects and situations and other persons' actions by implicitly employing a kind of pre-conceptual attunement between oneself and the outer world: it is through the immediate, pre-reflexive perceptual linkage between myself and the other that I recognize another being as an alter ego and make sense of her actions. Attunement is a set of non-propositional skills, capacities and dispositions that bridge oneself with the world. Commonsense is ultimately constituted by those abilities that function before one can make sense of one's own experiences. To be attuned means to share with other people one's primary engagement with the world, conveying one's direct, pre-reflective and practical grasp of the world. These abilities are rooted in corporeality and emotional life. It is supposed that the basis of commonsense is intercorporeality, the perceptive bond between one's self and another person based on one's possibility to identify with the other person's body by means of a primary, built-in, spontaneous perceptive tie. Intercorporeality is never fully evident, but it is the bearing support of all interaction connected with behaviour, already active and present ahead of any explicit communication. Intercorporeality is the primary bond of perception by which one recognizes others as being similar to oneself. I can identify with my partner's body that I perceive over there. I perceive his body as like my own. I recognize the other as an 'alter ego' through an immediate perceptual linkage with his body. Intercorporeality is also the prerequisite for understanding other minds. Proprioception is involved in understanding other persons through body-to-body attunement. This is compatible with embodied simulation theory; according to this, we understand the others' actions by watching them and virtually reproducing them in our own body (Gallese and Goldman, 1998).

I will only mention in this chapter theory of mind (TOM, Baron-Cohen *et al.*, 1994), maybe the most challenging paradigm to account for the phenomena in other contexts called 'commonsense'. It goes beyond the scope of this chapter to describe and discuss TOM in detail (see Carpendale and Lewis, this volume, Chapter 2) and to point out in detail analogies and differences between it and commonsense theories.

The place of the lived body in the constitution of self-awareness, object-awareness and intersubjectivity

Phenomenology mainly endorses the commonsense as attunement theory. In this section I extend the hypothesis of the central role of embodiment in the constitution of the world we are used to live in, to pave the way to my discussion of the way in which this 'common' world breaks down in schizophrenia. Since the beginning of the twentieth century, phenomenology has developed a distinction between lived body (Leib) and physical body (Koerper), or body-subject and body-object. The first is the body experienced from within, my own direct experience of my body in the first-person perspective, myself as a spatiotemporal embodied agent in the world. The second is the body thematically investigated from without as, for example, by anatomy and physiology, a third person perspective. Phenomenology conceives of the lived body as the centre of three main dimensions of experience:

- the experience of my self, and especially of the most primitive form of self-awareness
- object-experience and meaning-bestowing
- the experience of other people, i.e. intersubjectivity.

I will now briefly outline the role of embodiment in minimal self-awareness and object-awareness.

In a state of minimal self-awareness, I experience myself as the perspectival origin of my experiences (i.e. perceptions or emotions), actions and thoughts. This primordial access to myself, or primitive form of egocentricity, must be distinguished from any explicit and thematic form of I-awareness since it is tacit and implicit, although experientially present. This primitive experience of myself does not arise in reflection, i.e. from a split between an experienced and an experiencing self, but is a pre-reflexive phenomenon. It is also immediate since it is an evidence not inferentially and criterially given. This form of primitive self-awareness is not a conceptual or linguistic representation of oneself, rather a primordial contact with myself or 'self-affection' in which who feels and who is felt are a one and one thing (Henry, 1965). It must also be distinguished from a kind of object-awareness, since it does not arise from an objectifying or observational perception of oneself. Henry uses the term ipseity to express this basic or minimal form of self-awareness. Thus, ipseity is the implicit, immediate, non-conceptual, non-objectifying sense of existing as a subject of awareness. It is prior to, and a condition of, all other experience.

Two basic and closely related aspects of minimal self-awareness are self-ownership and self-agency. Self-ownership is the pre-reflexive sense that I am the one who is undergoing an experience, and that this experience (e.g. the feeling of my hand as my hand) happens within the boundaries of my own self in a spatial/geometrical sense. It both implies a territorial as well as a legal/possessive sense of ownership. Self-agency is the pre-reflexive sense that I am the one who is initiating an action. The immediate awareness of the subjectivity of my experience or action involves that these are in some sense owned and generated by myself. These are the basic components of the experienced differentiation between self and non-self, my self and the object I perceive, and my representation of that object and the object itself. Merleau-Ponty (1945) emphasized that this basic form of self-experience is rooted in my bodily experience and its situatedness amongst worldly objects and other people. Ipseity to Merleau-Ponty is indiscernible from 'inhabiting' one's own world, i.e. being engaged and feeling attuned to one's own environment. It is the lived body that provides this engagement and attunement. Being conscious – says Merleau-Ponty (1945) – is dwelling in (*être-à*) the world through one's own lived body. There is good empirical evidence in developmental psychology that newborn infants are already equipped with this minimal form of self-awareness, that is embodied and attuned to the world. For instance, Rochat (2004) argues that children, long before they have developed a conceptual image of themselves, have a proprioceptive and ecological sense of their bodily self.

Regarding object-awareness and meaning-bestowing, the power of organizing world experience is grounded in motility and perception. Husserl (1952) showed that a modification in one's lived body implies a modification in the perception of the external world: 'The shape of material things as aistheta, just as they stand in front of me in an intuitive way, depends on my configuration, on the configuration of the experiencing subject, refers to my own body.' By means of the integrity of kinaesthesia – the sense of the position and movement of voluntary muscles – my own body is the constant reference of my orientation in the perceptive field. The perceived object gives itself as a flesh-and-blood, real thing existing out there through the integration of a series of perspectival appearances.

The lived body is not only the perspectival origin of my perceptions, but also the means by which I own the world, insomuch as it structures and organizes the chances of participating in the field of experience. The living body perceives worldly objects as parts of a situation in which it is engaged, of a project to which it is committed, so that its actions are responses to situations rather than reactions to stimuli. The body – as Merleau-Ponty put it – seeks understanding from the objects with which it interacts. I understand my environment as I inhabit it, and the meaningful organization of the field of experience is possible because the active and receptive potentials of my own body are constantly projected into it (Sheets-Johnstone, 1999). Knowledge is enacted (Varela *et al.*, 1991) or action-specific, and perception is always tangled up with specific possibilities of action; these possibilities for action are what we call 'meaning', since the meaning of an object is how we put it to use. Objects appear to my embodied self as something 'in-order-to', as 'equipment', 'ready to hand', for manipulating reality and so for cutting, sewing, writing, etc. I literally grasp the meaning of one thing, since this meaning is exactly the specific 'manipulability' (*Handlichkeit*) of one thing (Heidegger, 1927).

The place of the body in the psychopathology of schizophrenia

In this paragraph, I report the evidence for the role of disorders of embodiment in schizophrenia. Persons with schizophrenia display a morbidly intuited body. The most represented phenomena include (Cutting, 1997): violability (e.g. 'pips coming out of TV to hit her in the eye'); altered shape/structure (e.g. 'insides changing into a woman's'); false composition (e.g. 'legs and arms dropped off and bionic ones replaced them'); and altered regional sensitivity (e.g. 'blood rushes from brain to heart; odd feelings in legs'). This topic was developed by many authors during the last century, especially in France (e.g. Ey, 1973) and Germany (e.g. Huber, 1957). Huber (1957) described a subtype of schizophrenia named 'cenesthetic schizophrenia' characterized by abnormal bodily sensations as unusual sensations of movement, stiffness, heaviness, lightness, numbness, shrinking, etc. The main phenomenal characteristic of schizophrenic abnormal bodily sensations is, according to Huber, their being uncanny and quasi-ineffable: 'in our language, the expressive possibilities and adequate categories concerning these peculiar bodily sensations are completely lacking'. Most of the abnormal bodily phenomena described by Huber have been later incorporated by Parnas *et al.* (2005) in the Examination of Anomalous Self-Experiences (EASE), a semi-structured interview meant to explore the experiential or subjective disorders of minimal self-awareness. Other abnormal bodily sensations described in the EASE include morphological change, so-called mirror-related phenomena, bodily estrangement, psychophysical misfit and split, bodily disintegration, and spatialization of bodily experiences. Typically, one's body is experienced as deanimated and one's spirit as disembodied (Stanghellini, 2008). In persons with schizophrenia (relative to manic-depressives) there is a thematic predominance of violability, anomalous spatial position, disintegration, anomalous shape/structure and anomalous belonging (MacGilchrist and Cutting, 1995).

Phenomenological models of delusions in schizophrenia

In this section, I discuss two main models of delusions found in schizophrenia in phenomenological literature before I pass to the one I proposed, centred on the notion of disembodiment. Both involve the concepts of *epoché* and reduction. *Epoché* is a Greek word which means 'check' or 'cessation'. It is used to denote operations which involve suspending beliefs in something. It consists in methodical disengagement from the entire world of experience, as it is known in straightforward cognition. The reduction – which derives from Latin *reducere* (to lead back) – is what the method of *epoché* allows us to achieve. But let me raise first an epistemological point: paradigmatic models of delusions – defining what a delusion is in itself and what are its borders with similar phenomena – proved to be unsatisfactory in psychopathology. As Schneider and Huber (1975) put it: 'what counts in delusions is not the delusion itself . . . but snagging the course of the lived experience, rather than its product'. What we do need, in order to understand what delusions really are, are syntagmatic models – how delusions (in this case: delusions in persons with schizophrenia) are connected to other phenomena within a structure or a process. What we should look for, then, are the phenomena that contribute as motivationally (or causally) necessary vulnerability, i.e. the basic disturbance for the development of delusions. This logically implies that we need studying delusions *in fieri*, or the pathways that lead from more basic psychopathological phenomena to delusions themselves. This methodological move from crystallized delusions to delusions in-the-making is quintessential to define the subtle phenomenal invariant core that characterizes them and that emerges across the manifold facets of the world the deluded person lives in, and shapes these facets and keeps them meaningfully interconnected.

A syntagmatic model should account for (at least) three features of a delusion: abnormalities in symbolization (loss of commonsense meaning of a given thing or fact, and their re-symbolization within a new, idiosyncratic frame); formal aspects (e.g. revelation character, experience of centrality); and specificity of content (e.g. metaphysical tinge). It should also be compatible with those phenomena like self-disorders (loss of sense of ownership and of agency) that are entailed in most schizophrenic positive symptoms (e.g. verbal-acoustic hallucinations and experiences of alien control). Finally, it should keep meaningfully interconnected delusions with the transformations in life-world of persons with schizophrenia, e.g. changes in lived body, space, time, intersubjectivity.

First model: symbolization disorder

At the roots of delusions in schizophrenia there is a sudden, unexpected and ineffable decomposition of the person's understanding of the world. Delusions are portrayed as disorders of symbolization. In phenomenological literature, this model is based on Gruhle's (1932) observations on the pre-delusional atmosphere, that is 'the dissolution of a fundamental categorical structure, that of the formal, transcendental symbolic contents' (Callieri, 1982). The formal characters of the pre-delusional atmosphere are the following: suspension of the fulfilling of meaning, dissolution of the transcendental, symbolic contents, and a subsequent abnormal attribution of meaning. The pre-delusional atmosphere is explained as the outcome of a 'radical erosion of the constituting subject' (Wiggins *et al.*, 1990), that is of one's set of knowledge through which one usually makes sense of the world. Evidently, some kind of cognitive failure is supposed to be at play here. At the origin of delusions in schizophrenia there is a breakdown in one's 'primary theory' of the world one uses to typify others' behaviours, course of actions and one's own attitudes. As Blankenburg (1969) put it, 'There is an abdication of commonsense.' In this frame, delusions are the person's reappropriation of the world using other meanings, due to the apparent evanescence, ephemerality, of common meanings.

The phenomenological paradigm that shapes this account of the formation of delusions in schizophrenia can be traced back to the phenomenological practice called eidetic reduction: this is a means to grasp the essential or core feature of a given phenomenon through the bracketing of its commonsensical, everyday meaning. Both in the practice of eidetic reduction (that is performed actively by the phenomenologist) and the process of constitution of delusions (that is passively suffered by persons with schizophrenia) there is the suspension of commonsense meanings; i.e. the meanings through which we usually typify reality, the turning of interest away from the world as it is usually perceived and understood. The eidetic reduction should allow things 'to speak by themselves' – to reveal their essential character (*eidos*). This is exactly the subjective feel described by persons with schizophrenia who experience delusions.

There are though five main criticisms of this model that need be addressed. First, it is an exclusively mentalistic interpretation postulating an entity named 'transcendental categorical structure', a sort of phantom encyclopedia of the commonsense meanings (i.e. what we called earlier the primary theory of the world) to be attached to things in the world. Second, it also postulates another entity named 'constituting subject', disembodied and desituated. Third, it is unclear how the 'constituting subject' can act as an intermediate entity between the 'transcendental categorical structure' and the world. Fourth, it does not convincingly account for the shift from meaninglessness (pre-delusional atmosphere) to meaningfulness (delusion). Finally, it does not account for transformations in lived body, space, etc., that we observe in the world of the person with delusions.

Second model: hyperreflexivity

Another phenomenological theory sees delusions in schizophrenia as the effect of an over-monitoring of processes and phenomena that would normally be confined in the tacit dimension (Sass, 1992). Persons with schizophrenia tend to be more and more engaged in self-monitoring when they are not able to make pre-reflective sense of what it is happening. This has two main consequences. First, there is the emergence of the implicit as explicit. Second, parts of the self are perceived as non-self (morbid objectification). Mental phenomena that would usually happen implicitly become objects of focal awareness. For instance, one's interior dialogue that usually remains in the background in the process of self-reflection or decision taking, may come to the foreground. As they become objects of focal awareness, mental phenomena that are usually sensed as parts of the self tend to be objectified and spatialized – that is, felt as existing in an 'outer' space. For instance, thoughts may be felt as existing in some special part of the brain. Symptoms can be seen as the epiphenomena of heightened awareness of processes and phenomena that would normally be experienced in the tacit dimension (hyperreflexivity, Sass, 1992) and of a concomitant diminishing in the sense of existing as a subject of experience (diminished self-affection) that are typically accompanied by a loss of cognitive or perceptual 'grip' (Sass and Parnas, 2003).

This account is in contrast with the hypothesis that delusions in schizophrenia (especially delusions of control), as well as other positive symptoms of schizophrenia like verbal-acoustic hallucinations, are the outcome of a metacognitive failure, namely the breakdown of self-monitoring (Frith, 1992). According to Frith's model, this breakdown of self-monitoring is essentially a disorder of the sense of self-agency. Contrary to this, the hyperreflexivity theory claims that there is an excess of self-monitoring in persons with schizophrenia – not a failure in the basic self-monitoring processes (Gallagher, 2004). Persons with schizophrenia may have problems with monitoring their own actions, but this occurs typically since they direct their attention to certain 'unusual', hidden aspects of experience.

This account of delusions in schizophrenia is called transcendental reduction: this phenomenological practice consists in the suspension of the natural attitude that orients one's attention from the world as it appears in straightforward cognitions to the condition of possibility of this appearing. The transcendental reduction shifts attention from the way things appear (*noema*), to the way they are constituted in/by consciousness (*noesis*). It takes the world as a phenomenon and reflects upon the way consciousness constitutes it. It brings into view 'constitutive subjectivity', i.e. the way transcendental subjectivity is involved in appropriating worldly objects to itself and giving meanings to them.

This very process is supposed to take place, although involuntarily, in persons with schizophrenia (Stanghellini, 1997). Whereas the phenomenologist performs the transcendental reduction actively and voluntarily, the person with schizophrenia passively undergoes a similar process. After performing (or undergoing) the transcendental reduction, the world will not be experienced as existing per se, but as the correlate of one's subjectivity. In its extreme form, one would experience that the world exists only as the creation of one's own mind. This phenomenon, called solipsism, is quintessential to delusions in schizophrenia. One of the main criticisms that may be directed to this model is that it does not fully account for the disorder of symbolization which occurs in the early stages of schizophrenia. In what way would hyperreflexivity entail the crisis of commonsense meanings? One possible answer is that hyperreflexivity brings about a preoccupation with the usually implicit, and a backing away from the usual encounter with the practical (commonsensical) external world.

Third model: disembodiment and the lifedrive reduction

In this section I try to develop a model of delusions in schizophrenia that places embodiment in the front stage. This model is consistent with the idea that typically delusions express an impairment of minimal self-awareness, of meaning-bestowing as well as of intersubjective attunement and our 'common' way to engage with the world. The central philosophical claim is that the categorical activity (meaning-bestowing and intersubjectivity) presupposes corporeality. The central psychopathological claim of this model is that in the condition of disembodiment the cancellation of commonsense practical engagement in the world occurs and a new enactment or action-specific knowledge takes place.

Within the disembodiment model of delusions in schizophrenia, the basic disorder is the disruption of one's basic indwelling and engagement in the world, bringing about a disruption of readiness-to-hand, i.e. of a specific framework of enacted knowledge – an interconnection involving embodiment, world, action and meaning. In delusions in schizophrenia, the commonsense framework in which body/world/action/meaning are usually set breaks down and a new enactment arises, having its own specific (idiosyncratic) meanings. The kind of reduction at work here is neither eidetic nor transcendental; rather, it is the one called by Scheler (2008) the lifedrive (*Lebensdrang*) reduction.

For Scheler this kind of reduction is neither a question of the cancellation of an act of cognitive judgement, i.e. of an attribution of meaning which is appropriate to the cultural and historical context, nor an act of reorientation of awareness, i.e. the turning away of one's focal attention from the way the world appears to the condition of possibility of its appearance. Rather, it is the switching off of a drive-based function which renders the reality of the world as given.

Lifedrive means the basic drive through which factual reality is given and happens to us. The lifedrive is what makes one feel practically engaged in the world and see things in the world as equipments for one's survival, e.g. a cave is a shelter, a stone is a weapon, a goat is food, etc. Thanks to the lifedrive, one sees things in the world as provided with 'existentially-relative handles' through which one can manage and put them to use. That things have 'handles' means that one's vital drive-based attention is directed to those features of existing things which have a vital relevance to the living organism. Scheler explains that all the main dimensions of human existence (minimal self-awareness, object-awareness, meaning-bestowing and attunement) undergo deep transformation if the lifedrive is wiped off. The lifedrive reduction switches off the 'urgency of life' – the root of all drives, needs and vital attention. What sorts of new givennesses are revealed in the lifedrive reduction?

First, this will modify the relationship between oneself and one's own body. The part of us called lived body is switched off and the body becomes objectified. What is objectified is the 'animal' part of oneself. One becomes a *geistiger Person* – a person with only mental, intellectual dimensions – and considers oneself as having (not being), possessing or dominating one's body or animality. Second, if one's drive-based involvement in the world is switched off, one's grasp of the world will fade away too. This implies a loss of 'practical references' to the world – those vital relevancies that are of use and therefore normally enter one's awareness. If the lifedrive is switched off, the commonsense 'handles' of things will disappear too. The outcomes of this are twofold. Parallel to the loss of practical grasp, things will change into mere objects without a practical relevance for one's body. Depending on the disappearance of the 'reality moment', there grows in meaningfulness an ever-intuitively given fullness of free-floating qualities, as the quality of an object's colour, a surface colour, etc., and of forms. Forms (roundness, triangularity, etc.) become independent objects. The reduction enacts an essentialization of the world, it transforms the world into an 'idea'. The appearance of the world is reduced to the realm of images (*Bildsphaere*). One's body cannot affect any object out there, and objects do not have any causal relationship with each other. Spatial as well as temporal relations among bodies and objects, which are dynamically conditioned qualities depending on bodily movements, undergo a profound change. It is a perfectly adynamic world.

The second consequence of this loss of practical grasp of the world is a metamorphosis of meaning-bestowing. The lifedrive blocks off all those potential significations which do not have a relevance for that living organism. From all the manifold meanings of things one extracts only that small fraction which is appropriate to one's cultural and historical environment. The suspension of the lifedrive allows for a new kind of 'perspectival view' or enactment to appear, focusing on 'theoretical' aspects of experience, e.g. what makes reality appear as it appears?

Third, there is a switching off of one's sense of cohesion and embodied resonance with other human beings. The sense that the others are living beings like oneself is swept aside and all conventional expressions of one's common interpersonal situations are cancelled.

A disembodied world

This kind of *epoché*, which suspends 'the subservience to life's drives', entails a free-floating state of consciousness. 'My awareness (of myself, of him, of the room, of the physical reality around and beyond us) instantly grows fuzzy. Or wobbly,' writes Elyn Saks (2007), a woman with schizophrenia and now an academic engaged in making the experience of schizophrenia more understandable to scholars and lay people: 'Consciousness gradually loses its coherence,' she continues. 'One's center gives away. The center cannot hold. The "me" becomes a haze, and the solid center from which one experiences reality breaks up like a bad radio signal' (p. 12). Within this new frame of hazy consciousness, the self feels like 'a sand castle with all the sand sliding away in the receding surf' (p. 12).

The world parallels the self in undergoing its own metamorphosis. Scheler describes in detail the way the world appears to such a self – lacking a solid centre, fuzzy and wobbly, sliding away like the sand of a sand castle – during his quasi-mystical 'experiments' of suspension or neutralization of the lifedrive, the outcome of which very closely resembles self-descriptions of persons with schizophrenia. In the last part of this chapter, I will use the case of Renée (Sechehaye, 1951) as a clinical example of the way Scheler's doctrine of the lifedrive reduction applies to schizophrenia. In particular, I suggest that there are at least six main features of Renée's world.

First, there is the cancellation of practical meanings of things. We understand worldly things as body-relative utensils. Disembodiment entails the loss of practical grasp of things. There is the cancellation of practical meanings of things, the divorce from things and their ready-to-hand meanings: 'When, for example, I looked at a chair or a jug, I thought not of their use or function – a jug not as something to hold water and milk, a chair not as something to sit in – but as having lost their names, their functions and meanings' (pp. 55–56). And 'I attempted to escape their hold by calling out their names. I said, "Chair, jug, table, it is a chair." But the word echoed hollowly, deprived of all meaning; it had left the object, was divorced from it, so much that on one hand it was a living, mocking thing, on the other, a name, robbed of sense, an envelope emptied of content' (p. 56).

Second, in Renée's world there is a cancellation of the meanings of the other persons' gestures. We understand the others' actions as gestures, i.e. purposeful movements meant to handle things and put them to use. Disembodiment implies the lack of body-to-body resonance through which we make sense of the others' movements by virtually reproducing them in our own body. For Renée others' gestures become movements without meaning: 'People turn weirdly about, they make gestures, movements without sense' (p. 44). And 'Their gestures and their noises [became] more artificial, detached from the other, unreal, without life' (p. 45).

A third quality of Renée's is the disembodiment of the other persons. We normally perceive others as expressive embodied selves, flesh-and-blood animated persons. Disembodiment implies perceiving others as soulless bodies, emotionless mechanical automatons. Renée, for instance, perceives 'robots or puppets moved by invisible mechanisms (. . .) my friend unreal like a statue' (p. 24). And 'Only their bodies were left with them (. . .) moving like a kind of automaton and their movements were deprived of emotions and feelings' (p. 50).

A fourth quality of Renée's experience involves a metamorphosis of space. We usually perceive space as a practical space oriented around the physical structure of the body and its needs; near and far, within reach and out of touch, are relative to one's bodily motility, including the body's capacities and limitations in its pursuit of its goals. In the condition of disembodiment, space becomes mere extension lacking magnitude and measurability: 'Around us the fields spread away, cut up by edges or clumps of trees, the white road ran ahead of us, the sun shone in the blue sky and warmed our backs. But I saw a boundless plain, unlimited, the horizon infinite' (pp. 36–37).

A fifth quality of Renée's experience could be described as the cancellation of causal relations between things. It is thanks to our embodied practical engagement in the world that we see things as equipments for living. Our body and things in the world can have effects on each other. With the cessation of one's practical engagement in the world, one will see things as a sum of 'realia' which fill up the geometrical space. The world would become a perfectly ghostly world, a mere collection of objects which stand one next to the other just 'proximally'. 'A mineral, lunar country, cold as the wastes of the North Pole. In this stretching emptiness, all is unchangeable, immobile, congealed, crystallized' (p. 44). And 'I am lost in it, isolated, cold, stripped, purposeless. A wall of brass isolates me from everybody and everything' (p. 44). And 'I saw things, smooth as metal, so cut off, so detached from each other' (p. 55).

Finally, a sixth quality of Renée's experience involved the cancellation of borders between things and images. Worldly things are not mere images since they offer resistance to our own body. Devoid of their relation to one's own body, one sees things nearly as geometric disembodied entities distributed within a purely geometric space: 'Objects are stage trappings, placed here and there, geometric cubes without meaning' (p. 44). And 'With heart empty, despairingly empty, I reach home. There I find a pasteboard house, sisters and brothers robot' (p. 38).

Disembodiment and the metaphysical enactment

In the course of this kind of metamorphosis, an unusual perspective on the world takes place. New concerns – the quest for what is real versus unreal, meaningful versus meaningless, true versus false, subjective versus objective – emerge from this experience of self and world transformation. Delusions in schizophrenia are the outcome of transformations in the structure of experiencing (Bovet and Parnas, 1993), which through the lens of the disembodied model of delusions in schizophrenia are seen as a consequence of suspension of the lifedrive. Things in the world and people's behaviours lose their incarnated givenness and their at-hand meaningfulness: Do things exist per se or are they the product of someone's mind, or of a technological device? Are the meanings of things authentic or inauthentic and 'made up'? Are others flesh-and-blood persons or mechanical puppets? Are the others' behaviours purposefully tricky and ambiguous?

Delusions typical in schizophrenia express these 'philosophical' concerns, like ontological, eschatological, charismatic and epistemological ones (Jaspers, 1913; Bovet and Parnas, 1993; Stanghellini and Ballerini, 2007) that dominate at the expense of worldly elements and the factuality of things. All these follow a phase that is dominated by doubts and uncertainties. For instance, in ontological delusions, after a period of tension during which the meanings of things in the world appear fleeting and evanescent, the person feels that he has discovered the essence (*noumenon*) of reality whereas other people are ignorant and merely aware of the appearance of phenomena (Kepinski, 1974).

Conclusions

> Philosophy and psychosis have more in common than many people (philosophers especially) might care to admit. The similarity is not what you might think – that philosophy and psychosis don't have rules, and you're tossed around the universe willy-nilly. On the contrary, each is governed by very strict rules. The trick is to discover what those rules are.
>
> (Saks, 2007: 38)

What the philosophical practice called lifedrive reduction and the psychotic condition called schizophrenia have in common is the experience of disembodiment. Disembodiment entails the crisis of embodied object-awareness, meaning-bestowing, and of body-to-body attunement. A disembodied self sees things in the world as unreal and as deprived of their existentially-relative handles – thus useless, meaningless. I have suggested that this is not the outcome of the cancellation of some ghost encyclopaedia where the meanings of things are inscribed, or a disorder of some disembodied meta-cognitive capacity; rather, it is the effect of the disruption of the embodied praxis of manipulating things according to one's practical engagement. This model of delusions in schizophrenia has two main advantages: first, on the phenomenal level it rather coherently accounts for all the most prominent features of the schizophrenic life-world; second, it is partly compatible with an account of phenomena typical of schizophrenia based on the concept of embodied simulation.

References

Baron-Cohen, S., Tager-Flusberg, H. and Cohen, D.J. (1994). *Understanding other minds. Perspectives from autism.* Oxford: Oxford Medical Publications.

Blankenburg, W. (1969). Ansaetze zu einer Psychopathologie des 'Commonsense'. *Confinia Psychiatrica*, *12*, 144–163.
Blankenburg, W. (1971). *Der Verlust der Natuerlichen Selbstverstaendlichkeit. Ein Beitrag zur Psychopathologie Symptomarmer Schizophrenien*. Stuttgart: Enke.
Bovet, P. and Parnas, J. (1993). Schizophrenic delusions: A phenomenological approach. *Schizophrenia Bulletin*, *19*, 579–597.
Callieri, B. (1982). *Quando vince l'ombra*. Roma: Città Nuova.
Cutting, J. (1997). *Principles of psychopathology. Two worlds–two minds–two hemispheres*. Oxford: Oxford University Press.
Ey, H. (1973). *Traité des hallucinations*. Paris: Masson.
Frith, C.D. (1992). *The cognitive neuropsychology of schizophrenia*. Hove, UK: Lawrence Erlbaum Associates Ltd.
Flavell, J.H. (1979). Metacognition and cognitive monitoring: A new area of cognitive-developmental inquiry. *American Psychologist*, *34*, 906–911.
Gallagher, S. (2004). Neurocognitive models of schizophrenia: A phenomenological critique. *Psychopathology*, *37*, 8–19.
Gallese, V. and Goldman, A. (1998). Mirror neurons and the simulation theory of mind-reading. *Trends in Cognitive Sciences*, *2*, 493–501.
Gruhle, H.W. (1932). Die Schizophrenie. Allgemeine Symptomatologie. In O. Bumke (ed.), *Handbuch der Geisteskrankheiten*. Berlin: Springer.
Heidegger, M. (1927). *Being and time*. [Engl. transl.] Oxford: Blackwell.
Henry, M. (1965). *Philosophie et Phénoménologie du Corps*. Paris: Presses Universitaire de France.
Huber, G. (1957). Die Coenaesthetische Schizophrenie. *Forstschritte der Neurologie und Psychiatrie*, *25*, 491–520.
Husserl, E. (1952). *Ideas pertaining to a pure phenomenology and to a phenomenological philosophy. II. Studies in the phenomenology of constitution*. [Husserliana IV, Engl. transl.] Dordrecht: Kluwer, 1989.
Jaspers, K. (1913). *General psychopathology*. [Engl. transl.] Chicago: University of Chicago Press, 1963.
Kepinski, A. (1974). *Skizofrenia*. Warsaw: Panstwowy Zakland Wydawnictw Lakarskich.
MacGilchrist, I. and Cutting, J. (1995). Somatic delusions in schizophrenia and the affective psychoses. *British Journal of Psychiatry*, *167*, 350–361.
Merleau-Ponty, M. (1945). *Phenomenology of perception*. [Engl. transl.] London: Routledge & Kegan Paul.
Parnas, J., Moeller, P., Kircher, T., Thalbizer, J., Jansson, L., Handest, P., *et al.* (2005). EASE: Examination of anomalous self-experience. *Psychopathology*, *38*, 236–258.
Rochat, P. (2004). *The infant's world*. Cambridge, MA: Harvard University Press.
Saks, E.R. (2007). *The centre cannot hold. A memoir of my schizophrenia*. London: Virago Press.
Sass, L.A. (1992). *Madness and modernism: Insanity in the light of modern art, literature, and thought*. New York: Basic Books.
Sass, L.A. and Parnas, J. (2003). Schizophrenia, consciousness, and the self. *Schizophrenia Bulletin*, *29*, 427–444.
Scheler, M. (2008) *The constitution of human being: From the posthumous works,*

Volumes 11 and 12 [translated by J. Cutting.] Milwaukee: Marquette University Press.
Schneider, K. and Huber, G. (1975). Deliri. In *Enciclopedia Medica*. Firenze: Uses.
Sechehaye, M. (1951). *Autobiography of a schizophrenic girl*. [Engl. transl.] New York: Meridian, 1994.
Sheets-Johnstone, M. (1999). *The primacy of movement*. Amsterdam: Benjamins.
Stanghellini, G. (1997). *Antropologia della vulnerabilità*. Milan: Feltrinelli.
Stanghellini, G. (2005). Schizophrenic consciousness, spiritual experience, and the borders between things, images and words. *Transcultural Psychiatry*, *42*, 61–629.
Stanghellini, G. (2008). *Psychopathology of commonsense*. Milano: Cortina. New English Edition forthcoming: *Disembodied spirits and deanimated bodies. The psychopathology of commonsense*. Oxford: Oxford University Press.
Stanghellini, G. and Ballerini, M. (2004). Autism. Disembodied existence. *Philosophy, Psychiatry, and Psychology*, *11*, 259–268.
Stanghellini, G. and Ballerini, M. (2007). Values in persons with schizophrenia. *Schizophrenia Bulletin*, *33*, 131–141.
Varela, F.J., Thompson, E. and Rosch, E. (1991). *The embodied mind*. Cambridge, MA: MIT Press.
Wiggins, O.P., Schwartz, M.A. and Northoff, G. (1990). Towards a Husserlian phenomenology of initial stages of schizophrenia. In M. Spitzer and B.A. Maher (eds), *Philosophy and psychopathology* (pp. 21–34). New York: Springer.

Chapter 9

Deficit of theory of mind in depression and its correlation with poor clinical outcomes

Shigenobu Kanba, Kazuo Yamada and Yumiko Inoue

Introduction

According to the social brain hypothesis, in order to adapt to complex society humans evolved both phylogenetically and ontogenetically in their ability to engage in social relationships, or in other words, they developed social intelligence. This neuronal base comprises the unique cerebro-neural networks seen in humans and other social animals (Brothers, 1990; Dunbar, 1998). The social brain is a highly developed faculty that assumes the role of data processing in the midst of the complexity of social interactions in order to understand the goals, intentions, beliefs and inferences of others, so making possible interpersonal psychological interactions. The social brain is covered by social cognitive neuroscience and 'theory of mind' (TOM) is thought to play an important role in social cognitive function.

In this chapter, we begin by giving a simple review of the social brain and TOM. We then introduce the results of our study of TOM ability directly post-treatment and TOM ability and social functioning one year after treatment of depressive patients. Based on these results, we then examine prospects for future research.

The social brain

During the course of evolution, the human brain has constructed unique neural networks in order to adapt to complex society. The social brain is one such important neural network that governs intelligence during social living, including the cognitive functions that occur during interpersonal interactions (Brothers, 1990).

The function of the social brain in governing social recognition renders possible information processing based on highly developed cognitive functions. These include the acquisition of social knowledge, perception of social information and processing of representation that are necessary in order to lead an optimum existence in the environment. While also being affected by emotions, controlled social cognition, which simultaneously represents and distinguishes between the intentions and behavior of oneself and others, makes it possible for an individual to lead a social existence. This results in the development of social intelligence, which leads to social success. Through the workings of the social brain, interpersonal psychological interaction becomes possible even in the midst of the complexity of social interactions, and social communication is established. Furthermore, social cognition leads to new intellectual ability by experiencing a mental state called cognitive fluidity through learning via environmental influences. Through repeating this cycle, humans have acquired the ability to conversely manipulate their environment, developing the intelligence advantageous for personal gain (Machiavellian intelligence). As well as being a particular feature of the physical world, social cognition is also engaged in understanding metaphysical concepts. So, along with being a higher brain function acquired during the process of evolution, social cognition can also be thought of as the essence of the human mind (Dunbar, 1998).

Face, expression, line of vision and TOM are among the main factors in social cognition (Dunbar, 1998) and of these, the cognition forming the basis of the social brain is TOM.

Theory of mind and the social brain

The term 'a theory of mind' was first used in 1978 by Premack and Woodruff (1978) in their paper, 'Does the chimpanzee have a theory of mind?' They defined possession of a theory of mind as the ability to suppose internal emotions such as goals, intentions, knowledge, beliefs, inferences, cogitation, skepticism and the like, in other words, mental states of oneself and others. They also used the term 'imputes mental states', and assumed that behind the behavior of others there is a specific mental action.

Assuming that the difference in science between 'phenomenon' and 'theory' corresponds with 'behavior' and 'mind', 'theory', events that cannot be directly observed, can be replaced with 'mind'; and 'phenomenon', directly observable events, with 'behavior' (Fletcher *et al.*, 1995). As events that cannot be directly observed are thus being treated as 'mind', this system of inferences is a 'theory', and following on from this, it is called 'theory of mind'. In actual studies, as stated by Brüne *et al.* (2003), it is used to express a 'theory of other minds', and has been defined as the ability to suppose the mental states of others.

Criticism was leveled at Premack's experiments that 'there is the possibility that the mind of oneself and others are being viewed as the same, rather than a difference being inferenced between them.' In response to this, Perner and Wimmer (1985) proposed that the ability to solve a 'false belief task' constitutes an understanding of the difference between a person's own mind and that of another. A false belief task tests whether the subject understands the relationship that 'Person A falsely believes that Object X is in Place Y', a first-order-representation (Perner and Wimmer, 1985; Baron-Cohen *et al.*, 2000). Carrying out false belief task experiments on children shows that they cannot be solved by children under the age of three, but from the age of four inference becomes possible. Additionally, when they reach the ages of nine to ten they can understand the relationship that 'Person B falsely believes that Person A thinks Object X is in Place Y'. This is a second-order-representation, or meta-representation (Baron-Cohen *et al.*, 1985, 2000; Perner and Wimmer, 1985). This is a further development of *n*-dimensional representation ability, which is requisite in understanding complex human relationships and makes it possible to understand oneself from the viewpoint of others. Add to this ability the manipulation of others' behavior and deceitful acts become possible (Brothers, 1990; Byrne, 1999; Baron-Cohen *et al.*, 2000).

The area of the brain relating to social intelligence is known as the social brain, and this appears to mainly involve the fronto-orbital cortex, the superior temporal gyrus and the amygdala (Brothers, 1990; Baron-Cohen *et al.*, 2000). In neuroimaging studies of TOM task execution, the likelihood of frontal lobe participation has been directly shown (Evelyn *et al.*, 2002). When subjects are required to reason about someone's false belief, medial prefrontal cortex (MPFC), medial precuneus and bilateral temporo-parietal junction (TPJ) are recruited (Saxe *et al.*, 2006). Mentalizing about a similar other engaged a region of ventral MPFC linked to self-referential thought, whereas mentalizing about a dissimilar other engaged a more dorsal sub-region of MPFC (Mitchell *et al.*, 2006). Activity in the MPFC was positively correlated with the mentalizing ability in alexithymic subjects (Moriguchi *et al.*, 2006).

In structural neuroimaging studies of depressed patients, well replicated findings include an increased rate of deep white matter hyperintensities, and a reduction in size of the frontal lobe, hippocampus, cerebellum, caudate and putamen (Steffens and Krishnan, 1998). Bipolar disorder has been reported to be associated with an increase in the size of the third ventricle, basal ganglia and amygdala. Functional imaging studies have indicated that both metabolism and blood flow in depressed patients are decreased in the dorsolateral prefrontal cortex and left hippocampus and increased in the amygdala, ventrolateral and posterior orbital cortex (Taylor and Fink, 2006). In addition, reductions in the volume and metabolism of the sub-genual prefrontal cortex (SGPFC) have also been reported (Drevets, 2001).

Therefore, the areas in which impairment is suspected in depressed patients show significant overlap with the areas responsible for TOM ability.

Mental disorders and theory of mind

Dysfunction of any region of the social cognition neural network mechanism will generate impairment of social cognitive function. This leads to an inability to build appropriate relationships with others and ensuing dysfunction of social life. Various pyschosocial impairments are potential causes or exacerbating factors of mental disorders. There have previously been reports observing deficiency in social cognition, including TOM, or social brain dysfunction in various mental disorders such as autism (Baron-Cohen *et al.*, 2000) and schizophrenia (Brüne, 2001; Pinkham *et al.*, 2002; Inoue *et al.*, 2006a).

Regarding mood disorders, a general impairment in recognition of emotional facial expressions was reported in depressed patients (Wexler *et al.*, 1994; Lanbenecker *et al.*, 2005; Lee *et al.*, 2005). Specific TOM performance was similarly impaired in euthymic state of major depressive disorder (Inoue *et al.*, 2004) and medication-free depressed patients (Wang *et al.*, 2008). Regarding bipolar disorder, euthymic and stable patients showed TOM deficits (Bora *et al.*, 2005; Olley *et al.*, 2005; Lahera *et al.*, 2008). Also, as introduced below, the authors' own research shows that in patients with major depression, the existence of defective TOM ability bears a strong relation on treatment outcome and prognosis, including recurrence rate (Inoue *et al.*, 2006b).

Frith (1992) proposed that TOM impairments in psychotic patients may explain the genesis of psychotic symptoms such as paranoid delusions. However, non-psychotic depressed patients or bipolar patients without previous psychotic symptoms showed deficit in TOM, as well as symptomatically remitted patients with schizophrenia (Herold *et al.*, 2002; Inoue *et al.*, 2006b). Further work is required to determine how TOM deficit is related to psychotic symptoms.

Clinical evaluation of the social brain through evaluation of social cognition function, including TOM, in patients with various mental disorders allows not only information regarding the cognitive attributes of the patient to be obtained but is also useful for building treatment strategy, including prevention of recurrence.

TOM performance and one-year outcome of major depression

The authors focused on social cognitive dysfunction and investigated the presence of TOM ability impairment in mood disorder patients (Inoue *et al.*, 2004, 2006b). In task execution experiments that are too simple, it was difficult to ascertain differences between the disorder group and the healthy group. We therefore used a four-frame comic strip by Willhelm Bush (a nineteenth-century German artist; see Figure 9.1).

The subjects were asked to put the four pictures in sequence, which were presented in the same order (Inoue *et al.*, 2004). If they failed to sequence the picture story correctly, a correction was made by the rater and the picture story was continuously presented in the right order for subsequent

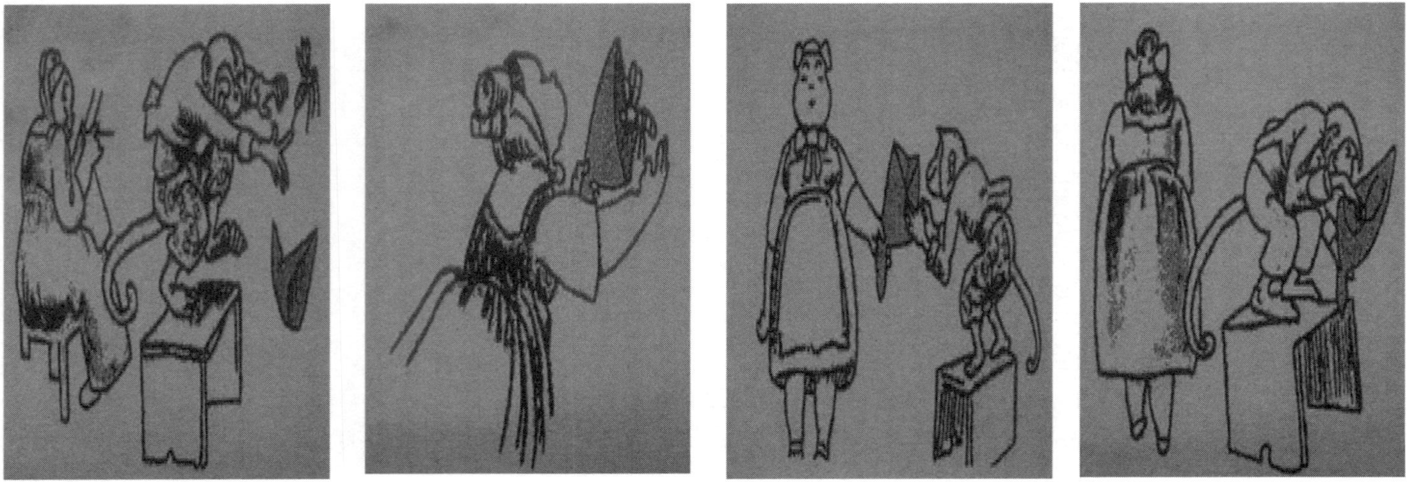

Figure 9.1 Theory of mind (TOM) battery.

Source: Inoue *et al.* (2004).

TOM testing. The subjects were then given a verbal description of each picture as follows. 'A woman catches a bee in a paper bag (first picture). She presents the paper bag to the monkey (second picture). The monkey curiously reaches into the paper bag (third picture). The monkey is stung by the bee (fourth picture).' After the description of the action, the first-order false belief was examined. The subjects were asked to answer a question 'What does the monkey think is in the bag?' and subsequently 'What is really in the paper bag?' The subjects were then asked 'What does the monkey think the woman intends to do?' to examine the second-order false belief question. Then the subjects were asked the reality question again ('What was actually in the bag?'). Finally, the subjects were asked 'What does the woman intend to do?' (a tactical deception question). The maximum summed score of the cartoon TOM task was four (for correct sequencing, and correct answering of the TOM tasks, including the reality questions).

The subjects were 50 patients (depression group) with an IQ = 79 who were in remission following a major depressive episode, and who met the *DSM-IV* criteria (American Psychiatric Association, 2000) for major depressive disorder (n = 34) or bipolar I type disorder (n = 16); and 50 healthy patients not suffering from mental disorder matched for gender and age (healthy group). Both groups comprised 22 men and 28 women. In the mood disorder group the average age of onset was 44.5 ± 8.5 years (mean ± SD) and average IQ was 106.6 ± 10.4. The average age of the healthy group was 44.3 ± 10.7 years and average IQ was 107.3 ± 13.1. Respectively, there was no statistical difference between the two groups.

Impairment in handling sequence, a first-order false belief question, a second-order false belief question and a tactical deception question were investigated in all 100 subjects. In addition, a follow-up was conducted for one year and interpersonal skills and social functioning were evaluated.

In the sequence, first-order false belief question, and tactical deception question tasks, no significant difference was seen between the groups in the number of correct answers. However, in the second-order false belief question, the correct answer was given in 48 cases (96 per cent) in the healthy group, as opposed to only 31 cases (62 per cent) in the mood disorder group, which shows a statistical significance (Fisher's exact test, $p < 0.0001$; odds ratio, 14.71; 95 per cent confidence interval: 3.20–67.62). These results show that in many mood disorder patients, even those in remission, deficiency in the second-order false belief question area of TOM ability was observed.

They were divided into those who answered the second-order false belief question correctly (n = 28) and those who answered incorrectly (n = 19) and followed up over one year. In the group who answered correctly (C-group), recurrence of mood disorder within one year was observed in only two cases (7.1 per cent) while in the group who answered incorrectly (I-group)

Table 9.1 Theory of mind (TOM) and relapse

	TOM second-order false belief question	
	Incorrect (I-group)	Correct (C-group)
Relapse	11	2
Not relapse	8	26

Fisher's exact text p < .0001; relative risk = 8.105; 2.202 < 95% CI < 32.54

recurrence of mood disorder was observed in 11 cases (58 per cent) (Fisher's exact test, $p < 0.0001$; relative risk = 8.105; 95 per cent confidence interval: 2.202, 32.54) (Table 9.1). Also, in differences in scores for the global assessment of functioning (GAF) scale of the *DSM-IV* from the start of the study to one year later, a 16.6 ± 15.8 point improvement was observed in the correct answer group against a 9.8 ± 17.7 point worsening observed in the incorrect answer group ($t = 5.25$, $p < 0.00001$). These results show that in mood disorder patients demonstrating deficiency in second-order false belief question area of TOM ability, recurrence occurs more easily, a decrease in social function is observed and prognosis is poor in many cases.

Discussion

Deficiency in TOM ability, especially in second-order false belief question tasks, can be observed in many mood disorder patients, even those in remission. Also, deficiency in TOM ability in mood disorder patients bears a strong relation to treatment outcome and prognosis, including recurrence rate (Inoue *et al.*, 2006b).

Patients in whom deficiency in second-order false belief question tasks is observed have a high possibility of early recurrence, and the possibility of decrease in overall quality of life (QOL) reflected in the GAF score was also implied. These results imply that TOM ability deficiency in mood disorder patients is not generated as a direct symptom of a major depressive episode. However, the causes of the deficit can be multifold. Many factors are known to affect TOM performance such as innate trait, as well as poor attachment, poor reference on mental states in social conversation with adults since infancy, social isolation, poor socio-economic status, or trauma history.

Looking at the cause of TOM deficiency in mood disorder, it is possible that brain areas and associated networks related to mood disorders and brain areas related to TOM, including mirror neuron system areas (Rizzolatti *et al.*, 2006), are already vulnerable before pathogenesis. In depression, hypofunction of frontal cortex (Taylor and Fink, 2006) is consistently reported in the central area of mirror neuron system. Representing the mental state of another as if it was one's own (simulation theory) requires involvement of the mirror neuron system, as well as understanding of the intentions of others (Iacoboni and Dapretto, 2006). Patients with major depression might have difficulty in interpersonal relationship that triggers onset of depressive episodes because of impairment of representing the mental state or understanding of the intentions of others.

As Ingudomnukul *et al.* (2007) identified, there is the possibility that the body's internal environment during fetal life such as elevated fetal testosterone has an effect. Factors such as parents' divorce or abuse that provide an unfavorable environment during early childhood developmental stages leading to insufficient contribution being made to emergent regions of the brain areas related to TOM are also potential causes. As described above, poor attachment, social isolation, poor socio-economic status, or trauma history are considered to play a significant role in causing the emotional, cognitive and metacognitive features of post-traumatic symptoms (see Liotti and Prunetti, this volume, Chapter 12).

In addition, it is possible that gene clusters which endow specified cognitive tendencies that are beneficial in a particular environment may, under the environment present at onset of the disorder, cause maladaptation, and the lack of adaptive behavior may thus cause pathogenesis of a mood disorder. TOM ability deficiency, which is thought to be strongly related to mirror neuron system (MNS) vulnerability, is possibly linked to decrease in memory recall ability of others' feelings or mental state, and may lead to a decreased level or lack of sympathy or mistaken assumptions (false belief). Also, this may lead to the inability to distinguish between the mental states of oneself and others, which generates cognitive confusion and a breakdown of cognitive fluidity that in complex environments or new situations causes inability to display regulated cognitive ability and difficulty in interpersonal psychological interactions. These results generate stressors in human relationships which may cause mood disorder recurrence or decrease in QOL.

Previous reports have observed deficiency in social cognition, including TOM, or social brain dysfunction in various mental disorders such as autism, schizophrenia and mood disorders. The results show observation of social brain dysfunction in patients with various mental disorders, exceeding the current borders of illness classification. This may indicate the need for a cross-sectional diagnostic system that transcends existing diagnostic classifications.

Conclusion

Predicting social brain dysfunction from a clinical point of view through evaluation of social cognitive function, including TOM ability, in patients with various mental disorders, is useful in gaining valuable information about the patient's cognitive tendencies. Moreover, a therapist can help a patient to develop a capacity to mentalize self-states and state of mind and motivations of others in order to avoid interpersonal problems (Bateman and Fonagy, 2004), which may result in recurrence prevention.

Born of evolutionary and developmental psychology, TOM is now being considered psychopathologically, and further studied regarding its relation to localized functions of the brain. We can therefore expect development of comprehensive treatment strategies including programs to improve or acquire TOM.

References

American Psychiatric Association (2000). *Diagnostic and statistical manual of mental disorders, 4th edn (DSM-IV)*. Washington, DC: American Psychiatric Association.

Baron-Cohen, S. Leslie, A. and Frith, U. (1985). Does the autistic child have a 'theory of mind'? *Cognition, 21*, 37–46.

Baron-Cohen, S. Tager-Flusberg, H. and Cohen, D.J. (2000). *Understanding other minds*. Oxford: Oxford University Press.

Bateman, A.W. and Fonagy, P. (2004). *Psychotherapy for borderline personality disorder: Mentalization-based treatment*. Oxford: Oxford University Press.

Bora, E., Vahip, S., Gonul, A.S., Akdeniz, F., Alkan, M., Ogut, M., *et al.* (2005). Evidence for theory of mind deficits in euthymic patients with bipolar disorder. *Acta Psychiatrica Scandinavica, 112*, 110–116.

Brothers, L. (1990). The social brain: A project for integrating primate behavior and neurophysiology in a new domain. *Conceptual Neuroscience, 1*, 27–51.

Brüne, M. (2001). Social cognition and psychopathology in an evolutionary perspective. *Psychopathology, 34*, 85–94.

Brüne, M., Ribbert, H. and Schiefenhövel, W. (2003). *The social brain evolution and pathology*. Chichester: Wiley.

Byrne, R. (1999). *The thinking ape: Evolutionary origins of intelligences*. Oxford: Oxford University Press.

Drevets, W.C. (2001). Neuroimaging and neuropathological studies of depression: Implications for the cognitive-emotional features of mood disorders. *Current Opinion in Neurobiology, 11*, 240–249.

Dunbar, R.I.M. (1998). The social brain hypothesis. *Evolutionary Anthropology, 6*, 178–190.

Evelyn, C., Ferstl, D. and von Cramon, Y. (2002). What does the frontomedial cortex contribute to language processing: Coherence or theory of mind? *Neuroimage, 17*, 1599–1612.

Fletcher, P.C., Happé, F., Frith, U., Baker, S.C., Dolan, R.J., Frackowiak, R.S., *et al.* (1995). Other minds in the brain: A functional imaging study of 'theory of mind' in a story comprehension. *Cognition, 57*, 109–128.

Frith, C.D. (1992). *The cognitive neuropsychology of schizophrenia*. Hove, UK: Lawrence Erlbaum Associates Ltd.

Herold, R., Tenyi, T., Lenard, K. and Trixler, M. (2002). Theory of mind deficit in people with schizophrenia during remission. *Psychological Medicine*, *32*, 1125–1129.

Iacoboni, M. and Dapretto, M. (2006). The mirror neuron system and the consequences of its dysfunction. *Nature Reviews Neuroscience*, *7*, 942–951.

Inoue, Y., Yamada, K., Tonooka, Y. and Kanba, S. (2004). Deficiency of theory of mind in patients with remitted mood disorders. *Journal of Affective Disorders*, *82*, 403–409.

Inoue, Y., Yamada, K., Hirano, M., Shinohara, M., Tamaoki, T., Iguchi, H., *et al.* (2006a). Impairment of theory of mind in patients in remission following first episode of schizophrenia. *European Archives of Psychiatry and Clinical Neuroscience*, *256*, 326–328.

Inoue, Y., Yamada, K. and Kanba, S. (2006b). Deficit in theory of mind is a risk for relapse of major depression. *Journal of Affective Disorders*, *95*, 125–127.

Inqudomunkul, E., Baron-Cohen, S., Wheelwright, S. and Knickmeyer, R. (2007). Elevated rates of testosterone-related disorders in women with autism spectrum condition. *Hormones and Behavior*, *51*, 597–604.

Lahera, G., Montes, J.M., Benito, A., Valdivia, M., Medina, E., Mirapeix, I., *et al.* (2008). Theory of mind deficit in bipolar disorder: Is it related to a previous history of psychotic symptoms? *Psychiatry Research*, *161*, 309–317.

Lanbenecker, S.A., Bieliauskas, L.A., Rapport, L.J., Zubieta, J.K., Wilde, E.A. and Berent, S. (2005). Face emotion perception and executive functioning deficits in depression. *Journal of Clinical and Experimental Neuropsychology*, *27*, 320–333.

Lee, L., Harkness, K.L., Mark, A., Sabbagh, A. and Jacobson, J.A. (2005). Mental state decoding abilities in clinical depression. *Journal of Affective Disorders*, *86*, 247–258.

Mitchell, J.P., Macrae, C.N. and Banaji, M.R. (2006). Dissociable medial prefrontal contributions to judgments of similar and dissimilar others. *Neuron*, *50*, 655–663.

Moriguchi, Y., Ohnishi, T., Lane, R.D., Maeda, M., Mori, T., Nemoto, K., *et al.* (2006). Impaired self-awareness and theory of mind: An fMRI study of mentalizing in alexithymia. *Neuroimage*, *32*, 1472–1482.

Olley, A.L., Malhi, G.S., Bachelor, J., Cahill, C.M., Mitchell, P.B. and Berk, M. (2005). Executive functioning and theory of mind in euthymic bipolar disorder. *Bipolar Disorders*, *7*(Suppl. 5), 43–52.

Perner, J. and Wimmer, H. (1985). 'John thinks that Mary thinks that'. Attribution of second-order beliefs by 5- to 10-year-old children. *Journal of Experimental Child Psychology*, *39*, 437–471.

Pinkham, A.E., Penn, D.L., Perkins, D.O. and Lieberman, J. (2002). Implications for the neural basis for the study of schizophrenia. *American Journal of Psychiatry*, *160*, 815–824.

Premack. D. and Woodruff, G. (1978). Does the chimpanzee have a theory of mind? *Behavior & Brain Science*, *4*, 515–526.

Rizzolatti, G., Fogassi, L. and Gallese, V. (2006). Mirrors in the mind. *Scientific American*, *295*, 54–61.

Saxe, R., Moran, J.M., Scholz, J. and Gabrieli, J. (2006). Overlapping and non-overlapping brain regions for theory of mind and self reflection in individual subjects. *SCAN*, *1*, 229–234.

Steffens, D.C. and Krishnan, K.R. (1998). Structural neuroimaging and mood disorders: recent findings, implications for classification, and future directions. *Biological Psychiatry*, *15*, 705–712.

Taylor, M.A. and Fink, M. (2006). *Melancholia: The diagnosis, pathophysiology, and treatment of depressive illness*. Cambridge: Cambridge University Press.

Wang, Y.-G., Wang, Y.-P., Chen, S.-L., Zhu, C.-Y. and Wang, K. (2008). Theory of mind disability in major depression with or without psychotic symptoms: A componential view. *Psychiatry Research*, *161*, 153–161.

Wexler, B.E., Levenson, L., Warrenburg, S. and Price, L.H. (1994). Decreased perceptual sensitivity to emotion-evoking stimuli in depression. *Psychiatry Research*, *51*, 127–138.

Chapter 10

Interpersonal problems in alexithymia

A review

Stijn Vanheule, Ruth Inslegers, Reitske Meganck, Els Ooms and Mattias Desmet

Introduction

A substantial number of psychiatric patients have difficulty grasping what is going on in their own minds and bodies. In emotionally arousing situations, affects overwhelm them and challenge their subjective integrity. Affective experiences burden them with intense but vague sensations of unease that give rise to dysfunctional and often destructive reactions, ranging from intense panic to numbness, and from violent outbursts of anger to avoidant behaviour. A frequently used concept for characterizing these problems in metacognitive monitoring is alexithymia.

Alexithymia is most often defined within the four-component structure developed by Taylor *et al.* (1997) as a combination of:

- difficulties identifying feelings and distinguishing between feelings and the bodily sensations of emotional arousal
- difficulties describing feelings to other people
- constricted imaginal processes, as evidenced by a paucity of fantasy life
- a stimulus-bound, externally oriented cognitive style.

These characteristics prove to be helpful in characterizing a broad range of psychiatric patients, ranging from those with eating disorders, somatization, mood disorders, psychosis and various personality disorders (Taylor *et al.*, 1997; Dimaggio *et al.*, 2007; Lumley *et al.*, 2007). A substantial number of patients with these diagnoses have problems when experiencing sensations of internal arousal and understanding to which emotions these sensations refer. Reflecting on subjective determinants of affective experiences is also difficult for them, and as a consequence their mental life typically gives an impression of emptiness and inconsistency. In therapeutic interactions these patients tend to focus their thoughts on external events rather than on their own mental states. In general, communicating about affective experiences is difficult (Vanheule, 2008).

As Taylor and colleagues (1997) make clear, alexithymia is not conceptualized as a categorically distinct mental disorder. Alexithymia is a characteristic that can be present to various degrees in patients with a range of different disorders. The concept enables us to grasp a specific dimension of psychopathological mental life, and helps us focus on a patient's capacity for regulating affective experiences.

At a macro level the concept can be used to gain insight into clinical characteristics that typically co-vary with alexithymic traits, and also helps us to refine our knowledge on the antecedents, dynamics and consequences of poor metacognitive functioning. For example, in a study on depression we observed that it was possible to discern a subgroup of alexithymic depressed patients. This group differed from non-alexithymic depressed patients with respect to the precise nature of their depressive symptoms as well as their interpersonal attitude. At the level of symptoms they had more vital-somatic depressive complaints, and in their contacts with others they displayed a more distance-taking position (Vanheule *et al.*, 2007b). This symptomatic and interpersonal profile indicates that these patients are more 'silent' in the expression of what is going wrong, and rely less on others for solving their problems. These two characteristics pose a challenge for the therapists working with them.

At a micro level, in clinical practice the alexithymia construct can be used in diagnostic situations to get a better understanding of patients' affective experiences. This helps therapists to tailor their approach and focus on how to work with specific alexithymic difficulties. This is very important. One observation that persists since the early work with alexithymic patients is that therapeutic success is low. Strongly alexithymic patients are harder to treat than non-alexithymic patients (Ogrodniczuk *et al.*, 2005; Taylor *et al.*, 1997; Grabe *et al.*, 2008). Research must be adjusted to make treatment more effective, and the interpersonal style of alexithymic patients is an important area of investigation. Due to their typically detached attitude, alexithymic patients tend to evoke rejecting or angry reactions in others. In therapeutic contexts these reactions are counterproductive, yet they often occur.

In this chapter we review the literature on the interpersonal problems associated with alexithymia. We also present a theoretical frame that can hopefully give a better explanation of them. We propose that alexithymia should be understood as a problem in the metacognitive monitoring of affective states, which is inherent to a typical relational modus. The relation between alexithymia and the metacognitive monitoring of the self and others will be explored.

Initial insights on interpersonal problems in alexithymia

Alexithymia was first coined by Nemiah and Sifeos in the 1970s. Based on their clinical experience with psychosomatic patients, the authors understood alexithymia as a form of restricted mental functioning and strongly focused on the intra-psychological side of the problem. The authors discerned two main characteristics. First, alexithymia should be understood as 'a striking incapacity of the verbal description and expression of feelings', hence the choice of the concept; 'a-lexis-thymos' or 'no words for emotions' (Nemiah and Sifeos, 1970: 159). Second, the thoughts and associations of these patients were described as largely referring 'to external events and actions rather than to internal fantasies' (Nemiah and Sifeos, 1970: 159). According to the authors, the thoughts these patients expressed and the answers they gave to questions came across as superficial. Their personal accounts did not come across as lived experiences and were not marked by subjectivity. The standard definition of Taylor and colleagues (1997) is faithful to the descriptive characteristics outlined by Nemiah and Sifeos, and can be understood as a more nuanced version of them.

In their initial descriptions Nemiah and Sifeos (1970: 159) made very interesting observations on the subjective effect that alexithymic patients had on them as psychiatrists. No doubt informed by the fact that countertransferential reactions are important to take into account, the authors remarked that their 'own introspections revealed a sense of frustration when interviewing the patients, and a feeling that they were dull, lifeless, colorless and boring. . . . The general effect was a lack of communication between doctor and patient that frequently gave to their relationship the quality of being sterile and unproductive' (Nemiah and Sifeos, 1970: 159). It seems that the alexithymic patients enervated them just as they fascinated them, a reaction frequently reported in alexithymia literature. Unfortunately, however, these comments remained largely anecdotal and did not give rise to more fundamental considerations of the interpersonal stance or broader metacognitive monitoring of alexithymic patients.

For example, in *Psychosomatic illness: A problem in communication* (Nemiah and Sifeos, 1970) the authors introduce the case of a 37-year-old man, a union steward, who makes a consultation for psychosomatic problems. The case largely focused on this man's difficulty in naming what he was experiencing emotionally. The discussion revealed that his affective difficulties were situated in the context of tense professional relationships. At work, this patient was pressed between an employer who refused to meet compelling demands from employees, and increasingly angry colleagues who exerted pressure on him to fight for their case. The key problem that the patient faced was the question of how to deal with these pressures. From different sides he was confronted with demands that were placed upon him; the context, so to speak, was a situation where an act was expected of him. His dumbfounded reaction indicates that it was precisely the act of taking a subjectively meaningful position in relation to others that constitutes his problem. Indeed, it was his interpersonal difficulties that emerged as being the only relevant context within which his affective problems could either be expressed or understood. The patient gave no evidence of elaborate social cognitions, and obviously lacked the necessary social skills to react adequately to these demands. His answer is a-lexical and blank: no clear position towards others could be taken, no personal stance that would locate him as an 'I' within a perhaps embarrassing situation was occupied.

No doubt this same blank attitude is what returned in his relationship with the interviewing doctor. With respect to the relationship during the clinical interview, Nemiah and Sifeos (1970: 156) conclude that 'the patient remains seemingly detached, unconcerned and distant' and that 'the entire relationship appears to be pale, colorless, lifeless, dull and without any of the human warmth and resonance that usually develop between two people over a period of time' (Nemiah and Sifeos, 1970: 156). The same remark could probably be made for the patient's interpersonal contacts at work, yet Nemiah and Sifeos do not link this. In sum, it is remarkable that Nemiah and Sifeos discuss this patient's difficulties in naming affective experiences, but neglect the dynamic link with the interpersonal difficulties. The effect is that the man's difficulties in the metacognitive monitoring of his own affective states are disconnected from the question of further metacognitive difficulties in the social sphere.

In later clinical literature, interpersonal problems of alexithymic patients are frequently indicated. Pierre Marty and colleagues (1963, 1980) focused on a similar clinical picture and described individuals with a poor representational life as 'operational' in their thinking and living. By 'operational' the authors principally mean that their mental life is strongly limited to the actual and the factual, and is marked by poor phantasmatic activity. The authors suggest that such individuals have difficulties in processing affective states and that this 'operational' way of living implies poor psychic investment in the surrounding world. These patients do not care too much about others and social relationships. Marty (1980: 62) describes their relation to others as 'devitalized' and 'decathected', in that the degree of preoccupation with others is low, and that they function in a pattern of relative detachment from and unconcern for others. Alexithymic persons may take a physical distance from others, and close connections will be avoided.

In addition to the distance-taking tendency of alexithymic patients, a marked vulnerability for conflict and emotionally tense situations has also been described (e.g. McDougall, 1974; Krystal, 1979; Marty, 1980; Mitrani, 1995). This interpersonal problem is not that surprising. As a result of their poorly elaborated social cognitions, alexithymic individuals lack a sophisticated representational system that would work towards the interpretation of others and their actions. Those who make a strong appeal to them despite the distance-taking attitude typically cause confusion, destabilize these individuals and will easily be experienced as intrusive.

What has empirical research taught us?

A question we can ask is whether the above insights, which are gathered through intensive clinical contacts with relatively small groups of patients, are generalizable to alexithymic patients as such. We believe that detailed observation in clinical contexts is an invaluable tool for developing insight into psychiatric disorders, but empirical research with standardized methods can help to solve the question of generalizability. We will review and discuss a number of these studies with the aim of gaining more insight into the interpersonal functioning characteristic of alexithymia. Most of these studies make use of self-report questionnaires. Such questionnaires are popular in psychological research. They have the advantage of being less time consuming, where large groups of patients can be assessed with minimal effort. On the other hand these instruments tend to be imprecise in measuring the concept they intend to measure, which is why replication by independent researchers is important.

The self-report questionnaire that is most frequently used for measuring alexithymia is the 20-item Toronto Alexithymia Scale (TAS-20; Bagby *et al.*, 1994a, 1994b). This instrument measures three of the four characteristics of alexithymia defined by Taylor and colleagues (1997): difficulty identifying feelings (DIF); difficulty describing feelings (DDF); and externally oriented thinking (EOT). While the TAS-20 is psychometrically acceptable, it has been observed that the EOT subscale is not as strongly related to the DIF and DDF subscales as one would theoretically expect (Meganck *et al.*, 2008). A weakness in the current alexithymia research is that usually the TAS-20 is used as the sole instrument for measuring alexithymia. The authors of the TAS-20 advise against this and recommend the use of multiple methods to measure alexithymia. We believe that interview-based measures, such as the Toronto Structured Interview for Alexithymia (TSIA; Bagby *et al.*, 2006) and free response tasks, such as the Levels of Emotional Awareness Scale (LEAS; Lane *et al.*, 1990), should be included in upcoming studies.

In the last decade, a first series of studies addressed the question of interpersonal problems typical of alexithymia by using the TAS-20 in combination with the Inventory of Interpersonal Problems (IIP; Horowitz *et al.*, 2000). The IIP is a self-report questionnaire that measures eight categories of interpersonal problems:

- 'domineering/controlling', which indicates difficulties in relinquishing control over others
- 'vindictive/self-centred', which describes problems of hostile dominance and the tendency to fight with others
- 'cold/distant', which refers to low degrees of affection for and connection with others

- 'socially inhibited', which refers to the tendency to feel anxious and avoidant in the presence of others
- 'non-assertive', which measures problems in taking initiative in relation to others and coping with social challenges
- 'overly accommodating', which indicates an excess of friendly submissiveness
- 'self-sacrificing', which indicates a tendency to affiliate excessively
- 'intrusive/needy', which describes problems with friendly dominance.

Based on the clinical observations mentioned above, it could be expected that cold and distant functioning would be typical for alexithymia.

Weinryb and colleagues (1996) applied the IIP to psychology students (n = 118) and discovered that specifically the cold/distant subscale was related to alexithymia (measured with two self-report instruments). Spitzer and colleagues (2005) studied psychiatric inpatients (n = 149) before and after an intensive group psychotherapy program. They observed that cold and socially avoidant behaviour were typical for alexithymic patients, and also found that therapy did not change this pattern. In a mixed group of psychiatric outpatients (n = 404) and psychology students (n = 157) we observed that cold/distant and non-assertive social functioning was strongly related to alexithymia (Vanheule *et al.*, 2007a). We also observed that, in a group of depressed outpatients (n = 134), strongly alexithymic patients differed from others in terms of more pronounced cold/distant functioning. The association between alexithymia and interpersonal functioning explored by these independent research groups indicates that cold/distant functioning is typical.

Research that uses other self-report instruments further supports these findings. For example, studies examining the characteristics of adult and peer attachment relations associated with alexithymia found that experiences of attachment insecurity are typical. Alexithymic persons tend to develop avoidant attachments with others in general (De Rick and Vanheule, 2007; Meins *et al.*, 2008) and with therapists in particular (Mallinckrodt *et al.*, 1998). Research into the relation between alexithymia and personality disorders shows that schizoid, avoidant and antisocial personality disorder traits are related to alexithymia (De Rick and Vanheule, 2007). These personality disorders share as a common feature social isolation or detachment in interpersonal relationships. In the schizoid personality, social isolation is accompanied by restricted affectivity; in the avoidant personality detachment comes with overwhelming fear (see also Dimaggio *et al.*, 2007); whereas in the antisocial personality disorder, detachment is characterized by lack of empathy. These questionnaire studies indicate that alexithymia is concomitant with distance taking in interpersonal relations.

Empirical research using alternative measurement methods to study detachment in alexithymia are scarce. Such research is required if we are to avoid the typical sources of bias that are inherent to self-report questionnaires (e.g. the tendency to give socially desirable answers, and the tendency of people to over-estimate or under-estimate their own capacities). Scheidt and colleagues (1999) have used the Adult Attachment Interview and a related Q-sort coding method to assess attachment relations. These attachment measures primarily tap into a person's state of mind regarding his or her attachment in his or her family of origin. They observed that dismissing and deactivated attachment patterns were significantly related to alexithymia scores, in particular to the 'externally oriented thinking' subscale of the TAS-20. Their findings support the association found between interpersonal detachment and alexithymia, and the authors generalize these findings to patterns of attachment in childhood. Moreover, a longitudinal study that examined attachment to parents and patterns of affect expression over a period of two years in 12- to 36-month-old children found that poor parental bonding and difficulties in affect regulation coexist (Lemche *et al.*, 2004). Using the Strange Situation Procedure (an attachment test in which a child is observed playing for 20 minutes while caregivers and strangers enter and leave the room), the authors observed that insecurely attached children have serious difficulties in verbalizing inner experiences. This was particularly noticeable for the socially avoidant children, that is, those who seem to lack clear strategies for dealing with separation from their parents or dealing with unknown adults. These children display not only a generalized poor bonding to others, but simultaneously lack the linguistic 'tools' to process emotions and to understand causes and consequences of affects. The results from this study indicate that social detachment and alexithymic functioning (or poor metacognitive self-monitoring) coexist. Implicit measures have also been used to measure alexithymia. In a sample of psychiatric outpatients, we used lexical content analysis to measure both alexithymia (in combination with TAS-20) and their level of involvement in social processes. We observed that alexithymia, and especially the externally oriented thinking subscale of the TAS-20, was related to social detachment and unconcern for others (Vanheule *et al.*, in review). The outpatients with poor metacognitive self-monitoring proved to be less concerned about social processes and had a poor range of mental representations in relation to social processes. In two studies mapping central relationship patterns that pervade self–other interactions through detailed coding of clinical interviews, the same pattern of detachment was observed. One study examined psychiatric outpatients (Vanheule *et al.*, 2007c) and the other chronic fatigue patients (Vanheule *et al.*, 2007d). In both cases the Core Conflictual Relationships Theme (CCRT) method was used (Luborsky and Crits-Christoph, 1998). This method maps the wishes and intentions that pervade people's interactions; their subjective perceptions of how the other responds in relation to them; and their own typical responses to the other. In these studies we observed that alexithymia is related to a double interpersonal indifference: not much is expected from others, nor is there a personal urge felt to fulfil the expectations of others.

The observation that social detachment is associated with alexithymia indicates that alexithymic patients avoid interaction with others, but leaves us with the question as to why. A plausible hypothesis is that alexithymic patients have problems in 'mentalization'. By mentalization we refer to the ability by which people 'read' and understand the minds of others, such that their actions can be framed as meaningful and predictable (Fonagy *et al.*, 2002). A normal capacity for mentalization enables people to react to others' actions in flexible and adaptive ways; it gives them the capacity to account for others' immediately observable actions in terms of mental state constructs (e.g. in terms of desires or beliefs). Poor mentalization implies that others are an enigma rather than knowable, and that interacting with them is strange and unpredictable rather than agreeable. We suggest that the tendency of alexithymic patients to withdraw from others can be interpreted as an effect of their poor mentalization. To the extent that others are blank entities, alexithymic persons will not solicit them, hence their distant attitude. If others persist in their attempt to obtain a deeper connection, these attempts can have a destabilizing effect. On the other hand, the cold or distant attitude that these patients display may result in rejecting reactions by the therapist, who no longer wants to work with them. The patient of Nemiah and Sifeos (1970) and their own reactions to this type of patient illustrate both points.

Research on the topic of mentalization and mind reading in alexithymia is still in its infancy. We believe that it constitutes an important line of research that may connect two related fields of research. It may also lead to a more holistic understanding of metacognitive functioning in relation to self and others (Dimaggio *et al.*, 2008). Our finding that alexithymic individuals have less concern about social processes compared to non-alexithymic individuals and a poor range of mental representations concerning social processes indicates this connection (Vanheule *et al.*, in review). Research on emotional awareness, for its part, indicates that awareness of one's own emotions tends to be proportional to having awareness of others' emotions: complex representations of one's own emotions usually lead to complex representations of others' emotions; poor representations of one's own emotions tend to correlate with poor representations of others' emotions (Lane *et al.*, 1990; Lane, 2008). Nevertheless, the connection between mentalization and alexithymia needs to be tested more explicitly.

Guttman and Laporte (2002) observed that alexithymia is inversely related to the capacity for empathy. The authors used self-report data from patients with anorexia and borderline personality disorder and their parents. Alexithymic individuals differed from non-alexithymic individuals in that they had more problems in perspective taking (the cognitive capacity to see things from the perspective of the other) and empathic concern (the tendency to experience the affective reaction of sympathy, concern and compassion for other people undergoing negative experiences), while experiencing more feelings of distress and discomfort in witnessing other people's negative experiences. These results point to problems with mentalization, and support the clinically formulated idea that alexithymic persons have a marked vulnerability for tense interpersonal situations. Moriguchi and colleagues (2006) confirmed this finding in a study that compared alexithymic to non-alexithymic college students. These researchers observed that alexithymic participants perform worse in a theory of mind task that makes an appeal to mentalization. By means of fMRI they also examined brain activity during the execution of this theory of mind task. They detected that in the alexithymic group neural activity in the medial prefrontal cortex (the brain area concerned with the representation of mental states) was decreased. These results suggest that a common component like perspective taking, reflective awareness or mind-mindedness is involved in both alexithymia and mentalization. In both alexithymia and poor mentalization, interpreting inner states through vague cues (physiological signs in case of alexithymia and ambiguous visual or auditory information in case of mentalization) poses a problem. Meins *et al.* (2008) further studied alexithymia and mind-mindedness in students. Starting from a task that evokes stories about others, these authors coded whether participants were mindful to other people's experiences and examined whether this score was related to alexithymia. It was observed that the more alexithymic a person is, and particularly the more strongly a person's tendency towards externally oriented thinking is, the more likely it is that this person will not describe or explain the behaviour of other people in terms of internal states.

Early theoretical considerations

Current research in alexithymia rarely builds upon theoretical models. The a-theoretical starting point of Nemiah and Sifeos seems to have paved the way. This might be a reason why the link between alexithymia, interpersonal functioning and mentalization is studied so infrequently. This is surprising since most of the theoretical models that were developed on the topic of alexithymia touch on interpersonal issues.

Henri Krystal (1979) and Joyce McDougall (1974), two psychoanalysts and pioneers of clinical alexithymia studies, formulated ideas on the connection between the mental and interpersonal functioning of alexithymic patients. Building on Freud's metapsychological theory on the binding of somatic sensations to mental representations, Krystal (1979) proposed an ontogenetic model of affect development that connects alexithymic patients' affective problems to their cognitive style of operational thinking and their detached interpersonal functioning. He regards alexithymia as the consequence of a failure or arrest in affective development. Two crucial steps in human affect development that Krystal discerns are affect differentiation and affect verbalization. Krystal (1979) argues that emotions are primarily manifested as undifferentiated pleasurable or painful somatic sensations that respectively evoke a state of contentment or distress in the child. A child experiences these primitive affects as overwhelming, which might lead to abreaction by means of physical action. Yet the appropriate method of mastering these affective experiences is through the mental act of verbalization. By naming, somatic sensations are gradually 'de-somatized' and turned into differentiated mental representations.

Krystal and McDougall placed the problem in the mental encoding of somatic arousal in a broader affect-regulatory framework that is essentially interpersonal in nature. McDougall (1974) attributes a crucial role to the maternal function early in human development. She indicates that it is of crucial importance that mothering caregivers are available for a child and that they give meaning to the inner experiences an infant communicates non-verbally. If mothers fail to fulfil their function as a shield against the various stimuli to which a baby is subjected, the process of naming is not properly developed. This will inhibit the child's capacity to acquire meaning in relation to what he experiences and to attach psychical representations to his impulses. Krystal (1978) argues that mothering caregivers also have a role in permitting the child to mentally bear affective tension. A caregiver not only gives names to a child's affective experience, but also provides the child with an example of how affective responses can be regulated within the context of certain norms for affective expression. Conversely, in cases where these mothering roles are not or only partially occupied, a state of psychic trauma may develop. If emotions are not differentiated or verbalized, reflective self-awareness of emotions will likewise be poor. As a result the child will remain in a blank intrapsychic world. Typical for alexithymia is that the inner void becomes filled by a preoccupation with details from external reality, hence the so-called operational way of living. In cases where the affective life remains largely somatic and undifferentiated, emotion will fail to supply 'colour' to experience and memory, hence the result that others experience them as cold and unemotional in social contexts (Krystal, 1979).

Illustrative in this respect is the case of Karen, a chronically fatigued young woman who consults one of the authors. Her fatigue started in a context of strong emotional burdens and stress, by which she hardly seemed to be affected. In a short period of time her parents divorced; her mother with whom she still lived engaged in a new and turbulent relationship that finally fell through; her brother developed cancer; and she broke up with her boyfriend. Remarkable is that Karen did not complain about any of these events, which she described in neutral terms. For example, during the course of his disease she constantly took care of her brother: she visited him in hospital, nursed him at home, and combined these activities with her full-time job. Her mother, conversely, seemed to be emotionally distant from the whole situation and appeared hardly involved. The mother's apparent lack of concern affected her brother deeply: he told Karen several times that the situation weighed on him, and even declared that his cancer was caused by the emotional distress in the family. However, she reported the details of the whole situation without showing any signs of distress. At the time she obviously acted in an operational way, and likewise, there are no verbal or non-verbal indications of distress in her current account of the situation either. The therapeutic mistake that is easily made with a patient like this is that one could consider her as fundamentally unable to relate to others or as unmotivated, which would be most counterproductive as it would reinforce the patient's initial failure to recognize or name their subjective reactions. What the treatment of alexithymic individuals needs is patience, and a therapist who can offer the opportunity to get in touch their subjectivity. In the case of Karen, for example, the therapist repeatedly expressed his surprise that despite the events this woman went through she was not mournful; he noted that many other people would indeed express displeasure. She initially reacted to this comment with indifference, but it finally brought her to express elements of dissatisfaction. Via outbursts of tears she gradually came to tell stories of events that affected and hurt her.

Later theoretical developments

Later theoretical models, such as Lane and Schwartz's emotional awareness theory (1987; Lane, 2008), Bucci's multiple code theory (1997a, 1997b), and Verhaeghe's theory of actualpathology (2002; Verhaeghe *et al.*, 2007) further elaborate Krystal's basic idea that alexithymia is essentially a problem in the binding of affective arousal to mental representations.

Lane and Schwartz (1987) elaborate this idea within a Piagetian developmental framework, and argue that emotional awareness is a cognitive skill that develops in a stage-like way. The authors discern five stages in affective development, which range from awareness of sensations of emotional arousal, to the creation of increasingly complex cognitive emotional schemas: 'The five levels of emotional awareness in ascending order are awareness of physical sensations, action tendencies, single emotions, blends of emotions, and blends of blends of emotional experience (the capacity to appreciate complexity in the experiences of self and other)' (Lane, 2008: 216). This model has received substantial neurological support. An interesting feature of this model is that it considers awareness of one's own emotions and awareness of the emotions from others as two parallel processes. However, the authors do not sufficiently explain how this parallel should be understood.

Bucci's multiple code theory and Verhaeghe's theory of actualpathology are in this respect more explanatory. Both authors link the problem of mentally encoding affective arousal to recent findings from attachment theory. This accounts for the association between alexithymia and attachment difficulties. The original emphasis of early attachment theory was on the infantile attachment style and its determining effects on adult relationships. However, nowadays several authors reformulated the goal of attachment as consisting of the creation of a symbolic representational system through which affect regulation, the development of a self and the development of capacities to mentalize the mind of others (Fonagy *et al.*, 2002; Lemche *et al.*, 2004; Verhaeghe *et al.*, 2007) is developed. Attachment theorists have found substantial empirical support for the idea that identity arises through the caregiver's mirroring of the child's internal experiences of arousal whereby affect regulation is acquired (Fonagy *et al.*, 2002). In moments of distress the infant performs attachment behaviour, such as proximity-seeking and proximity-maintaining, in an effort of self-preservation and protection. In response to this appeal, caregivers will react by 'mirroring' the child's distress. This means that the caregiver will mentally process the infant's state-expressive behaviour, interpret it, and typically react to it in a soothing and regulating way. Through this interaction with the caregiver, automatic primary affects are transformed into differentiated representations. Adults transfer these representations to the child as an adequate mirror for the child's distress. During this process a representational system is created which permits the child to gradually acknowledge and master its own bodily arousal. However, for this to occur, the other's mirroring must meet a number of conditions. Fonagy and colleagues (2002) indicate that mirroring must be congruent (but not identical) with the emotional state of distress in the child. The mirroring of the child's experience in a modulated form makes this experience manageable. On the other hand, it is important that the child realizes that the reaction of the other is not real, but merely a reflection of the child's inner state. This occurs through 'marking', which is an exaggerated parental imitation of the child's experienced emotions. This finally results in the child's construction of a separate second-order representation of the primary somatic and affective experience, which has the effect of making this experience manageable. In other words: through the internalization of representations coming from significant others, arousal becomes regulated, and simultaneously by acquiring representations a mental map of the other is created (see also Verhaeghe *et al.*, 2007).

The models by Bucci (1997a, 1997b) and Verhaeghe (2002; Verhaeghe *et al.*, 2007) further elaborate the idea on the binding of arousal, and integrate it in a non-linear model of cognitive-emotional functioning (Bucci) or of the process of subject-formation (Verhaeghe). In contrast to the earlier linear theories, Bucci (1997a, 1997b) argues that the subsymbolic processing of emotions is not abandoned when verbal and logical processing is acquired. The author states that before sensory arousal experiences can be connected to language, connections with specific non-verbal imagery of emotions are necessary. In Bucci's opinion alexithymia reflects a problem in making connections or 'referential links' between non-symbolic emotional arousal, non-verbal imagery of emotions, and verbal cognitive schemata (Bucci, 1997b). Consequently the problem of alexithymia might reflect difficulties in connecting basic mental images to subsymbolic somatic arousal sensations, as well as difficulties in connecting a verbal code to these nonverbal representations of emotion. The effect of poor referential linking is that arousal will not be encoded optimally, and will be expressed at a visceral, somatic, motoric or sensory level. This may form the pathway in which an alexithymic condition could manifest (Taylor *et al.*, 1997).

In his theory of subject-formation, Verhaeghe stresses the socially mediated role of representation-building (Verhaeghe, 2002; Verhaeghe *et al.*, 2007). Representations (constituted through imagery and language) are seen as the most stable ways to master somatic arousal and are acquired through interaction with others, especially within close attachment relationships. In the wake of adopting these representations, a template for social bonding and a set of beliefs and expectations with regard to others is created. If an appeal to someone's representational system is made, the relational template, as well as the set of expectations and beliefs, will be actualized. In a case of alexithymia blankness is pivotal at all of these levels. The power of this model is that it enables us to understand the metacognitive self-monitoring typical for alexithymia to problems in the metacognitive monitoring of others, as well as to typical relationship patterns that emerge each time an appeal to metacognitive monitoring is made.

Conclusion

Research investigating the interpersonal functioning of alexithymic patients took several years to commence. Both clinical and empirical research demonstrates that distance-taking tendencies and vulnerability to conflict and emotionally tense situations are typical for alexithymia. We believe that the theories by Bucci and Verhaeghe are the most comprehensive and interesting frameworks for understanding these interrelations and their association with problems in mentalization. Future research must closely examine the relation between alexithymia, interpersonal problems and mentalization. In this chapter we hopefully demonstrated the relation between these phenomena, yet for the time being research investigating this is scarce. As these concepts are complex, we recommend the use of refined and clinically-based approaches for future research.

References

Bagby, R. M., Parker, J. D. A. and Taylor, G. J. (1994a). The twenty-item Toronto Alexithymia Scale – I. Item selection and cross-validation of the factor structure. *Journal of Psychosomatic Research*, *38*, 23–32.

Bagby, R. M., Taylor, G. J. and Parker, J. D. A. (1994b). The twenty-item Toronto Alexithymia Scale – II. Convergent, discriminant, and concurrent validity. *Journal of Psychosomatic Research*, *38*, 33–40.

Bagby, R. M., Taylor, G. J., Parker, J. D. A. and Dickens, S. E. (2006). The development of the Toronto Structured Interview for Alexithymia: Item selection, factor structure, reliability and concurrent validity. *Psychotherapy and Psychosomatics*, *75*, 25–39.

Bucci, W. (1997a). *Psychoanalyis and cognitive science*. New York: Guilford Press.

Bucci, W. (1997b). Symptoms and symbols: A multiple code theory of somatization. *Psychoanalytic Inquiry*, *17*, 151–172.

De Rick, A. and Vanheule, S. (2007). Alexithymia and DSM-IV personality disorder traits in alcoholic inpatients: A study of the relation between both constructs. *Personality and Individual differences*, *43*(1), 119–129.

Dimaggio, G., Semerari, A., Carcione, A., Nicolò, G. and Procacci, M. (2007). *Psychotherapy of personality disorders: Metacognition, states of minds and interpersonal cycles*. London: Routledge.

Dimaggio, G., Lysaker, P., Carcione, A., Nicolò, G. and Semerari, A. (2008). Know yourself and you shall know the other . . . to a certain extent: multiple paths of influence of self-reflection on mindreading. *Consciousness and Cognition*, *17*, 778–789.

Fonagy, P., Gergely, G., Jurist, E. and Target, M. (2002). *Affect regulation, mentalization and the development of self*. New York: Other Press.

Grabe, H. J., Frommer, J., Ankerhold, A., Ulrich, C., Groeger, R., Franke, G. H., *et al.* (2008). Alexithymia and outcome in psychotherapy. *Psychotherapy and Psychosomatics*, *77*, 189–194.

Guttman, H. and Laporte, L. (2002). Alexithymia, empathy, and psychological symptoms in a family context. *Comprehensive Psychiatry*, *43*, 448–455.

Horowitz, L. M., Alden, L. E., Wiggins, J. S. and Pincus, A. L. (2000). *Inventory of interpersonal problems. Manual*. London: Psychological Corporation.

Krystal, H. (1978). Trauma and affects. *Psychoanalytic Study of the Child*, *33*, 81–116.

Krystal, H. (1979). Alexithymia and psychotherapy. *American Journal of Psychotherapy*, *33*, 17–31.

Lane, R. D. (2008). Neural substrates of implicit and explicit emotional processes: A unifying framework for psychosomatic medicine. *Psychosomatic Medicine*, *70*, 214–231.

Lane, R., Quilan, D., Schwartz, G., Walker, P. and Zeitlin, S. (1990). The levels of emotional awareness scale: A cognitive-developmental measure of emotion. *Journal of Personality Assessment*, *55*, 124–134.

Lane, R. and Schwartz, G. (1987). Levels of emotional awareness: a cognitive-developmental theory and its application to psychopathology. *American Journal of Psychiatry*, *144*, 133–143.

Lemche, E., Klann-Delius, G., Koch, R. and Joraschky, P. (2004). Mentalizing language development in a longitudinal attachment sample: Implications for alexithymia. *Psychotherapy and Psychosomatics*, *73*, 366–374.

Luborsky, L. and Crits-Christoph, P. (1998). *Understanding transference*. Washington: American Psychological Association.

Lumley, M. A., Neely, L. C. and Burger, A. J. (2007). The assessment of alexithymia in medical settings: Implications for understanding and treating health problems. *Journal of Personality Assessment*, *89*, 230–246.

McDougall, J. (1974). The psychosoma and the psychoanalytic process. *International Review of Psycho-Analysis*, *1*, 437–459.

Mallinckrodt, B., King, J. L. and Coble, H. M. (1998). Family dysfunction, alexithymia, and client attachment to therapist. *Journal of Counseling Psychology*, *45*, 497–504.

Marty, P. (1980). *Les mouvements individuels de vie et de mort – Vol. 2, L'Ordre psychosomatique* [The individual movements of life and death – Vol. 2, The psychosomatic order]. Paris: Payot.

Marty, P., de M'Uzan, M. and David, C. (1963). *L'investigation psychosomatique* [Psychosomatic investigation]. Paris: Presses Universitaires de France.

Meganck, R., Vanheule, S. and Desmet, M. (2008). Factorial validity and measurement invariance of the 20-item Toronto Alexithymia Scale in clinical and nonclinical samples. *Assessment*, *15*, 36–47.

Meins, E., Harris-Waller, J. and Lloyd, A. (2008). Understanding alexithymia: Associations with peer attachment style and mind-mindedness. *Personality and Individual Differences*, *45*, 146–152.

Mitrani, J. (1995). Toward an understanding of unmentalized experience. *Psychoanalytic Quarterly*, *64*, 68–112.

Moriguchi, Y., Ohnishi, T., Lane, R. D., Maeda, M., Mori, T., Nemoto, K., *et al.* (2006). Impaired self-awareness and theory of mind: An fMRI study of mentalizing in alexithymia. *Neuroimage*, *32*, 1472–1482.

Nemiah, J. C. and Sifeos, P. E. (1970). Psychosomatic illness: A problem in communication. *Psychotherapy and Psychosomatics*, *18*, 154–160.

Ogrodniczuk, J. S., Piper, W. E. and Joyce, A. S. (2005). The negative effect of alexithymia on the outcome of group therapy for complicated grief: What role might the therapist play? *Comprehensive Psychiatry*, *46*, 206–213.

Scheidt, C. E., Waller, E., Schnock, C., Becker-Stoll, F., Zimmermann, P, Lücking, C. H., *et al.* (1999). Alexithymia and attachment representation in idiopathic spasmodic torticollis. *Journal of Nervous and Mental Disease*, *187*, 47–52.

Spitzer C., Sieble-Jürges, U., Barnow, S., Grabe, H. J. and Freyberger, H. J. (2005). Alexithymia and interpersonal problems. *Psychotherapy and Psychosomatics*, *74*, 240–246.

Taylor, G. J., Bagby, R. M. and Parker, J. D. A. (1997). *Disorders of affect regulation. Alexithymia in medical and psychiatric illness*. Cambridge: Cambridge University Press.

Vanheule, S. (2008). Challenges for alexithymia research: A commentary on 'The construct of alexithymia: associations with defence mechanisms.' *Journal of Clinical Psychology*, *64*, 332–337.

Vanheule, S., Desmet, M., Meganck, R. and Bogaerts, S. (2007a). Alexithymia and interpersonal problems. *Journal of Clinical Psychology*, *63*, 109–117.

Vanheule, S., Desmet, M., Verhaeghe, P. and Bogaerts, S. (2007b). Alexithymic depression: Evidence for a depression subtype? *Psychotherapy and Psychosomatics*, *76*, 135–136.

Vanheule, S., Desmet, M., Rosseel, Y., Verhaeghe, P. and Meganck, R. (2007c). Relationship patterns in alexithymia: A study using the Core Conflictual Relationship Theme (CCRT) method. *Psychopathology*, *40*, 14–21.

Vanheule, S., Vandenbergen, J., Desmet, M., Rosseel, Y. and Inslegers, R. (2007d). Alexithymia and core conflictual relationship themes: A study in a chronically fatigued primary care population. *International Journal of Psychiatry in Medicine*, *37*, 87–98.

Vanheule, S., Meganck, R. and Desmet, M. (in review). Alexithymia, social relating and mental processing: An explorative study.

Verhaeghe, P. (2002). *On being normal and other disorders: A manual for clinical psychodiagnostics*. New York: Other Press.

Verhaeghe, P., Vanheule, S. and De Rick, A. (2007). Actual neurosis as the underlying psychic structure of panic disorder, somatization, and somatoform disorder: An integration of Freudian and attachment perspectives. *Psychoanalytic Quarterly*, *76*, 1317–1350.

Weinryb, R. M., Gustavsson, J. P., Hellström, C., Andersson, E., Broberg, A. and Rylander, G. (1996). Interpersonal problems and personality characteristics: Psychometric studies of the Swedish version of the IIP. *Personality and Individual Differences*, *20*, 13–23.

Chapter 11

Different profiles of metacognitive dysfunctions in personality disorders

Livia Colle, Stefania D'Angerio, Raffaele Popolo and Giancarlo Dimaggio

Patients with personality disorder (PD) show a variety of difficulties in interpersonal relationships. They acknowledge their own desires and intentions, or fail to take others' perspective, and therefore they cannot successfully manage conflicting interactions. Metacognitive (or mentalizing) dysfunction seems to underlie the social impairments that are typical of PDs (Fonagy *et al.*, 2002; Bateman and Fonagy, 2004; Semerari *et al.*, 2007). The lack of a nuanced mental state understanding makes these patients unable to face subjective psychological suffering, to modulate interpersonal behaviour according to its ever-changing demands and to solve complex psychological problems.

Metacognitive impairments also affect the therapeutic process because the therapeutic relationship, as in any interpersonal process, requires good metacognitive capacities in order to be effective (Semerari, this volume, Chapter 16). For example, it is known that patients with alexithymia have poorer psychotherapy outcome (Vanheule *et al.*, this volume, Chapter 10). This seems to be mediated by the reduced ability of these patients to describe positive emotions and by the consequent loss of motivation on the part of the psychotherapist, leading towards a poorer therapeutic alliance (Ogrodniczuk *et al.*, 2005). Because of the low emotional involvement therapist and patient are distant from each other, and this results in a weak bond.

This chain effect leads us to consider metacognitive impairments as a core problem in PDs, and, therefore, their improvement is one of the major goals in psychotherapy. As extensively shown in this volume, metacognition is a multifaceted skill and includes a number of specific abilities interacting with each other (Dimaggio and Lysaker, this volume, Introduction), which can operate separately and which can be selectively damaged. For example, a patient could be unable to understand the cause for a depressive episode but still be capable of inferring a colleague's mood from her emotional expressions. Another patient might understand what causes his personal feelings but be unable to understand the covert intentions guiding others' behaviours. Therefore, a current research challenge concerning metacognitive impairments in PDs is to understand the relationship between different metacognitive dysfunctions and specific PDs.

Even though metacognitive or mentalizing dysfunctions in PDs are considered relevant by many authors (Choi-Kain and Gunderson, 2008), several questions remain unanswered:

1 Whether selective impairments in different aspects of metacognition can be found – for example, an impairment in understanding others' mental states in presence of good self-reflection. Preliminary data support the existence of a variety of metacognitive disorders within PDs (Semerari *et al.*, 2003, 2007), but such a hypothesis still needs to be tested in different PDs.
2 Whether different profiles of metacognitive dysfunction in different PDs can be identified. We will show, through clinical material and experimental results, that impaired metacognition can show in diversified clinical pictures, though with lower correlations between the patterns of metacognitive dysfunction and different PDs formerly hypothesized (Semerari *et al.*, 2007). Therefore, we will provide some possible explanations of these unexpected results.
3 Whether the severity of the metacognitive impairment could be related to the severity of the overall personality pathology (as defined for example by the total number of PD criteria met).

We discuss each of these questions in the next paragraphs. To do so we review research on PDs and provide a clinical picture of metacognitive disorders through transcripts of psychotherapy sessions and metacognitive interviews. We finally hint at implications on the therapy process of PDs, a topic covered in other parts of this volume (Dimaggio *et al.*, Chapter 15; Semerari, Chapter 16).

Different metacognitive functions and selective damages in PD

Clinical reports list and describe, often using different labels, a number of metacognitive impairments in PDs, thus portraying a complex and fragmented picture. We discuss here research from various sources on some PDs to show how the same impairment can be shared between different diagnoses and how, within the same diagnosis, different dysfunctions can be manifested.

Persons with narcissistic personality disorder (NPD) and avoidant personality disorder (APD) are described, for example, as impaired in identifying their own emotions – i.e. are alexithymic (Vanheule *et al.*, this volume, Chapter 10) – and in understanding their eliciting factors (Dimaggio *et al.*, 2007a). Persons with narcissism have further difficulties in accessing their own need of interpersonal relationships (Kernberg, 1975). Patients with narcissistic and avoidant PD actively try to keep negative thoughts and feelings out of their awareness. This then results in emptiness and alexithymia (Millon, 1981). However, poor emotional awareness is not the only metacognitive impairment in these patients. Avoidant PD patients, for example, show difficulties referring their automatic thoughts and assuming a critical attitude towards these thoughts (Beck *et al.*, 1990). These patients can, at least to a certain extent, identify feelings and beliefs but they actively strive to keep their emotions, both positive and negative, out of consciousness (Taylor *et al.*, 2004).

Moreover, both avoidant and narcissistic patients seem to have problems inferring the mental states underlying others' behaviour (Dimaggio *et al.*, 2007b; Lawson *et al.*, 2008). Their difficulty in analysing interpersonal exchange in terms of emotions and intentions makes their interpretation of relationships rigid, egocentric and scarcely empathic. A lack of empathic concern and an impairment in adopting the other's point of view have also been suggested to be present in the antisocial spectrum, from conduct disorders to psychopathy (Dolan and Fullam, 2007). Even in those persons, lack of empathy has been associated with worse performance at recognizing some specific negative emotions, especially sadness and fear (Blair *et al.*, 2004).

However, most of the experimental findings in this field have focused on borderline personality disorder (BPD). These patients display subtle dysfunctions in interpreting complex emotional facial expressions and present a bias toward over-attribution of fear and slower performance in recognizing surprise (Minzenberg *et al.*, 2006; Domes *et al.*, 2008). This impairment was associated with interpersonal antagonism, particularly suspiciousness and impulsiveness.

High emotional arousal seems to reduce borderline PD patients' ability to mentalize (Bateman and Fonagy, 2004). The specific context of attachment relationships is supposed to disrupt borderline's mentalization and to induce characteristic mental processes such as psychic equivalence and pretend mode. Psychic equivalence refers to difficulties in distinguishing between fantasy and reality and a suspension of the 'as if' dimension by which everything appears to be real. This dysfunction does not allow for any possible alternative interpretation of mental events. Persons with borderline PD might fancy, for example, that the absence of an expected phone call is a clear signal of the partner abandoning or betraying them.

In the pretend mode thoughts and feelings are perceived as dissociated and decontextualized and it is almost impossible for the patients to find meaning in them. The metacognitive dysfunctions in borderline PD are related to interpersonal disturbances. Patients hold rigid schemas of others' behaviour and mental states and use them to construct extreme and unrealistic representations that cannot be corrected by the communicative signals they receive (Bateman and Fonagy, 2004). These rigid interpersonal schema make it impossible for borderline patients to attribute nuanced meanings to changes in the interpersonal world. For example, if at a certain moment a partner is gentle he can be perceived as 'all good', but if a few minutes later he is concentrating on his work and does not pay attention he is suddenly perceived as a 'persecutor', without any memory of the former representation. This makes the relationship continuously strained by the abruptly changing attitudes these persons have towards others. Finally, the polarized 'good/bad' representations make them unable to make sense of what appears to be an inconsistent representation of the shifting relationships (Clarkin *et al.*, 2006; Semerari, this volume, Chapter 16).

Summing up, alexithymia, lack of distinction between fantasy and reality, poor integration, poor mindreading and lack of empathy are among the metacognitive impairments affecting PDs, supporting the hypothesis of a multifaceted metacognitive disorder in PDs. Such components seem to affect PDs differently: that is, with narcissistic or avoidant patients being more impaired in recognizing inner states and borderline PD patients able to describe emotions but unable to take critical distance from their states. Therefore, a second question that arises is whether specific metacognitive profiles can be detected in different PDs.

Different profiles in PDs

In order to track different dysfunctions in PD sufferers, a model of metacognitive disorders has been proposed in which part of the metacognitive system, or in some cases the system as a whole, can be damaged (Dimaggio and Lysaker, this volume, Introduction). This hypothesis has been mostly investigated through single-case process research, using the Metacognition Assessment Scale (MAS; Semerari *et al.*, 2003). The MAS assesses metacognition as manifest in individuals' verbalizations and detects its fluctuations over the course of psychotherapy. MAS focuses on three domains of metacognition: *awareness of one's own mind*, *awareness of the mind of the other* and *mastery* or the ability to use one's own knowledge of mental states to cope with stressors and solve interpersonal problems and conflicts. A second research tool has been recently developed, the Metacognitive Assessment Interview (MAI), a semi-structured interview eliciting life narratives and allowing a quick assessment of metacognition (Semerari *et al.*, 2008).

We provide here examples of various metacognitive impairments in the patients' discourse, using session transcripts or interviews, in order to offer a taste of their multifaceted phenomenology. The excerpts will vividly show how a network of dysfunctions works in PDs, with one dysfunction triggering another. We will describe each component and provide clinical examples for each impairment. Two subfunctions, differentiation and mastery, will be described in the same section since the patient's transcript showed evidence for both.

Monitoring of inner states

Monitoring concerns the ability to detect and refer to an addressee one's own thoughts and emotions. Patients suffering from a monitoring disorder appear unable to provide emotional descriptions of events and to understand the eliciting factors for their experience. Narratives typically describe facts, with only vague references to mental states, and as a result their minds appear opaque – and their behaviours decontextualized – both to themselves and to others. A sense of emptiness and social withdrawal might be created by monitoring disorders, as well as emotional dysregulation and impulsiveness.

Sandra is a 39-year-old woman diagnosed with avoidant PD and depressive PD, with dependent and passive-aggressive traits and a widespread personality dysfunction – 20 SCID-II criteria met (Structured Clinical Interview for *DSM-IV-TR* Axis II Personality Disorders) – who came to psychotherapy for a depression following an unexpected divorce. During the MAI she refers to a recent depressive episode in connection with the time when her new boyfriend, whom she met a few months after her divorce, told her he was not fully in love with her anymore, and he apologized if he gave her a different impression.

Sandra: I felt as if all my world was breaking down, since I believed I was important for him.

Interviewer: What emotions did you feel when he said that?

Sandra: I didn't have a clue. His attitude was the opposite until then. He seemed in love with me, so when he said that, many things came to my mind. Maybe I might have misunderstood him. I don't even remember what I thought. I was disappointed. I was wondering how it was possible to behave like he did and then say what he said.

Interviewer: You said you were hurt, disappointed. Could you explain to me these feelings a bit more? What did you feel?

Sandra: I don't know, I can't explain. I was feeling bad. I felt refused, as if I had already lost that person.

Interviewer: What did you think in that moment?

Sandra: I could not understand how it was possible. I don't know. . . but I was quite confused. I was wondering whether it was my fault, whether I misinterpreted his behaviour, or whether I was too involved and he wasn't.

Interviewer: What was the link between the emotions you described and your thoughts?

Sandra: I don't know.

Interviewer: You said: 'I was hurt, disappointed' and you thought 'I cannot understand, how is this possible?' How can you put together your feelings and your thoughts?

Sandra: I have no idea of a link between them. I felt that and I thought that, I don't know if there is any link between them.

Sandra finds it difficult to describe emotional nuances. She only mentions that she felt disappointed but seems unable to mention more specific emotions. In other parts of the transcript she remained concentrated on her boyfriend's behaviour, unable to focus on herself. However, the most relevant disorder here is what we call *relations among variables*, that is, the ability to understand the psychological links between thoughts, affects and behaviours. When the interviewer focuses on the relationship between emotion and thought, Sandra identifies her thoughts but cannot tell how those elicited her feelings, so she cannot tell why she was disappointed and hurt.

The MAI of Luca, a 29-year-old soldier diagnosed with narcissistic PD, provides another example of poor self-monitoring. He came to psychotherapy after he moved back to a big town referring to 'a lack of self-confidence which causes chain reactions in many aspects of my life . . . I need to make some changes'. At the beginning of psychotherapy he described himself as confused about his goals and pessimistic about his future.

Luca: In September I got closer to my ex-girlfriend. Everything seemed to be going well and this was recharging for me. Now all falls down and I'm naked, it has been worse than last year. . .

Interviewer: Do you remember a specific episode with your girlfriend?

Luca: It was a weekend we should not have seen each other. She was busy at the university. But I had been sent to her town for work; I took this opportunity and asked her to meet up. She said she didn't know. I called her the day after insisting on having a rendezvous and she said she was busy and reacted very badly.

Interviewer: How did you feel?

Luca: I don't know how I felt. I was astonished, feeling bad, I cannot find now a specific word. I couldn't even reply immediately, I've spent ten minutes without knowing what to say and what to do.

Interviewer: Did you remember what you felt reading the text message?

Luca: It was a shock, I cannot find the words now, it was a supershock, I was feeling bad.

Interviewer: Do you remember a specific feeling?

Luca: I was feeling bad, I did not understand what was going on, I had to stop.

Interviewer: Why did you feel like that?

Luca: I didn't think it could . . . maybe I have overestimated that.

Interviewer: What exactly?

Luca: I have been a bit pushy; in my opinion she could have reacted differently, she exaggerated.

Luca cannot find the words to describe his feelings, nor can the interviewer infer them, no matter how intense and painful they were. The interviewer unsuccessfully strives to elicit descriptions beyond 'bad' and 'astonished'. In this transcript Luca also does not grasp the link between the event and his negative feelings. Luca's monitoring seems even poorer than Sandra's, since he failed to identify basic emotions, whereas Sandra was able to refer at to least some emotions, though she still could not grasp the events that triggered those emotions. Of note, a mastery deficit was evident in the excerpt, with Luca paralyzed by the situation and his lack of recognition of inner states, thus unable even to think about a course of action that might be started to change the state of affairs.

Differentiation between fantasy and reality and mastery

Differentiation refers to the ability to attribute mental contents to the right mode of thought, that is, distinguishing feelings experienced in a dream or in memories from the past from the tingeing everyday experiences. It also includes the capacity to adopt different perspectives on aspects of social life.

Differentiation disorders emerged in all four borderline PD patients whose first year therapy transcripts were analysed with the MAS (Semerari *et al.*, 2005). Moments of poor functioning tended to decrease during therapy in all four patients. Those patients could successfully monitor but could neither distinguish their fantasies from external reality nor question their own judgement. Paranoid PD patients also show severe problems in differentiation. They think people are deceiving, humiliating or attacking them and almost never look at their dysfunctional beliefs with a doubtful attitude (Dimaggio *et al.*, 2007b). These results support the idea that different metacognitive functions can be selectively damaged in PDs.

Another aspect of metacognition, which we name mastery, is the ability to use psychological knowledge to solve social problems and to cope with problematic experiences. Poor mastery emerged in all 18 patients' therapy transcripts analysed with MAS. Mastery was severely damaged and even when patients became able to paint detailed pictures of their own and others' mental states they barely used such knowledge to change the course of their life or to feel better (Carcione *et al.*, in press).

Both differentiation and mastery dysfunctions emerged clearly in Grace's MAI, a 28-year-old woman diagnosed with borderline PD with subthreshold narcissistic PD and obsessive-compulsive PD. She asked for psychotherapy to soothe her longstanding anxiety. She came to the first meeting with a friend because she could not move alone. She felt anxious in many circumstances, scared of making any decision, of losing control or becoming ill. She complained that she was anxious when she was away from her family. During the MAI she described how she had an anxiety crisis while at home on her own one evening when suddenly she felt sick, with stomach ache, tachycardia, tremors and fainting. When she took benzodiazepines those symptoms disappeared, leaving her in a state of undifferentiated negative arousal: 'I was afraid but I didn't know exactly of what.' She felt unable to cope with her problems and could not sleep all night.

Interviewer: Do you remember what you were thinking at that moment?

Grace: I thought I would never be able to feel better, I was scared of getting crazy, of losing control, of not being able to calm down anymore.

Interviewer: In that moment, how much did you believe that those thoughts were a correct picture of reality? Did you consider other interpretations?

Grace: In that moment I believed it 100 per cent. I was sure it was permanent.

Interviewer: Did you consider other hypotheses?

Grace: I was considering even my physical state as associated to my psychological state. I didn't even think I could have some real illness. It was only related to my mind, to my anxiety.

Interviewer: Thinking about it now, does your point of view differ somewhat?

Grace: If I think that right now, when I'm relatively okay, I realize that it was probably less tragic than what I was thinking at that moment. In any case I'm convinced this is a severe problem. It is not 100 per cent real, but I still think it's maybe 90 per cent true.

Interviewer: So you have the impression that that episode was not so dramatic. What leads you to such a different evaluation?

Grace: I realized that if I was really mad or I had a really severe problem, as I believed at that moment, I could not even have handled it as, instead, I did. In my opinion I could not even recognize such a state, nor think about it. I was becoming mad and that's it. I think I have a problem but it is not as severe as I thought at that moment. If I can laugh about it during these five minutes, it might be because I've exaggerated in that moment. This feeling is not consistent, it is not what I think all the time.

Poor differentiation appears when Grace considers her inner feelings as objective events, not as hypotheses. Grace could sometimes take a dialectical attitude towards her own beliefs but this was not a steady acquisition. In particular she is unable to do so when she is anxious, which is her dominant state. Grace also features poor relations among variables, not being able to tell what made her feel scared. Moreover, Grace had severe mastery problems. She felt paralysed, unable to cope with the situation and to figure out a way to overcome her anxiety. Such complex metacognitive dysfunctions carry an important question. What is the relationship between different metacognitive dysfunctions and which dysfunction triggers the others? We contend that Grace's monitoring and mastery impairments were the result of a differentiation disorder. When someone cannot recognize that the course of events is not headed towards catastrophe, it is impossible to find a way to stop the experience of being in a never-ending fall and to reduce the emotional arousal, which in turn leads to confusion and then the inability to keep one's concentration stable enough to discover the subtleties of one's inner world. Moreover, poor differentiation leads to a dramatic drop of mastery. This has been evident during all the therapy where Grace always felt controlled by outside forces, in particular by her mother. When she fell into anxiety states she looked for a friend's help, with only marginal and momentary benefits. She never arrived at considering her ideas subject to change.

Patients with differentiation impairments find it very hard to accept alternative interpretations of events provided by their therapists. They often stick to the matter of facts, refusing the therapist's discrepant perspective. Sometimes they can even be suspicious about the reasons why the therapist is offering a positive interpretation which conflicts with their own. Thus the therapeutic alliance could be profoundly compromised by differentiation impairments. In this volume both Dimaggio and colleagues (Chapter 15) and Semerari (Chapter 16) describe therapeutic techniques and strategies for when and how to overcome this dysfunction. However, differentiation is not the unique metacognitive component that can be selectively damaged and sometimes triggers other impairments.

Integration

Integration regards constructing a bird's eye view of oneself relating with others and solving any inconsistencies among different representations. Integration includes the ability to have a range of goals and action plans and to organize and narrate them in a clear order, according to a hierarchy of relevance, making evident which is the main goal or subplot topic and which are the secondary themes or goals. Integration allows for an understanding of how and why a person has changed over the course of their life.

Integration permits awareness of what caused a shift in states of mind. For example, it allows a person to notice being calm and relaxed while playing with his or her own children and then, suddenly, becoming angry and competitive because of a telephone call from work concerning a conflictual issue. With good integration, states of mind flow into our consciousness maintaining a certain degree of organization and context flexibility. Integration is, therefore, crucial in order to create a coherent narrative of memories and personal events and to pursue consistent goals as the interpersonal context changes.

Integration can be diachronic and synchronic. *Diachronic integration* allows persons to create a coherent mental representation which takes into account different states of mind over time. Keeping a self-representation stable over time allows persons to set context-appropriate actions. For example, it makes it possible for a person to remember that neglecting children's needs because of excessive work commitment leads children in distress, which in turn leads to feeling guilty. Thus, the person might in this example decide to avoid overwhelming deeds in order to spend time with the family.

Synchronic integration refers to the coherence of mental states in a specific moment. This skill is required when we perceive, contemporarily, mutually conflicting states of mind or when thoughts and feelings crowd together in a chaotic way (Dimaggio, 2006). The four borderline PD sufferers analysed with the MAS by Semerari and colleagues (2005) appeared unable to integrate different and contradictory aspects of their relationships with others and to portray a consistent picture of their mental states. This problem was still present, though less severe, at the end of the first year of therapy (see also Davidson *et al.*, 2007). Borderline PD patients have been suggested is exhibiting the most severe integration impairments. The problem in integration was, however, not evident in the four patients with avoidant or narcissistic PD analysed by Dimaggio and colleagues (2007a).

Laura, a 26-year-old medical student, has a very severe overall PD – 37 criteria met – and diagnosed with borderline, dependent, obsessive-compulsive, narcissistic, avoidant PDs (with histrionic and passive-aggressive traits). She asked for therapy because, after the death of her mother, the only member of her family still alive, she had an emotional breakdown. She was unable to study – though incredibly bright and with first-class preparation – had vomiting attacks lasting for days, depression, hypochondria, panic attacks and agoraphobia. In the following excerpt from a session during the end of the first year of therapy, the inability to integrate different representations of self with others and to give a hierarchical order to her narrative – indicating both synchronic and diachronic integration dysfunctions – was evident throughout, together with a severe differentiation dysfunction.

Laura: I am struggling to study, but I can't pass the exam.

Therapist: Why are you saying that? I had the feeling you knew almost everything.

Laura: I can't. I simply can't. I feel sickness is destroying me. I have no dignity at all, I am a terrible failure. I'm so cross with Ambra [a friend 20 years older than Laura] because she denied me the help I needed.

Therapist: Sorry, maybe I missed something. Did you ask her for some help?

Laura: She is so self-centred, she forgets things. I've spent the whole day last week talking with her about her husband's betrayal. I cooked her a soup and soothed her and yesterday I was so frantic, because I had to go to the hospital to sign a document and I have decided to go and buy myself a ring.

Therapist: Why did you do that?

Laura: I have not had a ring for years. Yesterday I was at home with Leonardo [a man 30 years older than Laura with whom she lived and whom she did not love]. It was terrible, everything was grey.

Therapist: In what sense everything was grey?

Laura: [*desperate, she puts her elbows on the desk, clutches the therapist's hand and holds it tightly*] Tell me I won't marry him!

Therapist: I'm not saying you have to marry him!

Laura: Please tell me I won't marry him!

Therapist: Why are you asking me this? Did you feel you ought to marry him?

Laura: I had this dream, a wedding ceremony and he was the spouse. I had a grey suit. I don't want to get married all dressed in grey. Please tell me I won't.

In this touching excerpt, Laura jumped from one theme to another, with no clear links between the different topics. But what drove her to shift from the sense of being unable to pass the exam to the anger of being abandoned by her friend? What was the relation between not being nurtured and the fantasy of a grey wedding? The therapist was puzzled and could not find a focus while Laura jumped from one dysregulated set of emotions and ideas to another. Laura also had a severe differentiation deficit. She could neither distinguish fantasy or a dream from reality – the actual possibility of marrying her partner – nor a wish from a duty. Monitoring was also affected: she could not explain, as in other passages of the session, why she felt the relationship was 'grey'. She was not even able to explain why passing the exam was so impossible for her; she did not justify her sense of being doomed to fail – to date, she had ranked highest in all the exams she had taken before. A mastery deficit is also evident. Laura felt that disembodied forces ruled her life, a dream was able to dictate her future and she was completely passive, thus making desperate requests for help she never felt arrived, remaining powerless and desperate despite the therapist's reassurances.

Again the transcript highlights qualitative different metacognitive dysfunctions, but in addition it shows how often such dysfunctions are intertwined with each other, with poor monitoring, Laura could not describe why she experienced the wedding as 'grey', triggers to poor differentiation. The idea of an obligatory wedding was just a dream, which in turn leads to a mastery deficit, Laura could not cope against a dictate from above. Understanding how specific dysfunctions trigger each other in cases like Laura's is an important issue for future research.

Decentration

Being able to decentre means on the one hand taking into account that others see things differently from ourselves and that many variables affect others' mental states. On the other hand decentration means the ability to recognize that others' thoughts and feelings do not have oneself as the centre of attention. For example, such a function allows a person to understand when their partner's disappointment is probably motivated by a work problem and is not a sign of hostility towards oneself.

Patients with decentring dysfunctions are incapable of questioning their own judgements as to what others think and feel and of using the others' communicative signals to adjust representations of others (Bateman and Fonagy, 2004). PDs tend to interpret others' behaviour according to their own dominant schemas without recognizing they are just holding hypotheses. Being able to decentre also requires some ability to differentiate between one's own ideas and the outside world.

Using MAS decentration Dimaggio and colleagues (2009) have analysed 16 therapy sessions of 14 patients diagnosed with different PDs: four borderline PD, three narcissistic PD, two avoidant PD, two dependent PD, two obsessive-compulsive PD and one paranoid PD. Patients showed difficulty in adopting the other's point of view by standing back from their own, and in grasping that others were driven by motivations independent from the relationship with themselves. On the other hand, the more basic mindreading skill was only occasionally impaired. All patients appeared egocentric but the worst functioning was found in the patient with paranoid personality disorder (PPD). These results suggest that decentration is a widespread dysfunction in PDs, above and beyond damages in a specific PD, though the idea that PPDs function worst still deserves to be investigated.

Poor decentration was a problem in Tommaso, a 35-year-old programming engineer diagnosed for borderline PD with depressive and passive-aggressive traits. Tommaso complained about difficulty in interacting with Maria, a friend who was likely to become his boss at work. One day

Tommaso protested to Maria and her husband that he thought they did not appreciate the help he had given them during difficult circumstances. To overcome the frustration Tommaso started drinking alcohol, and once drunk he began arguing with Maria. During the MAI Tommaso kept saying that he and Maria thought they were very similar.

Therapist: Why do you think your friend had such emotions and thoughts, as far as you know her?

Patient: Because she is like me. Worse, but like me.

Therapist: What do you mean?

Patient: She feels exactly the same, there is a mental connection between us. We understand each other, we do the same things, react in the same way. I do not speak only in terms of alcohol and drugs, or bingeing and vomiting. Well, I do not vomit, while she does. I talk about intensity. There are mental mechanisms which switch on for me and her in the same moments and circumstances. We spot the same people, we are both incredibly seductive, we are . . . I don't know . . . we have an incredible emotional connection.

In this short example Tommaso was unable to distinguish his own interpretation of events from his friend's perspective. He kept saying he knew exactly what she thought and felt, even without speaking. Though recognizing a special link with his friend he is not able to say why she had the same attitude as her husband, nor understand why she disagreed with him. Therefore, his mindreading was poor and in particular not decentred. He also felt he was centre of Maria's ideas, which was evidently not the case in this episode.

The decentration disorder in PDs could be caused by schema-driven attributions that distort the way PD suffereres construct ideas about others. They can portray nuanced pictures of others' minds, but they favour interpretations of others' behaviour as consistent with their own interpersonal schema (Veen and Arntz, 2000), ignoring communicative signals not foreseen by the schemas. Moreover, elements present in the others' minds can be shadowed or distorted by derogatory attitudes, stereotypes or self-serving biases (Dimaggio *et al.*, 2008).

Overall, the relations between specific PD and specific metacognitive dysfunction seem only partially to hold. Research with MAS in psychotherapy transcripts during the first year of therapy (Carcione *et al.*, in press) confirms that selected aspects of metacognition are damaged in PDs. At one end of the spectrum there are PDs mainly featuring poor emotional awareness, such as avoidant PD and narcissistic PD, with others more damaged in the ability to distinguish fantasy from reality and integrate different representations of self with others in the presence of good self-monitoring. However, no consistent diagnosis-specific pattern could be found, with many metacognitive problems disseminated along the PD spectrum.

Moreover, the low number of patients analysed is not representative of each PD. Thus further research is needed to understand how PDs differ in metacognitive competence from one another and to exclude the possibility of specific profiles. Nevertheless, another variable seems to be correlated with metacognitive functions and need to be investigated: the severity of personality pathology.

Metacognition and severity of personality pathology

Our final question concerns the relation between overall metacognitive disorder and severity of personality pathology, as evident in Laura. Preliminary data of 75 patients measured with MAI showed a correlation between the number of PD criteria met and metacognitive failures, so supporting the idea that broader personality dysfunctions are linked with the poorer overall ability to make sense of mental states. However, further analysis still needs to be performed in order to discover if specific aspects of metacognition correlate with pathology severity. Also, while compared with patients with only axis I 'neurotic' disorders, PDs appear to be much more impaired in all metacognitive functions.

Metacognition during treatment

A final note regards how metacognition evolves during therapy, at least during a treatment specifically devoted to improving it. MAS data, applied to patients mostly treated with metacognitive interpersonal therapy (Dimaggio *et al.*, 2007a), during the first year of therapy, highlights many metacognitive impairments, ones that tended to recede partially and quickly with appropriate treatment, but they showed a trend towards having a slower rate of improvement in the second part of the therapy year, one which persisted to the end of the year (Carcione *et al.*, in press; Dimaggio *et al.*, 2009). Impairments shifted with patients having alternate moments of better and poorer functioning, thus leading to the hypothesis that many factors from the context in which metacognition was used could play a role in impairing the metacognitive performance.

The most severely impaired dimension of metacognition was mastery; almost all the patients had severe problems in coping. Most struggled to be able to formulate different ideas concerning how to think about and respond to social problems. These difficulties in mastery appear to be stable across the time period studied, though in some patients it was less pervasive.

Summary and conclusion

Overall, the results from MAS and MAI seem to provide partial answers to the questions we posed at the beginning. We discuss each of them in light of the example provided.

A variety of metacognitive functions and their selective damage in PDs

Probably this is the most robust finding, consistent with our former hypotheses (Semerari *et al.*, 2003). Transcripts show how different dysfunctions appear in the discourse and can be differentiated from one another. Moreover, metacognitive functions can be selectively damaged; that is, it is possible to detect problems in taking somebody's else perspective while the person is still able to recognize the causes of his own emotions. On the other hand, monitoring disorders could be distinguished from the inability to differentiate fantasy from reality or to integrate different aspects of the self and the other.

Many patients, however, tend to present more than one metacognitive impairment. For example, besides Luca's poor monitoring, he had difficulties in forming a representation of his girlfriend's mental states, thus presenting both disordered self-reflection and understanding of the other's mind. We can expect that the interaction between different dysfunctions can lead to a complex dynamic inside the metacognitive system, triggering each other and amplifying psychopathology. A more refined formulation of the 'selective damage' hypothesis is that there are constellations of metacognitive disorders which can be affected together, leaving other aspects of the systems well functioning, as speculated in Dimaggio and Lysaker (this volume, Introduction). The existence of specific causal paths from one metacognitive disorder to the others is a matter for further speculation and research (see Dimaggio *et al.*, 2008).

PDs' metacognitive profile

In light of the examples provided below, the hypothesis that there are specific metacognitive dysfunctions for different PDs does not appear to be supported in full. Different PDs can share the same metacognitive impairments. For example, impaired monitoring appeared in Sandra, with primarily avoidant PD, and Luca, with narcissistic PD. On the other hand the problem of co-occurrence of PDs, present in most patients (Clarkin, 2008; Dimaggio and Norcross, 2008), prevents the possibility of telling which troubled aspect of personality is associated with each specific metacognitive dysfunction. In the case of Laura, for example, it is hard to tell whether her disorders in differentiation and integration could be ascribed to her borderline PD diagnosis, as earlier predicted (Semerari *et al.*, 2005) or to other disorders, such as dependent, obsessive-compulsive or narcissistic, from which she suffered. Different interpretations might be possible: first, a specific metacognitive dysfunction can underlie different disorders; second, an overall metacognitive impairment, involving at the same time self-reflection, understanding others and finding solutions to social problems might be a liability leading to a widespread personality dysfunction (Dimaggio and Norcross, 2008). A third possibility is that in the case of co-occurrence of PDs, poor metacognition is correlated with specific underlying personality traits, such as perfectionism, emotional dysregulation and unstable self-esteem, which can serve as liabilities to many PDs. For example, perfectionism can be a common trait of narcissistic PD and obsessive compulsive PD, which leads these persons to concentrate on moral standards as a guide for action, thus neglecting attention to their own feelings, and therefore it can be reflected in poor metacognitive monitoring. On the other hand, a poor capacity for metacognitive monitoring might hamper the ability to use arousal shifts as reliable guides for action, thus leading those persons to become perfectionistic in order to know how to behave properly.

Severity of metacognitive impairment and severity of personality pathology

The severity of metacognitive impairment is related to the severity of the overall personality pathology. From preliminary data collected from the MAI interview in a sample of PD patients emerges a correlation between PD severity and depth of the metacognitive disorder (Carcione *et al.*, 2008). Laura, the most affected patient with 37 criteria met, was a prominent example of a severe overall PD. Her metacognition was impaired in many aspects: differentiation, integration and mastery were the most evident and they remained largely dysfunctional during many years of therapy. Her diffuse metacognitive disorder would undermine the possibility of making sense of many areas of social life. As a consequence she was not able to live up to her work skills or have a normal romantic life and she left experiencing a wide array of symptoms. A greater amount of research is needed to understand whether metacognitive disorders are associated with a specific PD or to constellations of PDs. The correlation between severity of personality pathology and metacognition is a key point for future research.

These observations have important implications for therapy processes and technique. Clinicians could benefit from a quick assessment of metacognitive disorder in order to understand which set of disorders is present in a specific patient. The idea of a correlation between severity of PD pathology and how widespread metacognitive deficits are should lead clinicians not to using interventions which force patients to apply mentalizing skills they do not possess. It suggests, on the contrary, the formulation of interventions that stay within the metacognitive zone of proximal development, thus helping patients to make the minimal step towards better understanding of their own psychic process, steps they can make without stumbling. In addition, clinicians could swiftly focus on the key metacognitive dysfunction they considered more relevant in a specific moment of therapy, and make assumptions about the causal chains existing between different metacognitive impairments – for example, poor self-reflection can often foster poor mindreading (Lysaker, this volume, Chapter 4). Such a clinical picture should help the clinician to address first the part of the disorder more amenable to change. Finally, assessment could involve the relation between factors other than metacognition that, in return, affects these abilities, such as pattern of interactions, mood, emotions, emotional dysregulation. To investigate the many possible links between metacognition, personality traits and symptoms is the most promising line of research to spawn treatment tailored to the specific psychopathology of persons with PDs.

References

Bateman, A. and Fonagy, P. (2004). *Psychotherapy for borderline personality disorder: Mentalization-based treatment.* Oxford: Oxford University Press.

Beck, A.T., Freeman, A., Davis, D.D. and associates (1990). *Cognitive therapy of personality disorders.* New York: Guilford Press.

Blair, R.J.R., Mitchell, D.G.V., Peschardt, K.S., Colledge, E., Leonard, R.A., Shine, J.H., *et al.* (2004). Reduced sensitivity to others' fearful expressions in psychopathic individuals. *Personality and Individual Differences, 37,* 1111–1122.

Carcione, A., Semerari, A., Nicolò, G., Pedone, R., Conti, M.L., Fiore, D., *et al.* (in press). Metacognitive mastery dysfunctions in psychotherapy of personality disorders. *Psychiatry Disorders.*

Choi-Kain, L.W. and Gunderson, J.G. (2008). Mentalization: Ontogeny, assessment and application in the treatment of borderline personality disorder. *American Journal of Psychiatry, 165,* 1127–1135.

Clarkin, J.F. (2008). Clinical approaches to axis II comorbidity: Commentary. *Journal of Clinical Psychology: In-Session, 64,* 222–230.

Clarkin, J.F., Yeomans, F. and Kernberg, O.F. (2006). *Psychotherapy of borderline personality: Focusing on object relations.* Washington, DC: American Psychiatric Publishing.

Davidson, K., Livingstone, S., McArthur, K., Dickson, L. and Gumley, A. (2007). An integrative complexity analysis of cognitive behaviour therapy sessions for borderline personality disorder. *Psychology and Psychotherapy, 80,* 513–523.

Dimaggio, G. (2006). Disorganized narratives in clinical practice. *Journal of Constructivist Psychology, 19,* 103–108.

Dimaggio, G. and Norcross, J. (2008). Treating patients with two or more personality disorders: An introduction. *Journal of Clinical Psychology: In-Session, 64,* 127–138.

Dimaggio, G., Procacci, M., Nicolò, G., Popolo, R., Semerari, A., Carcione, A., *et al.* (2007a). Poor metacognition in narcissistic and avoidant personality disorders: Four psychotherapy patients analysed using the Metacognition Assessment Scale. *Clinical Psychology and Psychotherapy*, *14*(5), 386–401.

Dimaggio, G., Semerari, A., Carcione, A., Nicolò, G. and Procacci, M. (2007b). *Psychotherapy of personality disorders. Metacognition, states of mind and interpersonal cycles*. London: Routledge.

Dimaggio, G., Lysaker, P.H., Carcione, A., Nicolò, G. and Procacci, M. (2008). Know yourself and you shall know the other . . . to a certain extent: Multiple paths of influence of self-reflection on mindreading. *Consciousness and Cognition*, *17*(3), 778–789.

Dimaggio, G., Carcione, A., Conti, M.L., Nicolò, G., Fiore, D., Pedone, R., *et al.* (2009). Impaired decentration in personality disorder: An analysis with the Metacognition Assessment Scale. *Clinical Psychology and Psychotherapy*, *16*, 450–462.

Dolan, M. and Fullam, R. (2007). The validity of the Violence Risk Scale second edition (VRS-2) in a British forensic inpatient sample. *Journal of Forensic Psychiatry and Psychology*, *18*, 381–393.

Domes, G., Czieschnek, D., Weidler, F., Berger, C., Fast, K. and Herpertz, S.C. (2008). Recognition of facial affect in borderline personality disorder. *Journal of Personality Disorders*, *22*, 135–147.

Fonagy, P., Gergely, G., Jurist, E.L. and Target, M. (2002). *Affect regulation, mentalization, and the development of the self*. New York: Other Press.

Kernberg, O.F. (1975). *Borderline conditions and pathological narcissism*. New York: Aronson.

Lawson, R., Waller, G., Sines, J. and Meyer C. (2008). Emotional awareness among eating-disordered patients: The role of narcissistic traits. *European Eating Disorders Review*, *16*, 44–48.

Millon, T. (1981). *Disorders of personality: DSM-III, Axis II*. New York: Wiley.

Minzenberg, M.J., Poole, J.H. and Vinogradov, S. (2006). Social-emotion recognition in borderline personality disorder. *Comprehensive Psychiatry*, *47*, 468–474.

Ogrodniczuk, J.S., Joyce, A.S. and Piper, W.E. (2005). Strategies for reducing patient-initiated termination of psychotherapy. *Harvard Review of Psychiatry*, *13*, 57–70.

Semerari, A., Carcione, A., Dimaggio, G., Falcone, M., Nicolò, G., Procacci, M., *et al.* (2003). How to evaluate metacognitive functioning in psychotherapy? The Metacognition Assessment Scale and its applications. *Clinical Psychology and Psychotherapy*, *10*, 238–261.

Semerari, A., Dimaggio, G., Nicolò, G., Pedone, R., Procacci, M. and Carcione, A. (2005). Metarepresentative functions in borderline personality disorders. *Journal of Personality Disorders*, *19*, 690–710.

Semerari, A., Carcione, A., Dimaggio, G., Nicolò, G. and Procacci, M. (2007). Understanding minds: Different functions and different disorders? The contribution of psychotherapy research. *Psychotherapy Research*, *17*, 106–119.

Semerari, A., d'Angerio, S., Popolo, R., Cucchi, M., Ronchi, P., Maffei, C., *et al.* (2008). L'intervista per la valutazione della metacognizione (IVam): Descrizione dello strumento. *Cogniterismo Clinico*, *5*, 60–82.

Taylor, C.T., Laposa, J.M. and Alden, L.E. (2004). Is avoidant personality disorder more than just social avoidance? *Journal of Personality Disorders*, *18*(6), 571–594.

Veen, G. and Arntz, A. (2000). Multidimensional dichotomous thinking characterizes borderline personality disorder. *Cognitive Therapy and Research*, *24*, 23–45.

Chapter 12

Metacognitive deficits in trauma-related disorders

Contingent on interpersonal motivational contexts?

Giovanni Liotti and Elena Prunetti

Many adult psychiatric patients report childhood histories that have been plagued by traumatic experiences, sometimes quite severe, during a long period of their personality development. These patients are often diagnosed as suffering from a dissociative disorder or from borderline personality disorder (BPD), but they may also present other *DSM-IV* disorders (Davidson and Smith, 1990; American Psychiatric Association, 2000). A characteristic pattern of personality changes shared by many patients with a traumatic developmental history includes feelings of emptiness and hopelessness, hostility and distrust, social withdrawal and shame, dissociative feelings of alienation and unreality, loss of coherence in self-representations, irritability, pervasive problems with self-regulation, vulnerability to self-harm or to harm inflicted by others, and clinging dependency paradoxically coexisting with attachment avoidance (complex post traumatic stress disorder PTSD, Herman, 1992). The diagnostic label of complex PTSD may be instrumental for studying all trauma-related disorders as a continuum with PTSD (Classen *et al.*, 2006). It will be often used in this chapter, the aim of which is to evaluate the relationship between metacognitive deficits and all trauma-related psychopathology.

The chapter begins with a general review of studies on the relation between traumatic memories and hindered metacognition in adult populations. The next session focuses on the hypothesis that specific interpersonal contexts (rather than vehement traumatic emotions per se) hinder metacognition while remembering traumatic experiences. The third section offers an analysis, based on attachment theory, of the motivational features characterizing the interpersonal contexts that may influence the exercise of a patient's metacognitive skills, moderating or even causing deficits. Finally, the influence of motivational interpersonal factors on metacognitive processes is illustrated by excerpts from the transcripts of the psychotherapy sessions with a patient suffering from complex PTSD.

Trauma and metacognition

Psychological trauma is held to cause dissociation as a defence against overwhelming mental pain, although an alternative view is that disorganization of the integrative functions of consciousness and memory is a primary, non-defensive outcome of vehement painful emotions (see e.g. Meares, 2000). Dissociation is, according to its very definition – a failure of the integrative functions of memory, consciousness and identity – a type of metacognitive failure. The metacognitive capacity of patients suffering from the aftermaths of traumatic experiences may be hampered by both types of dissociative mental processes, compartmentalization and detachment from the lived experience of emotion, the body or the self. Compartmentalization involves a failure of metacognitive monitoring and integration of mental states, while detachment involves at least a deficit in the identification of emotions (Holmes *et al.*, 2005).

Besides the expected hindrance to metacognitive capacity coincident with dissociative mental processes, specific subtypes of metacognitive deficit have been assessed in PTSD and other trauma-related disorders. In correspondence with symptoms of disordered memory and defective emotion regulation, research studies have assessed the presence of two types of metacognitive deficit in clinical populations reporting traumatic memories. These deficits concern (a) the monitoring and critical appraisal of memory processes (source memory); (b) the ability to modulate the intensity and duration of emotions. The defect in source memory appears either in the form of *reality monitoring* (i.e. the capacity to discriminate between externally generated events and internally generated ones such as thoughts and fantasies) or in the form of *external source monitoring* (i.e. the ability to distinguish whether a given event occurred in one situation or in another). The defective capacity to monitor emotional experiences and understand their meaning has been the subject of extensive PTSD research under the heading of alexithymia: the tendency to recall traumatic events not as a fluent narrative but in the form of mental images. Somatosensory re-experiencing may be regarded as a form of alexithymia. Rather than regarding alexithymia and deficits in source memory as purely individual problems, it should be remarked that they are closely related to interpersonal difficulties (see Vanheule *et al.*, this volume, Chapter 11). Abnormal suspiciousness, hostility and social withdrawal are linked with the attribution to a real occurrence of one's own thoughts about possible negative intentions of others, or with erroneously remembering that a significant person expressed negative comments while in fact these were uttered by somebody else. A correct picture of one's own and another's feelings is related to the exercise of satisfactory interpersonal exchanges.

Defects in source memory

Source memory deficits in adult populations with histories of childhood traumas have been assessed in studies by Golier *et al.* (1997) and by McNally *et al.* (2005). The McNally *et al.*'s (2005) study reports that adults who experience recently recovered memories of child abuse exhibit more reality monitoring deficits than adults in two control groups: those with no history of abuse and those with continuous memories of childhood traumas. This finding suggests that traumatic memories per se, may not be the cause of the metacognitive deficit.

Defects in identifying emotions (alexithymia)

Empirical studies on trauma and alexithymia are quite numerous. Fukunishi *et al.* (1996), for instance, found high levels of alexithymia in patients undergoing rehabilitation after serious physical traumas (e.g. traumas involving the need for surgical amputations). The diagnosis of PTSD is related to the presence of higher alexithymia scores than the mere report of traumatic experiences. In a group of 55 refugees reporting traumatic experiences, Sondergaard and Theorell (2004) found higher scores on the Toronto Alexithymia Scale (TAS) in the 22 subjects suffering from PTSD. A similar finding is reported in a study of Holocaust survivors (Yehuda *et al.*, 2006).

High alexithymia scores are associated not only with PTSD symptom levels, but also with reported memories of childhood abuse and neglect (Frewen *et al.*, 2006; McCaslin *et al.*, 2006; McLean *et al.*, 2006). Interestingly, alexithymia scores in the McCaslin *et al.*'s (2006) study were not correlated with the cumulative level of critical incident exposure: vulnerability factors predisposing to adult PTSD may play a more relevant role in causing alexithymia than severity of trauma experience.

All these research outcomes converge in suggesting that both PTSD symptoms following recent traumas and memories of childhood maltreatment may negatively influence the metacognitive monitoring of emotions and the ability to reflect upon them, while single traumas in adult life are less likely to cause serious levels of alexithymia.

Other types of metacognitive deficit

The clinical features of PTSD suggest the involvement of other types of hindrance to metacognitive skills besides deficits in source memory and in emotion regulation. PTSD patients' reports of traumatic memories are often fragmented and incoherent. They have more difficulties than non-PTSD people in putting traumatic memories into the world and in controlling their remembrances (Megias *et al.*, 2006). Their narratives of traumatic events, including the inner narratives of internal dialogues, tend to be disorganized and incoherent because of intruding mental images (i.e. vivid and fragmentary memories of the event endowed with strong somatosensory components which interrupt the flow of verbal representations). A likely candidate for explaining this feature of the clinical picture is the deficit in the metacognitive monitoring of discourse and thought. Metacognitive monitoring (Main, 1991) is a necessary prerequisite for metacognitive integration and narrative coherence (Semerari *et al.*, 2005; Dimaggio, 2006). Another type of deficit that is likely to intervene in the metacognitive profile of PTSD concerns mastery over thoughts and memories (for an analysis of mastery as a subfunction of metacognition, see Semerari *et al.*, 2003). PTSD patients typically report a perception of diminished control over thoughts and mental images related to traumatic memories. This deficit of mastery over thoughts seems the consequence of attempts at suppressing trauma-related memories (Wenzlaff and Wegner, 2000). An interesting finding is that the incontrollable rebound of trauma-related thoughts following deliberate thought suppression is not specifically linked to PTSD: the same effect has been observed in non-PTSD samples (Beck *et al.*, 2006). Beliefs regarding the importance of controlling intrusive thoughts do not influence thought suppression ability (Broadbent and Nixon, 2007), contrary to the assumption that individual beliefs on the importance of controlling thoughts play a significant role in PTSD genesis and treatment (Wells, 2003).

Trauma, metacognition and interpersonal context

The mechanism that mediates the relationship between traumatic experiences and metacognitive skills may be a defensive one. In order to protect consciousness from overwhelmingly painful emotions and from the rehearsal of traumatic memories, these painful mental states may be avoided through dissociation and thought suppression. This defensive effort may involve strains and hindrances on memory and metacognitive processes. However, this hypothesis is far from being satisfactory. Narratives of traumatic experiences by PTSD patients tend to be longer and more complex than those of non-traumatic events, contrary to what the theory of defensive avoidance predicts (for a review, see Brewin and Holmes, 2003). Working with patients suffering from dissociative identity disorder (usually comorbid with complex PTSD), van der Hart *et al.* (2005) observed that not only traumatic but also emotionally charged non-traumatic life events were recalled with significant somatosensory components rather than in the form of verbal self-narratives. In support of this observation, deficits in the formation of source memory (evidenced by a shift from an 'I remember' to an 'I know' position) can be elicited in PTSD patients by words non-related to trauma (Tapia *et al.*, 2007). Therefore, the memory processing typical of

PTSD cannot be attributed straightforwardly to defence against traumatic memories. Cognitive, metacognitive and neurocognitive deficits that traditionally have been attributed by clinicians to the effect of psychological trauma and defence against mental pain may instead be aspects of vulnerability factors predisposing to PTSD (Parslow and Jorm, 2007).

The metacognitive deficits leading, as putative vulnerability factors, to trauma-related disorders may be revealed by specific emotional states. For instance, the poor general ability in the formation of source memory reported in Tapia *et al.*'s (2007) study is associated with anxiety. This finding may be matched with the one reported by Minzenberg *et al.* (2006) in their study of source memory in a group of BPD patients compared with a healthy control group (BPD is often comorbid with complex PTSD). Poorer self-referential source memory was assessed in the BPD group, but only in association with measures of suspiciousness and hostility. Minzenberg *et al.* (2006) hypothesize that heterogeneity in source memory function is specifically related to the hallmark interpersonal disturbances of BPD, independent of the effects of general negative affect or general memory impairment. Interpersonal contexts that are able to elicit hostility and suspiciousness (Minzenberg *et al.*, 2006) or anxiety (Tapia *et al.*, 2007) may therefore cause or increase metacognitive deficits in patients exposed to traumatic experiences. In other words, metacognitive deficits in trauma-related disorders could be regarded as widely contingent on the quality of past and present interpersonal transactions: they may be context-dependent.

This hypothesis is supported by the studies on the relevance of social and relationship factors in the genesis and course of PTSD. Lack of social support, both in the immediate aftermath of traumatic experiences and in the personal childhood history of adult trauma victims, plays a key role in the genesis of PTSD (Brewin *et al.*, 2000; Scarpa *et al.*, 2006; Schumm *et al.*, 2006; Lauterbach *et al.*, 2007). A social environment characterized by criticism or indifference after a traumatic experience predicts PTSD more than the simple lack of positive support (Ullman and Filipas, 2001). A role even more important than objective support after exposure to trauma may be played by the subjective ability to ask for support, perceive it and utilize it (Feng *et al.*, 2007). Studies based on attachment theory suggest that this ability is related to past attachment relationships. For instance, in the 9/11 study performed by Fraley *et al.* (2006), individuals with histories of secure attachment exhibited significantly fewer symptoms of PTSD than insecurely attached ones. Attachment insecurity, and particularly disorganization of attachment, was also related to increased risk for PTSD or to higher mean scores of post traumatic symptoms in other studies (Muller *et al.*, 2000; Appelmeier *et al.*, 2007; Bailey *et al.*, 2007; Elwood and Williams, 2007; Stovall-McClough and Cloitre, 2006). Studies evidencing the role of negative self-appraisal styles in the genesis of PTSD (e.g. Briant and Guthrie, 2007) provide further even if indirect support to the hypothesis that attachment processes and styles play a significant role in causing the emotional, cognitive and metacognitive features of post traumatic symptoms.

The role played by attachment processes in trauma-related disorders clarifies the main thesis of this chapter, namely that the metacognitive deficits observed in these illnesses may depend on contextual variables. In the presence of an insecure attachment style, these deficits may appear quite clearly in interpersonal and meaning contexts related to the activation of the attachment motivational system, and disappear in contexts where the attachment system is inactive. An example is provided by the recent study of a sample of adults with an insecure-avoidant attachment style. Edelstein (2006) evidenced deficits in working memory for both positive and negative attachment-related stimuli, but not for emotional stimuli unable to activate the attachment system. For a better understanding of the interpersonal contexts where the attachment system becomes active, we now turn to an overview of theoretical and empirical knowledge on the relationship between trauma and attachment (for a detailed discussion of this topic, see Liotti, 2004).

Trauma and attachment

The attachment motivational system evolved in birds and mammals with the function of protecting the individual from environmental dangers through the active search of proximity to a familial member of the social group (Bowlby, 1969/1982). The attachment system is one among a number of evolved systems regulating different aspects of social life. Different systems regulate social interactions aimed at caregiving, establishing the social rank of dominance and submission, cooperating towards the achievement of a shared goal, and sexual mating (Gilbert, 1989; Panksepp, 1998). Each of these motivational systems may be conceived as an encapsulated mental (and brain) module that, once activated, organizes mental and behavioural functions in view of the system's biosocial goal. Fear and pain, particularly if they are intense and prolonged, activate the attachment system 'from the cradle to the grave' (Bowlby, 1979: 129), while other organisms, environmental and social variables prompt other social motivational systems into action.

It follows from this definition that the attachment system is necessarily activated during traumatic experiences. The attachment style is an important factor in the capacity to cope with traumatic experiences. Reciprocally, traumas suffered at the hand of attachment figures throughout childhood and adolescence have a damaging effect on the attachment style (Lieberman, 2004). The attachment style is originated by the internal working model (IWM), a structure of implicit memory (Amini *et al.*, 1996) summarizing past attachment interactions and determining expectancies about what is likely to happen in later attachment interactions. Life events that activate the attachment system also activate the IWM of attachment.

The IWM of secure attachment, providing expectations to be soothed and helped by competent caregivers, acts as a protective factor, in the face of later traumas, against the development of trauma-related disorders. In contrast, the IWM of insecure attachments (ambivalent, avoidant and disorganized) increases the risk of pathological responses to traumas. A pre-existing disorganized attachment (expressed by utterly incoherent behavioural and attentional strategies towards the caregiver) is particularly likely to instigate dissociative reactions to new traumatic experiences (Cassidy and Mohr, 2001; Liotti, 2004, 2006). Attachment disorganization is produced because a frightened and/or violent caregiver becomes at the same time the source and the solution of a child's fear. Once established, the disorganized IWM is likely to yield poor stress-coping abilities (Schore, 2003) and multiple, dramatic, fragmented representations of self and others (Liotti, 2004, 2006) whenever the attachment system is activated by loneliness, fear or pain.

Almost all children who have been disorganized infants develop, before they reach school age, an organized interpersonal strategy toward their caregivers. They tend to exert active control of the parent's attention and behaviour either through caregiving or through domineering-punitive behaviour (Hesse *et al.*, 2003). This empirical finding can be explained as a defensive inhibition of the attachment system, achieved by co-opting another equally inborn interpersonal system. Whenever, because of fear or pain, these children's behaviour comes to be motivated by the attachment system, they tend to shift to a different motivation that, while preserving proximity to the parent, is as removed as possible from a straightforward request for help and soothing. The aim of this defensive strategy is to protect both the children and their relationships from the unbearably chaotic experience of disorganization. The activation of the caregiving system instead of the attachment system yields controlling caregiving strategies, while the activation of the ranking (dominance–submission) system yields controlling-punitive strategies. Besides the controlling-caregiving and controlling-punitive strategies that are widely studied in research on the sequels of infant disorganized attachment, the existence of controlling-submissive and controlling-sexualized strategies has been hypothesized on both theoretical and clinical grounds.

The controlling strategies limit the possibility of a reactivation of the IWM of disorganized attachment, but do not cancel it. Controlling children appear well oriented and organized in their thinking, behavioural and attentional strategies until they are shown pictures portraying situations that are able to powerfully activate a child's attachment system (e.g. parents leaving a child alone). Once the system is thus activated, the formerly organized strategies of thought and behaviour collapse in the controlling children: the underlying disorganization of their mental operations is suddenly revealed by the unrealistic, catastrophic and utterly incoherent narratives produced in response to the pictures (Hesse *et al.*, 2003). It could be argued that both mental pain and the process of making a new bond are potentially able to foster the activation of the attachment system and cause a collapse of the controlling strategies.

The collapse of the controlling strategies in the face of a powerful activation of the attachment system illustrates an important process in the pathogenesis of trauma-related disorders. The relative inhibition of the attachment system through the defensive activation of other equally inborn motivational systems allows for coherent styles of relating in people otherwise prone to disorganized states of mind and behaviour. These relational styles can meet social approval and be appraised as pleasant and healthy (as often happens with controlling-caregiving children and adults), or on the contrary they can be regarded as problematic but not necessarily indicative of a disorder (as with controlling-punitive people). Adults with a story of early attachment disorganization may therefore run altogether normal lives until the controlling strategy is forcefully suspended under the influence of a powerful stressor (e.g. a traumatic event). It is on these occasions that psychopathological symptoms may appear and involve all the consequences of attachment disorganization: emotional dysregulation and alexithymia (Schore, 2003), reduced mentalizing capacity (Bateman and Fonagy, 2004) and dissociative experiences based on dramatic, non-integrated self-representations (Liotti, 2004, 2006).

Support to the hypothesis that metacognitive deficits are contingent upon attachment-related interpersonal contexts (see Vanheule *et al.*, this volume, Chapter 11) is provided by a paper by Hill *et al.* (2008). In this study, insecure attachment at 18 months was associated, in five-year-old children, with indices of low metacognitive capacity in an emotionally laden doll's house scenario that is likely to activate a child's attachment motivation, but not in a neutral scenario that is unlikely to activate this motivational system. Also in keeping with the hypothesis are the findings reported by Prunetti *et al.* (2008) in a study based on coding the transcripts of psychotherapy sessions with the Metacognition Assessment Scale (MAS, Semerari *et al.*, 2003). During the second session of the psychotherapy of borderline patients, metacognitive successes and failures alternated in the patients' thought and discourse according to the degree of supportive emotional closeness conveyed by the therapist's interventions. Therapist's interventions fostering emotional closeness in the therapeutic dyad were followed by a decrease in the patients' exercise of their metacognitive skills, while emotionally neutral interventions allowed for the patients' better use of metacognitive capacity (Prunetti *et al.*, 2008). This seemingly paradoxical finding is interpreted by the authors as a consequence of the activation of a disorganized IWM caused by the therapist's expressed understanding and emotional support. The authors argue that successful psychotherapy gradually induced a change towards attachment security in the patients' IWM through corrective relational experiences, thereby allowing the patients to benefit from emotional closeness and support.

Metacognitive deficits in the psychotherapy process of complex PTSD

An illustration

Further support to the above hypotheses could be provided by coding the transcripts of psychotherapy sessions both with the MAS and with another operationalized system, called Assessing Interpersonal Motivation in Transcripts (AIMIT). The AIMIT codes different types of interpersonal motivation in transcripts of psychotherapy sessions: seeking care, help and soothing (i.e. attachment), offering care, dealing with sexual feelings, competing for dominance or displaying submissiveness (ranking), cooperating on equal grounds. Excerpts from the transcripts of two psychotherapy sessions with a patient suffering from severe complex PTSD, coded according to the MAS and the AIMIT manuals, provide illustration of the hypothesis that metacognitive deficits related to traumas depend on the interpersonal context where the trauma is narrated or rehearsed.

Eva, 32, single, asked for psychotherapy in search of relief from the manifold disabling symptoms of complex PTSD that had plagued her life since childhood. The only child of fragile, helplessly vulnerable and neglecting parents, she had been raised since she was six years old in an institution where she was sexually abused for many years by her teacher and tutor. On session seven of her treatment (weekly individual sessions), she reported having been sexually assaulted while she was going home after the preceding session.

Eva: I stopped at the central bus station because I needed to use the WC. While I was coming out of the toilet two men came in and . . . ah . . . they shut the door and . . . they asked for money. I then, yeah, I thought they were about to rob . . . and I immediately felt frightened . . . so that . . . [*prolonged pause*] in short I got near the wall, my fault, I trapped myself with this stupid move . . . They took my handbag. One of them started saying things . . . both of them came closer, I was trapped in the corner and . . . one of them put his hands on me, the other one laughed and said dirty words. I only said 'Leave me alone, I'll scream' – 'No, you are not even brave enough to do so' – I tried to defend myself as best as I could . . . my voice failed because yeah, I was so frightened that I was unable to speak . . . it would have been useless, anyway. Then . . . the other one, as I started to say something, I think they were afraid I could scream or something and . . . they . . . they shut my mouth. The other one got hold of me, in the meantime he stroked me and they tried to lay me down and then I tried to kick them and scratch them . . . I tried, for instance I even tried to bite the one whose hand was on my mouth but . . . oh hell there were two of them, I was helpless. And the eyes too, yeah, they, they pressed on my eyes, and this is because even . . . in the end it was not an infection, it was a . . . they hurt my cornea, because they pressed so hard that the lenses . . .

When formally analyzing this transcript with the MAS, the perhaps surprising result is that there is no evidence of metacognitive failure in it. Eva identifies mental states, names emotions properly, acknowledges thoughts, understands the minds of her abusers and is aware of the difference between her thoughts and reality. This efficient exercise of metacognitive abilities was not typical of Eva's dialogue with her therapist. Analysis with the MAS of other sessions' transcripts evidences Eva's frequent and severe metacognitive failures. A particularly striking example is the following, where Eva, a few months after the traumatic episode at the bus station, was reporting to the therapist her reaction to the recent sad news of the death of a man she had been very fond of in the past.

Eva: I was losing consciousness, I wanted to throw myself out of the car, I started banging my head on the window, and G [the friend who was driving the car and had just told her about this death] did not have a place to stop, so he held my arms because I was scratching myself really hard, I was hurting myself and then he stopped the car and he begun slapping me and told me to get hold of myself. I cried a lot, it hurt so much when I heard about his death, mainly because of the distance, because I couldn't do anything but pray for him. But yesterday for instance, you know, for instance, he said if I wanted to know about the illness and . . . you know . . . But every time I heard about it, mainly about a person so dear to my heart, I cried, I really let myself go. This time however I felt . . . I smoked a lot so when he was saying these things, something I usually do not do, but maybe it was a way to let myself go . . . all this smoking, I did not cry at all, but I was trembling, I was tense, I felt so bad but I was unable to show it. As a matter of fact I said, 'Look, I am sorry, I am sad. I feel really bad', and she [*a common friend? Eva does not clarify*] was telling me . . . and she cried and I felt like saying saying 'I am not expressing . . . really I am not . . . the pain I felt toward him' and this

> made me feel so bad. Indeed, just before coming here I went through a crisis but a crisis like losing consciousness. I did not know where I was and during the entire night I was worrying over everything he said, imagining all the time, having all these images and so on.

The metacognitive failure, so evident in this narrative, can be readily coded in the MAS two subcategories of deficits: (1) In understanding one's mind (e.g. 'a crisis like losing consciousness. I did not know where I was', 'G did not have a place to stop, so he held my arms' – how could he since he was driving? – the impossibility to stop the car); (2) Mastery (e.g. 'I started banging my head on the window', 'I was scratching myself really hard'). The fact that such a severe and generalized failure is not evident while Eva reported the recent traumatic event at the bus station requires an explanation. According to the theoretical model outlined in the previous paragraphs, an explanation may be found on the premise that metacognitive failures while reporting traumatic memories are caused by the activation of an insecure and particularly a disorganized IWM (i.e. negative, multiple and dissociated expectations about the consequences of expressing the need to be soothed). No metacognitive failure would be expected, according to the theory, when the attachment system is inhibited while reporting the event – for instance, inhibited by the activation of the competitive ranking system, either in the dominant-punitive or in the subordinate, yielding subroutine.

Indeed, when the excerpt of the session transcript 'Assault at the Bus Station' is coded according to the AIMIT, one notices only one short-lived utterance that hints at the activation of the attachment system at the beginning of the narrative: Eva names her painful feeling ('I felt frightened'), which is compatible with the expectation of being understood and soothed by her therapist. Immediately thereafter in her narrative, however, the AIMIT coding system allows the highlighting only of the durable and intense activation of the ranking system in organizing Eva's discourse. She insists on describing in detail her alleged ineptitude ('My fault, I trapped myself with this stupid move') and her yielding to the aggression. This is in keeping with the idea of a defensive, controlling strategy that uses the ranking system to inhibit the attachment system and keeps at bay the influence of a disorganized IWM on metacognition. Eva uses the memory of an event where, very likely, both her motivation for fight/flight and her motivation for ranking have been activated by the assault, in such a way as to inhibit any tendency to ask for the therapist's soothing and helping responses. Rather, she insists on despising and shaming herself in front of the therapist (shame is the hallmark of the activity of the ranking system in its submissive subroutine; Gilbert, 1989). This is precisely what could be expected if, after being an infant disorganized in her attachments, Eva as a child had learned to inhibit her attachment system through the development of a controlling strategy based on the immediate mobilization of motives, experiences and memories related to the ranking system.

In contrast, during the reporting to the therapist of the episode related to the loss of a beloved person, the AIMIT allows the assessment only of the activation of Eva's attachment system. Although her description of self-harming may hint at an activation of the ranking system (self-inflicted punishment), she does not express in words any self-despising thought or any intention of punishing herself. Rather, she repeatedly dwells on her painful feelings and on her crying, which is the hallmark of the activation of the attachment system. Without the inhibitory influence of a controlling strategy, the IWM of disorganized attachment emerges and causes, according to our theory, dissociative phenomena and the related metacognitive failure.

After two years of treatment, while reflecting anew on traumatic events she had never reported to the therapist (an abortion, the memory of a rape when she was 11), Eva began to relinquish her defensive controlling strategy and to allow the activation of her attachment system in the therapeutic dialogue in such a way as to suggest some beginning, albeit still uncertain, security in her attachment to the therapist.

> *Eva*: I don't want to hurt your feelings, or make you think that I don't trust you, but I must say that I find it difficult to deal with sexual things with you . . . you are married, you accepted the challenge of having children, which is something I did not accept. On the contrary, I destroyed, I undid everything [*Eva hints at an abortion, an event that she was able to discuss with the therapist during the following sessions.*] I was afraid to tell you, because if you think that I don't trust you, well, it's not true.

The AIMIT coding of this passage still reveals, as usual for this patient, the concurrent activation during the clinical exchanges of the attachment and the ranking system (in the subordinate subroutine) – Eva's customary controlling strategy. The activation of the ranking motivational system is betrayed by the utterance 'you accepted the challenge of having children . . . I did not . . . On the contrary, I destroyed . . .', where Eva states that she sees herself as inferior to her therapist. The activation of the attachment system in a beginning secure modality is suggested by the repeated assertion that she trusts her therapist's willingness and capacity to help. However, Eva's disorganized IWM may have not been fully corrected in the therapeutic process. The MAS coding of the passage highlights a slight transient metacognitive failure concurrent with the activation of the attachment system. While Eva is able to use her metacognitive capacity for an efficient description of her state of mind and for a reasonable guess at the therapist's state of mind ('I do not want to hurt you . . . you may believe that I am not trusting you . . .'), she does not yet master her problematic state of mind ('I find it difficult to deal on sexual things with you').

The therapist's reply was aimed at fostering the activation of the cooperative system, by stating repeatedly that she saw their dialogue as a joint enterprise aimed at achieving a shared goal. In the following patient–therapist exchanges of this session, Eva seemed to accept perceiving their dialogue as motivated basically by cooperation on equal grounds. The transcript of the second part of the session evidences no metacognitive failure during the description of traumatic events.

Therapist: You're right that you need to feel safe when you discuss and share this part of your life with me. If Dr S can help you do this, that's very good.

[*Dr S is a clinician who covered the maternity leave of the therapist a few months before, and who Eva asked to go on meeting even after her therapist resumed the treatment.*] Our idea of cooperating, the three of us, in the dialogue was also meant as an opportunity for dealing more safely with these difficult aspects of your experience.

Eva: The only aspect I began to tell to Dr S was about a person who helped me with my sexuality . . .

Therapist: When did this happen?

Eva: It was 19**, he was my psychiatrist.

Therapist: Was he your first psychiatrist?

Eva: No, the first was another one, but the experience was devastating. He used hypnosis, and I felt so bad because it was the first time I talked about my childhood, and he tape-recorded what I said during the hypnosis and made me listen to the tapes afterwards. All the things that happened when they raped me. I did not remember those things. It has been hard, really hard. Like being abused again.

Therapist: I understand.

Eva: Well, that's what happened. . . .

Therapist: And then you met this second psychiatrist, the one who helped you with your sexuality. How long did this second treatment last?

Eva: Six months, then he was sent to another hospital, in another city. Far away.

Therapist: I see. Was this disappointing?

Eva: Not so much, because he had already helped me with trusting other people more than I ever did. For instance, he helped me to change my attitude toward Q. I still thank him for that, there were things I did not allow Q to do, even if I liked Q showing affection to me. I remember Q's affectionate gestures as the first ones I ever experienced since childhood, but there were moments when I was afraid of him.

According to the AIMIT, Eva's utterances that indicate activation of her attachment system in this transcript (e.g. 'he helped me') are contextualized within the narrative of her relationship with her second psychiatrist. There are no indicators of an activation of the patient's attachment system within the ongoing dialogue with the psychotherapist in this excerpt. The ongoing exchange is motivated by the cooperative system in both members of the therapeutic partnership. The MAS does not evidence any type of metacognitive failure in the excerpt, even if memories of traumas that are probably unresolved are surfacing (the rape, the abortion).

Concluding remarks

Anecdotal evidence such as that provided by the excerpts of Eva's psychotherapy would come as no surprise to clinicians experienced in psychodynamic and relational approaches to the treatment of patients suffering from complex trauma-related disorders (Verhaege and Vanheule, 2005; Stein and Allen, 2007; Schottenbauer *et al.*, 2008). The idea that metacognitive failures while reporting traumatic memories depend on the motivational systems organizing the clinical dialogue – although it is not stated explicitly in the literature on psychodynamic treatments of complex PTSD reviewed by Schottenbauer *et al.* (2008) – permeates both case formulation and the logic of the intervention. Insistence on felt security in the transference or on the prompt repair of ruptures in the therapeutic alliance as prerequisites for achieving a satisfactory exercise of metacognitive capacity while reflecting on traumatic memories is in keeping with the hypothesis that metacognitive failures related to traumas are linked to an insecure and probably disorganized attachment system motivating the relationship with the person to whom the trauma is being reported. To this widespread albeit often implicit belief of dynamic psychotherapists, this chapter adds the idea that metacognition while reporting traumatic memories may be preserved not only by cooperative motivations (e.g. underpinning a good therapeutic alliance) or earned security of attachment (e.g. through corrective experiences in the therapeutic relationship), but also through the defensive inhibition of the attachment motivational system (achieved through controlling strategies). Controlling strategies however, while they can momentarily minimize metacognitive deficits (e.g. allowing the reporting of traumatic events in a ranking mentality rather than in an attachment mentality involving needs for help and soothing), leave the patient at the mercy of dissociation and metacognitive failures whenever the activation of the attachment system overpowers the defensive activation of another motivational system.

Highly structured therapeutic interventions on PTSD that do not involve activation of the patient's attachment system in the therapeutic relationship (e.g. eye movement desensitization and reprocessing, EMDR, or cognitive-behavioural interventions) may foster metacognition and allow integration of the traumatic memories without changing the patient's IWM of attachment or fostering his or her propensity to engage in cooperative interpersonal exchanges outside therapy. This possibility may explain both the positive outcome and the high rate of relapses (and also the high rates of nonresponders and drop-outs in patients with complex PTSD; Schottenbauer *et al.*, 2008). Even if momentarily successful, treatments that do not address security of attachment and motivation to cooperate on equal grounds may fall short of what many PTSD patients need in order to achieve a durable capacity to cope with traumatic memories through the satisfactory exercise of their metacognitive abilities.

While there is evidence that an IWM of disorganized attachment may be particularly detrimental to metacognition (Fonagy *et al.*, 2003; Bouchard *et al.*, 2008), controlled research studies are needed in order to support the hypothesis that the satisfactory exercise of metacognitive abilities depends on the motivational systems underpinning inner and outer ongoing dialogues. These studies could provide evidence to what clinical experience and anecdotal evidence such as Eva's suggest: that a disorganized IWM hinders metacognition whenever the attachment motivational system becomes active in the dialogue, and less so during interactions motivated by other systems. Such could be studies of the psychotherapy process of patients suffering from trauma-related disorders, assessing metacognitive abilities (e.g. through the MAS) during their reports of traumatic events while they are motivated by the attachment system and while they are motivated by other systems (as assessed, for instance, through the AIMIT) in the interaction with the therapist. Should the hypothesis be confirmed, the aim of psychotherapy of trauma-related disorders would not be limited to the integration of traumatic memories or to the correction of maladaptive beliefs regarding traumatic events, but should also address security of attachment and the ability to activate the cooperative system rather than the ranking, the caregiving or the sexual system whenever painful feelings related to traumas surface.

References

American Psychiatric Association (2000). *Diagnostic and statistical manual of mental disorders, 4th edn (DSM-IV)*. Washington, DC: American Psychiatric Association.

Amini, F., Lewis, T., Lannon, R., Louie, A., Baumbacher, G., McGuinnes, T., *et al.*

(1996). Affect, attachment, memory: Contributions toward psychobiologic integration. *Psychiatry*, *59*, 213–239.

Appelmeier, J.E., Elliott, A.N. and Smith, C.H. (2007). Childhood sexual abuse, attachment and trauma symptoms in college females: The moderating role of attachment. *Child Abuse and Neglect*, *31*, 549–566.

Bailey, H.N., Moran, G. and Pederson, D.R. (2007). Childhood maltreatment, complex trauma symptoms, and unresolved attachment in an at-risk sample of adolescent mothers. *Attachment and Human Development*, *9*, 139–161.

Bateman, A.W. and Fonagy, P. (2004). *Psychotherapy for borderline personality disorder: Mentalization-based treatment*. New York: Oxford University Press.

Beck, J.G., Gudmundsdottir, B., Palyo, S.A., Miller, L.M. and Grant, D.M. (2006). Rebound effects following deliberate thought suppression: Does PTSD make a difference? *Behavior Therapy*, *37*, 170–180.

Bouchard, M., Target, M., Lecours, S., Fonagy, P., Tremblay, L., Schachter, A., *et al.* (2008). Mentalization in adult attachment narratives. *Psychoanalytic Psychology*, *25*, 47–66.

Bowlby, J. (1969/1982). *Attachment and Loss Vol. 1: Attachment*. London: Hogarth Press.

Bowlby, J. (1979). *The making and breaking of affectional bonds*. London: Tavistock.

Brewin, C.R., Andrews, B. and Valentine, J.D. (2000). Meta-analysis of risk factors for posttraumatic stress disorder in trauma-exposed adults. *Journal of Consulting and Clinical Psychology*, *68*, 748–766.

Brewin, C.R. and Holmes, E.A. (2003). Psychological theories of posttraumatic stress disorder. *Clinical Psychology Review*, *23*, 339–376.

Briant, R.A. and Guthrie, R.M. (2007). Maladaptive self-appraisals before trauma exposure predict posttraumatic stress disorder. *Journal of Consulting and Clinical Psychology*, *75*, 812–815.

Broadbent, J.C. and Nixon, R.D.V. (2007). Maladaptive beliefs and suppression of negative autobiographical memories. *Behaviour Change*, *24*, 125–134.

Cassidy, J. and Mohr, J.J. (2001). Unsolvable fear, trauma and psychopathology: Theory, research and clinical considerations related to disorganized attachment across the life cycle. *Clinical Psychology: Science and Practice*, *8*, 275–298.

Classen, C.C., Pain, C., Field, N.P. and Woods, P. (2006). Posttraumatic personality disorder: A reformulation of complex post traumatic stress disorder and borderline personality disorder. *Psychiatric Clinics of North America*, *29*, 87–112.

Davidson, J. and Smith, R. (1990). Traumatic experiences in psychiatric outpatients. *Journal of Traumatic Stress*, *3*, 459–475.

Dimaggio, G. (2006). Disorganized narratives in clinical practice. *Journal of Constructivist Psychology*, *19*, 103–108.

Edelstein, R.S. (2006). Attachment and emotional memory: Investigating the source and extent of avoidant memory impairment. *Emotion*, *6*, 340–345.

Elwood, L.S. and Williams, N.L. (2007). PTSD-related cognitions and romantic attachment styles as moderators of psychological symptoms in victims of interpersonal trauma. *Journal of Social and Clinical Psychology*, *26*, 1189–1209.

Feng, S., Jan, H., Benjamin, A., Wen, S., Liu, A., Zou, J., *et al.* (2007). Social support and post-traumatic stress disorder among flood victims in Hunan, China. *Annals of Epidemiology*, *17*, 827–833.

Fonagy, P., Target, M., Gergely, G., Allen, J.G. and Bateman, A.W. (2003). The developmental roots of borderline personality disorder in early attachment relationships: A theory and some evidence. *Psychoanalytic Inquiry, 23*, 412–459.

Fraley, R.C., Fazzari, D.A., Bonanno, G.A. and Dekel, S. (2006). Attachment and psychological adaptation in high exposure survivors of the September 11th attack on the World Trade Center. *Personality and Social Psychology Bulletin, 32*, 538–551.

Frewen, P.A., Pain, C., Dozois, D.J. and Lanius, R.A. (2006). Alexithymia in PTSD: Psychometric and FMRI studies. *Annals of the New York Academy of Sciences, 1071*, 397–400.

Fukunishi, I., Sasaki, K., Chishima, Y., Anze, M. and Saijo, M. (1996). Emotional disturbances in trauma patients during the rehabilitation phase: Studies of posttraumatic stress disorder and alexithymia. *General Hospital Psychiatry, 18*, 121–127.

Gilbert, P. (1989). *Human nature and suffering*. London: LEA.

Golier, J., Harvey, P., Steiner, A. and Yehuda, R. (1997). Source monitoring in PTSD. *Annals of the New York Academy of Sciences, 821*, 472–475.

Herman, J.L. (1992). Complex PTSD: A syndrome in survivors of prolonged and repeated trauma. *Journal of Traumatic Stress, 3*, 377–391.

Hesse, E., Main, M., Abrams, K.Y. and Rifkin, A. (2003). Unresolved states regarding loss or abuse can have 'second-generation' effects: Disorganized, role-inversion and frightening ideation in the offspring of traumatized non-maltreating parents. In D.J. Siegel and M.F. Solomon (eds), *Healing trauma: Attachment, mind, body and brain*. New York: Norton.

Hill, J., Murray, L., Leidecken, V. and Sharp, H. (2008). Specificities in continuities between attachment security at 18 months and mentalising abilities at age 5 years. Manuscript submitted for publication.

Holmes, E.A., Brown, R.J., Mansell, W., Fearon, R.P., Hunter, E.C.M., Frasquilho, F., *et al.* (2005). Are there two qualitatively distinct forms of dissociation? A review and some clinical implications. *Clinical Psychology Review, 25*, 1–23.

Lauterbach, D., Koch, E.I. and Porter, K. (2007). The relationship between childhood support and later emergence of PTSD. *Journal of Traumatic Stress, 20*, 857–867.

Lieberman, A.F. (2004). Traumatic stress and attachment: Reality and internalization in disorders of infant mental health. *Infant Mental Health Journal, 25*, 336–351.

Liotti, G. (2004). Trauma, dissociation and disorganized attachment: Three strands of a single braid. *Psychotherapy: Theory, Research, Practice and Training, 41*, 472–486.

Liotti, G. (2006). A model of dissociation based on attachment theory and research. *Journal of Trauma and Dissociation, 7*, 55–74.

McCaslin, S.E., Metzler, T.J., Best, S., Liberman, A., Weiss, D.S., Fagan, J., *et al.* (2006). Alexithymia and PTSD symptoms in urban police officers: Cross-sectional and prospective findings. *Journal of Trauma Stress, 19*, 361–373.

McLean, L.M., Toner, B., Jackson, J., Desrocher, M. and Stuckless, N. (2006). The relationship between childhood sexual abuse, complex post-traumatic stress disorder and alexithymia in two outpatient samples: Examination of women treated in community and institutional clinics. *Journal of Child Sexual Abuse*, *15*, 1–17.

McNally, R.J., Clancy, S.A., Barrett, H.M. and Parker, H.A. (2005). Reality monitoring in adults reporting repressed, recovered or continuous memories of childhood sexual abuse. *Journal of Abnormal Psychology*, *114*, 147–152.

Main, M. (1991). Metacognitive knowledge, metacognitive monitoring, and singular (coherent) versus multiple (incoherent) models of attachment. In C.M. Parkes, J. Stevenson-Hinde and P. Marris (eds), *Attachment across the life cycle*. London: Routledge.

Meares, R. (2000). *Intimacy and alienation: Memory, trauma and personal being*. London: Brunner-Routledge.

Megias, J., Ryan, E., Vaquero, J. and Frese B. (2006). Comparison of traumatic and positive memories in people with and without PTSD profile. *Applied Cognitive Psychology*, *21*, 117–130.

Minzenberg, M.J., Fisher-Irving, M., Poole, J.H. and Vinogradov, S. (2006). Reduced self-referential source memory performance is associated with interpersonal dysfunction in borderline personality disorder. *Journal of Abnormal Psychology*, *20*, 42–54.

Muller, R.T., Sicoli, L.A. and Lemieux, K.E. (2000). Relationship between attachment style and posttraumatic stress symptomatology among adults who report the experience of childhood abuse. *Journal of Traumatic Stress*, *13*, 321–332.

Panksepp, J. (1998). *Affective neuroscience: The foundations of human and animal emotions*. Oxford: Oxford University Press.

Parslow, R. and Jorm, A. (2007). Pre-trauma and post-trauma neurocognitive functioning and PTSD in a community sample of young adults. *American Journal of Psychiatry*, *164*, 509–515.

Prunetti, E., Framba, R., Barone, L., Fiore, D., Sera, F. and Liotti, G. (2008). Attachment disorganization and borderline patients' metacognitive responses to therapists' expressed understanding of their states of mind: A pilot study. *Psychotherapy Research*, *18*, 28–36.

Scarpa, A., Haden, S.C. and Hurley, J. (2006). Community violence victimization and symptoms of posttraumatic stress disorder: The modulating effect of coping and social support. *Journal of Interpersonal Violence*, *21*, 446–449.

Schore, A.N. (2003). *Affect dysregulation and the repair of the self*. New York: Norton.

Schottenbauer, M.A., Glass, C.R., Arnkoff, D.B. and Gray, S.H. (2008). Contributions of psychodynamic approaches to the treatment of PTSD and trauma: A review of the empirical treatment and psychopathology literature. *Psychiatry*, *71*, 13–36.

Schumm, J.A., Briggs-Phillips, M. and Hobfall, S.E. (2006). Cumulative interpersonal trauma and social support as risk and resiliency factors in predicting PTSD. *Journal of Traumatic Stress*, *19*, 825–836.

Semerari, A., Carcione, A., Dimaggio, G., Falcone, M., Nicolò, G., Procacci, M., *et al.* (2003). The evaluation of metacognitive functioning in psychotherapy: The Metacognition Assessment Scale and its applications. *Clinical Psychology and Psychotherapy*, *10*, 238–261.

Semerari, A., Carcione, A., Dimaggio, G., Nicolò, G., Pedone, R. and Procacci, M.

(2005). Metarepresentative functions in borderline personality disorder. *Journal of Personality Disorders*, *19*, 690–710.

Sondergaard, H.P. and Theorell, T. (2004). Alexithymia, emotions and PTSD: Findings from a longitudinal study of refugees. *Nordic Journal of Psychiatry*, *58*, 185–191.

Stein, H. and Allen, J.G. (2007). Mentalizing as a framework for integrating therapeutic exposure and relationship repair in the treatment of a patient with complex post-traumatic psychopathology. *Bulletin of the Menninger Clinic*, *71*, 273–290.

Stovall-McClough, K. and Cloitre, M. (2006). Unresolved attachment, PTSD and dissociation in women with childhood abuse histories. *Journal of Consulting and Clinical Psychology*, *74*, 219–228.

Tapia, G., Clarys, D., El Hage, W., Belzung, C. and Insigrini, M. (2007). PTSD psychiatric patients exhibit a deficit in remembering. *Memory*, *15*, 145–153.

Ullman, S.E. and Filipas, H.H. (2001). Predictors of PTSD symptom severity and social reactions in sexual assault victims. *Journal of Traumatic Stress*, *14*, 369–389.

van der Hart, O., Bolt, H. and van der Kolk, B.A. (2005). Memory fragmentation in dissociative identity disorder. *Journal of Trauma and Dissociation*, *6*, 55–70.

Verhaege, P. and Vanheule, S. (2005). Actual neurosis and PTSD: The impact of the Other. *Psychoanalytic Psychology*, *22*, 493–507.

Wells, A. (2003). Anxiety disorders, metacognition and change. In R.L. Leahy (ed.), *Roadblocks in cognitive-behavioral therapy*. New York: Guilford Press.

Wenzlaff, R. and Wegner, D. (2000). Thought suppression. *Annual Review of Psychology*, *51*: 59–91.

Yehuda, R., Steiner, A., Kahena, B., Southwick, S., Zemelman, S. and Giller, E. (2006). Alexithymia in Holocaust survivors with and without PTSD. *Journal of Traumatic Stress*, *10*, 93–100.

Part III

Treatment of metacognitive disturbances in severe adult disorders

Chapter 13

Metacognitive capacity as a focus of individual psychotherapy in schizophrenia

Paul H. Lysaker and Kelly D. Buck

Metacognition in schizophrenia: why a possible focus for psychotherapy

As has been discussed at length earlier in this volume, schizophrenia may be understood as a disorder, at least in part, of metacognition. This is to say that an individual with schizophrenia often experiences a reduced capacity for the following:

- thinking about his or her own thinking
- thinking about the thinking of others
- recognizing the independent relationship others have with one another
- thinking actively about the self as he or she seeks to confront psychological challenges.

As a result, he or she may have difficulties characterizing their own emotional states and psychological challenges. It may also be more difficult to appreciate the motives and intentions of others and, in joint conversation with others, to chart a course to wellness, one replete with a sense of agency and realistic hope of a meaningful life. On the small scale of day-to-day activity, unexpected problems or matters which call for a break in the expected routine may be difficult to cope with and a person with schizophrenia may consequently tend to respond with avoidance and withdrawal. As a consequence problems may remain unsolved or, even worse, tasks and relationships may be increasingly abandoned. On a larger scale, without the ability to detect nuances in self experiences and the behaviour of others, it may be difficult to construct and continue to evolve a narrative complex enough to make sense of one's larger life course (Lysaker and Buck, 2007). As a consequence, persons with schizophrenia may feel they have no substantial life story or are not even worthy of one (Lysaker and Lysaker, 2008).

With this in mind, we would suggest that it is a natural intuitive leap to begin to think about the possibility of treatments to address deficits in metacognition in schizophrenia. In other words, in addition to interventions intended to lessen symptoms, provide general support, help one to dismiss maladaptive beliefs, to manage his or her illness better and to succeed in specific psychosocial roles (e.g. work or family relationships), it would seem a matter of great promise also to seek a means to help an individual with schizophrenia to strengthen his or her capacity for metacognition. If interventions could be defined that help one better to monitor and think about their inner states, to strengthen his or her capacity to think about others in relationship to the individual and to each other, it would seem likely that the chances of success at other tasks might greatly increase.

For example, consider the patient who has difficulties in recognizing his or her emotions until they are at the level of rage and then they explode and quit their job or ruin their friendships by yelling at others. If that patient could begin better to recognize the nuances in his or her experience of sadness and frustration, he or she might be able to recognize and communicate their needs before the point of crisis. In this way, just as many serious physical injuries commonly require concurrent rehabilitation approaches – such as physical therapy together with occupational therapy to strengthen damaged muscles and tissues – interventions that strengthen the capacity for metacognition might also help those with schizophrenia to take advantage of other treatment opportunities and regain a larger range of previously lost functional capacity. For instance, consider the patient who receives a vocational placement but struggles to be able to recognize the emotions of others on the job. It seems likely that a psychotherapeutic intervention which helps that patient to become better able to critically examine their beliefs about others might increase their chances of vocational success. In this chapter we focus on the potential of just one of many interventions which might strengthen metacognitive capacity for those with schizophrenia: individual psychotherapy. We have chosen psychotherapy because it seems one which naturally requires persons to practise metacognitive acts. In psychotherapy, across diverse schools, the individual is commonly afforded opportunities to decide or explore what he or she feels and thinks about the self and others, and to challenge those ways of understanding. Specifically this chapter will address three broad questions:

- How might an integrative psychotherapy be conceptualized as addressing metacognition in schizophrenia?
- What would be involved at the concrete level of assessment and intervention in such a form of psychotherapy?
- Would such a psychotherapy be viable as a contemporary treatment for schizophrenia?

To address these questions, we first begin with a discussion of the traditional objections to the psychotherapy of schizophrenia and note some of the general requirements that any contemporary psychotherapy for schizophrenia must meet in order to be viable. Following this we offer one way to conceptualize how psychotherapy might be an opportunity for the exercise, practice and development of an atrophied metacognitive capacity. We then propose a series of concrete suggestions about what would be involved in terms of initial assessment, the process of intervention and finally ongoing evaluation of outcome.

Basic requirements for a viable psychotherapy of schizophrenia

Once touted as a key element of treatment, if not the treatment of choice for persons with psychosis (e.g. Karon and Vanden Bos, 1981), interest in research and theoretical considerations in the psychotherapy of schizophrenia have diminished dramatically in the last 50 years. One reason for this is that many of the same authors who argued vehemently for the potential benefits of psychotherapy for persons with schizophrenia also asserted that schizophrenia was fundamentally a psychological disturbance which was the direct result of faulty family dynamics. These remarks were largely seen as irresponsible and destructive, and a firestorm ensued leading many utterly to reject intensive psychotherapy (Drake and Sederer, 1986). As a consequence, it is clear that for any psychotherapy which addresses metacognition to be viable, one requirement is that it must be clearly distanced from early models which blame families or deny the complex roles that biology and social forces probably play in the development of the disorder.

A second and third requirement of a viable contemporary psychotherapy for schizophrenia is that its outcomes be measured and its procedures compatible with other treatments. Recovery from schizophrenia is well documented as a realistic and desirable point that generally can be reached in some form. Recovery is also a phenomenon that can be promoted by existent rehabilitative practices and can be assessed objectively (Lysaker and Buck, 2008). Also, psychotherapy cannot exist as an isolated practice conducted without regard for other useful rehabilitation practices (e.g. vocational rehabilitation). Its conceptualization must involve potential interface and synergistic interaction with existing and developing rehabilitative and pharmacological strategies. Thus, any viable psychotherapy that addresses metacognition must offer clear methods for the assessment of its utility and be capable of being integrated within larger psychosocial practices.

A final and perhaps more controversial discussion arises around the issues of social power and stigma. Ample research has indicated that many with schizophrenia experience themselves as possessing little power or intrinsic worth, in part as a result of stigma or stereotyped social beliefs about mental illness. These stereotypic beliefs, which include assumptions that mental illness is synonymous with dangerousness or incompetence, lead persons with mental illness to see themselves as such and, therefore, leave them especially vulnerable to demoralization, hopelessness and social withdrawal (Link *et al.*, 1989; Ritsher and Phelan, 2004). With this in mind, a final criterion we would suggest for the viability of any treatment concerned with metacognition is that it does not promote stigma or oppressive power relationships.

Psychotherapy and metacognition in schizophrenia

Basic conceptual principles

It seems necessary to begin with a model of how psychotherapy could address metacognition in the first place within the parameters just addressed above (e.g. in a manner that does not blame families, promote stigma, etc.). Should metacognitive deficits in schizophrenia be thought of as a matter of deficient knowledge and, therefore, addressed primarily through education? Are they a matter of erroneous ways of thinking and, therefore, to be corrected primarily through cognitive interventions?

In response to these questions, we suggest that metacognitive deficits in schizophrenia should be thought of as deficits in the capacity for metacognition. In other words, many with schizophrenia vary in their capability to perform acts of metacognition along a continuum from good to limited. With that said, we propose that psychotherapy can be conceptualized as aiding in the recovery of metacognitive capacity by providing a place in which such capacities can be practised and exercised in order of increasing complexity. We suggest that psychotherapy can offer clients a chance, in the manner of physical therapy, to develop over time the capacity to engage in acts they were once better able to perform. With such exercise and practice, metacognitive capacities that have atrophied or been damaged may be reclaimed such that more complex metacognitive acts can be performed with greater ease in regular life. Following the metaphor of physical therapy, practising these capacities may be difficult and painful, but incremental progress is to be expected given the plasticity of the human organism.

Following the metaphor of physical therapy further, a psychotherapy concerned with metacognition should not be one which hinges on a single global intervention. As different kinds of leg injuries may require different forms of physical therapy, so should different kinds of deficits in metacognitive capacity. According to Semerari and colleagues (2003) in their synthesis of the literature, there are at least four semi-independent forms of metacognition (i.e. four different foci of metacognition which may call upon semi-dependent metacognitive capacities): awareness of oneself;

awareness of others; awareness of the world as a place in which I am not the centre of the world (referred to as decentration); and awareness of myself as someone confronting and coping with psychological challenges. Further, as detailed in our last chapter and elsewhere again in this volume, each of these different kinds of metacognition may involve different neurocognitive and psychological processes in such a way that persons may have deficits in certain capacities but not others. They may be able to successfully make a metacognitive judgement about one particular subject but not about another (e.g. I may have an aptitude for discerning the emotions of others but be less able to discern my own emotions, or understand the nuances of a relationship two other people have with one another which does not involve me).

Thus, a psychotherapy concerned with metacognition must not only consider that its aim is not always the development of capacity in general but of specific capacities, each of which may call for somewhat different interventions. For instance, clients with schizophrenia struggling with limited self-awareness and others struggling to attain awareness of relationships between others into which they do not intrude may both use psychotherapy to develop those capacities but each may require somewhat different interventions.

Initial assessment

In the preceding section, we proposed that psychotherapy could be thought of as providing opportunities for the development of different kinds of metacognitive deficits, based upon client need. Raised by this general conceptual point, however, is the issue of how one might go about assessing metacognitive deficits at the outset. If psychotherapy is to address different metacognitive deficits, how should it do so? Based upon our own work and the model proposed by Semerari and colleagues, we suggest that the modified Metacognition Assessment Scale (MAS; Semerari *et al.*, 2003; Lysaker *et al.*, 2005) may be used by clinicians to concretely and theoretically determine in a collaborative manner with clients the types and forms of metacognitive deficits they are struggling with.

As noted in our earlier chapter and others, the modified MAS not only points to four distinct foci of metacognition which may be imperiled, but it also offers a continuum along which a client's capacities for making metacognitive judgement about each focus (e.g. oneself, others, etc.) may vary according to complexity. In other words, it provides an estimate of the degree of complexity with which clients can perform each of the four forms of metacognition. To accomplish this, the modified MAS divides each focus of metacognition into a series of increasingly complex steps. These steps are arranged in a hierarchical order such that to accomplish any given level of complexity one has to be able to accomplish the levels below it. In this way a point may be identified at each level of metacognition the client can attain. One client, for instance, might be said to have the capacity to perform the first through fifth step of the scale which culminate in the ability to recognize the fallibility of one's own thoughts, but not the sixth step which requires knowing expectations have no impact on reality. Another client might be said to be able to perform only the first three steps which culminate in knowing one's thoughts are one's own but not more. Accordingly, the first client would be thought to have greater metacognitive capacity on a given scale relative to the second client, but would also have room for growth. This first client might, for example, not yet be able to construct a complex personal narrative, tying together thoughts and feelings across epochs of their lives.

To illustrate this we will lay out and then discuss the nine steps that the modified MAS identifies for awareness of one's own mind. To be aware of one's own mind, the first step suggested by the modified MAS is acknowledgement by clients that they have mental functions. The second step involves clients being able to see that they have their own ideas. The third step requires that they are able to distinguish and differentiate cognitive operations (e.g. remembering, imagining, having fantasies, dreaming, desiring, deciding, foreseeing and thinking). The fourth step calls for clients to define and distinguish their emotional states. The fifth step requires that clients recognize that their ideas about themselves and the world are fallible. The sixth stage calls for the ability to recognize the limited impact that expectations, thoughts and desires have on reality. The seventh step calls for clients to recognize that their behaviour may be determined by one specific mode of cognitive or emotional functioning and to see the influence of interpersonal relationships. In the eighth step the client must demonstrate the capacity to construct a complete description of his or her own mental state and/or of the interpersonal processes in which they are involved, distinguishing cognitive and/or emotional elements. Finally, the ninth step involved in metacognition about oneself calls for clients to integrate into a coherent and complex narrative their different modes of cognitive and/or emotional functioning.

Thus it can be seen that each step on this scale calls for an act more complex than the last and it is unlikely that someone with schizophrenia could perform a specific step without being able to perform the ones below it. For instance, to be able to meaningfully link behaviour with thoughts and feelings, the client would have to be able to identify his or her own feelings, know his or her thoughts are fallible and recognize that wishes are not synonymous with reality.

To illustrate, let us consider two clients with schizophrenia who we will discuss later when talking about specific interventions: Purcell and Grieg. As described elsewhere (Lysaker and Lysaker, 2008), Grieg is a man in his fifties who experiences considerable levels of positive symptoms and Purcell is a man in his forties with considerable levels of cognitive and disorganization symptoms. Both were living on their own in the community – Grieg for years and Purcell for only a few months – when they enrolled in psychotherapy. Both were prescribed atypical antipsychotic medication. On the MAS based on clinical interview, Purcell appeared as someone who was struggling to know that his thoughts and behaviours were his own. When he described making a decision to come to the clinic, it was unclear who was thinking what or even what led to those thoughts. Purcell certainly had the capacity for the first step of awareness of one's own mind; he had mental functions. Uncertain about origin of his thoughts and feelings, however, he could be seen to struggle with the second step, which is to know that one's own thoughts are one's own. Grieg, on the other hand, was clear about why he came in and how he decided to (he was irritated with a previous therapist whom he felt was inconsistent). He could be said to have attained the first three steps of awareness of one's own mind. He knew his thoughts were his own, but he could not articulate anything about what he felt.

Using the MAS as an assessment tool we suggest that it is possible to see the very different metacognitive needs of two clients with schizophrenia on a single dimension of metacognition: Grieg was struggling to distinguish his feelings while Purcell was struggling to recognize his thoughts as his own. As might be imagined, ratings on the other three MAS scales could also be used to further determine the needs of both clients and present specific tasks for psychotherapy.

Early aspects of interventions

In the previous section we suggested that the MAS could identify specific needs with regard to metacognitive capacities along four different dimensions. This naturally raises the next question of whether one exercises metacognitive capacities in psychotherapy. While a full response to this would probably fill a volume larger than this, in this section we discuss issues that pertain to forming a working relationship with clients with schizophrenia and metacognitive deficits, and then present examples of interventions.

To lay out a possible set of basic concepts underlying interventions targeting metacognition, we will present material abstracting the guiding principles from the psychotherapy of Grieg and Purcell. Of note these were conducted in an outpatient clinic by a clinical psychologist and involved weekly voluntary sessions closely coordinated with medication and rehabilitation services. Beginning then with the presenting complaint, Grieg explained he was seeking therapy as a result of people at the supermarket staring at him because a television celebrity loved him and also because others who were jealous of the attention he received were plotting to kidnap him. As noted above, he knew his thoughts were his own, and could distinguish different cognitive functions from one another, but seemed completely unable to recognize any affect. With this in mind, psychotherapy could be conceptualized as offering him an opportunity to develop the capacity to understand and distinguish his own affects, but what would this involve?

Certainly the first matter to be addressed here – as it would in any psychotherapy – is the development of a therapeutic alliance (Norcross, 2002). To develop an alliance in this case, the therapist began by listening while refraining from interrupting Grieg in a way that called for the recognition of emotion. The therapist did not, for instance, say 'You are angry', as Grieg largely lacked the capacity to recognize internal states. The therapist also avoided the temptation to argue with the delusions; Grieg lacked the capacity to regard his thoughts as matters which were fallible. What the therapist offered instead, along with interest and respect, were comments about the quality of his thoughts – something that someone who has managed the third stage of awareness of one's own mind can understand. The therapist noted things like 'You can only think about the celebrities today' or 'You are consumed by thoughts about being kidnapped and there is no room for other ideas or people.' Indeed, Grieg recognized these as accurate and empathic reflections and an initial alliance was built around his experience of being consumed by these thoughts.

Turning to Purcell, his initial complaint was more difficult to discern. He stated, 'I wouldn't know lifestyle demand . . . Lifestyle demand is irrelevant anymore to me because the reason I say it's irrelevant is because the words are more important, and yet they decrease your style of living for the benefit that there's no bad actions, you know. That way, you're liable to forget you see, and I can understand that, but if I wanted to put something intact this immediate, it would be mine.'

As noted above, Purcell was conceptualized as struggling with the second stage of being aware of his own mind. He was unsure regarding the ownership of his thoughts. In initially responding to him, the therapist – as in the case of Grieg – avoided reflecting emotions or offered comments on the accuracy of thoughts. Even more so than for Grieg, these comments would have been without real meaning to Purcell. Instead, the therapist worked within what he estimated Purcell's abilities to be: when Purcell spoke of a metaphorical snake, the therapist responded by saying, 'You think I am a snake.' When Purcell mentioned someone from his past, the therapist merely noted, 'You are remembering someone.' Each fragmented thought was noticed but not tied to any subsequent or preceding thought. No effort was made on the part of the therapist to connect these into a large whole. The therapist merely tried to talk directly about their early and very turbulent relationship in a way that Purcell could process. As with

Grieg, this was accepted as empathic and formed an agreed upon basis for treatment: 'I need to recuperate.'

Turning to the issue of intervention (once a therapeutic alliance has been reasonably established), we find the metaphor of physical therapy again potentially useful. Using this metaphor, the therapeutic relationship can be seen as serving two functions. First, the relationship empowers the therapist to encourage the client to try and think about things which are painful, much as a physical therapist might offer essential encouragement to move a leg in ways which are painful. Second, the relationship itself may also function as a brace or prosthesis. Just as a brace might help someone to walk and exercise muscles that could not be exercised otherwise, the therapist may within the therapeutic relationship operate in some sense as a cognitive prosthetic. Therapists may, for instance, offer assistance in filtering, recalling and considering material relevant to the client's deepest concerns in a flexibly abstract manner.

The therapist in both cases chose interventions according to an estimate of the client's metacognitive capacity (i.e. what stages they are capable of achieving). During the early work with Grieg, the therapist challenged him to examine what he might possibly feel in a certain situation: 'Mr Grieg, you described a situation in which X and Y happened, but you did not mention how you felt.' If Grieg could not answer the therapist pushed: 'Do you have any ideas of what you could have felt?' 'You are unsure about how you felt', or 'How do you think I would feel in such a situation?' The therapist might also offer periodic summaries of what had been said in session as if serving partially as a filter to help Grieg see the key points made so far. The therapist highlighted times when affects were noted fleetingly: 'You were sad', or 'You were angry with your brother.' Reflections were made in the second person (i.e. 'you') and in essence offered Grieg an image of himself in the 'you' mentioned such that it could be considered jointly by both parties (i.e. by Grieg and the therapist). In response to this, Grieg slowly began spontaneously to describe more distinct emotional states (e.g. envy, feelings of inadequacy, rage). It appeared that where previously he had used delusions to explain distressing states, he could now describe those states directly with the result that the report of delusional thinking lessened dramatically. He also developed a new shared goal of not wanting to be dominated by thoughts. He said he did 'not know how to love' and wanted to be able to do that, something that the therapist interpreted as a desire to further the capacity to discern feelings of love for others.

As for Purcell, after he offered disorganized or highly abstract thoughts, the therapist reworded these into a statement that highlighted the second person as if to challenge Purcell to form a thought that he might own. For instance, when Purcell stated, 'The people of this earth shun the wounded like they don't know them in their back alleys', the therapist replied, 'You are shunned.' Purcell replied, 'The head of the body is in pain,' and the therapist said in return, 'You have a headache.' Again, interventions did not address matters in a way that called for metacognition beyond Purcell's capacity. For example, at this stage no attempt was made to construct any larger state of affairs, such as, 'You are angry because you feel you have been shunned, and now have a headache.' As in the case of Grieg, each time a thought was clearly articulated by Purcell it was emphasized by the therapist: 'You think . . .'. Here it was not viewed as important that the therapist's comments were by some standard correct, but rather that they successfully recognized Purcell's ownership of his own thoughts. Purcell was quick to dismiss incorrect translations of his speech into the second person and to laugh with some delight when he thought they were correct. For example, he began a session, 'In this country it is killing them with kindness.' When the therapist said, 'You want to be kind to me,' Purcell calmly shook his head no. The therapist tried again, 'You want to kill me.' With that, Purcell laughed with an air of being pleasantly surprised but also angry.

With regard to the function of the therapist as a prosthetic, as in the case of Grieg, the therapist often served as a voice which repeated multiple things Purcell said. This seemed less a presentation of choices to pursue and more an offering of a kind of working memory that could be used to access an account of what had taken place so far in the session. Indeed, as Purcell was to say to the same therapist several years into his therapy, 'You make me remember my life which is why I hate you.'

In summary, we have suggested in this section that psychotherapy may offer persons with schizophrenia an opportunity to exercise and develop metacognitive capacity after the establishment of a therapeutic relationship. In the two cases we presented, this was done by first ascertaining the level of metacognition the client had achieved in the area of awareness of one's own mind and then offering back in the second person observations or challenges about matters appropriate to that level. If the client was struggling to recognize his thoughts as his own, comments were offered about the thoughts he had. If the client was struggling to recognize his own distinct emotions, comments were directed towards that.

We did not intend to offer a description of every possible intervention that could be tied to a given level of a given domain of metacognition. Much more work is needed in this area, and we anticipate that the approach described in this section is ultimately an integrative one. Techniques from a range of perspectives can be meaningfully utilized to address metacognitive deficits as long as they are sensitive to the client's existent capacities. Additionally, we did not address above work on the other three domains of metacognition on the MAS for reasons of space. The initial capacities for awareness of other's minds, decentration and mastery were assessed and certainly much work was done in these areas. As a brief note, this followed the same principles as noted above. After the formation of the therapeutic alliance, work was offered in the second person, for example: 'You are unsure about how your ex-wife feels', or 'You were overwhelmed and unsure about what to do and so you walked away.'

Progress and conceptualization during interventions

As the work in these two cases progressed over a period of months and then years, improvements were noted. As a result, metacognitive capacities on all the MAS scales were reconsidered routinely and work was adjusted accordingly. For example, the therapist offered a routine and somewhat more complex summary of Purcell's reflections during a session: 'You think that if you try to get along it will all go bad and people will shun you.' Purcell laughed giddily and said, 'Yeah, that's right.' 'Why?' the therapist asked. Purcell proceeded to contextualize this mutually constructed observation, bringing together several very clear historical experiences centred on feelings of abandonment. He recalled how relatives had raised him away from his siblings and how he was angry at having been separated in this way. At the time he felt as if his surrogate parents had not really loved him, although he now confessed to perhaps not having given them a chance, particularly since he had come to learn that the grandmother who raised him had also struggled with mental illness. He noted that since then he had lived a life of self-neglect as the only way to survive. The therapist responded, 'That's the story of how you became the king of self-neglect.' Purcell laughed, 'But that is not a good way to be.' In this snippet we would assert that a capacity to distinguish affects is growing along with the beginning of the possibility to develop the understanding of the subjectivity and fallibility of his own thoughts. Additionally, referring to Purcell as the 'king of self-neglect' not only communicated an observation in a non-judgemental manner but it also provided a scaffolding, so to speak, for him to continue to tell his story as one who is neglectful of his own needs.

Highlighted in this example, moreover, is the fact that as progress is made the therapist must respond accordingly in the moment. Additionally, there are three separate points that are essential to the evolution of the work. First, while Purcell is thinking about other people, his own feelings and also the issue of coping or mastery, it would be naive to think that each would be addressed in a separate section of the session. All may naturally emerge or not emerge according to some logic to which the therapist will never be privy. Thus, there should be no 'pre-session plan' to address a certain metacognitive ability or stage, as progress is fluid and variable from session to session.

Second, while there is progress in this particular session, in the following session there was regression. In the case of Purcell, Grieg and others (e.g. Lysaker *et al.*, 2007), progress was rarely linear. While estimates of metacognitive capacity trended upwards over time in a statistically significant manner, losses often followed gains, suggesting that as persons regained metacognitive capacity it often faltered before it became established. As a corollary, changes in one domain of metacognition did not translate automatically into changes in another. Both Grieg and another case study formally analysed with blind raters (Lysaker *et al.*, 2005, 2007) suggested that awareness of one's own mind improved substantially before there were any changes in awareness of the other's mind.

A third and equally important point is that the therapist's ability to observe progress was contingent on the formulation of goals and the assessment of progress in terms of capacities rather than solutions to certain problems, states or conflicts. If the development of metacognition is the purpose, key issues do not include finding the solutions needed to get out of specific dilemmas, the resolution of particular conflicts or the changing of isolated beliefs. While certainly still important issues, none are central to development of metacognitive capacity. Coping with problems and resolving troublesome emotional states and behaviours are both essential for recovery from schizophrenia and it would be inappropriate to ignore them for either Grieg or Purcell. The aim of a metacognitive psychotherapy, though, is the development of the capacities that would enable clients to find adaptive ways to solve those and other problems more often on their own. Addressing problems would be meaningful in such psychotherapy mostly in terms of whether and how it provided the client with an opportunity to practise and develop metacognitive capacities.

As an illustration, consider the following example. At one point, to become more active, the therapist assisted Grieg to figure out how to utilize the area's bus system. This involved helping him learn how to get a ticket, how to insert it in the ticket reader, where and when to find the returning bus, and so on. It was mutually agreed that he would try this once a week and come and see the therapist for an additional visit and cup of coffee. Certainly there were problems to be solved and the experience had to be discussed over and over (e.g. the first time he could not find the bus stop, panicked and called an expensive taxi to return him home). Nevertheless, the point was not only that he successfully arrived and departed, but also that he decided to come in, followed through and experienced different emotions throughout the process. On days when he did not come in for the extra visit, the point was not only to find out how to help him make it there the next time but also to process how it was he decided not to come in. Thus, whether he successfully rode or did not ride the bus was as much the issue as how he decided to travel or not travel. Had he thought about it the evening before? Was he tempted to turn around? What did he feel after making the trek only to discover no cup of coffee because the therapist was ill? Raising these issues, for instance, brought out how he 'felt institutionalized and resented' with others making demands upon him. It also brought out the recognition in general that when the world was not as he pleased, he felt inadequate, blamed himself and said hostile things to others. The same principle held true and applied to the issue of dysfunctional or discrete maladaptive beliefs. Purcell believed that he was of no value socially and was likely to fail should he attempt to work. Certainly these were matters that were addressed, but in addressing them the goal was not only to help create more adaptive thought patterns but also to use the discussion as an opportunity for the exercise and strengthening of the capacity to think about one's own thinking.

To expand this point, let us consider a possibly more complex example. As both Grieg and Purcell moved towards recovery they naturally struggled to find ways to resolve conflicts and repair relationships with family and friends. Purcell called it his 'rude awakening'. Grieg wondered about several things: whether he was lovable in the eyes of another person; his feelings of jealousy for his more successful siblings; and the torment of having a mentally ill parent when he was a vulnerable child. Some might respond to these issues by seeking to resolve a particular psychological conflict. In contrast, the metacognitive perspective we would like to evolve – as in the above example – would not see the resolution of conflictual feelings as the goal but instead as an opportunity for the exercise and development of metacognitive capacity during this process.

Thus, the metacognitive perspective offers a chance to easily avoid the temptation to solve clients' dilemmas for them, a practice which while superficially appearing to be benign might instead reinforce stigmatizing beliefs that a mentally ill person is not capable of making his or her own decisions. It also allows for therapists to avoid the destructive and often irresponsible practice of framing family dynamics as necessarily playing a causal role in psychosis. As we have discussed elsewhere (Lysaker and Daroyanni, 2006), metacognitive deficits might make it difficult to solve the psychological conflicts that characterize the psychic life of many, and the failure to solve those conflicts may exacerbate symptoms. This may also provide a way to understand the basis for faulty observations regarding psychological conflicts as primary causes of psychosis. Addressing conflicts led to symptom reduction in Grieg's case. However, this was not because these conflicts caused the symptoms, as some have supposed, but possibly as a result of deficits in metacognition it was especially difficult to live with these conflicts and they then exacerbated symptoms.

Outcome and ongoing assessment

Thus far we have suggested that once a therapeutic alliance has been formed, psychotherapy may offer clients an opportunity to practise and develop metacognitive capacities. To illustrate we have offered clinical material from two cases and suggested that in both the therapist purposefully crafted interventions in order to offer them opportunities to work on specific forms of metacognition at achievable levels. We have also suggested that the improvements which follow are not linear and that changes in one domain may be independent of another. We have noted the need in this form of therapy for the therapist to sustain a view of progress in terms of opportunities for exercise and the actual growth of metacognitive capacities rather than merely the solution of problems, states or conflicts. We have also suggested – consistently with basic requirements of contemporary psychotherapy of schizophrenia – that this form of psychotherapy may easily remain compatible with rehabilitation and in no way blame families or stigmatize clients.

A final question to be raised pertains to the objective assessment of progress in such a form of treatment. In what is probably a highly anticipated response, we offer the final suggestion that growth may be tracked in terms of performance on the modified MAS. If psychotherapy results in changes in metacognitive capacity, blind assessments using the MAS should reveal significant changes over time.

Indeed, one method for doing this is to assign a point to each modified MAS scale level attained such that a score can be generated estimating metacognition within the semi-independent scales of the MAS as well as overall metacognition (i.e. overall metacognition may be estimated as the sum of the scales). For instance, if Purcell was judged to successfully master the second step of awareness of one's own mind, he would be given a score of two for that scale and that scale score would be summed with the other scale score to provide a total. As published elsewhere, we have found that blind raters can reliably rate metacognition from both psychotherapy transcripts and personal narrative obtained outside of therapy by a semi-structured interview (Lysaker *et al.*, 2005, 2007; Lysaker and Daroyanni, 2006).

As an illustration of the viability of this procedure, in Figure 13.1 we present bimonthly ratings of Grieg's psychotherapy transcripts using the modified MAS over a period of 51 months of psychotherapy. As can be seen in this graph, ratings of the MAS total can be seen to rise in a non-linear fashion over a period of two years and then slowly to sustain an elevated level over time, suggesting the gradual attainment of metacognitive capacity. Interestingly and true to experience, growth appears slow with gains often followed by increasingly brief periods of loss. As an aside, the total score for the MAS may reach 28; thus Grieg reaches a ceiling which suggests he has not achieved the most complex levels of metacognition.

Summary, limitations and conclusions

At the outset of this chapter we asked whether an integrative psychotherapy conceptualized as addressing metacognition was viable as a contemporary psychotherapy for schizophrenia, and if so what the technical requirements

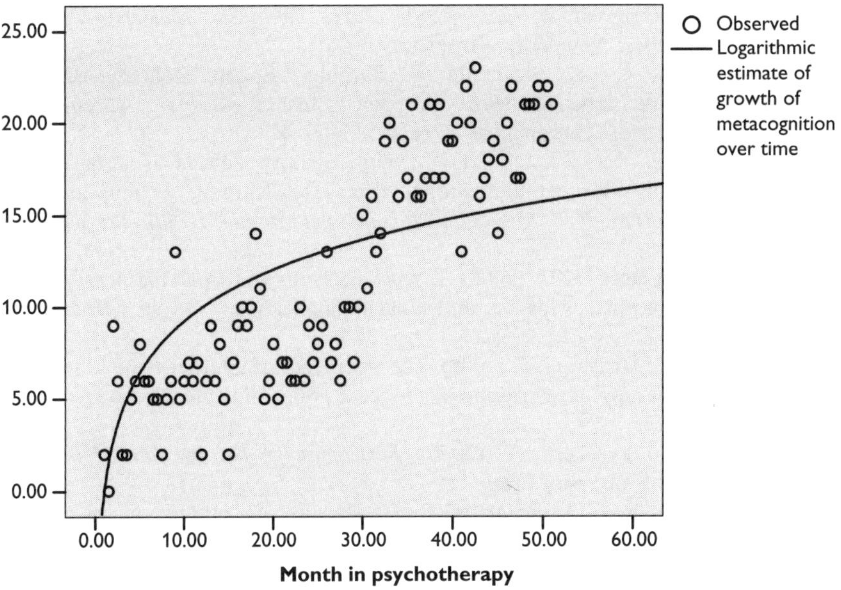

Figure 13.1 Modified metacognition assessment total score over 51 months: case of Grieg.

of such a psychotherapy would be and then how to assess outcomes. In response we have suggested that psychotherapy may offer opportunities for the practice and development of metacognition by considering metacognition as composed of a range of domains in which capacity may vary considerably. We have suggested that this begins with an accurate assessment of the individual's capacities and the timing of interventions based on ongoing assessments. We believe our case examples have also suggested such an intervention is fully compatible with existent forms of recovery oriented rehabilitation practices, has outcomes that should be measurable and carries with it no risk of stigmatizing mentally ill persons or their families.

There do, however, remain important limitations to our report. There exist no randomized controlled trials of this treatment and the only supporting evidence is the case reports cited above which were conducted at one site. Future work is needed to further define and study this intervention and to provide more detailed guidance for practitioners.

References

Drake, R.E. and Sederer, L.I. (1986). The adverse effects of intensive treatment of schizophrenia. *Comprehensive Psychiatry*, *27*, 313–326.

Karon, B.P. and Vandenbos, G.R. (1981). *Psychotherapy of schizophrenia: The treatment of choice*. New York: Aronson.

Link, B.G., Frances, T.C., Struening, E., Shrout, P.E. and Dohrenwend, B.P. (1989). A modified labeling theory approach to mental disorders: An empirical assessment. *American Sociological Review*, *54*, 400–423.

Lysaker, P.H. and Buck, K.D. (2007). Neurocognitive deficits as a barrier to psychosocial function: Multidirectional effects on learning, coping and self conception. *Journal of Psychosocial Nursing and Mental Health Services*, *45*, 24–30.

Lysaker, P.H. and Buck, K.D. (2008). Is recovery from schizophrenia possible? An overview of concepts, evidence, and clinical implications. *Primary Psychiatry*, *15*(6), 60–65.

Lysaker, P.H. and Daroyanni, P. (2006). The emergence of interpersonal relatedness in the psychotherapy of schizophrenia: A case study. *Bulletin of the Menninger Clinic*, *70*, 53–67.

Lysaker, P.H. and Lysaker, J.T. (2008). *Schizophrenia and the fate of the self*. Oxford: Oxford University Press.

Lysaker, P.H., Davis, L.D., Eckert, G.J., Strasburger, A., Hunter, N. and Buck, K.D. (2005). Changes in narrative structure and content in schizophrenia in long term individual psychotherapy: A single case study. *Clinical Psychology and Psychotherapy*, *12*, 406–416.

Lysaker, P.H., Buck, K.D. and Ringer, J. (2007). The recovery of metacognitive capacity in schizophrenia across thirty two months of individual psychotherapy: A case study. *Psychotherapy Research*, *17*, 713–720.

Norcross, J.C. (ed.) (2002). *Psychotherapy relationships that work*. New York: Oxford University Press.

Ritsher, J.B. and Phelan, J.C. (2004). Internalized stigma predicts erosion of morale among psychiatric outpatients. *Psychiatry Research*, *129*, 257–265.

Semerari, A., Carcione, A., Dimaggio, G., Falcone, M., Nicolò, G., Procacci, M., *et al.* (2003). How to evaluate metacognitive functioning in psychotherapy? The metacognition assessment scale its applications. *Clinical Psychology and Psychotherapy*, *10*, 238–261.

Chapter 14

Empathic and theory of mind processes

The dialogical core of a metacognitive approach to psychiatric rehabilitation

Ilanit Hasson-Ohayon, Shlomo Kravetz and David Roe

Social, affective and cognitive impairments and disabilities are major challenges confronting persons committed to providing mental health and psychiatric rehabilitation services to persons with severe mental illness (SMI). These impairments and disabilities play a central role in the inadequate social functioning that the *DSM-IV* (American Psychiatric Association, 1994) requires for all mental illness diagnoses. According to recent theories of schizophrenia and other SMI, impairments of metacognition (i.e. empathy, theory of mind, TOM, mind reading) are major sources of these communication and interpersonal limitations (Frith, 1992; Lee, 2007).

The present chapter differentiates between empathy and TOM within a dialogical framework of metacognition and uses this differentiation critically to review interpersonal and metacognitive rehabilitation interventions for persons with SMI. These interventions are pioneering efforts that have recently been developed to improve the communication and interpersonal skills of persons with schizophrenia. A major aspect of these interventions is their inclusion of techniques for correcting the mind reading errors that often distort the interpersonal perception and communication of persons with SMI. In this sense, they deal with the limitations of empathy and TOM. This chapter will show how dialogue can significantly enhance these techniques for dealing with these limitations.

A dialogue about knowing and not knowing the other in schizophrenia

Metacognitive processes have been hypothesized as playing major roles in the impairments and disabilities of persons with schizophrenia, especially those associated with the difficulties these persons experience as participants in interpersonal relationships and activities (Frith, 1992; Lee, 2007). On the one hand, according to Frith (1992), due to impaired metacognition, persons with schizophrenia have difficulty formulating ideas about their own goals and intentions and often misconstrue the intentions of others. Such deficits and distortions of one's own dispositions and intentions and of the intentions and dispositions of others are thought to result in difficulties with social behaviour often experienced by persons with schizophrenia (see Schaub *et al.*, this volume, Chapter 5). In addition, persons with schizophrenia have difficulty interpreting social cues and even have distorted views of the affective states of others. Thus, schizophrenia is conceived of as a disorder of intuitive attunement that constitutes a fundamental deficit of the development and maintenance of social relationships (Lee, 2007; Stanghellini, this volume, Chapter 8). On the other hand, persons with schizophrenia are estranged from others, in part, due to stereotypes that attribute to them interpersonal awkwardness and insensitivity (Corrigan, 2007).

The above situation would seem to be somewhat paradoxical. If metacognition and empathy entail knowing and experiencing the other as she or he knows and experiences herself or himself, then not acknowledging the other's limited metacognition and empathy could be defined as deficient metacognition and empathy even when such an acknowledgement is considered a negative stereotype. However, because many individuals with schizophrenia do not acknowledge their limited metacognition and empathy, attributing to them limitations that they do not avow may also constitute a breach of metacognition and empathy. This paradox raises the question as to whether one can be empathic with someone she or he considers inherently lacking on empathy.

The above issue was raised in connection with schizophrenia in a 1957 dialogue between Carl Rogers and Martin Buber (Agassi, 1999). Buber and Rogers disagreed as to whether therapists and patients can achieve complete symmetry. Rogers claimed that ultimate therapeutic change takes place when moments of complete symmetry occur, whereas Buber argued that the therapist's striving after such moments posits asymmetry between the therapist and the patient and thus inherently limits their achievement.

In his efforts to explore the above point of contention, Buber asked Rogers whether he would make the same claim for his work with individuals with paranoia and schizophrenia. After admitting that he had limited experience in working with such persons, Rogers answered, 'I would say there is *no* [italics in the original] difference in the relationship that I form with a normal person, a schizophrenic, a paranoid – I don't really feel any difference' (Agassi, 1999: 257). Buber's response introduced what he termed 'the concept of limits' and added 'I do something, I try something, I will something, and give all my, all my existence-*into* [italics in the original] this doing. And I come, at a certain moment, to a wall, to a boundary, to a limit that I *cannot* [italics in the original] ignore . . . So even in dialogue, full dialogue, there is a limit set' (p. 258).

The position adopted in this chapter is closer to that of Buber than to that of Rogers' position in the above dialogue. We will provide clinical and empirical support for the claim that dialogue between the self and other is essential for the development and maintenance of empathy and TOM. We will make an attempt to show how the self, as object and subject, incorporates those aspects of metacognitive processes that are paradoxical and how, in this respect, the manner in which schizophrenia leads to persistent difficulties with developing and maintaining interpersonal relationships may only be an exaggeration of the less severe and persistent interpersonal difficulties of persons without SMI. Finally, the model of mind reading as an interpersonal capacity grounded on the interaction between empathic processes and TOM mechanisms that is monitored by dialogue will be used to critically evaluate a number of attempts to develop interventions based on metacognitive accounts of schizophrenia. Dialogue between the person with a SMI and her or his care provider as to the limits of both the care provider's and the care user's mind reading should be an especially effective and non-stigmatic way of coming to terms with these limits.

The relation between TOM and empathy in schizophrenia

Different terms such as metacognition, theory of mind, empathy and mind reading have been used to refer to the processes that contribute to an individual's capacity for and interest in experiencing and reflecting on herself or himself and the other as a distinct person. Differences between these terms are not always clear and are often used interchangeably. However, explications of theoretical controversies regarding the essential nature of the metacognitive process sometimes adopt stipulative definitions of these terms to identify sides to the controversy.

On the basis of a review of the literature on the neuronal underpinnings and ontogeny of empathy and mind reading (i.e. TOM), Singer (2006) suggests that empathy and TOM may refer to different capacities with different underlying neuronal circuitry and ontogenetic trajectories. Singer associates the capacity to develop a TOM with the ability to make attributions about another person's propositional attitude (desires, beliefs, intentions). However, she associates empathy with the sharing of sensations and emotions of others.

A model of mind reading that integrates TOM and empathic accounts of understanding the other is highly consistent with Langdon's theory of the relation between metacognition and schizophrenia. Langdon (2005) maintains that whereas deficits in a TOM module generally responsible for representing the desires, beliefs and intentions of others appear to account for mind reading deficits in autism, the capacity for mind reading of persons with schizophrenia seems to be compromised by distorted empathic perspective-taking. Langdon (2005) describes two related sets of the possible consequences of compromised empathic processes in persons with schizophrenia. One of these refers to the tendency of persons with schizophrenia occasionally to lose a sense of themselves in interpersonal interactions due to the loss of boundary experiences. The other set of consequences consists of the retreat of these persons into a solipsistic and alienated world that is often accompanied by the distrust of others and persecutory thoughts.

Empathy, metacognition and dialogue

Establishing and maintaining a sense of the self and the other

On the basis of the above stipulated differentiation between empathy and TOM, interpersonal understanding could be considered to be a function of the interaction between these processes. TOM constructs could modulate the intensity and structure of the process of empathic perspective-taking. Loss of boundary experiences and over-identification with the other at one end of a complex continuum and alienation and solipsism at the other end could constitute the limits of this interaction.

Actually, Beck (1978) uses the term 'mind reading' to denote one of the major common cognitive biases. Beck defines mind reading as the belief that one knows what a person is thinking solely on the basis of her or his behaviour. According to Beck, mind reading is classifiable as a pathological cognitive bias when it is produced by a rigid schema about reality and the self and when one of its consequences is negative feelings about the self. In keeping with this chapter's view of mind reading as a function of the interaction between empathic processes and TOM mechanisms, mind reading that is pathological would seem to be a function of TOM constructs whose rigidity and negative emotional impact distorts and prevents corrective genuine empathic perspective taking. In a certain sense, this suggested account of distorted mind reading is keeping with Saxe's (2005) attribution of prevalent errors in mind reading to naive theories of mind. Although, as Beck points out, certain forms of mind reading may be dysfunctional, the approach to mind reading adopted by this chapter is that both pre-reflective empathy and the more critical TOM processes are essential ingredients of interpersonal conduct. Actually without these ingredients such fundamental phenomena as parent–child relationships and such sophisticated cultural activities as art and science would be unimaginable. However, due to the limitations of empathy (Langdon, 2005) and TOM (Beck, 1978; Saxe, 2005; Schaub *et al.*, this volume, Chapter 5), this conduct sometimes goes astray. For certain persons, such as persons with schizophrenia, these limitations may be so rigid that they require special attention. In this chapter, we describe how combining dialogue with psychosocial metacognitive interventions may be an effective way of dealing with these limitations.

Cognitive restructuring is one of the major innovations used by cognitive behavioural therapists in their attempts to modify mind reading when mind reading loses its openness and flexibility and begins to bias cognition with dire consequences for individual and social functioning and quality of life (Beck, 1970). Socratic dialogue is usually one of the first therapeutic techniques used when engaging persons seriously troubled by cognitive biases in cognitive restructuring (Freeman, 2005). Within the framework of cognitive behavioural therapy, Socratic dialogue is a therapeutic technique for generating questions aimed at facilitating the client's exploration of beliefs, images, desires and intentions connected to the problem that brought him or her to therapy.

In this chapter, dialogue refers to a norm of intentional communication (Tirassa, 1999; Carpendale and Lewis, 2004). According to Tirassa (1999), intentional communication is characterized by processes derived from theories of cognitive pragmatics that describe what goes on in the mind of a person who is involved in a communicative interaction with another person. Tirassa (1999) claims this approach to communication is based on the assumptions that communication is a form of social activity rather than a linguistic activity and that it therefore requires cooperation between the participants.

Viewing dialogue as an ideal intentional communication is consistent with the above assumptions and with Tirassa's designation of the communicative act as an overt attempt to create a situation that is relatively satisfactory to the participants in the dialogue. In this sense, successful dialogue, in part, consists of coupling the cognitive dynamics of these participants. Thus, dialogue as intentional communication depends upon mind reading.

Tummolini *et al.* (2006) describe the development of the capacity for mind reading in terms of an early innate capacity in the infant to openly share experiences with other people that eventually is transformed by sophisticated TOM mechanisms. They denote the early stage of TOM development as sharedness and define it as an agent's ability to experience her or his mental states as mutually known to a partner. In terms of the putative distinction between empathy and TOM that was formulated in the first part of this chapter, sharedness can be considered as an early form of empathy.

These theoreticians also suggest that during early development children cease to share all of their mental states with their caregivers. They specify this stage as the beginning of true mind reading and relate it to the emergence of freedom and autonomy. Thus, the origin of sophisticated mind reading does not coincide with sociality but rather with the restrictions that TOM places on unbounded empathic sharedness. Because at this stage of development children begin to exercise some control over the experiences they attempt to reveal to the other, this stage is also the origin of intentional communication. Positioning the emergence of the capacity for dialogue at a developmental interval where empathic sharedness interacts with metacognitive TOM mechanisms to allow for the differentiation between private and communicative action is very much in line with dialogical conceptualizations of the self.

According to Salgado and Hermans (2005), internalization of dialogue is the source of the individual's inner voice which she or he comes to articulate as the self and a variety of potential others. This experience of the dialogical self, like every intersubjective experience, has a subjective and private side. The dialogical self also dynamically links one's awareness of the self with one's awareness of the other (Dimaggio *et al.*, 2008). In a similar vein, Stam (2006) concludes his discussion of the dialogical self with the following related statements: 'The self that is in dialogue is made possible by that very dialogue' and 'Dialogue is the double negotiation of that dependence and agency' (p. 115). Accordingly, empathic dialogue is characterized by the tension between the transparency and opacity of the experience of the self and the other. A breakdown of this tension might result in a shift to the extreme interiority and, subsequently, the alienation of paranoia, the breakdown and loss of self of schizophrenia, or the rigid and negative mind reading of depression and anxiety and obsessive-compulsive disorders.

Reinstating the sense of the self and the other

Dialogue and interventions with persons with schizophrenia

Very recently, metacognitive training programmes have been developed to help persons with schizophrenia to become aware of and to gain control over the metacognitive sources of their cognitive biases and deviant behaviour. Assumptions underlying these programmes are that impairments of metacognitive, TOM and empathic mechanisms and processes are responsible for the cognitive distortions and personal and interpersonal deficiencies and excesses experienced by persons with SMI. For example, Moritz and Woodward (2007) describe a metacognitive training programme (MCT) that they developed whose feasibility, treatment adherence and subjective efficacy they evaluated.

The MCT programme includes eight modules that address a variety of cognitive errors and problem-solving biases associated with schizophrenia and other disorders such as bipolar disorder and severe personality disorder (Moritz and Woodward, 2007). Each module is reproduced with parallel exercises so that the participants in the training programme can repeat the training twice. These modules deal with the following biases: increased self-serving bias (module 1); a jumping to conclusion bias (modules 2 and 7); a bias against disconfirmatory evidence (module 3); deficits in TOM (modules 4 and 6); over-confidence in memory (module 5); and depressive cognitive patterns (module 8). Modules are presented in a group format, consisting of three to ten persons. Homework assignments are also used in conjunction with the modules.

In the MCT programme described here, metacognition refers both to thinking about one's own thoughts and experiences as well as thinking about the thoughts and experiences of others. TOM and empathy are treated as synonyms and are considered a subcategory of metacognition that deals with thinking about the thinking and experiences of others. Because this chapter emphasizes the interpersonal nature of metacognition, a concise description of module 6A, labelled To Empathize II, will be provided as an example of the MCT programme.

Module 6 is concerned with how we evaluate what others are thinking and experiencing. In this module's initial tasks, a list of social cues (i.e. posture, hands, language, clothes) that are often used to identify the emotional states, beliefs and intentions of others are presented, followed by a list of the advantages and disadvantages of these social cues. These lists are accompanied by such questions for discussion as: When you get to know someone, where do you look first? and How reliable are these cues? Subsequent tasks require the participants in the programme to complete, rearrange and interpret cartoons that illustrate how the misuse of social cues can lead to interpersonal misunderstanding. The final tasks link the former tasks to problems with interpersonal relationships often experienced by persons with SMI.

Moritz and Woodward (2007) compared the MCT programme to CogPack (Marker, 2003), a computerized cognitive remediation programme for persons with schizophrenia that is administered individually. The programmes did not differ with regard to attendance, feasibility and acceptance whereas a number of questions about subjective efficacy indicated that the MCT programme was characterized by a statistically significant higher level of subjective efficacy than CogPack. Moritz and Woodward (2007) are cautiously optimistic about MCT's potential to reduce metacognitive deficit, though note the limitations of their work to date which they label as a pilot study.

As mentioned above, the developers of the MCT programme neither differentiate between empathic and TOM aspects of the metacognitive impairment of persons with schizophrenia, nor do they seem to view the latter interpersonal metacognitive impairments as more central contributors to the disabilities of persons with schizophrenia than are the intrapersonal metacognitive impairments. Thus, in module 4A, labelled To Empathize I, ways of exploring the thoughts and experiences of another person are presented, such as referring to knowledge about that person or about that person's environment/situation. Although the MCT manual encourages lively discussions between the participants and instructs the group leaders to provide enough time for the participants openly to exchange their views, activities that may enhance the affective components of metacognitive communication, the possibility of communicating with that person and asking about her or his thoughts and experiences are not included in the list of examples of ways of improving empathy. In terms of this chapter's emphasis on dialogue as empathic communication, such a process should be a major way of improving empathy with another person. Due to its sensitive and complex nature, this process could require one or more separate modules.

Another example of a metacognitive intervention is the Social Cognition and Interaction Training (SCIT) programme which was developed to improve both the social cognition and social functioning of person with schizophrenia spectrum disorders (Combs *et al.*, 2006; Penn *et al.*, 2007). Although the title of this intervention refers to cognition rather than metacognition, actually it is designed to help persons with schizophrenia with such metacognitive issues as jumping to conclusions and theory of mind that are also the concern of the MTC programme. However, SCIT emphasizes the interpersonal nature of the latter issues. Thus, one of the rationales for the SCIT programme's focus on social cognition is Brothers' (1990) claim that social cognition is concerned with mental operations underlying social interactions such as the human ability and capacity to perceive the intentions and dispositions of others. Accordingly, this intervention would appear to be more in keeping with this chapter's emphasis on the centrality of the interpersonal aspects of metacognition.

SCIT is divided into three phases – emotion training, figuring out situations and integration – that span 24 weeks of 50-minute sessions. Training in each of these sessions is provided by one to two therapists who make use of a manual and a DVD and a VHS supplement. Goal and procedures vary across the programme's phases.

The goals of the emotion training phase are to provide information about emotions in general and about the basic emotions in particular. Commercially available computer-based programmes are used to improve the participants' emotion perception and to facilitate their differentiation between justified and unjustified suspiciousness. During the figuring out phase, a variety of materials and activities is used to inform the participants about the dangers associated with jumping to conclusions, to increase their cognitive flexibility in social situations, and to help them distinguish between personal and situational attributions, and between social facts and guesses.

In the final integration phase, under the guidance of the therapists, the participants put into practice what they learned in the first two phases. During this phase, problematic interpersonal situations from the participants' life histories are used to exemplify identifying other person's affect, differentiating between facts and guesses, avoiding jumping to conclusions, and coming up with a solution or action plan. This action plan could include engaging in a conversation with another person to explore that person's beliefs and feelings. Role plays with the therapist or other participants are used to strengthen the participants' social skills in this phase of the programme.

Pilot testing of the SCIT programme with 17 persons with schizophrenia has been carried out. This testing indicated that SCIT improved these persons' perception of emotion and theory of mind and reduced their attribution of hostile intent. After treatment, 94 per cent of the participants agreed with statements as to the understandability of the programme's materials, the programme's usefulness, and the degree to which it helped them think about their social situation and improve the way they related to other people. Furthermore, in another study, five clinicians not affiliated with the research team that developed the programme agreed with statements as to the helpfulness of the programme's manual and as to the programme's positive contribution to their clients' social cognition and interaction. Obviously these preliminary findings must be qualified due to the limited number of participants in the intervention and the lack of control groups and comprehensive outcome criteria (Combs *et al.*, 2006).

Integrating dialogical processes in rehabilitation interventions with persons with schizophrenia

Metacognitive psychiatric rehabilitation interventions for persons with psychiatric disabilities are in the pioneering stage. These interventions are based on the relatively general assumptions that such disabilities are, in part, the consequence of impaired metacognitive abilities and that training in metacognitive task performance will improve these abilities and reduce the disabilities associated with the psychiatric condition. In this way, these interventions share the directive and pragmatic aspects of more established interventions such as cognitive behaviour therapy (Morrison, 1998), illness management and recovery (Mueser *et al.*, 2006) and family psychoeducation (McFarlane *et al.*, 2003).

However, in this chapter theoretical arguments and empirical evidence were presented for distinguishing developmentally and neuropsychologically between the empathic and TOM facets of interpersonal understanding and communication (Langdon, 2005; Singer, 2006). Elaborating the dialogical elements of the above reviewed metacognitive and social cognitive interventions could make this integration of the empathic and TOM aspects of metacognition more explicit and possibly more effective. The claim has been presented that dialogue both within the individual and between the individual and others contributes significantly to the development of a coherent sense of self and that disruptions of internal and external dialogue could account for the various kinds of disorganization of the self experienced by persons with SMI (Lysaker and Lysaker, 2001, 2002).

Accordingly, metacognitive psychiatric rehabilitation interventions that are structured around improving the persons' capacity for dialogue may both enhance the empathic processes involved in the perception and communication of affective states and facilitate the integration of these processes with the metacognitive processes involved in critically examining the desires, beliefs and intentions of the other. Follow-up investigations of the implementation of such interventions should inform us of the extent to which they are effective in improving the interpersonal quality of life of persons with psychiatric disabilities and of the extent to which the assumptions underlying these interventions are valid.

As was suggested with regard to the manner in which cognitive and metacognitive psychosocial interventions overlap, psychosocial interventions, in general, due to their reflexive nature, may implicitly contain metacognitive elements. In keeping with this chapter's emphasis on an essential link between dialogue and metacognition, the dialogism that also often characterizes aspects of psychosocial interventions may contribute to the above metacognitive elements. Accordingly, an emphasis on the encounter and dialogue with the other are major relatively recent developments of Rogers' person-centred psychotherapy. Schmid (2001) believes that these developments in part stem from Rogers' dialogue with Buber described above. This emphasis constitutes an acknowledgement of the value of empathy together with an appreciation of empathy's limits. Schmid (2001) suggested that this acknowledgement reflects an openness toward the other's concrete, typical and unique way of being.

Consequently, to a certain extent, integrating dialogism with the existing metacognitive psychosocial interventions for persons with SMI entails making the implicit dialogical elements of these interventions explicit and expanding them. According to a definition adapted from SAMAHA's (2000) guide to participatory dialogue, a dialogical metacognitive psychosocial intervention is a relationship in which two or more persons participate as equals to explore the empathy and theory of mind problems attributed to a mental illness diagnosis. Persons who work with the process of dialogue consider establishing a context of trust as a necessary first step toward developing the above described symmetrical relationship. A dialogue oriented metacognitive module should facilitate establishing a trusting and symmetrical relationship in which the group facilitator and the group members learn how to use empathic and theory of mind processes appropriately. The following is an example of the implementation of such a module.

D is a 40-year-old woman who received the diagnosis of schizophrenia at the age of 25. D has been able to maintain herself in a hostel in the community for the last two years after a long period in which she alternated short periods of residence in the community with short hospitalizations. In a number of the hostel's staff meetings in which D's difficulties have been discussed, her extremely isolated and lonely life style has been attributed to her tendency to externalize her problems. This tendency has sometimes been labelled paranoia by a number of the hostel's staff. One of the goals of the psychosocial metacognitive intervention group in which D participates is to modify such perverse mind reading.

In a group session, D complains bitterly about the hostel's insistence that she accept the necessity of having to take medication for the rest of her life. She accuses the psychologist who facilitates the group as suggesting this because of a lack of hope and faith in her ability to achieve mature autonomy. The psychologist employs role playing, specifically role reversal, as a major step towards entering into a trusting and symmetrical dialogue with D with regard to the beliefs that D attributes to her. She adopts the role of the client and thus genuinely attempts to explore with D her own belief that the appropriate use of medication is crucial for D's recovery. In discussing the role play, D says, 'I now understand how I make you feel. You keep on suggesting ways of helping me and I keep on rejecting them. I also understand how difficult it is for you to understand how hopeless I feel.' This example shows how a technique based on a dialogical approach can engender a trusting and symmetrical relationship and, thus, facilitate both empathy and the realization of how terribly difficult it is at times to appreciate and empathize with other persons' internal states.

An intervention that has at its core dialogue between the care provider and the care user and that takes seriously the difficulties which persons with SMI may experience when engaging in such dialogue (Lysaker and Lysaker, 2001, 2002; Semerari *et al.*, 2004) would also be consistent with the above example and its theoretical rubric. Furthermore, in their review and updating of Engel's biopsychosocial model of suffering, illness and disease, Borrell-Carrio *et al.* (2004) suggest that interventions based on a dialogic model require empathy on the part of both care provider and care user. Accordingly, a relationship that evolves from an attempt at mutual empathy may resolve the tension sometimes experienced by the care provider due to her or his concern for both the autonomy and needs of the care user and lead to '"autonomy in relation" – an informed choice supported by a caring relationship' (p. 579).

Summary

Thus, adopting a dialogical approach to metacognition in general and to the metacognitive challenges that SMI poses in particular can provide a framework for developing concrete ways of dealing with major tensions associated with psychiatric rehabilitation. The capacity for empathy and the possession of TOM are considered essential characteristics of what being human means. Therefore, attributing deficient empathy and TOM processes to a person with a SMI diagnosis, even if this attribution is relatively valid, may be a major source of the extreme stigma from which the above-mentioned tensions may arise. However, as this chapter has pointed out, although empathic and TOM processes are the grounds for much of what is positive and creative about human society, empathy and TOM in the form of inappropriate mind reading can breed destructive proclivities in persons both with and without a SMI diagnosis. Accordingly, this chapter describes dialogical processes that arise in infancy and accompany our interpersonal development throughout our lifespan as focused attempts to achieve genuine mutuality. These processes can serve as the basis for attempts to help persons with a SMI navigate the human disposition for either extreme or deficient empathic and TOM processes in their striving for an understanding of the self and others.

References

Agassi, J.B. (1999). *Martin Buber on psychology and psychotherapy: Essays, letters and dialogue*. Syracuse, NY: Syracuse University Press.

American Psychiatric Association (1994). *Diagnostic and statistical manual of mental disorders*, 4th edn. Washington DC: American Psychiatric Association Press.

Beck, A.T. (1970). Cognitive therapy – nature and relation to behavior therapy. *Behavior Therapy*, *1*(2), 184–200.

Beck, A.T. (1978). *Anxiety checklist*. Philadelphia, PA: Center of Cognitive Therapy.

Borrell-Carrio, F., Suchman, A.L. and Epstein, R.M. (2004). The biopsychosocial model 25 years later: Principles, practice, and scientific inquiry. *Annals of Family Medicine*, *2*(6), 576–582.

Brothers, L. (1990). The social brain: A project for integrating primate behavior and neurophysiology in a new domain. *Concepts in Neuroscience*, *1*, 27–61.

Carpendale, J.I.M. and Lewis, C. (2004). Constructing an understanding of mind: The development of children's social understanding with in a social interaction. *Behavioral and Brain Sciences*, *27*, 79–151.

Combs, D.R., Adams, S.D., Penn, D.L., Roberts, D., Tiegreen, J. and Stem, P. (2006). Social cognition and interaction training (SCIT) for inpatients with schizophrenia spectrum disorders: Preliminary findings. *Schizophrenia Research*, *91*, 112–116.

Corrigan, P.W. (2007). How clinical diagnosis might exacerbate the stigma of mental illness? *Social Work*, *52*(1), 31–39.

Dimaggio, G., Lysaker, P.H., Carcione, A., Nicolò, G. and Semerari, A. (2008). Know yourself and you shall know the other . . . to a certain extent: Multiple paths of influence of self-reflection on mindreading. *Consciousness and Cognition*, *17*, 778–789.

Freeman, A. (2005). Socratic dialogue. In A. Freeman, S.H. Felgoise, C.M. Nezu,

A.M. Nezu and M.A. Reincke (eds), *Encyclopedia of cognitive behavior therapy* (pp. 380–384). New York: Springer.

Frith, C.D. (1992). *The cognitive neuropsychology of schizophrenia*. Hove, UK: Lawrence Erlbaum Associates Ltd.

Langdon, R. (2005). Theory of mind in schizophrenia. In B. Malle and S. Hodges, (eds), *Other minds*. New York: Guilford Press.

Lee, K.H. (2007). Empathy deficits in schizophrenia. In T. Farrow and P. Woodruff (eds), *Empathy in mental illness*. Cambridge: Cambridge University Press.

Lysaker, P.H. and Lysaker, J.T. (2001). Psychosis and the disintegration of dialogical self-structure: Problems posed by schizophrenia for the maintenance of dialogue. *British Journal of Medical Psychology*, *74*, 23–33.

Lysaker, P.H. and Lysaker, J.T. (2002). Schizophrenia and the collapse of the dialogical self: Recovery, narrative and psychotherapy. *Psychotherapy*, *38*, 252–260.

McFarlane, W.R., Dixon, L., Lukens, E. and Lucksted, A. (2003). Family psycho-education and schizophrenia: A review of the literature. *Journal of Marital and Family Therapy*, *29*(2), 223–245.

Marker, K. (2003). *COGPACK manual version 5.9*. Ludenburg: Marker Software.

Moritz, S. and Woodward, T.S. (2007). Metacognitive training for schizophrenia patients (MCT): A pilot study on feasibility, treatment, adherence and subjective efficiency. *German Journal of Psychiatry*, *10*, 69–78.

Morrison, A.P. (1998). Cognitive behavioral therapy for psychotic symptoms in schizophrenia. In N. Tarrier, A.Wells and G. Haddock (eds), *Treating complex cases – the cognitive behavioral therapy approach* (pp. 195–216). Chichester: Wiley.

Mueser, K.T., Meyer, P.S., Penn, D.L., Clancy, R., Clancy, D.M. and Salyers, M.P. (2006). The illness management and recovery program: Rationale, development, and preliminary findings. *Schizophrenia Bulletin*, *32*, 32–43.

Penn, D.L., Roberts, D.L., Combs, D. and Sterne, A. (2007). The development of the social cognition and interaction training program for schizophrenia spectrum disorders. *Psychiatric Services*, *58*(4), 449–451.

Salgado, J. and Hermans, H.J.M. (2005). The return of subjectivity: From a multiplicity of selves to the dialogical self. *Journal of Applied Psychology*, *1*(1), 3–13.

SAMAHA (2000). *Participatory dialogues. A guide to organizing interactive discussions on mental health issues among consumers, providers, and family members*. Washington, DC: US Department of Health and Human Services: Substance Abuse and Mental Health Services Administration Center for Mental Health Services. Consumer information series, vol. 3.

Saxe, R. (2005). Against simulation: The argument from error. *Trends in Cognitive Sciences*, *9*(4), 174–179.

Schaub, D., Abdel-Hamid, M. and Brune, M. (this volume). Schizophrenia and social functioning: The role of impaired metacognition.

Schmid, P.E. (2001). Acknowledgement: the art of responding. Dialogical and ethical perspectives on the challenge of unconditional relationships in therapy and beyond. In J. Bozarth and P. Wilkins (eds), *Unconditional positive regard*. Ross on Wye: PCCS Books.

Semerari, A., Carcione, A., Dimaggio, G., Nicolò, G. and Proacci, M. (2004). A dialogical approach to patients with personality disorders. In H.J.M. Hermans and G. Dimaggio (eds), *The dialogical self in psychotherapy* (pp. 220–234). New York: Brunner-Routledge.

Singer, T. (2006). The neuronal basis and ontogeny of empathy and mind reading: Review of literature and implications for future research. *Neuroscience and Behavioral Review*, *30*, 855–863.

Stam, H.J. (2006). The dialogical self and the renewal of psychology. *International Journal for Dialogical Science*, *1*, 99–117.

Stanghellini, G. (this vol). Common sense, disembodiment, and schizophrenic delusions.

Tirassa, M. (1999). Communicative competence and the architecture of the mind/brain. *Brain and Language*, *68*, 419–441.

Tummolini, L., Castelfranchi, C., Tirassa, M., Bosco, F.M. and Colle, L. (2006). Sharedness and privateness in human early social life. *Cognitive Systems Research*, *7*, 128–139.

Chapter 15

Enhancing mental state understanding in over-constricted personality disorder using metacognitive interpersonal therapy

Giancarlo Dimaggio, Giampaolo Salvatore, Giuseppe Nicolò, Donatella Fiore and Michele Procacci

Leaving aside their specific diagnosis, many personality disorder (PD) patients display a series of recurring characteristics:

- Poor comprehension of mental states, i.e. lack of metacognition, and in particular a difficulty in defining their own affects and the relational causes behind them.
- Restricted sense of identity because there are only a few goals driving their actions and they also lack strategies for achieving them (Dimaggio and Semerari, 2001) and do not see certain parts of the self as belonging to them so that, as a result, these are not included in their self-narratives.
- A coarctated and stereotyped representation of interpersonal relationships, rendering social life impoverished, dysfunctional and unsatisfying.
- Limited or flat affects and over-regulation of impulses and emotions.

As well as having difficulty identifying them, these persons tend to undervalue their emotions and repress them, whether positive or negative. They fail to use them as a reliable guide to social action and rely rather on general theories about human functioning or on rigid moral standards.

Such individuals are usually diagnosed for avoidant, obsessive-compulsive, paranoid, narcissistic, passive-aggressive, dependent, depressive or schizoid PDs, or any comorbidity among them, whether it is a question of a full diagnosis or one of the presence of a few traits. Overall such patients are described as over-constricted or inhibited PD (Millon and Davis, 1996; Livesley, 2003; Lynch and Cheavens, 2008; Dimaggio *et al.*, in press).

Federico, a 27-year-old manager, illustrates the prototype. He is intelligent and active and has excellent career prospects in an expanding firm. His motivation for seeking therapy is difficult to decipher immediately. In his opinion there is almost nothing wrong. He is successful at work, has had a relationship for nine years with a girl whom he loves and respects but who has, nevertheless, pushed him into asking for therapy.

Federico: I'm rather reserved and cold and they often point this out to me.

He takes over his girlfriend's suggestion. The diagnosis of the SCID II interview (Structured Clinical Interview for *DSM-IV-TR* Axis II Personality Disorder) for PDs is: narcissistic and paranoid disorders with obsessive-compulsive – excessively dedicated to his work, over-scrupulous and morally inflexible, incapable of delegating – and depressive – criticizes himself and others and has a concealed low opinion of himself – traits. To sum up, Federico is a narcissist with perfectionist standards and a need to control. He fears negative consequences for himself and the reaction others have to him which he cannot control and for this reason is more cautious than distrustful. When he believes he has not complied with his personal standards he tends to morally despise himself. He theorizes about his problems in the abstract but contributes few autobiographical episodes to support this. He over-controls his emotions and measures every word he says. In the interview, the reason he gives for seeking therapy is a feeling of unease he ascribes to the fact that interior conflicts have surfaced because he is less frenetic and hot-headed than in the past, thanks to the stability of his relationship and of his work. He wants to know himself better and uncover his emotions, which he finds disturbing but can scarcely identify. He also wants to modify his personality:

Federico: My excessive intransigence, towards both others, because I'm extremely self-critical, because I feel guilty when I realize I've made a mistake.

In his first session, on the contrary, his narrative shows that he feels his emotions sometimes take over from his rationality, not a good sign for him. He accepts the therapist's (GD) suggestion that he provide some narrative episodes – of note, the first step in our intervention procedure – to illustrate the question and help both of them to understand the hitherto vague nature of his problems. Federico relates as follows.[1]

Federico: I'd delegated some tasks to a young assistant. She's intelligent but talks too much and mixes up friendships and professional relationships. I can accept joking up to a certain extent, because it's fair that there should be a moderately intimate atmosphere at work, but she goes too far. I criticized her for something but tried to do it tactfully. Maybe she was offended but didn't say anything to me. A few days later I found out

1 Unlike the other session extracts, transcribed in their entirety from the recordings, this is a summary.

> that she had complained to my superiors about my excessively aggressive manner. I think her conduct was incorrect. I also went with this same colleague on a work trip. The train journey went OK. There was the same relatively cheerful atmosphere but not the sort of intimacy I'd have with my girlfriend or a close friend. We got to the hotel. I'd forgotten my toothpaste. It was 6 pm, a time of day when there's nothing wrong in knocking on a room door, and I asked to borrow her toothpaste. I used it and gave it back to her. That evening we had dinner with some colleagues from there and the atmosphere continued to be relaxed. Next day we had a good work meeting. But in the following weeks a rumour got around that I'd made sexual advances to her. It was she who deduced this from the fact that I'd knocked on her door. I realize I was imprudent. I need to keep a better control of my actions.

The therapist asks him why the episode was problematic and Federico's reply is that his superiors would have had a negative opinion of him because he had discriminated against the colleague, which is against the firm's rules. Moreover the rumors spread by her could have damaged his image. Then he adds another 'disturbing' episode:

> *Federico*: Another female colleague, who is very nice and conscientious, had carried out a part of the tasks for which I am responsible. I pointed out some inaccuracies in what she did, trying to be as polite as possible. I don't know if I was too aggressive, but her face started to tremble. I immediately explained that there was nothing wrong. I didn't want her to suffer for what I'd said. My girlfriend said that it was almost as if I wanted to dry her tears. These are problems I'm unable to solve. I can't understand why I act like that. I need to control myself more but don't know how.

The traits of someone with an over-constricted PD can be seen in these stories. From a metacognitive point of view, Federico has difficulty describing his emotions – using abstract terms instead – and identifying the motivations behind his actions. Furthermore he does not acknowledge one of his personality traits, perfectionism and need to control, mistaking it for its opposite – impulsiveness!

He uses a limited range of interpersonal schemas: he seeks perfection, control and order so as to avert negative opinions that might hamper his ambition. He voluntarily represses his affects and prefers to resort to standards of moral behavior, to be followed by everyone. Pleasure plays a limited role in his life. In other episodes he describes how he has always found it difficult to think of relaxing, enjoying a sex life and having fun.

These personality characteristics are overshadowed by his search for success and moral approval. He thus has a narrow identity.

Metacognitive interpersonal therapy

General aspects and developments

Federico was treated using metacognitive interpersonal therapy (MIT), developed and manualized by the Third Center of Cognitive Psychotherapy (Dimaggio *et al.*, 2007). This is aimed at treating PD patients, including the over-constricted type described here. MIT is designed to tackle metacognitive dysfunctions emerging during interpersonal relationships and widen the range of schemas driving the latter.

MIT attacks the dysfunctions underlying the PD and the vicious cycle of interaction among them. A limited awareness of emotions and/or symptoms, the impact on others of dysfunctional behavior driven by pathogenic schemas and a failure to acknowledge the impact that such behavior has on others are among the elements hindering treatment planning and construction of a therapeutic relationship. A therapist reacts negatively both to patients with limited ability to describe their inner states – because they appear reticent or defensively withdrawn – and to those who are distrustful because they cannot perceive well-disposed intentions and good faith. Vice versa a bad therapeutic relationship worsens metacognition: if patients feel that their therapist is hostile or embarrassed, they stop thinking about themselves. They may fear criticisms or intrusions and, in thinking about how to protect themselves from them, they shut off and lose contact with affects and painful memories. MIT works immediately to improve the therapeutic relationship, with the idea that this increases access to mental states, which in turn improves the relationship and makes it possible to access, modify and enlarge the patient's meanings system.

In describing the dysfunctions underlying over-constricted PD we shall focus principally on the problems found in Federico and then show how they were treated.[2] Using his case, we shall develop MIT beyond the manual, with a formalization of step-by-step procedures aimed at improving metacognition, widening a patient's range of schemas and maximizing the effectiveness of interventions. These procedures help to tailor interventions to the level of metacognitive skills which a patient displays at a particular moment, optimize agreement on goals and solve therapeutic relationship problems (Dimaggio *et al.*, in press). For space reasons we

2 For a more detailed description of over-constricted PD see Dimaggio *et al.* (in press). For a systematic classification of poor metacognition in PDs see Colle *et al.*, this volume, Chapter 11.

shall concentrate on the technical aspects of treatment, with only a brief mention of the work required to maintain a good therapeutic relationship.

Poor metacognition and stereotyped schemas in over-constricted personality disorder

Poor metacognition

As described in this volume (Dimaggio and Lysaker, Introduction; Colle *et al.*, Chapter 11), PD patients have problems with metacognition, which is the range of skills required for: (a) ascribing and identifying mental states in oneself and others on the basis of somatic states, facial expressions and behavior; (b) reflecting and reasoning on mental states; (c) using psychological information for deciding, solving psychological and interpersonal problems or conflicts, and mastering subjective suffering.

Federico, like many patients with over-constricted PD, has difficulty describing his emotions and the motivations behind his reactions. Situations in which he loses control bewilder and frighten him. He does not see that his emotions are in accord with the event provoking them. He does not, therefore, integrate aspects driven by emotions into his self-narrative. He does not realize that they have every right to be part of him or that they are adaptive. When faced with the apparent contradictions among his ways of acting or attitudes towards others, he is struck by doubts he cannot rationally overcome. For example, he feels he loves and appreciates his girlfriend and finds her pretty, very intelligent (she is an excellent cellular biologist) and able to listen to him sensitively and stimulate him to reflect on himself. On the other hand, when he dwells on her presumed physical defects – slight tendency to put on weight – he feels repulsion and doubts he loves her because she is imperfect. A dream: a shot of the face of a girl he saw one day, in reality, on the beach in the town where he comes from in Northern Italy.

> *Federico*: I've known perfection. The dream and memory of that face are a clear demonstration that it exists. My girlfriend does not embody it entirely.

Adding shortly afterwards:

> *Federico*: You see, it's like Michelangelo's *Pietà*. It's perfect just as it is. If you add two kilos to the *Pietà*, you've not only added two kilos, you've destroyed perfection! This is why I complain to my girlfriend when she puts on a little weight. She doesn't become objectively fat. But she's imperfect.

The therapist points out how he swings from states in which the other is desired and Frederico enjoys the time they spend together to states in which he detaches from the other and despises her. Shortly before telling about his dream he had talked about spending a nice morning with his girlfriend, during which they had had satisfying sexual relations. On the other hand, however, his ideal of perfection leads him to reject experiences that he himself goes through. He agrees with this observation:

Federico: Yes, I'm aware of that. I've got two dimensions inside me, day-to-day reality and the ideal, which are unrelated.

The term 'unrelated' illustrates his poor metacognitive integration. Federico does not construct a unified representation such as: 'I love my girlfriend and feel all right with her, even if from time to time I dream about a perfection that exists only in a dream world or in art', with which he would be able to experience his relationship with her in a more relaxed way.

With regard to understanding others' minds, Federico correctly decodes facial emotions and makes sophisticated hypotheses about the motivations of others' actions. However, he over-utilizes his moral reasoning in interpreting behavior and often speculates about what others should have done, instead of attempting to understand why a person, in a specific context, acted in a particular way. Under stress he does not decentre, that is, he does not take another's point of view and leave his own aside. This problem emerges when he feels that the other does not support him. When he tells his partner that he has got the offer of a job abroad in a leading company in his sector, an offer Federico is very keen on accepting, she gives her approval but looks sad. Federico gets angry because he sees his girlfriend's reaction as an attempt to restrict his personal liberty. He relies on his recurring life theme – 'others do not support my choices' – and probably thinks that his girlfriend is only suffering in the face of the idea of being separated from him – the city he is going to does not have any leading cellular biology facilities – and of having to leave the city in which they live and which she loves.

We shall come back to this point but saying that patients have problems decentring does not mean that the goal of therapy should be to force them to take the other's point of view! Doing this prematurely is useless or counter-productive (Dimaggio *et al.*, 2007, in press). Patients would be likely to see a therapist as hostile, almost as if allied with the person obstructing them. We shall see later when we consider it beneficial to work at stimulating decentered readings of others' minds.

The most dysfunctional part of Federico's metacognition, as in the majority of PD patients (Carcione *et al.*, in press) is Mastery, that is, the ability to use psychological information to solve problems, negotiate interpersonal conflicts and get out of distressing mental states. Federico has almost only one strategy – controlling behavior and emotions rationally – and the immense effort this entails often blocks him. He barely realizes that over-controlling is dysfunctional and fears that acting spontaneously could be dangerous for both himself and others. He is incapable of exploiting memories from his personal history to understand why he has developed such a limited range of strategies for handling the difficulties which social life involves.

Dysfunctional and stereotyped interpersonal schemas

A dysfunctional construction of relationships between self and others is, by definition, at the heart of PDs and gnaws at the quality of an individual's social life (American Psychiatric Association, 2000). Patients construe others in accordance with predefined schemas that they use pervasively and automatically as relational contexts evolve. These schemas influence their expectations as to how the other will respond to them. They also predispose patients to paying more attention to information consistent with their self-image – a schema involving fear of criticism generates a bias in attention towards signs of criticism – and influence the reactions others have towards the self. Moralistic attitudes make others in turn reactive and critical, which aggravates the core idea of being judged for one's moral imperfections, thus generating an interpersonal cycle (Safran and Muran, 2000).

Federico's identity is based on only a few goals. He is ambitious and competitive. He expects recognition for his qualities and works hard to obtain it. However, his competitiveness is activated in inappropriate contexts. Competition is dominant in his family relationships, where the whole family values everything on the basis of performance and a superiority/inferiority scale.

The minimum elements necessary for a relationship schema are: motivation behind self's actions (i.e. seeking support); a self-representation (i.e. deserving support); a representation of how the other will respond to the request (i.e. criticizes and despises); and self's reaction, i.e. hurt (Luborsky and Crits-Christoph, 1998). Based on the values ascribed to himself and others, Federico's dominant interpersonal pattern is despising/despised, consistent with his narcissistic PD (Ryle and Kerr, 2002; Dimaggio *et al.*, 2007).

Federico sometimes undervalues people around him but feels more often that he is the victim of criticism and disdain from his father, who scorns any action on his part which does not comply with the family's rules or is up to its standards. Federico reacts to this disdain either by withdrawing emotionally, which leads to the suppression of affects, or by activating his perfectionist schema: 'If I achieve the required standard, I will be accepted and admired.' The other core schema derives from his desire to be recognized and accepted. Federico represents himself as deserving this but needs the other person to confirm it. However, the other person is described as being invalidating and incapable of giving him recognition and this provokes anger, frustration and pain. Lastly, Federico has the idea that, if he reacts spontaneously, this will harm either himself or others, and this further hampers his expression of affects. Note that such expectations are internalized psychological structures, but Federico treats them as a matter of fact and thus has difficulty distinguishing fantasy from reality (Fonagy and Target, 1996). Overall, therefore, his limited access to certain emotions, the narrow range of schemas he uses as guides in his relational life and his protective over-controlling of affects restrict Federico's identity and make him a prototypical over-constricted PD.

General features of MIT

Metacognitive interpersonal therapy uses methods and strategies in line with the general principles for successful treatment (Castonguay and Beutler, 2006). The therapist should try: to show support and encourage the belief that treatment will be useful; be empathetic and show positive regard; cooperate; manage countertransference and self-disclose when appropriate; repair ruptures in the therapeutic alliance; and make accurate interpretations of thinking and acting patterns and deliver them promptly. MIT involves flexibility and ongoing reassessments and changes in strategy in order to adapt to the current problem, rather than complying a priori with a particular model (Livesley, 2008).

To achieve these goals when treating over-constricted PD, MIT follows a step-by-step procedure (Dimaggio *et al.*, in press), a series of logical sequences to guide therapists as to what to do and when, based on the problems appearing during sessions. Therapists need to continuously assess the clarity and richness of patients' narratives, their metacognitive dysfunctions, therapeutic relationship quality and responses to earlier interventions. They should pass from one action, i.e. identifying an emotion, to the next, i.e. understanding what triggered it, according to the patient's responses to earlier interventions and, in particular, the latter's level of metacognitive functioning.

An intervention should be in the metacognitive zone of proximal development (Vygotsky, 1930/1978; Leiman and Stiles, 2001; Allen *et al.*, 2008), that is, it should stimulate growth in the skill which is the closest possible to that which patients display of their own accord. Interventions outside this zone are unlikely to be effective. For example, it is pointless explaining to patients that they get angry when others impose something on them when they are not even aware of being angry.

Where there are relational problems, these should be tackled before any other step. Interventions are most successful when relational tension is low and emotions well modulated. Therapists need to continuously monitor the consequences of their actions (Safran and Muran, 2000). We consider an intervention effective when it leads to: increased telling of memories (Weiss, 1993); increased shared psychological knowledge; better expression of affects or modulation of disturbing affects; changes in mental state during sessions – i.e. signs that a patient really is reacting to an intervention and not just doing it to please; increased metacognition; and maintenance of therapeutic relationship quality or repairs to ruptures in the alliance. If some of these results are visible, one could pass to interventions requiring a greater metacognitive effort or which might elicit negative affects. The therapeutic actions to be taken are as follows:

1 (a) Eliciting detailed narratives; (b) identifying problematic thoughts and emotions.
2 Establishing causal links among relational events, emotions, thoughts and actions.
3 Stimulating memories associated with previous narratives.
4 Reconstructing existing schemas.

Operations 1 to 4 constitute the stage setting, where the ground is prepared for actions aimed at change. The next steps depend on the quality of the self–other relationships found. When they are ego-dystonic, e.g. fragile self/rejecting other one could pass to the following:

5 Distinguishing fantasy from reality.
6 Accessing the healthy self and exploring new forms of relationship.
7 Integrating previously dissociated self-aspects or finding points of view to explain incongruities.
8 Acknowledging one's own contribution to the creation of problems.
9 Decentering.

If self–other representations are ego-syntonic, e.g. grandiose self/others an obstacle, the steps change and are as follows:

5 Rrefraining from attacking these representations.
6 Returning to point 1 and investigating the self-narratives further until ego-dystonic aspects emerge.

From here on the intervention follows the same sequence as before, with the addition of the new painful relational focus, except that the sequence continues with an extra point:

10 Adopting a critical distance from one's ego-syntonic schemas (i.e. understanding that one's grandiose self-image is pursued compulsively).

The above sequence would not necessarily start from step 1 and does not represent treatment stages. One should start from the point where the patient is in session. If they relate of their own accord why they experienced an emotion and its consequences, one could pass directly to looking for other stories in which similar episodes occurred. If, on the contrary, the causes of an emotion are not clear, one should continue to look for them before stimulating associated memories. When, during therapy, therapists find new areas of a patient's personality requiring treatment, they may return each time to the beginning, i.e. gathering prototypical narrative episodes.

Step-by-step procedures

Eliciting detailed autobiographical narratives

The first step is to construct a rich, informative and reliable text for patient and therapist to 'consult' without any problems. The most reliable texts for this purpose are self-narratives, which contain the essence of how patients construe their relationships with others on the basis of their motivations (Angus and McLeod, 2004). A good narrative takes place within defined spatial (*where*) and time (*when*) boundaries. The actors (*who*), the subject they engage in dialogue about (*what*) (Hermans and Dimaggio, 2004) and the purpose for which the story is told (*why*) should be identifiable (Neimeyer, 2000). A therapist should ask, even insistently, for specific episodes, explaining that the more detailed a story is, the easier it will be to understand together what is happening. The episodes in which a colleague of Federico's spread rumours about his sexual advances and in which he criticized another colleague and made her cry were the first he related and subsequent steps were based on them.

Access to dominant thoughts and emotions

Therapists can now concentrate on understanding what patients felt and thought at a precise moment in their narrative. Focused observations such as 'You were angry' or 'You were afraid of being harmed' help a patient to provide specific information. If the patient uses vague terminology ('I felt uneasy; it irritated me'), as long as the description of inner experience is unclear, therapists need to suggest more specific expressions or concentrate on non-verbal language, nuances or changes in tone of voice and posture.

These attempts may fail if patients defensively withdraw. In this case one should avoid using pressure and concentrate the conversation less on inner states and more on topics with which the patient feels at ease until new signs indicate the possibility of exploring the emotions. In the episode described, Federico found it overall quite easy to identify thoughts and emotions (over-controlling, fear of causing or suffering harm, guilt and anger).

Stimulating the psychological links between thoughts, emotions and actions

When the contents of the story are clear to both parties, the next step is to identify the causal links between and logical and psychological implications of elements of experience. PD patients often act without knowing why or are overwhelmed by symptoms without understanding what triggered them. Clinicians should pose questions or proffer hypotheses about what caused an emotion or triggered a reaction, and if particular thoughts caused particular actions or affects, should explore the links between details in a narrative – what someone said or did – and a patient's actions. A lack of psychological links is often a fundamental part of the PD metacognitive dysfunction (Dimaggio *et al.*, 2007; Semerari *et al.*, 2007).

We would stress that all intervention steps should be agreed upon explicitly during the therapeutic dialogue. However, to understand the psychological connections, a therapist should first summarize the elements of a patient's discourse internally and find plausible causal links. Only after hearing what Federico says about his relationship with his colleagues and recalling similar scenes he talked about in the first assessment session does the therapist express out loud his own interpretation of the narrative:

> *Therapist*: You give me the idea of always needing to set limits in your life . . . you've got . . . some weighing scales, you're always very attentive, cautious and precise, goal-orientated . . . attentive to . . . the consequences of your actions . . . the impression is that in all the stories you've chosen . . . there's the same outcome. When there's greater intimacy or emotionality . . . when you stop being able to control the situation . . . you get harmed. You make an unpardonable mistake, knocking on a lady's door at 6 pm and this leads to . . . gossip . . . at this point you try to be even more reserved . . . when you feel riled for a moment, you raise your voice just a little, you go perhaps just a little bit further than is advisable. In my opinion it's totally normal . . . this causes distress in the other person, your colleague, who then causes problems for you. Or else you make the girl suffer and say immediately, 'No, I didn't want to! . . .' To avoid any damage . . . Try to be yet more shrewd. Agreed?
>
> *Federico*: Absolutely!

Federico's reaction at this point is surprising. He opens his eyes wide and says:

> *Federico*: That's how it is with my parents too. As long as I was spontaneous, a total mess! When I said: let's try to make this work, things started to go better.

Federico has thus spontaneously achieved the next step in the intervention: associating an episode with similar scenes occurring at other times.

Evoking autobiographical memories correlated to the self-narrative

PD patients are disinclined to think that problems are in their own minds and often attribute the causes of their suffering and poor adaptation more to the outside than to their own ideas or behavior. Identifying that problems which lie within how one thinks or feels about situations is an indispensable therapeutic step. To get there, asserting that a single fact is a schema – a stable personality structure – is arbitrary. Patients are likely to stick to the matter-of-fact value of the episode and uphold that their partner or boss really is unbearable and causes their problems. One should, therefore, evoke similar episodes and ask for other scenes from the past linked to aspects of the narrative. Once these memories have been retrieved, a therapist has several examples of one and the same prototype and can review with the patient whether there are any regularities depending more plausibly on his or her way of functioning than on, to paraphrase Lemony Snicket's books, 'a series of unfortunate events' (2006).

Federico carries out this operation on his own in response to the therapist's reconstruction, an excellent sign of therapeutic progress. In the next session he recalls how his parents were critical, easily hurt by his actions and how their disdainful and angry reactions were often unpredictable. He describes his mother as unable to assert her own ideas but prone to outbursts of anger:

> *Federico*: My mother internalizes everything and then . . . explodes . . . once she threw a shoe at me while we were in the kitchen when I was little and it broke the window.

He describes his father:

> *Federico*: More self-controlled but much more threatening . . . In our old house the toilet flush didn't work. A minute later my father arrives and gives me a slap. My mother said: 'No, it's not working. I tried it first

myself.' And he says, 'Anyway, a slap is always good for him.' . . . I have a feeling of having been wronged and . . . of subjection towards him.

Therapist and patient now possess a historical background that enables them to put the latter's need for emotional control and perfectionism into a context.

Identifying regularities

Once associated memories have been recalled, one can pass on to identifying and interpreting together. The therapist hypothesizes that there are similarities between the patient's stories in terms of emotions, interaction patterns or wish outcomes. The stories may have different plots, but with one being the cause of the other; often the one recalled by association contains the real problem, while the original story describes dysfunctional ways of coping. In Federico's case, for example, his attempts at controlling at work serve to protect him from a sensation of impending catastrophe and from destructive criticism, which go back to his relationship with his parents. The therapist points out the similarities between his family and work stories. He also notes the adaptive value of looking to control: Federico hopes that, if he keeps things under control, he will avoid being slapped! He retrieves new memories:

Federico: I had the best marks of anyone at our high school. When I saw them I was delighted. . . . I telephoned my father and said, 'I almost feel like taking a holiday.' My father reacted as if he was crazy. 'Oh yes! Now we stop everything. Now anything's allowed. No more rules!'

Federico remembers the devastating sensation when, with the highest marks possible, he obtained this violent reaction instead of a prize or the relaxation he hoped for. He thought his father seemed frightened by the chaos his son was creating by thinking for even one moment of abandoning their strict rules.

If the narrative reconstruction has been carried out with attention to detail and the therapist's observations employ the patient's language, the latter will generally acknowledge that the therapist's hypotheses are valid, with little risk of conflict or ruptures in the alliance. Tensions are nevertheless inevitable in the therapeutic relationship and the work described here is an attempt to minimize them. When they arise, one should focus attention on the dysfunctional patterns present in the therapeutic relationship. These become the 'on-line' narrative episode and one should address them in order to, on the one hand, understand their structure and, on the other, to overcome them.

Metacognitive differentiation in the case of ego-dystonic schemas

At this point patients know what themes recur in their thoughts. One could then help them to grasp how their memories of the past guide the imaginal constructions with which they give meaning to their relationships with others. It is a question of acquiring metacognitive differentiation or distinguishing between fantasy and reality (Fonagy and Target, 1996). Patients need to adopt a critical distance from the themes that have been problematic across the course of their lives.

Federico starts to accomplish this operation when he understands that his over-controlling at work not only depends on the firm's rules but is also an automatism of his to avoid violent, unexpected and frightening reactions like his father's.

A few sessions later the therapist works at stimulating differentiation further. Federico receives the offer of an interview for a job abroad with a leading company in his sector. Federico is excited and – in addition to his understandable ambitions, which the therapist validates – has grandiose expectations. He describes the new firm as being a professional Eden, where everything is perfect with top level efficiency, honesty and performance.

Grandiosity, a founding theme in Federico's identity, should not be attacked. We repeat that differentiation should be stimulated as regards ego-dystonic schemas, while ego-syntonic ones should be dealt with only after patients have enlarged the repertoire of meanings with which they construe the world. The therapist therefore avoids criticizing Federico's grandiose aspects, as he considers this would be to adopt the latter's invalidating parents' role.

The work therefore concentrates on another theme: Federico's coldness and anger towards his girlfriend Monica. When he enthusiastically tells her that he might get the job, she seems sad and the idea of him leaving distresses her, even if she approves and supports his choice. Federico accuses her of constraining his personal freedom, without any concern for her understandable distress and neglecting the fact that she supports him openly.

In session Federico is tense and close to losing his temper. The therapist senses that this is the moment at which the therapeutic relationship is most at risk. If he miscalculates the focus of his intervention, Federico would turn his anger on him. MIT pays particular attention to these situations in which the alliance could be broken and aims at identifying a point in the patient's experience that can be validated and with which to empathize in an atmosphere where conflict is minimized. The therapist realizes at that moment that he tends to take Monica's side and decides that working on stimulating greater comprehension by Federico of his girlfriend's point of view would break the alliance, as the patient would see him as hostile. He therefore avoids working in this direction. On the contrary, he concentrates on Federico's recurring need for support and approval, together with the idea that if he is spontaneous – in this case pursues a desire – the other suffers. To start with, the therapist validates Federico's ability to recall detailed memories in an atmosphere of trust in the therapist, and stresses that these indicate rapid therapeutic progress and an ability to work productively. He then stresses that Federico is dominated both by the idea that he has no right to his own wishes and his anger when he realizes that others are hindering him. Federico agrees. The therapist notes that the problem is that it was not Monica's real suffering that caused his anger but clashing once again with reference figures suffering (colleague, mother in other stories, father, girlfriend), or hostility (father) in reaction to his assertions of independence. This intervention brings relief to Federico, as he understands that the problem is not an external obstacle but his own proneness, rooted in his development history, to feel guilt and then anger if not supported. Therapist and patient agree that the need for support continues, pointlessly, to require gratification. At the session end Federico knows he will undertake the interview without any problems and returns to seeing that his relationship with Monica is solid. To sum up: his development memories – threatening internal fantasies – have returned to their place and have not got the better of external reality; his girlfriend was in fact supportive and was simply suffering because they were going to be separated.

Treatment steps aimed at restructuring and changing

Identifying the narrative background to a patient's problems and the psychological cause–effect links behind them does not constitute a once-and-for-all cure. Individuals need a large repertoire of interpersonal relationship procedures, a sense of identity that remains stable with variations in the flow of consciousness, and the ability to keep action goal-orientated despite obstacles, mood fluctuations and declines in motivation. Lastly, an articulated view of others is indispensable to avoiding conflicts and negotiating one's desires. Interventions of this level are to be attempted only after the achievement of the objectives described previously. The changing steps are as follows:

1 Enrich the patient's personality repertoire, integrate emerging features into a new narrative, and encourage the use of meaning constructions and more adaptive behaviours, as they surface in therapy.
2 Construct sophisticated and decentered readings of others' minds.
3 Recognize that one's actions impact on others and contribute to the problems from which one suffers.
4 Recognize one's self-serving biases (e.g. narcissistic self-enhancement), which generate inflated or selectively positive self-images.

Constructing new self-parts is indispensable in PD therapy. A normally effective and well-tolerated intervention is: first pinpointing with the patients where their treatment has currently reached and then explaining that further gains, in health and adaptation terms, require trying different routes. The goals of therapy are therefore to be renegotiated.

One needs to agree with patients on the safest relationship types and contexts in which to explore new self-aspects. Precisely because they are trying something new, unusual and often frightening, such experiments should be conducted tactfully. Federico's therapist encouraged him to adopt a more relaxed style, especially in situations where his perfectionist standards were less vital to him. He asked Federico, who always practised sports as if he were preparing for the Olympics, to try and enjoy the taste of physical exercise without measuring physiological parameters, and to then report the sensations that arose.

In such situations one should monitor patients' reactions carefully. Conversation should concentrate on discussing the results of the experiment, taking care to immediately note both the activation of usual modes of thinking and any positive effects generated by the new actions. The link between the well-being or freedom achieved and the change in ways of thinking and acting must be stressed.

For space reasons, we will deal with these aspects only briefly and all together. Moreover, Federico's therapy lasted only 20 sessions because of his transfer abroad. Thus many of these operations, which need to be carried out over the long term to provide valid and stable results, were only just started.[3] Therapist and patient agree to: acknowledge the latter's perfectionist tendencies and adopt less rigid standards; dedicate more time to relaxation and acknowledge that Federico's guilt feelings are left over from his development history; acknowledge his competitiveness and keep a distance from it when appropriate; and evaluate the impact of his behavior on others, but only when his internal motivations are firm and not undermined by uncertainties about their value or doubts about their right to exist. Between one session and the next, Federico himself monitors the emotional consequences of the new modes adopted.

The following transcript extract, taken from a session in the fifth month of his therapy, illustrates how Federico manages, in stressful conditions, to use psychotherapeutic work to adopt new strategies in contexts of great personal importance. He tells of an intense job interview with the firm he would like to join, an interview on which his future depends:

3 Federico was referred to a mentalization-based therapist (Fonagy *et al.*, 2002), both for the latter's compatibility with MIT and because there are skilled therapists of this school in the city where Federico now works.

Federico: Before the interview . . . I'd talked with Monica . . . she'd told me that often in competitive . . . situations, in which I'm not certain about the result . . . I tend to get a bit aggressive . . . rigid, formal . . . She encouraged me to be more calm and relaxed . . . I thought I didn't want to go trying to appear cleverer and more expert than I really am . . . better to go quite calm and relaxed, without too much emphasis on performance . . . obviously I wanted to be careful not only to try and do better but also try and understand how they worked and what they expected of me, and also pose these uncomfortable questions I'd decided to pose . . . That morning I woke up quite calm and rested . . . the outcome seems to have been very positive . . . all the management interviewed me.

Therapist: All the management?

Federico: Yes! All very official. Like they were giving me an x-ray. They had a very open approach. I reckon that overall the interviews went very well. I told them my experience . . . I believe I told them I've done something in their field and studied, that . . . I've been to Berlin, Seattle . . . but the evening before I'd said to myself, 'Don't expect at all that these people will think that what you've done is cool.' . . . I spoke without problems; of course it's not my mother tongue . . . It was more difficult with one of them. He was very forthright and direct, almost in a hurry, less interested . . . he asked me for some confidential data. I told him: what you are asking is not publicly available . . . for every little thing he wanted all the details . . . it was more difficult with him.

Therapist: You passed a test too. You were right not to give him that confidential information.

Federico: The interview was less relaxed then. Perhaps I was also more hesitant, but one way or the other I got through it. I reckon I gave quite a good impression. As regards them my impression was really very positive.

The therapist validates the aspects emerging in the transcript: the more relaxed style and the care to keep track of one's abilities and values (protecting confidential data) and nuances in others' behavior, rather than concentrating on achieving grandiose expectations and defending oneself from criticism. The therapist highlights the change compared to the past:

Therapist: I sense less of that feeling . . . of frenzy . . . last time [when he found out about the firm's interest] it was clearer . . . there'd been that conflict with Monica that meant you had to go there necessarily, as a sign of freedom of spirit . . . At the same time, before the interview you were describing the firm as the promised land. Now you have great prospects . . . rich in positive professional consequences. At the same time you no longer display that feeling of haste, conflict and coldness.

A little before this extract Federico talked about how he was helping Monica at her work and the therapist points to how he is able to handle others' problems without seeing this as a limitation to his freedom. The therapist also notes that Federico's view of life is now based less on extreme grandiose ideals and that, in the following extract, they interweave with the positive aspects of daily reality:

Therapist: Before you thought: 'How can I live with this reality when my ideal is so beautiful?' . . . In fact, it's interesting that, before talking about the interview, you included an introduction in which you devote yourself to Monica. Caring for a partner who's passing through a delicate transition period at work is no longer an obstacle to your ambition. They're dimensions that can co-exist. In the same way, the style with which you describe the interview with the firm is calmer. One could understand all the nuances, yours and the interviewers' . . . The other time we said that the dimensions were unrelated . . . now I sense that . . . on an emotional level it's all much more harmonious.

In response to this intervention, Federico replies with other recollections, in which a supportive reference figure finally emerges:

Federico: Yes . . . When I graduated, Monica really helped me a lot. I've got this strong memory inside me of her emotional support . . . for me it's absolutely natural being close to her when she's going through such situations.

Federico also feels understood and validated by the therapist and this helps him better to focus on his new state of well-being and on the positive effects, both internally and externally, of his less rigid and perfectionist style:

Federico: A strange thing . . . You described it very well: I felt very calm. During the last two weeks when we haven't even met, I've been consolidating certain thoughts, a joint result of our sessions and of the conversations with Monica . . . I can't explain why, which points to my inability to access . . . [*he laughs while joking about his difficulties in describing the motivations for his actions, a focus of his treatment since the beginning*].

Therapist: [*laughs*] Don't worry. If the interview went well, there are no psychological problems!

Federico: The days before the interview too.

Therapist: That's right! Already before the interview you devoted time to Monica. So you were relaxed and at peace with yourself.

Federico: I tackled the interview more serenely, without expecting to make heaven knows what impression. More realistic too, I'd say.

Without the therapist ever challenging his grandiose bias, Federico criticizes his tendency to self-enhance. Federico is now more able to feel pleasure. In fact, when modulating maladaptive schemas, this often almost automatically creates room for previously hidden aspects of his personality to emerge, and identity and inner experience are enriched:

Federico: I'm very happy about this. With Monica too the last two weeks, even if there's been stress . . . We've been more cheerful, we've made love more often, as if everything was calmer and more unified, less obsessed with perfection.

Treatment outcome

The therapy ends successfully by joint agreement after 20 sessions and Federico moves to the other country. Shortly before leaving, he marries Monica. On SCID II Federico no longer reaches the threshold for a formal diagnosis of any PD and the number of criteria met has dropped from 20 to two. Of course his therapy requires further work; there is some unfinished business. For example, his boss's disappointed reaction to the news of him changing his job makes him feel a traitor; he suffers deeply and has doubts about his choice. Thus he still tends to feel criticized, invalidated and guilty, and to become rigid and perfectionist under stress. Overall, however, he is more aware of his affects and reactions; masters better his tendencies to become cold and disdainful when others ask him for help, and to doubt his decisions and personal value when others criticize him. In fact, after some initial wavering and thanks to the therapist's support, he remains convinced about moving abroad. His identity is richer and embraces an ability to relax and enjoy life.

Conclusions

Patients with over-constricted PD have metacognitive problems. They are unable to identify the causes of their affects and reactions, fail to acknowledge parts of themselves and have difficulty constructing integrated narratives of self-with-other. MIT succeeds, as in the case described, in improving metacognition using a step-by-step procedure, starting with stimulating the recollection of detailed self-narratives and then focusing on affects and their causes and on interpersonal functioning schemas. Later MIT tries to stimulate differentiation between inner schemas and external reality, to create a more integrated self-narrative and encourage the enrichment of a patient's meaning and action repertoire. Patients are then helped to use the psychological knowledge achieved for problem solving and adaptation.

The present work depicts the technique used in a single case, and it is right to ask whether MIT, as applied here, works with over-constricted PD in general. For this purpose we are analysing several individual cases and conducting a naturalistic effectiveness study, evaluating whether MIT: (a) is an effective treatment (for PDs in general); (b) has the ability, described here, to improve metacognition. Another point not discussed here, given the shortness of the treatment, is how therapy proceeds when prolonged over time and whether other ingredients are needed for effectiveness to consolidate its beneficial results beyond the preliminary ones described by us here.

In Federico's case, work on the regulation of the therapeutic relationship can only be seen in the background, even if MIT (Dimaggio *et al.*, 2007; Fiore *et al.*, 2008) focuses constantly on this. A therapist should try continuously to validate any subjective experience that emerges, avoid criticizing problematic aspects and be attentive to ruptures in the alliance, such as conflicts or patients' withdrawal (Safran and Muran, 2000). In-session processing and repair of ruptures should be given priority over – or accompany – the technical interventions mentioned here. Federico's case was fortunate in this respect. Despite his diagnosis for narcissistic and paranoid PDs with a perfectionist trait, he was always cooperative and this is not ascribable solely to the therapy being carried out well. Patients with over-constricted PD – i.e. ones with narcissism, paranoia, avoidance, obsessive-compulsive or passive-aggressive traits – put therapists rigorously to the test. They challenge and criticize them, construe them negatively, refuse to cooperate and distrust treatment. As described elsewhere (Dimaggio *et al.*, 2007; Nicolò *et al.*, 2007), therapists therefore need to pay constant attention to their own negative reactions in order to avoid contributing to a relationship's poor quality.

Although these new developments of MIT are only at an initial stage, they seem promising. We have expressed them here in a detailed model that we hope is clear and empirically testable, which is one of the next steps in our research program.

References

Allen, J.G., Fonagy, P. and Bateman, A.W. (2008). *Mentalizing in clinical practice*. Washington, DC: American Psychiatric Publishing.

American Psychiatric Association (2000). *Diagnostic and statistical manual of mental disorders, DSM-IV-TR* 4th edn. Washington, DC: American Psychiatric Association.

Angus, L. and McLeod, J. (eds) (2004). *Handbook of narrative psychotherapy: Practice, theory and research.*Thousand Oaks, CA: Sage.

Castonguay L.G. and Beutler, L.E. (eds) (2006) *Principles of therapeutic change that work*. New York: Oxford University Press.

Carcione, A., Semerari, A., Nicolò, G., Pedone, R., Fiore, D., Conti, M.L. and Dimaggio, C. (in press). Mastery dysfunctions in personality disorders. *Psychiatry Research.*

Dimaggio, G. and Semerari, A. (2001) Psychopathological narrative forms. *Journal of Constructivist Psychology*, *14*(1), 1–23.

Dimaggio, G., Semerari, A., Carcione, A., Nicolò, G. and Procacci, M. (2007). *Psychotherapy of personality disorders: Metacognition, states of mind and interpersonal cycles*. London: Routledge.

Dimaggio, G., Salvatore, G., Fiore, D., Carcione, A., Nicolò, G. and Semerari, A. (in press). General principles for treating constricted personality disorder. Towards an operationalizing technique. *Journal of Personality Disorders.*

Fiore, D., Dimaggio, G., Carcione, A., Nicolò, G. and Semerari, A. (2008). Metacognitive interpersonal therapy in a case of obsessive-compulsive and avoidant personality disorders. *Journal of Clinical Psychology: In-Session*, *64*, 168–180.

Fonagy, P. and Target, M. (1996). Playing with reality: I. Theory of mind and the normal development of psychic reality. *International Journal of Psychoanalysis*, *77*, 217–233.

Fonagy, P., Gergely, G., Jurist, E.L. and Target, M. (2002). *Affect regulation, mentalization, and the development of the self.* New York: Other Press.

Hermans, H.J.M. and Dimaggio, G. (eds) (2004). *The dialogical self in psychotherapy*. London: Routledge.

Leiman, M. and Stiles, W.B. (2001). Dialogical sequence analysis and the zone of proximal development as conceptual enhancements to the assimilation model: The case of Jan revisited. *Psychotherapy Research*, *11*, 311–330.

Livesley, W.J. (2003). *Practical management of personality disorders*. New York: Guilford Press.

Livesley, W.J. (2008). Integrated therapy for complex cases of personality disorder. *Journal of Clinical Psychology: In-session*, *64*.

Luborsky, L. and Crits-Christoph, P. (1998). *Understanding transference*. Washington, DC: American Psychological Association.

Lynch, T.R. and Cheavens, J.S. (2008). Dialectical behavior therapy for comorbid personality disorders. *Journal of Clinical Psychology: In-Session*, *64*, 154–167.

Millon, T. and Davis, R.D. (1996). *Disorders of personality. DSM-IV and beyond.* Chichester: Wiley.

Neimeyer, R.A. (2000). Narrative disruptions in the construction of self. In R.A. Neimeyer and J.D. Raskin (eds), *Constructions of disorder: Meaning making frameworks for psychotherapy* (pp. 207–241). Washington, DC: American Psychological Association.

Nicolò, G., Carcione, A., Semerari, A. and Dimaggio, G. (2007). Reaching the covert, fragile side of patients: The case of narcissistic personality disorder. *Journal of Clinical Psychology: In-Session*, *63*, 141–152.

Ryle, A. and Kerr, I. (2002). *Introducing cognitive analytic therapy. Principles and practice*. Chichester: Wiley.

Safran, J.D. and Muran, J.C. (2000). *Negotiating the therapeutic alliance. A relational treatment guide*. New York: Guilford Press.

Semerari, A., Dimaggio, G., Nicolò, G., Procacci, M. and Carcione, A. (2007) Understanding minds, different functions and different disorders? The contribution of psychotherapeutic research. *Psychotherapy Research, 17*, 106–119.

Snicket, L. (2006). *A series of unfortunate events: The complete wreck: Books 1–13*. New York: HarperCollins.

Vygotsky, L.S. (1930/1978). *Mind in society. The development of higher psychological processes* (M. Cole, V. John-Steiner, S. Scribner and E. Souberman, eds). Cambridge, MA: Harvard University Press.

Weiss J. (1993). *How psychotherapy works: Process and tecnique*. New York: Guilford Press.

Chapter 16

The impact of metacognitive dysfunctions in personality disorders on the therapeutic relationship and intervention technique

Antonio Semerari

In this book it is argued that disorders of metacognition, i.e. difficulties reflecting upon one's own and others' mental states, have an important role in severe pathologies such as personality disorders (PD), schizophrenia or post-traumatic disorders. These patients have difficulties thinking about their own thoughts, perceiving their emotions, comprehending others' intentions and effectively regulating their own mental processes. Such difficulties appear in different forms in different patients. In some of them certain aspects of metacognition can be impaired, but not others, or the dysfunctions can manifest themselves with various degrees of pervasiveness.

Although the evidence about the influence that metacognitive disorders have on severe pathologies has now reached a critical point where many researchers find it convincing, relatively few works focus on treating metacognition. For PDs two manuals concentrate on the need to stimulate metacognition: Bateman and Fonagy's (2004) *Mentalisation based treatment for borderline personality disorders* (BPD) and *metacognitive interpersonal therapy* (MIT) (Dimaggio *et al.*, 2007). Regarding schizophrenia, the works described in this book (Lysaker and Buck, Chapter 13; Hasson-Ohayon *et al.*, Chapter 14) are at the cutting edge of treatments aimed at improving metacognition.

Nevertheless, various authors have tackled the problem of metacognitive deficits, adopting other languages. One example is what some have referred to as integration disorder, characteristic, according to Kernberg (1975), of borderline personality organization, with patients swinging between opposite and inconsistent representations of self and other. Similarly, Ryle and Kerr (2002) describe an inability in BPD to form a consistent representation of multiple mental states. Dialectical behaviour therapy (DBT, Linehan, 1993) considers borderline symptoms to derive from a difficulty in identifying and effectively regulating one's emotional states, a concept similar to self-reflection and metacognitive mastery (see Colle *et al.*, this volume, Chapter 11; Lysaker and Buck, this volume, Chapter 13). With this premise, therapy is focused on a typically metacognitive goal: helping patients to identify, accept and regulate their emotions.

While techniques for stimulating metacognition in PDs are described elsewhere (Dimaggio *et al.*, this volume, Chapter 15), of interest here is how the relationship that forms in psychotherapy can be conceptualized as promoting enhanced capacites for metacognition. In doing so I will keep in mind the tactics–strategy distinction. Tactics involve how sessions and, in particular, the crises in the therapeutic relationship occurring during treatment of seriously affected patients, are handled. Strategy involves generic therapeutic principles that can foster and stabilize patients' metacognition. This distinction has, in part, only an explanatory usefulness, as some session-handling principles, when repeated continuously throughout a therapy, lead to long-term treatment goals. Two clinical vignettes, drawn from my experience, can give the reader an idea of the problems facing a therapist when treating patients with metacognition disorders.

Rossi

The patient has just sat down in front of me, on the other side of my desk. I know nothing about him, except for what I see: a man about 40 years old, with a grey jacket and corduroy trousers. There is nothing showy or bizarre to be found in his appearance. He appears to be a middle class man like many others. I ask him why he has asked for an appointment and he replies that he suffers from anxiety. But it is not his verbal response that strikes me. It is his look, inquisitive, attentive, concentrated on gathering every detail. It settles on my face and my eyes. It glides down to look at the papers scattered over the desk, and moves on to the pen I have in my hand to take notes and then the switched off computer screen.

I immediately feel a sensation that I have learned to recognize over the years: the claustrophobic feeling of being observed and spied on in every detail, and the impalpable impression of a suspicion hanging over me, an unsaid accusation from which one does not know how to defend oneself. This is like the paranoid atmosphere described by Kafka. The first thought that comes to my mind is: 'What does he want from me?' There was a hovering threat that I would tell the patient at the end of the session that it would be better if he were not treated by me. From reading Safran and Muran (2000) I have learned to pay attention to the play between patients' expressive markers and my inner states, signalling a break in the alliance. I ask myself then what the patient is doing to cause this state in me. The way he observes me and the things in my room gives me the answer. He is studying me, almost trying to read my mind. The brief replies he supplies to my questions shed no light on his problem. Frankly, he seems reticent. He does not want to speak until he is happy about my intentions.

But why is it so difficult for him? The social context, a psychotherapy clinic that he himself has chosen to go to, my professional stance, everything ought to tell him that my intention is to understand his problem in order to treat it. Other patients deduce this without even having to reflect upon it. Instead, no matter how eager for information about my mental contents, he is unable to arrive at a sufficiently reassuring representation of my mind, of what I am thinking and feeling.

I can see that he needs information and I try to fight my instinct to feel that I am under suspicion, which leads to my choosing to say the least amount possible for fear that anything might be used against me. I have become wary. I have the sensation that whatever I say could be interpreted in ways that could lead to a therapeutic catastrophe. I imagine, then, that his state of mind is similar to mine. He does not understand my intentions and, consequently, the use I might make of the information he provides me. I note, after these inner reflections, that I am becoming empathetic towards him again and I let myself be led by this. I start to explain the reasons behind each question I pose. For example:

> 'Is your anxiety greater when you're alone or when with other people? I'm asking you to understand whether it's connected more to your thoughts or to problems with others.'

Continuing like this, the patient becomes readier to provide information and, almost at the end of the session, reveals the core of the problem afflicting him. His surname is the equivalent in Italian of *Red* and when he hears this word or sees it written somewhere, he is assailed by the doubt as to whether it refers to the colour or to his name pronounced or written with denigrating intentions towards him. As soon as he reveals his problem, the suspiciousness, which seemed to have waned, starts appearing again. He begins to examine me inquiringly and to reply in monosyllables. I am perplexed for a moment and the patient is unable to keep from posing the crucial question: 'Do you find me mad, Doctor?' That he has asked me this openly is a good sign, but it does not make it easier to reply to. Openly contesting content close to delusion is advised against by all the experts in our field, but not being sincere with a patient with a desperate need for truth about others' mental contents seems just to be ill advised. I get over this with a reply that, although indirect, does not belie my point of view:

> 'Truthfully, it wasn't that I was thinking about. If you want a diagnosis, I'll give you one when we've got to know each other better. What I was thinking of was something else. You told me that you aren't sure that the word refers to your name. You have doubts and suspicions and the suspicions torment you. I was asking myself whether in your history there were some good reasons to explain this tormenting by suspicion. Naturally, not knowing you, I can't be sure of my hypotheses, but, if you agree, we can talk about this in our coming meetings.'

At least for now he seems reassured by my reply. 'Yes,' he agrees, 'you're right. I've got doubts and suspicions but I'm not sure about them.' After this he asks for information about how the therapy will be conducted.

Anna

That morning I got to the clinic very early. Nobody else was there yet. The first appointment was in more than two hours and I had time to read the newspaper and leaf through some articles. As a result, when the bell rang, I went to open it personally. A woman about 35 years old and evidently very agitated, with messy hair and a frightened look, threw herself through the door.

'I need an appointment!' she said, almost panting and mistaking me for one of the clerical staff. 'With Doctor Semerari, if possible.' I felt like smiling. 'You've already had one with Semerari,' I replied, introducing myself. 'I can see you immediately, but, if it's a question of psychotherapy, I have to warn you that I personally don't have room at present. I can refer you, however.'

Her face suddenly became relaxed, almost pretty. 'It's destiny then,' she said, completely ignoring the last part of what I said. However, her smile of relief and look of admiration made me feel, for one moment, the most famous psychotherapist in the world, a benefactor of suffering humanity and frightened women. This unexpected idealization of myself should have reminded me of something but there and then I did not take any notice.

It was the way in which Anna started as soon as she sat down that made me realize I was playing the role of an omnipotent saviour. 'You have to help me,' she said 'I've just left a man, a stalker, capable of anything.' I was dumbfounded and my feeling of omnipotence quickly became impotence. What sort of request was that? How could I help her with a problem like that? I refrained, however, from giving her the too obvious advice to contact the police. The sense of confusion I noticed reminded me of what I experience lots of times with borderline or dissociated patients when they confusedly describe their relationships. 'Tell me the story from the beginning,' I told her, to give myself time to clarify my ideas.

Anna started to tell me about her relationship with the stalker, which had begun eight years previously, after her divorce. He was divorced too with a son. The relationship was a continuous succession of breaking up and getting back together again. It was always Anna who left him because, she said, he made her life impossible with his obsessive jealousy, controlling and rows. I asked her to what extent her decision to start the relationship again each time was due to fear triggered by his threats.

Anna appeared surprised by my question. No, he had never really threatened her each time they separated. 'On the contrary, he courts me,' she pointed out. I was nonplussed. I had imagined a dangerously violent individual and now I learned that there had never been either violence or threats. I then asked why on earth she had reciprocated his courting, given that he made her life impossible, and what tied her to him.

At this point there was a radical shift in the story, which became that of an idyll. Moments of passion alternating with intimacy and tenderness. Anna told me she felt guilty. She had permitted herself to flirt and that had triggered his jealousy and made him suffer. Naturally, I was still confused about the real state of things, but I had a clearer idea about Anna's mind. She was full of multiple and contradictory representations of herself, her partner and their relationship. But this can happen to anyone experiencing a tormented love story.

The problem was that she was unable to reflect on these representations. She did not even seem to realize how contradictory they were and how much they were driving her into lines of action that were so incompatible that they cancelled each other out. In short, there was no metacognitive point of view with which to combine the representations in a synthesis that was consistent and capable of producing effective actions. When she selected one of the various points of view, she seemed to forget the others; it was the sole and absolute truth for her.

Moreover, Anna saw these representations as reality and not mental constructions. She was in a mental state defined equivalent mode (Fonagy and Target, 1996; Bateman and Fonagy, 2004), in which, as in dreams, each inner representation is seen as a fact occurring externally and each fantasy as equal to reality. We have defined this *differentiation disorder* (Semerari *et al.*, 2003), in that a patient is unable to differentiate among different types of representation: dreams, fantasies, hypotheses, beliefs or memories. A fantasy is seen as a fact, a memory as if it was occurring at that moment and a dream as something really happening. Thoughts become, ipso facto, true and, temporarily, patients become unaware that their behaviour is driven by beliefs and representations that might be false (Baron-Cohen *et al.*, 1985). In short, I had the idea that, at least temporarily, Anna was displaying two aspects of metacognitive disorder: she was incapable, on the one hand, of developing a metareflection on the various and contradictory representations she made of her relational situation and, on the other, of grasping the representative and mental nature of her various fragmented points of view.

This way of functioning confused me. I could not see which version of the story to focus my intervention on and I myself had alternating sensations of mastering the session and of impotence. I thought that my confusion reflected, at least in part, that of the patient and decided to focus my intervention on this. I disclosed to Anna that I felt a little confused. I had tried to put together a picture of her relationship with this man and I listed the representations that I was unable to match: him persecuting her like a stalker, their amorous and intimate idyll, or her wounding him by provoking his jealousy. I did not doubt that each of these versions was well motivated and deserving of being examined in detail and understood. But meanwhile it was important to understand whether the problem was not precisely one of being confused by contrasting images and stimuli, all equally intense and pressing, without achieving a synthesis with which to follow a consistent line of conduct. I hoped in this way to stimulate Anna to take a metareflexive point of view of the confusion and chaos in her mental states. The intervention seemed to work. Anna stayed silent, with the air of someone who is reflecting. She acknowledged that she passed continuously from one attitude to another. She moved about like a mouse in a cage, she said, never getting anywhere.

I then asked her if she really considered she was in danger. Anna shook her head strongly in denial. No, she did not consider the man capable of violence; it was a problem of hers, she hinted. She added that sometimes her emotionality made her lose sight of reality. I finished by saying that I would find a colleague that I trusted absolutely for her to contact and Anna willingly accepted a course of treatment, which is proceeding profitably.

Session management

I hope the examples provided above are good illustrations of the points that I consider to be central to successfully managing psychotherapy sessions with patients with serious metacognitive disorders:

1. The various metacognitive dysfunctions provoke difficulties in the therapeutic relationship that cause problematical mental states in the therapist, with a certain correspondence between type of dysfunction and mental state.
2. The covert operations by which therapists transform their problematic states into information useful for guiding session.
3. The conversational style the therapist adopts in order to promote metacognition.
4. The planning of any interventions needs to take into account which of a patient's metacognitive skills are intact and which are dysfunctional.

Metacognitive dysfunctions and problems in the therapeutic relationship

Metacognitive disorders cause problems to develop in the therapeutic relationship. Comprehending our own and others' minds is the tool with which we regulate our interpersonal interactions, and it is through an awareness of each person's intentionality that we can experience and understand a wide range of relationships and perceive the exceptions to and refutations of our expectations. An impairment of these functions creates a series of difficulties in modulating and handling relationships, including the therapeutic one.

Another question, however, emerges from the above clinical vignettes. With both Rossi and Anna the therapist noticed problematical mental states and difficulties in relating. But they were different and this seemed to be related to differences in the patients' metacognitive malfunctioning. With a patient whose difficulties are principally related to comprehending others' intentions, the therapist felt scrutinized: He noted that every gesture he made was being evaluated with certain criteria, the logic of which escaped him. This made him wary and attentive, with the risk of making his mind even more opaque to the patient.

In the case of the patient with integration disorder, the therapist instead felt confused, dragged into a kaleidoscope of relationship representations in which he felt he could lose the thread of his therapeutic intervention. The question therefore is: Is it possible to identify specific problems in the therapeutic relationship connected to particular metacognitive disorders? This hypothesis is consistent with our group's work (Semerari, 1999; Dimaggio *et al.*, 2007), inspired by the ideas of Clarkin *et al.* (1999), according to whom the severity of a disorder contributes to determining the nature of countertransference. The type of metacognitive disorder repetitively and recognizably influences problematical interpersonal cycles that, driven by the interpersonal schemas of the participants in a relationship (in particular of the patients), occur between patients and therapists (Safran and Segal, 1990; Safran and Muran, 2000). On the basis of their schemas, patients activate dysfunctional coping strategies to handle relationships they foresee as negative. These strategies, in turn, cause in the therapist problematical mental states and action tendencies that can damage the relationship.

These reactions are, however, influenced in quality and intensity by the type and severity of the metacognitive disorders. For example, patients with monitoring disorder, i.e. difficulties in identifying and relating emotions, thoughts and desires, tend to cause a sense of interpersonal detachment and withdrawal from the relationship in a therapist, often accompanied by boredom or irritation (see Vanheule *et al.*, this volume, Chapter 10). Detachment is the effect of monitoring disorder. The particular emotional tone, for example, boredom or irritation, depends on interpersonal schemas. It is easier to become bored when faced with a withdrawn avoidant patient and irritated when faced with a haughty narcissist. Such states lead therapists to easily become distracted and think of things outside a session.

Patients like Anna, on the contrary, with limited integration and differentiation, cause confusion and generally hyper-involvement. Therapists swiftly alternate between anxiety, anger, fear, attraction and so on, depending on the particular interpersonal schema active at that moment.

Rossi, for his part, represents an example of how patients poor at decentring and understanding others' minds can create an atmosphere of claustrophobia and paranoid suspiciousness. The fact that such states are found in therapists with different temperaments, experience, schools and cultures indicates how much they depend on the psychopathology in question, rather than the therapist's character (Clarkin *et al.*, 1999) and it is precisely this stereotypy and repetitiveness that make it easier to study them and learn to handle them.

Therapist inner operations

The techniques for treating relational problems caused by patients are traditionally psychodynamic, such as in transference focused therapy (Clarkin *et al.*, 1999), and are implemented in the cognitive field using metacognitive interpersonal therapy (MIT, Dimaggio *et al.*, 2007; Dimaggio *et al.*, this volume, Chapter 15).

These techniques are based on the assumption that seriously affected patients' therapists experience mental states similar or complementary to their patients. Clarkin and colleagues (1999) consider that the latter induce these states with defence mechanisms such as projection or projective identification. In Rossi's case there was a sharing of the internal climate of suspiciousness, while Anna, as a victim, led the therapist to play the complementary role of saviour in a shared atmosphere of confusion.

Seriously ill patients' role representations are negative, rigid and applied pervasively to almost all significant relationships (Weiss, 1993; Ryle and Kerr, 2002). In this situation the quickest way of handling the expectation that the other will do something negative to the self is to do the same negative thing to the other (role reversal). In the therapeutic relationship, patients act unconsciously in ways that put their therapists in the position in which they themselves feel they are or fear being a source of discomfort to the patient.

If therapists accept unpleasant feelings without reacting and reflect on the similarities between their transient mental state and their patient's habitual one, they can become empathetic more quickly. Let us return to Rossi. How long would it have taken for him to manage to verbalize the experience of feeling observed and controlled? And yet right from the start he offered the therapist an outline of his suffering, causing a similar state in the latter that then steered the interview.

For therapists to use their own problematical states requires a self-reflective focus to identify their contents. They should then focus on the patient by asking him how much of their state resembles the latter's feelings and his fears about the therapeutic relationship. They should not assume that what they feel is identical to the patient's experience, but rather identify the problematical theme behind the relationship: competition with the risk of being humiliated, detachment, ill-treatment, idealization or seduction. They should then concentrate on the experience aspects they consider they share with the patient at that moment.

As well as switching from a negative reaction ('the patient does not trust me') to an empathetic position ('there is a climate of mutual diffidence') therapists might ask themselves: 'How would I want another's approach to be when helping me to exit from this mental state?' On the basis of the reply to this question it becomes easier to overcome the impasse in the relationship.

Intervention style

The conversational style used in these interventions involves self-disclosure, validation and sharing techniques (Linehan, 1993; Bateman and Fonagy, 2004; Dimaggio *et al.*, 2007). The importance of self-disclosure with patients suffering metacognitive disorders is exemplified by Rossi. Patients with difficulties understanding others' intentions and motivations need frequent information on the reasons behind their therapist's actions to avoid serious misunderstandings and ruptures to trust.

Validation has been used with various meanings. I shall look here at its use in personal construct psychology (Kelly, 1955) and dialectical behaviour therapy (DBT, Linehan, 1993). For Kelly, validation means confirming the sense of the forecasts and evaluations that a person constructs: 'I understand that you can have this point of view about the world.' According to Linehan, validation is a therapist stressing the comprehensible and acceptable nature of at least a part of borderline patients' dysfunctional experience: 'I understand how you can feel like that.' The first therefore validates patients' views of the world; the second their affective experience.

Validation in the Kellyan sense also occurs in the treatment of delusions. Patients losing the ability to understand that behaviour is driven by beliefs which can be false and do not differentiate between a representation of the world and its reality can become confused and hostile if a therapist invalidates their beliefs, which for them coincide with the world.

In cognitive behavioural therapy (CBT) for schizophrenia (Kingdom and Turkington 1994; Turkington *et al.*,, 2006), for example, therapists respect a patient's perspective and do not try to convince her of the falsity of her beliefs. They investigate, rather, the stress-inducing factors preceding the delirium and only when this work is over do they propose an alternative, normalizing interpretation, based on the stress/vulnerability concepts and a shared and coherent account of the problem at hand which is acceptable from the patient's perspective.

A Kellyan validation attitude has been described by Lysaker and Buck (this volume, Chapter 13) in the treatment of schizophrenia. When treating Verdi (Lysaker and Buck, 2006), a patient with pervasive delusions of persecution, the therapist was aware that a radical confutation of the patient's delusional beliefs would have made him feel totally mad. For a long time, therefore, he adopted an attitude of curiosity and interest about how Verdi had got to his conclusions and asked him whether any information had not made him doubt them, thus empathizing with his uncertainty. Moreover, the therapist did not directly challenge the patient's delirious beliefs and supported the latter's perception that he had been devalued.

Regarding emotional validation, according to Linehan, borderline patients have grown up in an environment where the expression of their affects received aggressive, disdainful and sarcastic responses. This invalidating atmosphere makes the patients confused or scared, or leads them in turn to invalidate their feelings and emotions. Validation, therefore, creates an atmosphere of trust, in which patients can metacognitively reflect on experience with less fear of provoking rejection or refusal in themselves or the therapist.

Another form of validation aimed at improving metacognition which has been adopted by MIT (Dimaggio *et al.*, 2007), is reference to 'universal we'. Therapists here stress that at least part of a patient's experience is shared or capable of being shared by them in that it is typically human (Safran and Muran, 2000). For example: 'Do you feel in one of those moments of emptiness where everything seems meaningless *to us*?' Such an intervention is both a self-disclosure – therapists implicitly stating that it is an experience to which, as humans, they too could be subject – and a validation. Both by creating a trusting relationship, in which one can reflect on one's own experience, and by stimulating a process of mirroring and comparison between one's own and the other's mental states in an atmosphere of equality, it results in an improvement of metacognition.

Assessing patients' metacognitive level

Continuously taking account of a patient's metacognitive level is part of both intervention tactics and strategy: tactics as regards the handling of each single session and strategy as regards the fact that, by working in each session on a patient's functioning level, a therapist stimulates any impaired functions and tries to stimulate long-term higher and more stable levels of metacognition.

Several session markers help in intuitively and rapidly evaluating a patient's metacognition. The first is the therapist's overall representation of the patient's mental contents and responses to interventions. A clear and orderly impression of the patient's discourse indicates good functioning.

The sensation that the speech is opaque or flat indicates a likely monitoring disorder. A confused or chaotic representation suggests an integration disorder.

Regarding the semiotics of metacognitive dysfunctions in sessions: in the most severe cases, usually persons with schizophrenia, even the ability to describe oneself as a thinking and acting person is impaired and one does not seem to be an agent (Lysaker *et al.*, 2007). In monitoring disorders, i.e. a difficulty in identifying and describing elements of one's inner state as thoughts, memories and affects, narratives are factual or theorizing; patients describe behaviour but without referring to the desires, beliefs and fears motivating them.

Narrative themes that are rigid and repetitive, and handled with a total emotional involvement in – or on the contrary excessive detachment from – their dramatic contents, suggest limited differentiation between inner fantasy and external reality. Chaotic stories crowded with different thought themes and contradictory representations, as in Anna's case, indicate poor integration. Flat, stereotyped or hyper-generalized descriptions of other people indicate a poor understanding of other people's minds and little decenteration.

Lastly, the therapist should consider how a patient replies to questions eliciting specific skills. Questions like 'What did you feel?' or 'What did you think?' trigger monitoring. Questions requiring generalizations or explanations of shifts and changes in mental states require integrative skills. For example, 'Do you typically react like that? Can you give me another example?' or 'What stimulated the change in your mood?' Replies to questions like 'How much did you subjectively believe what you were thinking?' can provide a measure of differentiation. Questions concerning patients' opinion of others' behaviour can shed light on their ability to understand others' minds and decentre.

Naturally a patient may have problems in various metacognitive areas. In such cases it is important to choose which of the impaired functions it is best to deal with first. An intervention should start with the disorder hindering the session the most. For example, in Anna's case the therapist's assessment suggested that the main problem was poor integration, which was causing confusion and making it impossible to identify a focus for treatment. During patients' therapies, as the simpler functions are gradually used successfully by them and, for example, after an initial stage with difficulties describing inner states, they manage to identify their emotions, one can switch to encouraging more complex metacognitive skills. Therefore, once the contents of affects are available, one can stimulate the identifying of what provokes these affects and of the consequences for behaviour entailed by the patients' emotions (see Dimaggio *et al.*, this volume, Chapter 15, for a formalization of the order in which metacognitive problems may be tackled in psychotherapy).

Long-term strategy

I propose two types of strategy for improving patients' metacognitive functioning:

- stimulating impaired skills
- providing a scaffold for the impaired skill.

In the first case a therapist engages in helping patients to use their impaired functions. In the second he or she supplies explanations or pedagogical interventions involving mind-functioning models that patients can use as a metacognitive point of view to observe and understand their own processes. Examples of a continuous stimulus of defective functions can be found in the therapy of patients with chronic schizophrenia described by Lysaker and Buck (this volume, Chapter 13). At the start of their treatment the patients had basic metacognitive difficulties: they did not see themselves as intentional agents capable of their own thoughts and perceptions. Initially, to help them to develop these functions the therapist merely stressed, repeatedly and with an emphasis on the second person, the perceptions reported by the patients, no matter how minimal – 'you heard' and 'you watched' – fostering a space in which the patients could see themselves as actors in their own mental lives. Individual case studies (Lysaker *et al.*, 2005; Lysaker and Buck 2006) show how interventions that follow the hierarchical structure of metacognition from the simplest to the most complex function result in patients progressively placing thoughts and feelings in coherent self-narratives of their stories.

Similarly, Bateman and Fonagy (2004) recommend that interventions with borderline patients need to take into account the mentalizing skills which the patients display in a particular moment. Therapists should help them to bridge the gap between affective experience and symbolic representation and, like good caregivers, provide them with sufficient feedback to help them to identify affective states and the thoughts accompanying them. Attention should be focused on the mental states currently found in life episodes narrated about here and now, and the use of metaphors and interpretations which could confuse patients should be avoided. Moreover, therapists should try to create meaning bridges among the variations in patients' emotions and points of view so as to develop integrative points of view about the self against the background of flows in relational experience (Clarkin *et al.*, 1999).

To improve integration among dissociated self-parts, Clarkin and colleagues (1999) use transference and countertransference analysis. Once the contradictory representations of self and others are assessed, the therapist and patient should try to name each relational dyad – e.g. neglected/neglecting. Once the dyads have been identified and named, the therapist should point out any rapid role changes within a dyad and variations among dyads, thus stimulating integrative processes. Similarly, in borderline patients, cognitive analytic therapy (Ryle and Kerr, 2002) fosters integrated self-reflection as mental states and self/other relational roles evolve. The therapist should help the patient to identify and name role representations and the cognitive and affective contents linked to them and then focus on factors triggering shifts from one representation to another. The therapist can draw a diagram of role representations with the connected mental states and the causes for the interstate transitions. By analysing the diagram, patients can achieve a bird's eye view of their inner world (Ryle and Kerr, 2002).

The second strategic therapeutic step is to provide patients with general concepts, using psycho-educational explanations and interventions, with which to observe and make sense of psychological processes, so as to compensate metacognitive disorders. One example of this is the previously mentioned conceptualizations based on the concepts of stress and vulnerability used in CBT with patients with schizophrenia (Kingdom and Turkington, 1994). Therapists try to construct an alternative and normalizing explanation with which to give meaning to psychotic experience. They explain that delusional ideas or hallucinations are part of a continuum between physiology and pathology and that, in particular stress conditions, anyone can experience similar phenomena. They also explain that the level of stress necessary for provoking psychotic experiences depends on individual vulnerability in turn linked to temperamental factors and life history.

Note that these explanations are provided as part of an individual psychotherapy and need to be tailored to the individual patient. These new ideas can enrich the patient with non-dysfunctional points of reference from which to observe their symptoms and construct a metarepresentation thereof.

In the personality disorder field, MIT recommends talking openly with patients about their difficulties with metacognition, in particular the problems that these difficulties entail in daily life, so as to foster an alliance about the goal of developing metacognition. We saw an example of how to start this discussion in Anna's excerpt. The therapist began by disclosing his feeling of confusion. He then pointed out that maybe Anna also felt confused. At this point he proposed that her confusion depended on the multiple and contradictory self and other representations appearing in her mind and showed how this was preventing her from adopting consistent behaviour.

Once patients are aware of their confusion and the difficulties this entails in maintaining consistent action, a therapist can introduce the integration concept and propose the development of the ability to observe and reflect on variations in their mental states as a therapy goal.

In the case of patients with poor monitoring of their emotions, a therapist can explain that affects provide important information for finding our way in the world. Therefore difficulties in perceiving them can lead to ineffective choices; vice versa focusing on the emotions can enrich one's self-knowledge and generate more ego-syntonic and satisfying decisions.

This type of information can be supplied in groups too. For example, in DBT skill training groups (Linehan, 1993) borderline patients need help to learn emotional regulation skills, starting with a description of the nature of the emotions and their adaptive value. It is possible that the group psychotherapy included in mentalization based treatment (Bateman and Fonagy, 2004) makes it possible for patients to use others' perspectives of themselves to enrich their knowledge of their own inner states and, gradually, of the nuances present in others' minds.

Conclusions

Psychotherapeutic work with severely affected patients has produced a number of principles for treating persons with poor metacognition. First, when relating with these patients, a therapist should be prepared to experience situations of acute unease and take action to transform them into therapeutic opportunities. The inner operations with which relational difficulties in sessions can be overcome are based on an awareness of one's inner states and a consideration that they could be similar or complementary to those which patients are experiencing or fear experiencing. These inner operations help the therapist to regulate the course of the relationship.

The conversational style adopted needs to stress the valid and acceptable elements in a patient's experiences, so as to create a trust-based interpersonal atmosphere, facilitating the achievement of a reflective point of view by the latter. A therapist should, moreover, be aware of the difficulties encountered by patients in understanding the intentions and mental states of the person before them, and help them with suitable self-disclosure interventions.

Lastly, therapists should diagnose the patient's level of metacognitive functioning and intervene continuously on this level to stimulate the use of any impaired functions. They can also provide explanations, information and clarifications which the patient can use as a metacognitive point of view for observing and reflecting on his or her mental states and psychological processes.

Nevertheless, the fact that the application of these principles leads to good results in the treatment of seriously affected patients does not prove, on its own, that they affect precisely metacognitive functioning. They may promote a positive outcome through other possible change mediators by, for example, improving the therapeutic alliance. More in general, if the hypothesis that metacognitive disorders play an important role in causing and perpetuating serious pathologies can be considered relatively solid, the clinical implications that an improvement in metacognition entails an improvement in the pathology or that therapy works by stimulating metacognition are not as solid. For example, an analysis of three different BPD treatments demonstrated that only in psychodynamic therapies was there both a metacognitive and a clinical improvement, something not occurring in DBT (Levy *et al.*, 2006).

Evidence that the therapy of severe patients requires an improvement in metacognition comes especially from individual case studies (Lysaker *et al.*, 2007) and correlational research indicating that in schizophrenic patients better social adaptation and quality of life coincide with improved metacognition (Schaub *et al.*, this volume, Chapter 5). Further research on the psychotherapeutic process is necessary to show the effectiveness of the therapeutic principles that we have so far been able to describe on the basis of clinical experience and theory.

References

Baron-Cohen, S., Leslie, A. and Frith, U. (1985) 'Does the autistic child have a "theory of mind"?' *Cognition*, *21*, 37–46.

Bateman, A. and Fonagy, P. (2004). *Psychotherapy for borderline personality disorder: Mentalization based treatment*. Oxford: Oxford University Press.

Clarkin, J.F., Yeomans, F.E. and Kernberg O.F. (1999). *Psychotherapy for borderline personality*. New York: Wiley.

Dimaggio, G., Semerari, A., Carcione, A., Nicolò, G. and Procacci, M. (2007). *Psychotherapy of personality disorders: Metacognition, states of mind and interpersonal cycles*. London: Routledge.

Kelly, G.A. (1955). *The psychology of personal constructs*. New York: Norton.

Kernberg, O.F. (1975). *Borderline conditions and pathological narcissism*. New York: Aronson.

Kingdom, D. and Turkington, D. (1994). *Cognitive behavioural therapy of schizophrenia*. New York: Guilford Press.

Fonagy, P. and Target, M. (1996). Playing with reality: Theory of mind and the normal development of psychic reality. *International Journal of Psycho-Analysis*, *77*, 217–233.

Levy, K.N., Meehan, K.B., Kelly, K.M., Reynoso, J.S., Weber, M., Clarkin, J.F., *et al.* (2006). Change in attachment patterns and reflective function in a randomized control trial of transference-focused psychotherapy for borderline personality disorder. *Journal of Consulting and Clinical Psychology*, *74*, 1027–1040.

Linehan, M.M. (1993). *Cognitive behavioural treatment of borderline personality disorder*. New York: Guilford Press.

Lysaker, P.H. and Buck, K.D. (2006). Narrative enrichment in the psychotherapy for persons with schizophrenia: Single case study. *Issues in Mental Health and Nursing*, *27*, 233–247

Lysaker, P.H., Buck, K.D. and Hammond, K. (2007). Psychotherapy and schizophrenia: An analysis of requirements of individual psychotherapy with persons who experience manifestly barren or empty selves. *Psychology and Psychotherapy: Theory, Research and Practice*, *80*, 377–387.

Lysaker, P.H., Davis, L.D., Strasburger, A., Hunter, N. and Buck, K.D. (2005). Changes in narrative structure and content in schizophrenia in long term individual psychotherapy: A single case study. *Clinical Psychology and Psychotherapy*, *12*, 406–416.

Ryle, A. and Kerr, I.B. (2002). *Introducing cognitive analytic therapy: Principles and Practice*. Chichester: Wiley.

Safran, J.D. and Muran, J.C. (2000). *Negotiating the therapeutic alliance. A relational treatment guide*. New York: Guilford Press.

Safran, J.D. and Segal, Z.V. (1990). *Interpersonal processes in cognitive therapy*. New York: Basic Books.

Semerari, A. (ed.) (1999). *Psicoterapia cognitiva del paziente grave*. [Cognitive therapy of severe patients.] Milan: Cortina.

Semerari, A., Carcione, A., Dimaggio, G., Falcone, M., Nicolò, G., Procacci, M. and Alleva, G. (2003). How to evaluate metacognitive functioning in psychotherapy? The metacognition assessment scale and its applications. *Clinical Psychology and Psychotherapy*, *10*, 238–261.

Turkington, D., Kingdom, D. and Weiden, P.J. (2006). Cognitive behavior therapy for schizophrenia. *American Journal of Psychiatry*, *163*, 365–373.

Weiss, J. (1993). *How psychotherapy works: Process and technique*. New York: Guilford Press.

Chapter 17

Change in post traumatic stress disorder

An assimilation model account

Katerine Osatuke and William B. Stiles

Post traumatic stress disorder (PTSD) is one of the few *DSM-IV* (American Psychiatric Association, 2000) diagnoses where, in addition to symptoms, an external cause of pathology (having witnessed or experienced a traumatic event) is a diagnostic criterion. Yet many individuals who experience similar events do not develop PTSD. The differences may be due to the different ways in which people cope with traumatic experiences. Like others (e.g. Herman *et al.*, 1989; Herman, 1992; Hesse *et al.*, 2003), we suggest that successfully resolving a trauma requires its integration into the survivor's previous and ongoing experiences. This chapter explains how this integration happens using a theory of psychological change that we call the *assimilation model* (Stiles *et al.*, 1990; Stiles, 2002). The model describes a developmental process of coming to terms with problematic experiences, including traumas. Like other metacognitive models, it suggests that people get symptomatic and functional relief from PTSD as they develop more advanced ways to respond to their trauma, cognitively and socio-emotionally and that psychotherapy can facilitate this development.

Trauma affects aspects of metacognition in many ways (e.g. Widom, 1999; Allen, 2001; Liotti, 2004, 2006; McNally *et al.*, 2005; Parslow and Jorm, 2007; Vanheule *et al.*, this volume, Chapter 10; Liotti and Prunetti, this volume, Chapter 12), including the capacities to internally represent one's knowledge, to alter one's own cognitive processes (e.g. beliefs about self and others), to identify and distinguish emotions (alexithymia), and to regulate states of consciousness (dissociative tendencies or capacities). As Liotti and Prunetti (Chapter 12) have pointed out, dissociation of any sort is, by definition, a metacognitive failure.

Briefly, we understand these metacognitive dysfunctions as related to difficulties in assimilating the traumatic experiences into the rest of the self. As described in the next section, assimilation is manifested as smooth access between parts of the self. Assimilation is thus a way of describing metacognition – one part able to think about and draw upon another part. The pain of recalling a traumatic experience may block assimilation and hence smooth access. In effect, at low assimilation levels, the usual or familiar self tries to keep the memory of a traumatic experience at bay. When the part of the person that has formed around the traumatic experience is addressed by circumstances, however, it repeatedly tries to break through and express itself, producing the core symptoms of PTSD, including those in the avoidance, re-experiencing and hyperarousal clusters.

This chapter presents the assimilation framework and then applies it to explaining the presenting problems, patterns of client experience, and dynamics of change in PTSD. We note links between assimilation and other accounts of metacognitive processes. We suggest that, during therapy, the traumatic experiences from which PTSD symptoms originate can sometimes be integrated into the self following the developmental sequence described by the assimilation model. We then present a clinical example that illustrates the implications of the assimilation framework for understanding the treatment of PTSD.

Assimilation model

The assimilation model understands personality as made of multiple parts, or internal *voices*, which originate in different life experiences and are integrated (assimilated) to different degrees within people (Stiles, 1999, 2002). The voice metaphor underscores the theoretical proposition that traces of past experiences and activities are active and agentic within people. They are more than cognitive representations, and comprise affective, kinaesthetic, motivational, intentional and other aspects of the original experiences that formed them. Voices strive to express themselves through actions and words. They speak and act when addressed by other voices or when called forth by situations resembling the experiences that formed them. What they say or do reiterates elements of their formative experiences. In the assimilation framework, there is no personal agency separate from voices. Everything a person does, feels, thinks and says is seen as an expression of one voice or another.

The interlinked traces of already assimilated experiences and activities form a *community of voices* within the person. This is the psychologically dominant part of people: it encompasses their usual, familiar experiences, including the relationships and events of everyday life. Voices within the dominant community are psychological resources, available when circumstances call for their unique features and capacities. Among other things, a person's dominant community may encompass faith in a just and benign world. This may include beliefs that the world is safe and people are kind, feelings of trust and optimism, behavioural tendencies of being assertive, somatic perceptions of being light and full of energy, altruistic motives, visual impressions of people as beautiful, and so forth.

Assimilation generally proceeds smoothly, as the traces (voices) of new experiences become linked with and accessible from those of previous experiences. However, when a new experience conflicts with other active voices, it is problematic to the person, causing psychological pain that may halt further assimilation (Stiles *et al.*, 2004). Although not a conscious decision, the distress may cause people to avoid or ward off the unassimilated voice. We could describe the unavailability (or incomplete availability) of such an experience as a metacognitive dysfunction.

Even when separated from the rest of the self (through denial, avoidance, or active conflict and rejection), problematic experiences strive to express themselves when they are addressed. When acting from a problematic self-state, people may say or do something they dislike or disapprove in their usual (dominant) self-state. For example, a person may be ashamed of something she said or did from her problematic position when she looks at it from her dominant position (e.g. 'I'm an independent coper. I should not have asked for help'). At very low assimilation levels (dissociative states, denial), a person may be unaware of having had the problematic experience and may be shocked, pained or terrified when the experience emerges after being addressed by circumstances. In the case of warded off traumatic experiences, this emergence may be manifested as terrifying flashbacks or compulsive fight or flight reactions.

Difficulties in dealing with unassimilated material – traumatic experiences, painful memories, threatening feelings, or destructive relationships – bring people to therapy. The assimilation of problematic experiences through therapeutic dialogue could be described as a means of metacognitive integration (Hermans, 1999). In this process, previously non-communicating voices build *meaning bridges*. That is, they find signs (such as words, gestures, or other meaningful tokens) that both interpret in the same way, shared ways to represent the experiences and previously disjointed fragments. For example, previously intolerable traumatic experiences may become elements in an accepted narrative (Osatuke *et al.*, 2004). This shared framework or story can then be worked through and applied in daily life, extending the range of familiar or manageable experiences by incorporating previously rejected material, including memories of traumatic events.

A series of intensive case studies of therapy (see Stiles, 2002) has suggested that, in successful psychotherapy of various kinds treating people with varied problems, clients followed a regular developmental sequence of recognizing, understanding, and eventually resolving their problematic experiences. This sequence is summarized in the Assimilation of Problematic Experiences Scale (APES, see Table 17.1; Stiles *et al.*, 1987, 1991; Stiles, 2002).

Clients may enter treatment at any point along the APES, and any increase in levels represents therapeutic progress. Each stage builds upon the previous one. In theory, stages cannot be skipped, though they may not be detected by observers. Clients may have multiple problematic experi-

Table 17.1 Assimilation of Problematic Experiences Scale (APES)

0. *Warded off/dissociated.* Client seems unaware of the problem; the problematic voice is silent or dissociated. Affect may be minimal, reflecting successful avoidance. Alternatively, the problem appears as somatic symptoms, acting out, or state switches.
1. *Unwanted thoughts/active avoidance.* Client prefers not to think about the experience. Problematic voices emerge in response to therapist interventions or external circumstances and are suppressed or actively avoided. Affect involves unfocused negative feelings; their connection with the content may be unclear.
2. *Vague awareness/emergence.* Client is aware of the problem but cannot formulate it clearly – can express it but cannot reflect on it. Problematic voice emerges into sustained awareness. Affect includes intense psychological pain – fear, sadness, anger, disgust – associated with the problematic experience.
3. *Problem statement/clarification.* Content includes a clear statement of a problem – so mething that can be worked on. Opposing voices are differentiated and can talk about each other. Affect is negative but manageable, not panicky.
4. *Understanding/insight.* The problematic experience is formulated and understood in some way. Voices reach an understanding with each other (a meaning bridge). Affect may be mixed, with some unpleasant recognition but also some pleasant surprise.
5. *Application/working through.* The understanding is used to work on a problem. Voices work together to address problems of living. Affective tone is positive, optimistic.
6. *Resourcefulness/problem solution.* The formerly problematic experience has become a resource, used for solving problems. Voices can be used flexibly. Affect is positive, satisfied.
7. *Integration/mastery.* Client automatically generalizes solutions; voices are fully integrated, serving as resources in new situations. Affect is positive or neutral (i.e. this is no longer something to get excited about).

Notes

1. Assimilation is a continuum, with intermediate levels allowed: e.g. 2.5 represents a level of assimilation halfway between vague awareness/emergence (2.0) and problem statement/ clarification (3.0).
2. Versions of this scale have appeared in many papers, including several of those cited here. The first version appeared in Stiles *et al.* (1987).

ences, each at a different assimilation level with respect to the dominant community and to each other.

The assimilation model is a descriptive, not prescriptive, theory of client change in psychotherapy. It describes what happens in successful treatment of any type by specifying mechanisms and levels of integration of problematic (e.g. traumatic) experiences, rather than prescribing specific therapeutic strategies.

Metacognition and assimilation of traumatic experiences

The link between metacognition and assimilation starts with the concept of unavailability or availability of the traumatic (or other problematic) experiences to the person's awareness. At the lowest assimilation levels

(APES = 0, see Table 17.1), traumatic experiences are warded off and inaccessible except when triggered externally. This is the model's account of dissociation, that is, of metacognitive failure. Thus, dissociation is the opposite of assimilation: 'compartmentalization and detachment from the lived experience of emotion, the body or the self' (Holmes *et al.*, 2005).

At APES stage 1 (unwanted thoughts/active avoidance), problematic experiences are only partly available. They may be cognitively acknowledged but their implications and full significance are avoided (see Osatuke and Stiles, 2006 for elaboration and clinical examples). Clients may be alexithymic (Vanheule *et al.*, this volume, Chapter 10), as emotionally significant aspects of experiences are pushed away. Some cognitive aspects may be accessible, but full confrontation would be psychologically too painful, incongruent or shameful.

At APES stage 2 (vague awareness/emergence), clients characteristically experience inarticulate psychological pain as they confront and try to tell about the experience. There is vivid awareness of the experience, which may be confronted at a planned (but feared) moment in therapy. This intentionality distinguishes stage 2 from the externally triggered reliving of flashbacks at stage 0. It is the agonizing beginning of therapeutic retelling and restorying.

By APES stage 3 (problem statement/clarification) the problem is clearly stated, which implies some perspective-taking on both sides of the conflict. This might be described as metacognitive awareness without full metacognitive integration (Dimaggio and Lysaker, this volume, Introduction). Each side recognizes the other, but they lack a meta-perspective that synthesizes the opposing parts. The client can name and describe the trauma but cannot make sense or use of it. Such insight requires completing the semiotic meaning bridges – ways of understanding that provide smooth access between the dominant community and the traumatic experience (APES = 4). Once attained, such metacognitive links can be translated into in real-world coping – applying and adjusting the gained understandings to practical situations (APES = 5) until the experience of the former trauma becomes a resource (APES = 6).

APES stage 7 (integration/mastery) represents full integration, permitting seamless transitions between formerly conflicting experiences. The formerly traumatic experiences become, in effect, part of the person, automatically available as resources. This is precisely the concept of metacognitive mastery as assessed by the Metacognition Assessment Scale (Semerari *et al.*, 2007).

Attentional mechanisms of dissociation and assimilation

From the assimilation model perspective, dissociation always occurs in the present. It occurs only when the dissociated material would otherwise have emerged (i.e. when it is addressed by circumstances). Thus, dissociation is not an intrinsic characteristic of particular experiential content but an active process of one (problematic) experience relating to another (dominant) experience. Even though dissociation may be a very reliable feature of material that is extremely painful, it is not a passive, permanent feature.

A less extreme way in which unassimilated problematic experiences may limit metacognitive functioning is through attention being drained off by problematic material. We assume that there is a fixed quantity of attention to be deployed in the present; that is, one can attend to only so much at a given time (Miller, 1956). Theoretically, when problematic content is triggered, incompatible voices within the person (problematic and dominant) are addressed simultaneously (Stiles *et al.*, 2004). This incompatibility evokes arousal (in effect, excess attention); the coverage is automatically suppressed, including some of the content that was addressed (Stiles, 1972). Since this is understood as a continuing process (i.e. the addressing and the suppressing continue as long as the conditions triggering problematic material are present), the dominant perspective tends to monopolize attentional resources, and the kind of relaxed perspective taking needed for internal observation becomes attentionally unaffordable. This diversion of attention from all or part of the problematic content is unthinking and automatic. It is a consequence of the arousal (negative affect) that is produced when incompatible contents are addressed and activated simultaneously.

PTSD symptoms as an expression of low assimilation

PTSD originates in events that are extremely psychologically threatening or painful and therefore incompatible with most people's dominant experience. Its incompatibility is felt as intense psychological pain (fear, panic, rage, disgust) whenever the traces are reactivated by current events that resemble or recall it. The pain shuts off the problematic voice, producing automatic inattention to the traces of the traumatic experience. Consequently, traces remain unassimilated, incompatible and unavailable for dialogical exchanges with the other voices. This theoretical implication parallels what Dimaggio and Lysaker (this volume, Introduction), described as poor basic self-awareness contributing to poor integration. The inattention is manifested as the PTSD symptoms in the diagnostic cluster of avoidance. The short-term gains of the avoidance include prevention or an immediate decrease in confusion and psychological pain that would ensue from a sustained encounter (Stiles *et al.*, 2004). A long-term cost of avoidance, however, is shutting off a part of one's real past experience, so it is not assimilated and not available as a potential resource.

Avoided or not, every voice remains agentic. It retains its ability to express itself dramatically when it is addressed by circumstances, well illustrated by battle trauma flashbacks triggered by loud noises. Liotti and

Prunetti (this volume, Chapter 12) characterized this phenomenon as a motivational system that becomes activated by situational cues. As it is unprocessed and unmoderated by the rest of the self, the intrusions into the survivor's awareness are felt as discontinuous and unexpected – fragmentary and painful reliving of the trauma triggered by external events or chance (Varvin and Stiles, 1999; Liotti and Prunetti, Chapter 12). This struggle constitutes core PTSD symptoms in the diagnostic cluster of re-experiencing. The affective upset caused by encountering the dominant community result in symptoms in the diagnostic cluster of hyperarousal.

Assimilation of traumatic experiences

PTSD symptoms may be resolved if the traumatic experience is assimilated into the rest of the person. Note that assimilating the trauma does not mean containing the experience but rather making sense of it, finding ways to express and reflect upon the meaning of the traumatic experience that are compatible with the rest (the non-traumatized parts) of the self. In other words, the trauma can never be cured and forgotten, but instead the traumatized self can be expanded.

Becoming assimilated does not require that the trauma itself become viewed as a positive event; rather, the formerly denied experience becomes cognitively and emotionally understood so that its representation become smoothly accessible. They are not forgotten, but rather easily remembered and usefully mastered (Semerari *et al.*, 2007). The content emerges in awareness when it is wanted or useful for planning and choosing strategies to solve current problems and not at other times.

Smooth access to the traumatic experience thus allows the representation to change and become a resource rather than a problem. Indeed, some childhood sexual abuse survivors offer the counter-intuitive opinion that their traumatic experience had some positive aspects (McMillen *et al.*, 1995), and the survivors' assessment of their own levels of functioning appeared consistent with their interview behaviors and the adjustment rankings that researchers assigned (Himelein and McElrath, 1996). They appeared to have assimilated their traumatic experience enough to transform its lessons into tools, helping them navigate to their current lives better. They saw the voice of the abuse (including how they had dealt with the abuse) as having made them stronger and more self-sufficient, able to put their lives in order, take better care of themselves, and sustain open and trusting relationships with their children (making sure that their child would tell them if abuse happened). They empathized more with others who had similar experiences and felt more motivated and better able to protect their children and to take action against abuse in society.

The assimilation approach thus explicates instances where traumatic experience becomes a psychological resource. It addresses the full continuum of adjustment: not only symptoms and symptom reduction but also trauma-related growth (Cohen *et al.*, 1998; Calhoun and Tedeschi, 2001). In principle then, the model suggests that an ideal goal of therapy for PTSD is bringing clients to a state of mastery of their traumatic experiences. Admittedly, this may not be a realistic goal for many clients with severe PTSD or with limited personal resources or external support in their lives.

The clinical example below tracks changes across treatment in traces of experiences associated with one client's PTSD. It shows how assimilation stages of the traumatic experience can be used to understand the client's levels of metacognitive disruption and symptomatic distress.

The case of Michael

Michael was a Vietnam war veteran in his late fifties diagnosed with chronic PTSD and panic disorder with agoraphobia. His PTSD symptoms originated in several combat events. In one, several of Michael's friends were killed. In another, Michael was shell-shocked and trapped in a bunker after an explosion, with no lights, no food and no water. He could not estimate the extent of his injuries, tell the time or find an exit, and did not know what had happened to his buddies. Michael's reactions at the time of these events involved a sense of helplessness, acute vulnerability and shame. He felt 'weak', 'useless', at the mercy of 'random' events, and unable to change the outcomes. These reactions had remained largely unprocessed, cognitively and emotionally, as the fast-changing circumstances of combat left Michael no time or attention for this. Later, he 'tried to forget' because he saw 'no point in chewing on it' – but unsuccessfully. For years, Michael lived with recurrent intrusive memories of the visual scenes, which stirred up much distress as he struggled to put them out of his mind.

Michael had concentration difficulties and insomnia. He avoided television programmes (especially news), books, magazines, places, or people that reminded him of his time in Vietnam. He appeared hypervigilant, irritable, mistrusting of the therapist and reluctant to discuss his history, particularly the Vietnam era events. Michael admitted that he would never have come to see a psychotherapist had his physician not strongly suggested a possible psychological component to what Michael saw as his bodily failures (hyperarousal, startle responses, occasional panic attacks). Michael's panic attacks (pounding heart, sweating, trembling, shaking, suffocation, chest pain and fear of losing control) were not specifically connected to his flashbacks. A few happened in reaction to realizing his physical limits. For example, Michael once took offence at someone's 'random' (note the word) remark in the street, felt an impulse to physically attack the offender, then realized this was not an option because he was no longer as strong as 20 years ago – and immediately had a panic attack.

Michael's therapist saw both Michael's PTSD symptoms and panic attacks as organized around his main problematic experience: feeling inadequate, weak, small, and unable to take care even of himself, let alone important others. The worst of this experience for Michael seemed to be his sense of failing at the most elementary, bodily level, which caused him panic attacks, much anguish and self-directed contempt. Michael was more open to discussing his panic attacks than his PTSD symptoms. He saw his PTSD as 'stupid', 'more embarrassing', and less problematic – although, in his therapist's assessment, it caused him much more severe functional impairment than panic attacks did. That is, Michael initially denied the full impact of his traumatic experience (a stance consistent with APES stage 0, Table 17.1).

As therapy proceeded, Michael gradually became more amenable to talk about his trauma, although the therapist had to broach the topic and Michael would go along only so far (APES stage 1). These discussions increasingly brought up feelings of embarrassment and inadequacy. Michael expressed them vividly, mainly non-verbally (through his tone of voice, blushing, squirming in his seat, constricted body posture). He could not articulate or explain his own reactions, but seemed intensely disturbed by them (APES stage 2). He confirmed the therapist's interpretations of his affect as shame, and typically appeared even more ashamed.

Michael formulated his psychological pain while processing the meaning of a daily event that stirred him up greatly. He saw a mouse in a mousetrap; it struggled to get out, effortful but unsuccessful, visibly at the end of its strength, in much physical pain. When Michael saw it, he started sobbing and could not stop. He picked up the trap and let the mouse out, all the while feeling stupid for his extreme reaction and for not killing the household pest. When telling the therapist about what happened, Michael realized that during the combat events, he felt 'just like this' (which explained the intensity of his response). Even after making this connection, he still felt his reaction was stupid – but he also saw 'the point' of his 'going nuts' (see APES stage 3, Table 17.1). He understood his current PTSD symptoms as re-experiencing what he lived through during combat: a painful struggle with something uncontrollable, exceeding his understanding, and much bigger than him, such that no matter how hard he fought back, it still had a hold on him. After this realization, Michael told his therapist that PTSD, not panic attacks, was the main problem he wanted to work on in therapy; he decided to 'sort this out' (see APES stage 3).

After the core problem was formulated, in-therapy discussions focused on when and where it started and its current workings in Michael's life. Intrusive re-experiencing of the combat scenes became less frequent, presumably because traces of these experiences gained access to different means of expression. They were now actively discussed in therapy, albeit in a guarded or measured way. The therapeutic purpose was to put together the Michael 'from before' and the Michael 'from after'. In the assimilation model's terms, this involved facilitating the APES stage 3 to 4 transition (the transition from clearly stating the problem to understanding the dynamics that maintained it). In other words, the purpose was to build a meaning bridge between Michael's dominant sense of self and his problematic experience – combat events (when things were out of control and he felt weak, and helpless) and their aftermath (re-experiencing, pushing back the intrusive memories, distress that the constant struggle caused) – by articulating a perspective that would include them both – a metacognitive achievement.

Michael used the words 'weak', 'useless' and 'crazy' to describe both his emotional reactions during the combat and his present symptomatic state. Both experiences were completely 'against the grain' of who Michael thought he was: a strong, independent, self-sufficient leader and caretaker. From early years of life, this stance seemed to be his consistent role in the family and community; it became an essential part of how he saw himself as a person. The traumatic events presented him with an inconsistent experience, potentially shattering Michael's core assumptions and leaving him unsure how to live his life. His pronouncements about interpersonal relationships often seemed to come from two different perspectives, seemingly reflecting alternation between the leader-caretaker voice and the problematic 'I'm weak and useless and I give up' voice. Sometimes Michael expressed anger and disbelief about people's failure to take good care of their children or ageing parents, but he also occasionally stated that he no longer cared what happened to anybody who could not take care of themselves.

Once, in connection with a television show on famine and hungry children in a third world country, Michael stated that their parents would do better if they stopped trying to provide and let the children fend for themselves or die. He added that he himself lost any interest in supporting anyone in his community when such things were happening in the world: it was 'fighting a lost cause'. Such statements notwithstanding, the therapist knew Michael kept helping several people, both financially and with chores or errands. The therapist asked if Michael felt it would be all right for her to stop preparing the meals for her own daughter, given there were hungry children in the world. Michael replied this would be logical, something he 'sure' would do. Pointing out the inconsistencies of Michael's words with his caring real-world behaviour usually made him shrug, attribute it to a long-time bad habit of 'being stupid', and then become very angry with himself; so instead, the therapist said she felt responsible for her daughter. She added it pained her that some children went hungry and that she could do nothing to change this, but this made it even more important for her to ensure that 'this one' (pointing to the picture of her daughter) was well taken care of and never went hungry. Michael paused and did not give any immediate comments, but at the beginning of the next session he shared a vivid dream about the therapist in a conversation with her daughter at the dinner table, with 'any and all kinds of food you can imagine'. In the dream, Michael's therapist was telling her daughter she would take care of her as long as she lived, and make sure the daughter never went hungry. He saw himself standing nearby, wondering if it would be okay to approach or if he might be unwelcome. Through a guided imagery technique using the dream elements (e.g. the therapist's imagined reaction if he joined them at the table), Michael could emotionally experience, and then realize and state in words, that being hungry and accepting food and nurture was okay: that he would not be despised, or despise himself, for doing this. Processing this dream facilitated Michael's insight (APES stage 4) that at times he would like to accept, rather than offer, help and care.

Considering this therapeutic development in the context of internal working models of attachment (Liotti and Pruneti, Chapter 12), it could be understood as a switch in the attachment system. Michael moved from a problematic condition of inverted attachment (caring for others instead of asking for care when needed) to positive attachment with the therapist (asking for and getting care in the imaginal world). In assimilation terms, this transition seemed to reflect development of a meaning bridge permitting metacognitive access between his activity of caring for others and his extreme demand on himself that he be fully self-sufficient. The meaning bridge apparently began with the therapist's self-disclosure, was elaborated in the dream imagery, and then articulated through discussion with the therapist. His earlier avoidance of his own needs in nurture apparently constituted an interpersonal aftermath of his trauma (a problematic experience where his failing to be fully self-reliant became associated with danger and pain). Working through this aftermath (finding a meaning bridge between the caregiving and care-requiring parts of himself) was therefore an important therapeutic moment. After it, Michael became considerably more open to discussing situations when he (not other people) felt needy or helpless. These included his years in Vietnam, the time he was growing up and his life now. A re-evaluation of Michael's interpersonal needs was thus applied to specific relationships he had with family and friends (APES stage 5).

As Michael worked on recognizing what he needed and what he could offer to others without overburdening himself, his PTSD symptoms subsided, apparently because he developed a new way of dealing with the traces of traumatic experiences his symptoms carried. For example, he became able to recognize feeling overwhelmed, and respond to himself by thinking what or who could help with the situation at hand. He was still more comfortable with turning to a 'what' than to a 'who' for help with emerging needs; however, this response to himself in need represented substantial progress. Previously, failing at being self-sufficient was a short fleeting experience, not attended to or reflected upon, but immediately followed by an intense shame, then anger and self-contempt. We understand this sequence as reflecting a dialogue between Michael's disowned problematic voice (feeling overwhelmed), and dominant voice (experiencing himself as strong, independent, capable). Feeling weak clashed with the proud self-sufficiency, prompting shame, intense and painful enough that it motivated quick avoidance (an internal fleeing away from feeling needy). Suppressing the problematic experience left only anger, the response from the dominant voice. Michael's anger now had no particular target, and therefore was hard to resolve. It lingered for a long while, expressed at a bodily level (hypervigilant, keyed up), with a very limited acknowledgement of the angry affect and even less understanding of where it came from. Interestingly, Michael was able to discuss this sequence with his therapist only after it subsided: he recognized it in retrospect, from the new perspective of how the problem could have been handled differently.

Becoming more accepting of his 'weak' side (e.g. that he could not always win) also helped Michael cope better with the flashbacks. Before, when he had flashbacks of the episode where he lost several of his friends, Michael tried hard to push it back, felt ashamed as this did not succeed, and became angry. Now, when the visual memory emerged, he allowed himself not to fight it, but instead think the names of the friends he lost, the names of the commanders, and the other people who were there. Putting words to the picture made the visual scene recede. His memory shifted to right before and after the event, he allowed himself to dwell on this, be sad, think of his friends' families, then of the friends who were still alive, and how they were doing. Michael reconnected with several people from the Vietnam era whom he had avoided and talked with them about their military past – something he had never done before he started therapy. Apparently, Michael was not only coping better with his traumatic experience but was also making steps towards mastery (APES stage 7; see Semerari *et al.*, 2007): a state where the problematic experience itself becomes a tool for responding to current life demands. Michael developed closer bonds with several people around their shared experience in the military, an important reversal, as he had previously avoided people and conversations that reminded him of Vietnam.

We suggest that these symptomatic improvements reflected a greater assimilation between the dominant voice and Michael's experiencing himself as weak and helpless. The unassimilated experience initially felt problematic due to its conflict with the familiar way of being, but it gradually evolved to become an accepted, legitimate part of Michael's self. We suggest that this happened through a therapeutic dialogue that facilitated an encounter between Michael's usual and problematic perspectives, leading to assimilation. Initially, these perspectives did not want to talk to each other; communication depended on the facilitative presence of the therapist. For example, relating to his therapist's life (rather than his own) facilitated Michael's insight into his need sometimes to receive, rather than offer, nurture. A meaning bridge from Michael's dominant independent caretaker voice to Michael's problematic, needy, vulnerable voice was presumably less threatening, therefore easier to make, within transference-based material (a fantasy of joining the therapist and her daughter at the dinner table) rather than directly considering Michael's own life. Therapeutic dialogue thus provided new material supporting the client's progress along the assimilation sequence.

As another example, Michael's therapist asked him questions about the mousetrap: 'What does it remind you of? when did you feel this way before?' Michael's answers came from his traumatic experience of vulnerability in Vietnam; hearing it from himself helped Michael realize he had it within him. Here, the therapeutic dialogue possibly supported greater assimilation in two ways. First, the problematic voice was invited to elaborate its perspective. In response, Michael remembered feeling 'just like this' when in combat. Second, interpersonal conditions were supportive. Michael was clearly not rejected or despised by the therapist, a reaction he was usually getting from himself anytime he felt vulnerable. The therapist's voice within Michael may thus have served as a mediator between Michael's dominant and problematic voices. Whereas Michael's strong independent voice did not connect well with Michael's vulnerable voice at first, each of these voices connected to the therapist, and through her they gained access to each other as well. His internalized experience with an attachment figure may have become a new voice, into which both his experience of need and his experience of independence could be assimilated. In effect, perhaps Michael became more accepting of himself because he experienced his therapist as accepting.

We note that the assimilation model does not prescribe ways of building meaning bridges between the dominant and problematic voices; each school of therapy offers its own extensively elaborated recommendations. Michael's case offers just one example of how this might be done. The assimilation model focuses on describing, and Michael's story on illustrating, how the evolution in the dominant voice's way of relating to the problematic experience proceeds through the stages described in the APES.

To summarize, in Michael's case, higher APES levels appeared to correspond with more acceptance and interest in his problematic experience of 'weakness' (i.e. less avoidance of the problem, by his dominant voice). Higher APES levels also corresponded with more direct experience (i.e. less intrusive or uncontrolled experience) of the problematic voice, from the dominant perspective. Finally, higher APES levels corresponded with less emotional and somatic distress (i.e. less hyperarousal), as incompatible voices come to terms rather than painfully intruding. At least in Michael's case, the meaning bridges, manifested as a more direct (less avoidant) way of dealing with traces of his traumatic past experiences, were associated with a decrease in his distress, anger, and hypervigilance and a lessening in the unwanted re-experiencing of traumatic memories and scenes.

Conclusions

Like the other metacognitive models discussed in this book, the assimilation model is interested in mechanisms of psychological integration, measuring its levels and tracking changes (i.e. increases in assimilation) in treatment. Comparing assimilation progress during therapy with specific improvements in PTSD clients' lives yields observations on the psychological impairments that underlie the clinical dysfunctions we assess (see Semerari *et al.*, 2007). The case of Michael illustrates our suggestions that PTSD symptoms can reflect survivors' attempts to cope with traumatic experiences by avoiding them or warding them off and that they tend to improve with greater assimilation of the voices of the trauma (stronger meaning bridges, giving smoother, less painful metacognitive access).

We suggest that metacognitive problems in PTSD reflect poor assimilation; they are the consequences of incompatibility or limited connection between voices. Some of the distinctive features of this particular model are as follows. It offers accounts of both restricted and disorganized manifestations of PTSD, based on the degree to which the traumatic material is successfully or unsuccessfully warded off or avoided. Through the APES (Table 17.1), the assimilation model accounts for the entire continuum of integrating distressing experiential contents – not only gaining access to and resolving the problem, but also its transformation into a psychological resource. This theoretical scope helps bridge the gap between normal and clinically impaired functioning with respect to metacognitive abilities and levels of self-system integration. By explaining people in terms of discrete strands of experiences (rather than in terms of functions that operate across multiple experiential contents), and construing the strands as agentic voices, the assimilation model allows tracking the evolution of traumatic experiences in treatment.

References

Allen, J.G. (2001). *Traumatic relationships and serious mental disorders*. Chichester: Wiley.

American Psychiatric Association (2000). *Diagnostic and statistical manual of mental disorders, 4th edn, DSM-IV*. Washington, DC: American Psychiatric Association.

Calhoun, L. G. and Tedeschi, R. G. (2001). Posttraumatic growth: The positive lessons of loss. In R. A. Neimeyer (ed.), *Meaning reconstruction and the experience of loss* (pp. 157–172). Washington, DC: American Psychological Association.

Cohen, L. H., Hettler, T. R. and Pane, N. (1998). Assessment of posttraumatic growth. In R. G. Tedeschi and C. L. Park (eds), *Posttraumatic growth: Positive changes in the aftermath of crisis* (pp. 23–42). Mahwah, NJ: Lawrence Erlbaum Associates, Inc.

Herman, J. L. (1992). Complex PTSD: A syndrome in survivors of prolonged and repeated trauma. *Journal of Traumatic Stress*, *3*, 377–391.

Herman, J. L., Perry, J. C. and van der Kolk, B. A. (1989). Childhood trauma in borderline personality disorder. *American Journal of Psychiatry*, *146*, 490–495.

Hermans, H. J. M. (1999). Self-narrative as meaning construction: The dynamics of self-investigation. *Journal of Clinical Psychology*, *55*, 1193–1211.

Hesse, E., Main, M., Abrams, K. Y. and Rifkin, A. (2003). Unresolved states regarding loss or abuse can have 'second-generation' effects: Disorganized, role-inversion and frightening ideation in the offspring of traumatized non-maltreating parents. In D. J. Siegel and M. F. Solomon (eds), *Healing trauma: Attachment, mind, body and brain* (pp. 57–106). New York: Norton.

Himelein, M. J. and McElrath, J. V. (1996). Resilient child sexual abuse survivors: Cognitive coping and illusion. *Child Abuse and Neglect*, *20*(8), 747–758.

Holmes, E. A., Brown, R. J., Mansell, W., Fearon, R. P., Hunter, E. C. M., Franquilho, F., *et al.* (2005). Are there two qualitatively distinct forms of dissociation? A review and some clinical implications. *Clinical Psychology Review*, *25*, 1–25.

Liotti, G. (2004). Trauma, dissociation and disorganized attachment: Three strands of a single braid. *Psychotherapy: Theory, Research, Practice and Training*, *41*, 472–486.

Liotti, G. (2006). A model of dissociation based on attachment theory and research. *Journal of Trauma and Dissociation*, *7*, 55–74.

McMillen, C., Zuravin, S. and Rideout, G. (1995). Perceived benefit from child sexual abuse. *Journal of Consulting and Clinical Psychology*, *63*(6), 1037–1043.

McNally, R. J., Clancy, S. A., Barrett, H. M. and Parker, H. A. (2005). Reality monitoring in adults reporting repressed, recovered or continuous memories of childhood sexual abuse. *Journal of Abnormal Psychology*, *114*, 147–152.

Miller, G. A. (1956). The magical number seven, plus or minus two: Some limits on our capacity for processing information. *Psychological Review*, *63*, 81–97.

Osatuke, K. and Stiles, W. B. (2006). Problematic internal voices in clients with borderline features: An elaboration of the assimilation model. *Journal of Constructivist Psychology*, *19*, 287–319.

Osatuke, K., Glick, M. J., Gray, M. A., Reynolds, D. J., Jr., Humphreys, C. L., Salvi, L. M., *et al.* (2004). Assimilation and narrative: Stories as meaning bridges. In L. Angus and J. McLeod (eds), *Handbook of narrative and psychotherapy: Practice, theory, and research* (pp. 193–210). Thousand Oaks, CA: Sage.

Parslow, R. A. and Jorm, A. F. (2007). Pre-trauma and post-trauma neurocognitive functioning and PTSD in a community sample of young adults. *American Journal of Psychiatry*, *164*, 509–515.

Semerari, A., Carcione, A., Dimaggio, G., Nicolò, G. and Procacci, M. (2007). Understanding minds: Different functions and different disorders? The contribution of psychotherapy research. *Psychotherapy Research*, *17*(1), 106–119.

Stiles, W. B. (1972). A neurological theory of higher mental processes. Doctoral

dissertation, Department of Psychology, University of California, Los Angeles, California.
Stiles, W. B. (1999). Signs and voices in psychotherapy. *Psychotherapy Research*, *9*, 1–21.
Stiles, W. B. (2002). Assimilation of problematic experiences. In J. C. Norcross (ed.), *Psychotherapy relationships that work* (pp. 357–365_. New York: Oxford University Press.
Stiles, W. B., Morrison, L. A. and Haw, S. (1987). *Manual for assessing assimilation of problematic experiences in psychotherapy sessions*. Working paper, MRC/ESRC Social and Applied Psychology Unit, University of Sheffield, Sheffield, UK.
Stiles, W. B., Elliott, R., Llewelyn, S. P., Firth-Cozens, J. A., Margison, F. R., Shapiro, D. A., *et al*. (1990). Assimilation of problematic experiences by clients in psychotherapy. *Psychotherapy*, *27*, 411–420.
Stiles, W. B., Morrison, L. A., Haw, S. K., Harper, H., Shapiro, D. A. and Firth-Cozens, J. (1991). Longitudinal study of assimilation in exploratory psychotherapy. *Psychotherapy*, *28*, 195–206.
Stiles, W. B., Osatuke, K., Glick, M. J. and Mackay, H. C. (2004). Encounters between internal voices generate emotions. In H. H. Herrmans and G. Dimaggio (eds), *The dialogical self in psychotherapy* (pp. 91–107). New York: Brunner-Routledge.
Varvin, S. and Stiles, W. B. (1999). Emergence of severe traumatic experiences: An assimilation analysis of psychoanalytic therapy with a political refugee. *Psychotherapy Research*, *9*, 381–404.
Widom, C. S. (1999). Posttraumatic stress disorder in abused and neglected children grown up. *American Journal of Psychiatry*, *56*, 1223–1229.

Conclusion

Paul H. Lysaker and Giancarlo Dimaggio

Metacognition and mental illness

At the outset of this volume we began with the observation that many adults with significant forms of mental illness experience grave metacognitive difficulties. It is not merely a matter that they have difficulties processing information, recalling information or that symptoms interfere with life in certain ways. For many, suffering from a serious mental illness involves fundamental difficulties apprehending themselves and others as meaning-making beings whose richly varied thoughts and feelings could themselves be an object of consideration. These deficits represent barriers to well-being, social relationships, treatment and ultimately recovery.

In the face of this issue, this volume has brought together a range of researchers and thinkers who have offered literature reviews, empirical data and theoretical analyses exploring the biological and social underpinnings of metacognitive deficits, the different kinds of metacognitive dysfunctions potentially linked with distinct disorders and the implications for treatment. As we come to the close of this volume we have chosen to focus on how this work has addressed or pointed towards three different though related issues:

- the interplay of neurological and social bases of metacognition
- the different forms of metacognition that can be impaired and their appearances across different forms of mental illness
- the potential of psychotherapy and rehabilitation to promote the recovery of metacognitive capacity.

In reviewing these areas our intent in this final chapter is not to provide an authoritative summary so much as to stir up questions that might enhance the research and clinical work of those readers who are still trying to digest the many different things offered in this volume.

Interplay of neurological and social basis of metacognition

One powerful and naturally unavoidable theme that can be observed to confront all of the authors across chapters of this book concerns the processes which are required for metacognition and the processes which may disrupt metacognition. What allows, for instance, persons to perform well on theory of mind (TOM) tasks, to name their emotions when sitting in a therapist's office or watching a basketball game, or to tell complex stories of their lives gathered in private or research settings? Why do some adults fail to develop sufficient metacognitive capacities or lose metacognitive capacities as their lives progress, resulting sometimes in tragic levels of psychosocial failure? We read the work in this volume as suggesting that deficits in metacognition may result from a highly complex, and as of yet poorly understood, interaction between two different but distinct sets of forces. First, as outlined by Carpendale and Lewis (Chapter 2) Gumley (Chapter 3), as well as Liotti and Prunetti (Chapter 12), metacognition first develops in the context of a relationship to other persons. From a very early age, closeness and connection with others makes thinking about thinking possible for human beings. Persons form attachments, those attachments affect other people, interpretation of oneself and life are constructed and the process repeats with every experience building on previous experience and a history develops in which unique persons develop a unique set of metacognitive strengths and weaknesses. Important here is that not only is the development of metacognition rooted in development and attachment, but also for some, disturbances in the process, for example, disruptions in attachment due to trauma or other circumstances may leave persons with particular forms of diminished metacognitive capacity.

In parallel, research outside of that reviewed in this volume has suggested that a wide range of relationships including peer relationships are relevant for developing the ability to reason metacognitively. Role play pretence, that is, the ability to assume different imaginary roles in the 'pretend play' or 'as if mode' common by the age of four or five (Dunn, 1988) has been correlated with theory of mind skills (Lillard, 2001). Simulating the beliefs, desires, and emotional responses of a character while playing with peers may stimulate the development of a theory of that character's mind (Harris, 1994; Gordon, 1995). In pretend play children talk about mental states with each other more often than in other contexts (Hughes and Dunn, 1997), again stimulating the development of theory of mind (Dunn *et al.*, 1991). In socio-dramatic play, metacognition may also be developed as children negotiate many elements including who plays whom, what things the props stand for and what events should take place (Lillard, 2001). Indeed, pretend play with older siblings has been linked to the development of the ability to mentalize at an earlier age (Ruffman *et al.*, 1998).

From another frame, metacognition acts can be both complex and unruly. Performing increasingly complex forms of metacognition may require greater levels of overall brain function. As Saxe and Offen describe in Chapter 1, a set of semi-independent complex neurological functions is required for certain metacognitive acts. Neuroimaging studies suggest that different aspects of the metacognitive system may rely on overlapping but not identical cortical activity, thus providing support to one key assertion found throughout our book, that is, the idea that components of the metacognitive system are related with each other but partially independent from one another. For example, Modinos and colleagues (2009) found that self-reflection involved unique activation in the anterior insula while other-reflection was linked to activation in the precuneus, while both processes were also linked with activation of many other areas.

While neurocognitive function is not synonymous with metacognition, metacognition may rely on forms of highly coordinated brain activity. Certain levels of neurocognitive capacity may in this sense be at least one of several preconditions for certain kinds of metacognition. Consistent with this, studies of both participants with and without clinical disorders suggest that disruptions in basic levels of metacognition, such as ownership of own body, or the primary sense of agency ('I am the one forming this thought or moving my arm') might affect consciousness and have clear neurobiological correlates (Metzinger, 2008). Though not covered in our volume, neurobiological studies also point to another set of difficulties with metacognition, namely, pathology linked to hyper-mentalizing. In this light, data shows how increased self-focus and over-attribution to the self of negative emotion relies on specific forms of altered brain circuitry – subcortical-cortical midline structures – and may play a causal role in depression (Grimm *et al.*, in press). This is consistent with theories on schizophrenia in which pathology is associated with over-mentalizing, particularly in regard to the mental states of other people (Brüne, 2005). One possible hypothesis is that over-mentalizing or increased negative self-focus are the rebound effect stemming from difficulties in other parts of an intact metacognitive system, for example, the ability to recognize positive emotions in the case of depression or the absence of basic self-referential processes making people able to recognize self-experience as emanating from the self (for the importance of basic self-relatedness on human conscience, see Northoff *et al.*, 2006).

Coming back to how metacognition emerges and is sustained, genetics and the associated development of brain function and neurocognition may represent the second set of forces that may imperil metacognition. Persons with possibly congenital deficits which interfere with certain brain functions necessary for metacognitive acts may be at risk for metacognitive deficits found in personality disorders. One example is impulsivity, a genetically based disposition that might impair the ability to reason about mental states, often found in borderline personality disorder (Allen *et al.*, 2008).

Those persons, driven by a given urge, may lack the cognitive resources to reason metacognitively about what is happening and therefore resist acting on their impulses. In diseases such as schizophrenia or PTSD, the loss of neurocognitive capacity secondary to the disease process may rob some persons of previously held metacognitive capacities.

And then there is the interaction of social and attachment relationships with neurocognition. Poor development, for example, in the case of insecure attachment, itself affects brain development and may play a role in vulnerability to neurocognitive decline (Allen *et al.*, 2008). Also, as suggested by Lysaker (Chapter 4), neurocognitive decline may make social interactions frightening and lead persons to withdraw socially, weakening the attachments needed to recover metacognitive capacity or to make accommodations for lost neurocognitive functions. Certainly there are dozens more permutations, but highlighted here is that these two forces interact very closely and in the end research is needed in which early human interactions, temperament and changes in brain function are seen as affecting one another in an ongoing manner, resulting in a range of function from the healthiest to the tormented phenomenology described by Stanghellini (Chapter 8). In sum, illustrated by the developments in this volume and many elsewhere, there can no longer be a mind versus body, endogenous versus exogenous, or environment vs. genetic account of these issues.

Different forms of metacognition impairment and appearances across different forms of mental illness

A second set of issues each author has had to address in this volume concerns the many different kinds of activities involved in metacognition and which might be conceptualized as part of the larger cognitive structures that allow metacognition to occur. Here we are not referring to the antecedents of metacognition but the system itself which is involved in recognizing and reasoning about mental states. As reviewed by Bell and colleagues (Chapter 7), having a full and meaningful appraisal of the mental states of other persons is a final product, one that is potentially formed from many different components. Forming an understanding of another person's mental states may, for instance, involve having to grasp that person's intentions. It may call for the recognition of the kind of emotion in the other person's voice or facial expression (e.g. anger versus surprise) or for an understanding that this particular other person would rather be soothed than distracted when distressed.

As reviewed by Dimaggio and colleagues (Chapter 15), as well as Semerari (Chapter 16), Vanheule and colleagues (Chapter 10) and Lysaker (Chapter 4), awareness of one's own thinking is also a product of a range of different processes. To think meaningfully about oneself may require a sense of ownership of one's own thoughts and the sense of being an agent, the ability to name or be aware of one's emotional states, the ability to be aware of and distinguish thoughts which are closer to fantasy or to reality, as well as the ability to coherently integrate a range of different views of oneself and others. As illustrated by Morgan and David (Chapter 6), being aware of a psychiatric illness and making decisions about treatment may require a range of very different forms of self-appraisal.

Essential here is that thinking about thinking involves a range of different acts which are not identical or synonymous with one another and which function independently but in a coordinated manner within a larger network. One function may be impaired while another is intact (the ability to recognize emotion may be limited but the ability to surmise intentionality may function reasonably well). As illustrated in a range of clinical material in this volume, some persons may be well able to think about other people's emotions, but have little sense of their own emotions, or vice versa.

Turning to the issue of psychopathology, we also see painted with a broad brush hints that there are specific clusters of dysfunctions in the different kinds of psychopathology. Kanba and colleagues (Chapter 9) point to the prevalence of deficits in theory of mind in affective disorders, while Vanheule and colleagues (Chapter 10) and Liotti and Prunetti (Chapter 12) point to deficits in the ability to recognize one's own affects in PTSD. Lysaker and Buck (Chapter 13) point to profound deficits in self-reflectivity which may underlie psychosocial impairments in schizophrenia, while Schaub and colleagues (Chapter 5) and Bell and colleagues (Chapter 7) suggest a slightly different view pointing to deficits in theory of mind as root causes of social dysfunction. Semerari (Chapter 16) and Dimaggio and colleagues (Chapter 15) flesh out the role of difficulties in distinguishing reality from fantasy as playing a unique role in some forms of personality disorders.

At a finer level of analysis, though, we find that there are no clear boundaries between different kinds of metacognitive dysfunction and different forms of psychopathology. As pointed out by Colle and colleagues (Chapter 11), for instance, personality disorder with very different kinds of dysfunction may share similar kinds of metacognitive struggles, while nearly every form of psychopathology involved some degree of alexithymia. Additionally, in every disorder discussed it remains poorly understood how the existent metacognitive disturbances are related to symptoms or underlying pathophysiology. While the general correlates of poor metacognition have yet to be better understood, as evidenced by Bell and colleagues (Chapter 7), Lysaker (Chapter 4) and Schaub and colleagues (Chapter 5), there is some consistent evidence that metacognition is linked to social functioning, in particular in persons with schizophrenia, but possibly, as noted by Colle and colleagues (Chapter 11), also in persons with personality disorders.

Of note, one issue still to be addressed regards the difference between intact and pathological metacognition. Though there are well-validated measures, for example, for alexithymia, cut-off scores are still lacking for what may be empirically characterized as impaired versus not impaired metacognition. This is evident in Saxe and Offen (Chapter 1), who note how individuals in non–clinical samples make many errors when it comes to self-attribution as well as theory of mind (see Dimaggio *et al.*, 2008).

Potential of psychotherapy and rehabilitation to promote recovery of metacognitive capacity

A final issue to be considered here regards what is to be done. In response we find a range of views suggesting that psychotherapy might be adapted to help persons to recover metacognitive capacity. Of importance is the role that disturbances in interpersonal or affective regulation play in impairing metacognition Vanheule *et al.*, Chapter 10). For example, when threatened, persons with borderline personality experience a reduction in their ability to correctly infer mental states from facial expressions and may tend to overly attribute anger to others (Domes *et al.*, 2009). Accordingly, psychotherapy may be an arena for creating the optimal interpersonal and emotional environment (Semerari, Chapter 16) for persons to learn how to identify and overcome exactly these kinds of biases and misattributions.

In thinking about the many views of the role of metacognition in psychotherapy, we see a number of contrasting threads that might be pursued. From a more developmental and attachment perspective, Liotti and Prunetti (Chapter 12) point to a psychotherapy in which the therapeutic relationship might foster the development of either lost or never before attained abilities to think about thinking. Certainly such a psychotherapy is pointed to as well by Gumley's review (Chapter 3).

From a more cognitive view, Osatuke and Stiles (Chapter 17) discuss how in psychotherapy persons may come to assimilate increasing a deeper and richer view of themselves, developing more coherent accounts of themselves as individual human beings in relation to others. Semerari (Chapter 16), Dimaggio and colleagues (Chapter 15) and Colle and colleagues (Chapter 11) also talk about how a therapeutic relationship may be developed; which then challenges patients to find new ways to think about themselves. Importantly, interventions in the frameworks proposed by these authors are chosen which target specific metacognitive needs and call on the therapist to be mindful of the interpersonal context in which any metacognition is taking place. A basic tenet of this line of thinking is that metacognitive deficits create limits which the therapist must observe. It is pointless, for example, to ask patients to form complex ideas about mental states when a given person cannot name the emotions they are experiencing.

From perhaps an even more cognitive perspective, Lysaker and Buck (Chapter 13) suggest a kind of psychotherapy in which persons are encouraged to exercise atrophied or damaged metacognitive capacities in the manner in which physical therapy addresses atrophied or damaged tissue or cognitive remediation addresses the loss of brain function. In this model the therapist helps patients to practise metacognitive acts according to a careful assessment of their capabilities. Patients practice metacognition at a level they are capable of and only take on increasingly difficult metacognitive acts as they build the appropriate levels of strength. In a similar manner Hasson-Ohayon and colleagues (Chapter 14) discuss psychosocial rehabilitation as a place where persons can come to practise and develop more complex abilities to think about themselves and others. In contrast to the approach of Lysaker and Buck (Chapter 13) which stresses the role of underlying deficits in neurocognition, Hasson-Ohayon and colleagues uniquely talk about the role of stigma as a barrier to metacognition, particularly in persons with severe mental illness.

Summary

Taken together, the chapters in this book paint metacognition as a matter that is well beyond anything that can be framed as a unitary self seeing a reflection of itself or gazing into the eyes of another unitary person. For human beings to think about thinking, a wide array of functions is required, some of which may be impaired while others may appear fully intact. Different forms of impairments appear linked to different disorders when viewed from a distance, but no clear boundaries can be found between disorders, at least as demarcated by metacognition when matters are examined in detail.

Future research is thus needed in a range of different arenas. For one, many instruments exist for assessing metacognition. Some involve laboratory tasks, others self-report, others spontaneous speech or behavioural assessments. Certainly more work is needed not only to validate these instruments, but also to understand how closely they overlap and how well they speak to independent components of metacognition. As theoretical advances are made in understanding the different components of metacognition, it is likely that these instruments will need to be significantly evolved and new procedures developed. An important avenue for future research concerns, as a result, the correlation of metacognition with symptoms, including suicidality, dissociation, delusions, and so on.

While the need for better methodologies is clear, so is there a need for more careful studies of the role of metacognition as a predictor of treatment need and response. As we are better able to assess this phenomenon, we should be able to see how metacognition predicts the needs of the unique person as well as the natural course of psychiatric illnesses. For instance, do deficits in self-reflectivity point to a different set of difficulties for persons entering psychotherapy or rehabilitation than deficits in theory of mind? Do persons entering vocational rehabilitation with different levels of self-reflectivity fare differently over time in terms of work performance? Do those deficits require different interventions and or mediate the effectiveness of interventions in a predictable manner? Needed here are longitudinal studies with diverse groups of participants, and diverse forms of interventions. For instance, as medications are developed that have the possibility to enhance cognition, there will be chances to see whether they lead to improvements in metacognition. Different methodologies are called for including not only randomized clinical trials but also serial case studies employing mixed qualitative and quantitative methods.

In short, we look forward to future volumes like this which bring together research generally considered only within specific silos. We see that the work in this volume coupled with future work may offer increasingly nuanced syntheses and ever more transparent views of the complex processes by which human beings make meaning of their lives and the lives of others called metacognition. Such a sharpening understanding of metacognition as a global phenomenon and one composed of a range of components seems essential for further understanding as to what has gone awry in mental illness and the best approaches to helping those persons with mental illness to move back towards wellness.

References

Allen, J.G., Fonagy, P. and Bateman, A.W. (2008). *Mentalizing in clinical practice*. Washington, DC: American Psychiatric Publishing.

Brüne, M. (2005). 'Theory of mind' in schizophrenia: A review of the literature. *Schizophrenia Bulletin*, *31*(1), 21–42.

Dimaggio, G., Lysaker, P.H., Carcione, A., Nicolò, G. and Semerari, A. (2008). Know yourself and you shall know the other . . . to a certain extent. Multiple paths of influence of self-reflection on mindreading. *Consciousness and Cognition*, *17*, 778–789.

Domes, G., Schulze, L., Herpertz, S.C. (2009). Emotion recognition in borderline personality disorder: A review of the literature. *Journal of Personality Disorders*, *23*, 6–19.

Dunn, J. (1988). *The beginnings of social understanding*. Cambridge, MA: Harvard University Press.

Dunn, J., Brown, J., Slomkowski, C., Tesla, C. and Youngblade, L.M. (1991). Young children's understanding of other people's feelings and beliefs: Individual differences and their antecedents. *Child Development*, *62*, 1352–1366

Gordon, R. (1995). Folk psychology as simulation. In M. Davies and T. Stone (eds), *Folk psychology* (Vol. 3, pp. 60–73). Oxford: Blackwell.

Grimm, S., Ernst, J., Boesiger, P., Schuepbach, D., Hell, D., Boeker, H., *et al.* (in press). Increased self-focus in major depressive disorder is related to neural abnormalities in subcortical-cortical midline structures. *Human Brain Mapping*.

Harris, P.L. (1994). The child's understanding of emotion: Developmental change and the family environment. *Journal of Child Psychology and Psychiatry*, *35*, 3–28.

Hughes, C. and Dunn, J. (1997). 'Pretend you didn't know': Young children's talk about mental states in the context of pretend play. *Cognitive Development*, *12*, 477–499.

Lillard, A.S. (2001). Pretend play as Twin Earth: A social-cognitive analysis. *Developmental Review*, *21*, 495–531.

Metzinger, T. (2008). Empirical perspectives from the self-model theory of subjectivity: A brief summary with examples. In R. Banjeree and B.K. Chakrabarti (eds), *Progress in brain research* (Vol. 168, pp. 215–245). Amsterdam: Elsevier.

Modinos, G., Ormel, J. and Aleman, A. (2009). Activation of anterior insula during self-reflection. *PlosOne*, *4*, e4618.

Northoff, G., Heinzel, A., de Greck, M., Bermpohl, F., Dobrowolny, H. and Panksepp, J. (2006). Self-referential processing in our brain – A meta-analysis of imaging studies on the self. *NeuroImage*, *31*, 440–457.

Ruffman, T., Perner, J., Naito, M., Parkin, L. and Clements, W. (1998). Older (but not younger) siblings facilitate false belief understanding. *Developmental Psychology*, *34*, 161–174.

Index

locators in **bold** refer to major entries
locators in *italic* refer to figures/tables
locators for headings which also have subheadings refer to general aspects of that topic